# THE ENTREPRENEUR'S ROADMAP
## From Concept to IPO

Published by

CAXTON
Business & Legal inc.

# The Entrepreneur's Roadmap: From Concept to IPO

**Publisher:** Tim Dempsey

**Project Manager:** Matt Rosenquist

**Consulting Editor:** Bonnie Hyun, New York Stock Exchange

**Design and Composition:** Graphic World Inc.

**Printing and Binding:** Transcontinental Interglobe, Beauceville, Qc, Canada

**www.nyse.com/entrepreneur**

The Entrepreneur's Roadmap: From Concept to IPO
is published by:
> Caxton Business & Legal, Inc.
> 27 North Wacker Drive, Suite 601
> Chicago, IL 60606
> Phone: +1 312 361 0821
> Email: tjd@caxtoninc.com
> Web: www.caxtoninc.com

First published: 2017
ISBN: 978-0-9964982-2-7

The Entrepreneur's Roadmap: From Concept to IPO
© May 2017

**Front-cover artwork: © New York Stock Exchange**

## DISCLAIMER

# INTRODUCTION

New York Stock Exchange

Thomas Farley, President

The New York Stock Exchange has been at the center of capitalism for over two centuries. While the world has changed dramatically during that time, our core mission has remained the same: to help great entrepreneurs raise capital so they can continue to innovate, inspire, and shape the future and in doing so, help the world become a better place by improving the overall quality of life.

Our very history is paved by those inventors, entrepreneurs, and visionaries that have changed the course of history, from Thomas Edison to Jack Ma. Edison created the phonograph, the camera, and electric light bulbs. You may not know that during his early days, however, he supported himself as a telegraph operator at the New York Stock Exchange where he created his first commercially successful invention, a new iteration of the stock ticker. Years later when Edison needed financial backing, he again came to the NYSE where he, together with JP Morgan, listed General Electric, the NYSE's ninth-longest listed company.

We are proud of our role in helping entrepreneurs turn their dreams into realities. Every day—whether it's Jack Ma from Alibaba, the world's largest e-commerce company and its hundreds of thousands of jobs, or Adam Elsesser, cofounder of medical device and therapies company, Penumbra, which saves lives—we welcome captains of all industries to our historic 11 Wall Street building. In a very real sense we are the satellite offices for the most powerful and innovative companies in the world.

Along with our community of listed companies, the entrepreneurial spirit is also part of our own DNA. Every member of our team is tasked with the goal of looking at new and better ways to do things every single day. Our own ability to evolve and adapt is the very reason we continue to be one of the world's most iconic financial services brands and an enduring symbol of capitalism.

So with this in mind, the NYSE is proud to bring you *The Entrepreneur's Roadmap: From Concept to IPO*. We hope this guide provides a wealth of practical information and insights, but beyond that, we also hope it serves to empower and inspire you on your journey.

*TW Farley*

# FOREWORD

Revolution LLC

Steve Case, Chairman and CEO, Revolution LLC; Co-Founder, America Online

Entrepreneurship is vital to job creation, innovation, and economic growth. Across time and continents, entrepreneurs have contributed enormously to society by creating new products, improving existing concepts, and exploring new markets. Entrepreneurial activity drives the competition, productivity, and investment that fuel economies.

Those of us who are entrepreneurs know that we are drawn to the idea of being one before we fully understand what the word means. We are a unique group of dreamers and doers, compelled to think of—and create—new businesses and technologies. Today, popular culture glamorizes the profession. But there is often very little glamour involved in building a startup. I like to say that AOL was an overnight success 10 years in the making. It is hard work, and success requires intense dedication to a precious idea that others may not fully understand or appreciate.

Today, entrepreneurs face a challenging landscape, but one that offers the opportunity to dramatically change the way we live, work, and interact. In the First Wave of the Internet (late 1980s to 1990s), we saw companies like AOL and Cisco lay the foundation for people to connect to the Internet. In the Second Wave (roughly 2000 to the present), companies built on that foundation. Facebook and Google created social networks and search capabilities. Developers launched apps of every kind to meet a variety of needs. They acquired users rapidly and monetized. We are now entering what I call the "Third Wave," a period in which entrepreneurs will leverage technology to disrupt major real-world sectors—transportation, energy, food, and health care. Building companies in this new era will require a new mindset and new playbook. It will require what I refer to as the three Ps:

- First, entrepreneurs will have to focus on building constructive **partnerships**. There's an African proverb I like to quote: "If you want to go fast, go alone; if you want to go far, go together." This has never been more true. Companies in the Third Wave will need to forge relationships with organizations and individuals that have an intimate understanding of the industries that they seek to disrupt and that are connected to the industry gatekeepers they want—and need—to influence in order to succeed. Entrepreneurs also need the support of others in the ecosystem. The most successful entrepreneurs have many mentors and pay it forward by sharing expertise. This is particularly important for young entrepreneurs who may be learning how to start and scale a business for the first time.

- Second, Third Wave companies seek to transform regulated industries, and so they must have a fluent grasp of the **policy** issues they will encounter. They will also have to pay attention to—and engage with—government officials and regulators.

- Third, disruption in this new era will require **perseverance**. Entrepreneurs will need to temper the desire to "move fast and break things" with the recognition that Third Wave products present a number of critical and complex challenges that regulators will need to work through. Similarly, the government will have to balance its desire to regulate our health and well-being, our security, and our privacy with the enormous potential that the Third Wave represents.

That potential is about more than just making a great product. Because of the impact Third Wave industries have on our lives, some of the most successful startups will consider social benefit as a core tenet of their missions. That commitment will make them attractive to those who are seeking to change the world with their investments, and it will make them attractive to millennials who are looking to work at companies that don't find profit and purpose to be mutually exclusive aims. When I cofounded AOL, it was because I had an unwavering belief in the power of connectivity to democratize information and create stronger communities. Tomorrow's entrepreneurs have the opportunity to change the world for the better by directing their energies toward disruptions that create value not just for a company, but for the global community.

Entrepreneurship may be at its cultural apex in this country, but it is actually on the decline. Between 1978 and 2012, the number of companies less than one year old declined as a share of all business by 44%. This has enormous social and economic consequences. Startups account for nearly all net new job creation, so we have much to gain by promoting their development, not just in cities traditionally associated with startup activity, namely Silicon Valley, New York, and Boston, but in other locales—what I call the Rise of the Rest. As we move into the Third Wave, I predict this will start to happen naturally as startup ecosystems take root in cities where specific industry expertise exists. At its core, this movement is about more than just geographic diversity; it is about stopping the flow of capital from going to the same people, in the same places, with the same ideas. By making entrepreneurship more inclusive, we will produce a deeper and richer bench of products and services. We will also level the playing field so that more people in more communities have a shot at the American dream: a Third Wave that will benefit us all.

Entrepreneurs create the innovations that power our dreams of what tomorrow might bring. We aren't bound by tradition or orthodoxies. As the Internet of Things becomes the Internet of Everything, there is a world of possibility. It is incumbent on us to use our talents wisely, building businesses that add real value and make a real difference. I hope those reading this will welcome that challenge as I once did. Now, let's get started.

# TABLE OF CONTENTS

**Download the electronic version of the guide at:**
www.nyse.com/entrepreneur

# PART I

## THE SEED STAGE: STARTING A COMPANY

### THE EARLY STAGE: ESTABLISHING A COMPANY

### THE EARLY STAGE: ESTABLISHING INITIAL FINANCING

### THE EARLY GOVERNANCE: ESTABLISHING IP STRATEGY AND INSURANCE

# TEN THINGS TO CONSIDER BEFORE STARTING A STARTUP

Techstars

David Cohen, Co-CEO

There are so many things to think about when starting your own business. I've been involved in around 1,000 startups thus far in my career. Some of them seem to get off to a fast start and have no trouble attracting mentors, customers, and investors. Others struggle mightily. When I thought about what the best companies seem to do before starting, I came up with this list that I hope will be helpful to you as you embark on your own entrepreneurial journey.

## 1. ARTICULATE YOUR PURPOSE

When creating a company, there's nothing more important than purpose. Start with your "Why." This is not a marketing exercise. It's a vision of an improved world and the way in which your company will contribute to that future state. For example, at Techstars our purpose is "We believe that great startups can be built anywhere. In support of this, we're creating the best global ecosystem for founders to bring new technologies to market."

One of my favorite quotes is from Simon Sinek, who said "People don't buy *what* you do, they buy *why* you do it." Every startup founder should invest 20 minutes to watch the popular web video "Start With Why."

When I invested in the very first investment round of Uber, I believed in the purpose of the company. They wanted to make transportation as reliable as running water, everywhere for everyone. This purpose stated simply enabled me to invest in the people and the purpose before a single car was on the road. That's the power of purpose.

Many founders that I meet express their purpose in terms of the financial upside. This is not purpose, it's a beneficial side effect of successful execution of purpose. Don't confuse purpose with financial motivations.

Once you know your purpose, don't spend any time wordsmithing it. Just write it down. This is your reason for being. Make sure everyone knows it, including the people you hire, your investors, your mentors, and your community.

## 2. COMMIT TO AT LEAST 10 YEARS

Now that you have a clear purpose, make sure you can commit at least 10 years of your life to this purpose. If you can't, you'll likely fail because startups are too hard to build unless you actually care about solving the problem. It's too easy to quit, so be sure you have this long-term commitment before starting down the road.

In your life, you'll hopefully have three to five career segments. In my life, these have been technology coder, startup founder, angel investor, and venture capitalist. In each case, I made an emotional 10-year commitment to everything I've ever done. When I think about the one thing I've done that failed at the macro level, it was a startup to which I didn't consciously commit 10 years of my life in advance. It was hard, and I gave up too early. I wasn't driven by the purpose of that particular company. It wasn't "me," and as a result I wasted one of my bullets as a startup founder.

Startups take time. Be sure you are dedicated to your purpose for the long term.

## 3. GET FAMILY ON BOARD

I always say that entrepreneurship is a life choice, not a job choice. When you have a typical job it's possible to leave it at the office at the end of the day. It's possible not to feel fully responsible for the employees that work for you. When you start a company, there's nobody else who can pick up the slack for you. It all comes down to you.

Often, this burden rolls downhill toward your family. Your emotional ups and downs will affect your family. A lower-than-market salary and income will place additional strain on the family at times. The long hours can cause challenges in your relationships.

This is not a commitment you can make alone. Be sure your family supports you in your decision to start a business and understands the likely downstream implications before setting off on the long journey.

## 4. DEFINE YOUR CULTURE

Now that you have a long-term commitment, your family is on board, and you understand your purpose, it's time to define your company culture. Many founders let culture happen automatically and are not thoughtful about it in advance. I'd encourage the opposite; think carefully about what you want your culture to be and live it every day inside your business. Your culture can be defined as a set of values that you'll always protect. They should be simple and memorable. At Techstars, we have four core values that define our culture. They are:

1. Give first.

2. Do the right thing for founders.

3. Quality before quantity.

4. Network over hierarchy.

A great mentor of mine once drew a chart for me with an X- and Y-axis. The X-axis was labelled performance and the Y-axis was labelled cultural fit. He explained that you can move people along the X-axis if they're not doing well. That's something you can work on. But if someone is low on the Y-axis, you have to move quickly to fire that person or the individual will compromise your culture. This is not hard when X and Y are both low. But it's extremely hard when cultural fit (Y) is low and performance (X) is high. Firing people who are high performers and poor cultural fit is critical for maintaining culture over time and living your values. This way of thinking makes hard decisions very easy.

## 5. AVOID COFOUNDER CONFLICT

Dharmesh Shah has been a mentor at Techstars since 2009 and he wrote a chapter for the Techstars book entitled *Do More Faster* entitled "Avoid Co-Founder Conflict." In that chapter, his key pieces of advice are to clearly discuss and agree on the following things before starting the new business, among others:

• How should we split the equity?

• How will decisions get made?

- What happens if one of us leaves the company?

- Can any of us be fired? By whom? For what reasons?

- What are our personal goals for the startup?

- Will this be the primary activity for each of us?

- What part of our plan are we each unwilling to change?

- What contractual terms will each of us sign with the company?

- Will any of us be investing cash in this company? How will this be treated?

- What will we be paid? How will this change over time and who will decide?

- How will we fund the company and what happens if we can't raise capital?

By having these discussions up front, you're likely to avoid the most common types of cofounder conflict down the line. From investing in over 1,000 startups, I can tell you that cofounder conflict is a major source of company failure. Have the hard discussions early.

## 6. ASSUME YOU ARE WRONG

I've found that founders who start out assuming that they're wrong end up doing the best. They recognize that all of their assumptions are just their best guesses. They are active listeners and are objective about the results they get early on. They test every assumption before accepting that it's correct. They find ways to instrument their products so that they get data. Then they combine that with their gut feeling and intuition and test some more.

Rarely does a startup ultimately succeed based upon their exact original idea. Consider Facebook, which was started to be a private college directory. Consider Google, which was an Internet search engine that didn't make money that way. My favorite story is about PhotoBucket, a very successful company that started by trying to be a photo social network. By paying careful attention to the data, founders Alex and Darren realized that people were abusing PhotoBucket to store images for free that they linked elsewhere, such as on Craigslist. Rather than fighting it, they made it easier to do and ultimately built a very large important company. They paid attention to the data and leaned into what their users really wanted. You can do the same.

## 7. ENGAGE MENTORS

For any situation you'll face as you build your company, there is someone out there who has faced it before. Network is perhaps the most undervalued resource by most startup founders. Techstars, and programs like it that are all about mentorship, and accelerator programs are an obvious way to tap into local networks. But there are many other ways. I advise a quality-over-quantity approach when it comes to mentors. Find a few experienced mentors who give first and ask for nothing in return. These can be investors or just local entrepreneurs that you admire. You'll be surprised at how helpful successful entrepreneurs are willing to be when you approach them in the right way. In my popular blog post "Find and Engage Great Mentors" I have written about tactics for establishing and maintaining great mentor relationships. Among the keys are starting with small requests via email, closing the loop with those who offer feedback, and making it easy to engage with you as a mentee by going to their office for 15 minutes instead of inviting them to coffee or lunch. Target mentors who actually care about you and what you're building and leverage them early and often. But remember to give back to them and make sure they're getting something from the relationship.

Great mentor relationships eventually become two-way. And you'll find that the right ones can change your company in ways that are very impactful.

## 8. ESTABLISH THE COMPANY

A common mistake with startups is a lack of formality and documentation. There's no quicker way to kill a promising company than by neglecting to set up an appropriate structure. Consult an attorney early and pick one that is

5

experienced with startups. A great question to ask them is how many companies they've worked with that have attracted venture capital. That will give you an indication of their level of experience in working with promising companies. They'll help you understand what makes sense for you in terms of corporate structure and give you basic agreements you can use with early employees or contractors. That way you won't wake up one day and discover that all your hard work is worthless because you don't own the intellectual property. Setting up the company also protects you personally in case of downstream liability. And, if you're going to build a real company, well then, it needs to be a real company.

## 9. UNDERSTAND FINANCING OPTIONS

I've worked with around 1,000 companies that have successfully raised about $15 billion dollars in capital. The one question I always ask when I'm first approached by startup founders hoping to raise money is, "Do you need to raise money at all?" Bootstrapping is highly underrated. I can tell you from first-hand experience that owning your entire company when you sell it is very exhilarating. I often say that if you can bootstrap, you should bootstrap. It's the only way to stay totally in control of your own company and it's the only way to have it all be owned by your team when you eventually go public or sell it. So the first question you should be asking yourself is why you need to raise money in the first place. If you have no good answer, take that into consideration.

Of course, some startups will need outside capital to have a chance at being successful. In that case, recognize that there are several options available. I'll call them customer capital, venture capital, angel capital, and loans.

Anyone who has ever gone to a bank for a startup loan knows that this is not the business of banks. They will loan money only to people who have money and will not consider the startup any form of valid collateral in that equation. However, there are groups that make loans to startups, such as Lighter Capital. Generally these groups require you to already have substantial revenue in order to ensure you can pay back the loans.

Customer capital is another underrated option. It's how I started my first company. We took a $100,000 loan from a customer in order to deliver a free lifetime license to use our software in the future. This was a great option for us, because we didn't actually sell any of the company to get access to this capital.

Angel capital and venture capital are the most well known options, of course. Angels invest with their own money and venture capitalists invest on behalf of their limited partners. There are many great resources on the web to understand angel and venture capital, but a few of my favorites include Angel.co, avc.com, feld.com, and of course Techstars.com.

Whatever path you choose, it's important to work with capital partners that you trust, have a shared vision, and who will be supportive of what is ultimately in your best interests as a founder.

## 10. DON'T WAIT—START

The hardest thing about starting a startup is starting. Don't wait for permission—the world will not give it to you. Don't wait for approval—you don't need it. Just start building the future. You'll find that by doing things and working toward the future you want to create, resources and opportunities will become available to you. There's nothing like the clarity of doing. So don't wait. Don't find excuses. Just start doing.

Good luck on your journey toward startup success!

# 2

# TAKING THE PLUNGE—FROM IDEA TO INCORPORATION

**Bessemer Venture Partners**

Byron Deeter, Managing Partner

## DAY 0

All great companies start with a courageous founder who is willing to step out of the status quo and change the tide of innovation. Most founders look for a light bulb moment—an idea that leads them to stop in their tracks and start coding—but only a few, if any, companies are started through movie-like story arcs. Instead, most great startups begin with a founder or founders who have a drive to innovate and pursue a lot of very purposeful ideation.

As a repeat founder myself and an early-stage venture capital investor for over 13 years, I have met with thousands of founding teams and seen clear patterns for success in the early founding days. For entrepreneurs who feel this calling to dive in and change the world, there are three key elements that you should focus on immediately: (1) Find your killer idea, (2) Draft the all-stars, and (3) Make sure it is a real business.

## PART I: FINDING YOUR KILLER IDEA (PRODUCT CONCEPT)

It is rare to fall in love with one idea immediately. Instead, you should focus on learning and getting feedback on a number of ideas. Some founders I have met fear idea theft, but in the early stages it's much more risky to go forward without candid feedback from experts and customers. Use your early days of ideation as an opportunity to brainstorm with smart people you admire—this could be founders you look up to or colleagues you have worked with in the past.

### ANCHOR AROUND YOUR SUPER POWERS

Try to find some unfair advantage that you have over other teams and companies.

Some founders are best suited to fix pain points they have faced in industries they know very well. Jeff Lawson founded Twilio out of technical shortcomings he experienced as the early CTO of Stubhub. As did Isaac, Jose, and Tim when founding SendGrid out of deep empathy for developer pain points around transactional email systems. The Procore Technologies product vision came directly out of problems that Tooey Courtemanche observed in the construction industry, having previously been a builder and technologist. Ara Mahdessian and Vahe Kuzoyan at Service Titan are building a cloud business for plumbing, HVAC, and electrical business owners after watching their family businesses struggle with poor software. All these founders had unique market insights from deep personal experiences and immense customer empathy and credibility.

Super powers do not have to be related to the field you have worked in previously—they can also be core talents that you have developed based on previous experiences. For example, if you have spent the early parts of your career building beautiful product, then design and user interface can be a core advantage and point of differentiation. Or, if you've worked for large Fortune 500 companies and have access to channel partners or early product partnerships, those too can help provide some early advantage.

## LOOK FOR MACRO TAILWINDS

The goal is to be the winner in a massive market, but if you fall short of that goal, it is often better to be number three in a large market than number one in a medium or small market. Find your rising tide, your tailwind, or your hypergrowth market that is about to explode. It allows you to aim for the moon and still have a great outcome if you fall a bit short.

Admittedly, not all market sizes are obvious from the outside, and many so-called industry experts and analysts will read them incorrectly. The early days of "The Facebook" would have suggested a small market with little revenue targeting students on the Harvard campus, and similarly the massive potential of Google did not fully reveal itself until matched with a revenue model of paid search results. Often opportunity can come from finding large markets that you know are undergoing massive upheaval and disruption.

## CUSTOMER FEEDBACK PRE-PRODUCT

Getting advice from smart people in the field is important for idea generation, and then you refine it further by talking to real customer

prospects. Many founders will build surveys and organize focus groups to get the feedback of at least 100+ customers for small medium businesses (SMBs) and dozens of prospects for enterprise products. You do not want to fire your rocket off in the wrong direction, so the more refinement you can do in the early days, the more efficient your efforts will be as you build real product.

## BUILD A PROTOTYPE

Early customer feedback on design mock-ups is helpful, but real user feedback on a real product is even better. This can be done through a minimum viable product (MVP) on the SMB/consumer side or a product pilot with a large enterprise that can help you build a product that is robust enough for enterprise players. For enterprise products, it is essential to involve partner companies to ensure that you are building a product they will use and to validate the return on investment (ROI) and price points for the value you are creating.

## ITERATION

As with any early prototype, make sure you leave time for product iteration based on key customer feedback. Your first prototype should never be your last.

## PRODUCT VALUE PROPOSITION

Make sure you are able to succinctly describe what your product does and why it is best suited to deliver on a particular value proposition. Know why your product can be much better than all other existing approaches and competitive products in the market and why this is valuable to your future customers.

At the end of the ideation phase, you should have a tight and compelling product value proposition that is essentially your foundational idea. It is the product inspiration around which the early company will be built. While it will inevitably evolve—sometimes quite considerably—it is the cornerstone concept around which you will recruit and finance.

# PART II: BUILDING YOUR ALL-STAR TEAM

## TO COFOUND OR NOT TO COFOUND?

It is a personal choice whether you want to be the lone wolf or part of a founding team of 2+ cofounders. Past experience shows that both models can be equally successful. But whichever path you choose, you need to surround yourself with "founder-like" advisors, employees, and contributors.

Personally, I have always enjoyed having thought partners on board as cofounders and have specifically sought to design around my technical limitations by working with a strong technical counterpart. For technically minded founders, you may find the exact opposite and want to involve one or more business-oriented team members. There is no single right answer for everyone, just the right approach for you and the company you want to build.

Beyond just the cofounder decision, the hiring of your early team members is the most important action of the founding CEO. For technology businesses in particular, the core asset of the company is the team, and it's the main determinant in your ability to "out-execute" others in the market. Test your idea out with strong potential team members and get their candid feedback. The opportunity cost of your team members will far exceed your likely cost of early capital, so candid feedback from trusted early candidates can be some of your best feedback as you make the decision whether to launch the business.

## INCLUDING ADVISORS AND MENTORS

Founding a business often proves to be the biggest professional challenge most executives undertake, so you will want to build a deep bench of advisors to get you through the extreme highs and lows. After several years that will come in the form of a formal board of directors, but early on it comes in the form of an informal network of prior bosses and mentors, many of whom hopefully become angel investors and advisors as the business takes shape.

## IT'S OK TO CHALLENGE CONVENTIONAL WISDOM AND GO AGAINST THE EXPERT ADVICE AT TIMES

At Bessemer Venture Partners, we have used the knowledge accumulated over our years of investing in cloud companies around the "Ten Laws of Cloud Computing," and we encourage founders to challenge a known rule or two. We believe a challenger mentality can often bring forth real innovation. However, if you see yourself challenging a handful of assumed truths, you probably need to verify your assumptions.

One of my most frustrating experiences when founding Trigo Technologies was when the chief technical officer (CTO) of a large public company tore our idea apart. His exact words as we concluded the meeting were, "The number of miracles necessary to make this happen exceeds two." We thought hard about the input, talked to as many other smart folks as we could with very different opinions, and decided we disagreed. In fact, we used these words as our rallying cry and posted his quote on our office wall for the full team to see. Years later, when reaching profitability and getting ready to go public, we still referenced that meeting and that challenge.

# PART III: HAVE A CLEAR BUSINESS CASE

## DON'T WASTE YOUR TIME ON A BUSINESS PLAN, BUT DO HAVE A TIGHT BUSINESS CASE BEFORE FOUNDING YOUR BUSINESS!

Ultimately all businesses should be valued as a sum of their current and future profits. Assuming you want to found a for-profit business, that means you should ultimately have a strategy for generating gains. That means you need to develop a sense for all the basics of pricing, costs, and team size to build the business over time. You should use these basics to put together a succinct one- to two-page summary document that you can use for recruiting and financing.

## WRITING YOUR EXECUTIVE SUMMARY

It is often difficult for founders to distill a product they have worked on day and night to a few key bullet points. However, having a precise executive summary that is no more than two pages is incredibly helpful as you seek advice and pitch your company to investors. In addition to the team and product elements highlighted above that should be major parts of this executive summary, you should also make sure to address the market size, financing strategy, and any customer or revenue traction to date.

To be a credible venture capital candidate, you'll need to convince your prospective investors of your large market opportunity. Most investors make between one to three new bets a year, and they hope to make these bets in markets that can contribute to outsized returns. That means that you have to see a path to a large acquisition or an initial public offering (IPO). The best way to evaluate the probability of those outcomes is to calculate an honest review of the total addressable market (TAM). For example, if you are selling to SMB marketers, how many SMB marketers are there in the United States, and how much do they spend on average on marketing software? Beyond this basic calculation, you should address both an upside and downside case of being able to capture the market. Will you rely on word-of-mouth adoption or other acquisition channels to attract SMB marketers?

Financing strategy is also important to detail upfront to all prospective investors. Where do you think your first phase of capital is coming from? Some founders build initial prototypes based on capital from their own savings or friends and family investors. Other founders are advised to go straight to the venture community because their ideas have either been validated early in the market or their teams have had past startup success. Regardless of the path you choose, make sure you research how much

capital you need and what you will spend it on. Clarity in raising capital, from an investor's perspective, is always a good indication that the team and founder will manage money effectively.

Of course, the most powerful data you can include in a business description is real-world market research. With the rapidly decreasing costs of infrastructure services today, many founding teams are actually building and launching real products before raising their first financing dollars. Although that is not expected, or the norm, it is a huge positive if you can show some semblance of traction in your early product. For example, if you are building an enterprise product, make sure you have had real discussions with large enterprise players or even better, have locked down early pilots. For SMB or consumer-facing products, make sure your beta customers are coming back to your product and you have started to track daily or weekly user engagement. Any engagement or user growth increasing over time is a good indication that your company is finding relevant product/market fit.

Over time the executive summary will be complemented by other financing tools such as PowerPoint slides, product mockups, more detailed financials, and possibly a short introductory video. As investors, we often use the executive summary to decide whether to take the first meeting and the slide presentation to decide whether we want to go into deeper diligence around a potential investment.

## CONCLUSION

With a killer product concept ("idea"), your early team members identified, and a business case around the revenue model and funding strategy, you have the necessary ingredients to start building your business. Now the real fun begins!

# 3

# FOUNDING TEAM PITFALLS

Noam Wasserman

Founding Director, Founder Central Initiative

University of Southern California Marshall School of Business, Lloyd Greif Center for Entrepreneurial Studies

Author, *The Founder's Dilemmas: Anticipating and Avoiding the Pitfalls That Can Sink a Startup*

"Follow your heart." "Make your passion your business." "Intuition should rule the day." We are surrounded by messages that reinforce the impression that gut-driven entrepreneurial decisions will take us to glory, that we should build our startups on a foundation built on our natural inclinations.

Steve Jobs had a caution about this mode of entrepreneurial decision making: "Follow your heart, but check it with your head." Before defaulting to the gut, make sure you've also engaged the brain. Make sure you've thought ahead to the potential consequences of your decision. If the head and heart agree, then terrific: You're off and running. However, if they disagree, pull back on the reins before you default to what your gut is telling you, for it may be leading you into trouble rather than glory.

## ONE FOUNDER'S EXHORTATION, 16,000 FOUNDERS' EXPERIENCES

Jobs' message flies in the face of what many entrepreneurs want to believe but has been reinforced time and time again by my research. I focus on the early decisions founders make about the people they involve in their startups and how they involve them. These people include themselves (as "core founders"), cofounders (the people who come onboard around the time of founding to help build the startup), hires (who fill holes in the founding team or help it deal with growth issues), investors (outside providers of capital), and members of the early board of directors. To study them, I draw upon my own entrepreneurial experiences, my firsthand observations of dozens of founders, and a dataset of 16,000 U.S. founders that I have collected since 2000.[1]

The recurring theme of the research reinforces Jobs' wisdom: Founders who default to their heart without checking with their head heighten the chances that their founding teams will splinter, that growth will be harmed, and that they will be replaced as leader of the startup. When it comes to making product and market decisions, it's possible that following your heart will lead you to glory.[2] However, when it comes to making people decisions, checking with your head is particularly important. Despite all of the attention paid to product development and market-related issues within startups, among startups that fail, people problems are the leading cause by far, accounting for nearly two-thirds of the failures.[3]

## HEIGHTENED POTENTIAL, OR HEIGHTENED RISKS?

Founders add new people with the hope that they and their resources will heighten the potential of the startup. However, those decisions also add risks to the startup, introduce new dilemmas, and could dramatically change the dynamics with the team and the startup.

For founders, the key is to understand ahead of time when they will be making a key people decision and how the options they face could heighten the potential while increasing the risks.

Likewise, for potential hires and investors, the key is to understand which prior founding decisions should be assessed before deciding whether to become involved in the startup. Have the founders built a solid foundation of forward-looking decisions that will heighten potential while reducing risks? If so, then you should be more willing to get involved in the startup. Have they made ill-considered decisions that heighten the risk of team fragmentation or stunted growth? If so, that should be a red flag making you think twice about becoming involved.

In this chapter, I focus on the early decisions founders face about whom to involve in the founding team and how to involve them. We will briefly see that the patterns can be extended to early decisions about hires. The most central of those hires is the most important hire a founder might make: his or her successor as CEO, a key inflection point that will be covered in a later chapter but deserves attention here too.

## FOUNDING TEAM PITFALLS: THE 3RS

When it comes to founding-team decisions, the most common decisions we make when we are following our heart tend to be the most fraught with peril. This is true of all three major areas of founding-team decisions, which we will call "the 3Rs": the prior Relationships among the

cofounders, how they allocate the Roles and decision making, and how they allocate the Rewards.[4] For instance:

- Relationships: The most common prior relationships among cofounders are people who knew each other socially but not professionally—most centrally, friends and family. Yet, teams comprised of friends of family are the least stable in the long run.

- Roles and decision making: The most common titles taken by founders are C-level titles, and the most common approach to decision making is unanimity or consensus. However, over time, the title inflation comes back to haunt many startups, and the approach to decision making slows down the startup and increases tensions.

- Rewards: The most common approaches to splitting the most important reward, the equity ownership of the company, heighten the chances that the team will have disincentive to continue fully contributing to the startup and that it will not be able to deal effectively with a cofounder's leaving the team.

Let's delve into the most fateful early decisions, whether they tend to heighten potential or heighten challenges and whether there are ways we can reinforce the potential while reducing the challenges.[5]

### RELATIONSHIPS

Where do cofounders find each other? In my dataset, more than half of the startups were cofounded by people who were prior friends or relatives—those who had a social connection bringing them together. This is understandable. It's far easier to find and reach them and we already feel comfortable with them. As Steve Wozniak, Steve Jobs' cofounder at Apple, said, "To be two best friends starting a company. Wow. I knew right then that I'd do it. How could I not?"[6]

Yet, after an initial honeymoon period of 6 to 12 months, these "social" founding teams are significantly less stable than founding teams comprised of prior coworkers. (There are also hybrid teams in which friends later cofounded together, thus building a professional relationship on top of the social one, or in which coworkers became close socially.) Most striking to me when I saw the results of our analyses[7] was that social founding teams were even less stable than teams comprised of prior strangers or acquaintances. What could be going on here?

As I homed in on the challenges faced by social teams, two major factors emerged.

First, despite their seeming closeness, those teams were less likely to discuss the elephants in the room—the conflict-ridden issues that tend to get bigger and worse if we avoid them. Our natural conflict avoidance leads us to push off discussing those issues, especially with those with whom we are socially close.

When we cofound with people we barely know, we enter with eyes wide open, assessing each other's capabilities, watching for any disconnects in working style, and discussing goals and values to assess compatibility. We "date" before deciding whether to get "married." However, when we are socially close with cofounders, we make the bold assumption that we already know each other (and thus will be compatible in the very different professional arena) and that we already trust each other. We neglect to consider that social trust—"he'll have my back"—is very different from trusting professionally in the other person's competence and ability to execute. We bypass the dating, making bold assumptions about our compatibility.

The second factor arises when the team almost inevitably hits a bump in the road. For instance, a founder isn't scaling with the startup or the founders disagree about a key hire or change in strategy. As these tensions rise within the startup, they risk imperiling our cherished relationships outside the startup. Yet, we are much less likely to have protected those relationships, or, in the opposite direction, to protect the startup from blow-ups outside of it (e.g., when a couple who founded together get divorced).

When both of these factors are true—we avoid the difficult conversations and risk causing damage to our most-cherished relationships if things blow up—we are playing with fire. The more we play with fire, the greater the chance that we will get burned. As the Chinese proverb says, "If you mix family and business, you will lose both."

Regarding the first factor, teams should proactively increase the chances that they will discuss the elephants in room, either by taking to heart the data about team stability and using it to motivate them to reduce their risks together or by tapping a trusted third party to facilitate those conversations. Regarding the second factor, teams should force themselves to list and then prioritize the pitfalls they might face as they grow and create disaster plans for how to deal with them if they occur. If a founder isn't scaling, how should that be handled? If the two cofounders aren't agreeing on strategic direction or are fighting at home, which one should exit from the startup? When playing with fire, such firewalls can help protect both the startup and the cherished relationships outside of it.

Teams that follow these prescriptions are much more likely to become the glorious team that Steve Wozniak dreamed about having with his best friend rather than a team that can cause the downfall of even the best idea. Hires and investors who assess whether the founding team has realized the challenges it faces and has found productive solutions to those challenges should be even more impressed with that team's self-awareness and ability to deal with difficult issues.

## ROLES AND DECISION MAKING

Founding teams typically start out with a "one for all, all for one" culture. They involve everyone in every major decision and seek consensus in the quest for solid decisions that incorporate disparate points of view. The founders find it motivating to be equals.

When it comes time to adopt titles within the startup, whether at the beginning or when they first have to present themselves to an outsider, the founders take senior titles. Often, they are all "Chief-something": Chief Executive Officer, Chief

Technology Officer, Chief Operating Officer, Chief Financial Officer. (Maybe even Chief Yahoo, Chief Internet Evangelist, and other actual titles at prominent startups.) Layered on top of this title inflation is the fact that initially, when they haven't yet raised any outside capital, all of the founders usually sit on the so-called board of directors.

The result is a reinforcing set of expectations about roles and decision making that can come back to haunt the team. With growth, the team usually realizes the need to adopt a clear hierarchy, to have decisions made by a subset of employees, and often that experienced hires might need to be brought in above the early members of the team. At that point, the deeply ingrained "equals" model is extremely hard to change as people feel left out of key decisions and even demoted.

The "easy" early model, which might have made perfect sense in the beginning, has now come back to constrain the team's ability to change and to heighten tensions rather than reduce them. The heart fights against even the most rational head-driven change. Teams that understand this long-term evolution and set early expectations accordingly are much better at dealing with this transition.

## REWARDS

Nearly three-quarters of founding teams in my dataset split the equity within a month of founding. Those teams are much more likely to split the equity equally and quickly, what I call "the quick handshake." Are those common rewards decisions good ones?

Thomas Hellmann and I analyzed founding team equity splits to see whether the quick handshake was good for founders.[8] Succumbing to a quick handshake, i.e., avoiding a difficult conversation about potentially differing contributions, levels of commitment, and incentives, is not a good decision. For instance, startups whose founders adopt a quick-handshake equity split suffer a significant valuation discount when they raise their first round of financing (if they raise at all).

It's not simply that by avoiding a quick handshake you can avoid the valuation discount. Instead, there are inherent characteristics, such as conflict avoidance, immaturity, and weak negotiating skills, that may lead teams to adopt a quick handshake and might likewise harm their ability to raise capital. For instance, teams with fewer years of work experience are likelier to suffer the valuation discount.

I have also delved deeply into additional aspects of equity splits that have important implications for team stability. For example, the majority of teams don't allow for any future adjustments to the founders' equity stakes, instead adopting a static split that persists despite changes in roles, involvement, and other aspects of value creation. (After all, raising such an issue, in which you are voicing doubts about your cofounder's potential commitment to the startup, can lead to a tension-filled conversation. There are clear parallels to our avoidance of the prenuptial conversations that we avoid having with our future spouses!) Given the ups and downs of startup life, the likelihood that something will change is high, yet the typical split does not adjust despite some fundamental changes internally.

Relatively simple structural solutions exist, such as time-based vesting. However, those are effective only insofar as the team is able to effectively discuss the issues that lead to their adoption.[9] Once again, teams can benefit from having a trusted third party involved.

## ECHOES IN HIRING DILEMMAS AND FOUNDER-CEO SUCCESSION

The 3Rs also apply to hiring dilemmas, when you're deciding where to look for potential hires, what roles to fill, how to involve them in decision making, and how to reward them.

Some very pointed echoes come at the inflection point where the founder is considering making his or her most important hire and shift in roles: A successor who will replace the founder as CEO. The most gut-wrenching and startup-threatening successions occur involuntarily, when the board or investors push the founder to step aside. In my dataset, 73% of the succession events were involuntary.

In those cases, the founder almost always resists being replaced as the parent of his baby. The heart overrules any messages from the head about why to buy in to the transition. Jack Dorsey, the early founder-CEO of Twitter, captured poignantly the visceral reaction that founders have to being replaced. Of being fired as CEO of Twitter, he said, "It was like being punched in the stomach."[10]

In fact, in a "paradox of entrepreneurial success," the most successful founders—those who spark the fastest growth and who succeed at raising the most capital—are the ones who face a particularly heightened risk of being replaced involuntarily. In short, the fast growth outstrips their ability to learn about the evolving challenges their startup is facing, and raising outside capital shifts the power structure within the board away from the founders and toward outsiders.[11] Add to that the fact that their very success makes successful founders the least receptive to the message that the board wants to change CEOs, and you're heading toward a high-stakes inflection point in the life of the startup, both for the founder personally and for the company more broadly.[12]

Quantitative analyses of the 6,130 startups in my dataset highlight how during the early years of the startup, founder control of the CEO position and the board can be a benefit to the startup but can quickly turn into a detriment to the company's value as the company grows and evolves.[13] At that point, founders usually have to face a significant tradeoff between remaining kings of their startups versus growing the most valuable kingdoms, a tradeoff that few founders are willing to acknowledge or prepared to think through. It is also a key tradeoff for investors and board members to understand and consider in making decisions about leadership, funding, and governance.

## EARLY SEEDS GROW INTO LATER PROBLEMS

The seeds of trouble are planted early. Founding teams who architect a fragile 3Rs foundation often find ways to justify their decisions in the short run, only to find that they planted early seeds that have grown into later problems. At that point, it is often much harder to hit the Undo key on those decisions. Instead, founders should proactively learn about the forks in the road where they will be making key early decisions, and proactively reflect on their natural inclinations and how they might become sources of later fragility.

With a fuller roadmap and deeper knowledge of how their own weaknesses might need counterbalancing, their great ideas have a better shot at having deep, long-term impact on the world, to the point where their startups can become large public companies realizing the founders' vision.

## REFERENCES

1. These data come from the largest two industries in the U.S. for high-potential startups, high tech and life sciences. Those two industries receive by far the most venture capital and account for the most IPOs.

2. At the same time, the core thrust of the Lean Startup movement seems to question even this assertion, for its best practices are geared to checking the founder's product intuition using A/B testing, data-driven hypothesis assessment, and quantitative metrics.

3. See Gorman, M., & Sahlman, W. A. 1989. What do venture capitalists do? *Journal of Business Venturing*, 4(4): 231–248; and Kaplan, S. N., & Stromberg, P. 2004. Characteristics, contracts, and actions: Evidence from venture capitalist analyses. *Journal of Finance,* 59: 2173–2206.

4. There is another very legitimate option for some types of founders in some types of startups that would help them avoid the challenges involved with the 3Rs: solo founding. However,

only 16 percent of the startups in my dataset were solo founded, making it very much the path less taken within American high-tech and life-sciences startups. For more details and data, please see Chapter 3 of *The Founder's Dilemmas.*

5. For further details and data on each of the 3Rs, please see Chapter 4 (Relationship Dilemmas), Chapter 5 (Role and Decision Making Dilemmas), and Chapter 6 (Reward Dilemmas) of *The Founder's Dilemmas.*

6. Wozniak, S. 2006. *iWoz: Computer Geek to Cult Icon: How I Invented the Personal Computer, Co-Founded Apple, and Had Fun Doing It.* W. W. Norton. Page 172. Later, the former best friends fought over many substantial issues (e.g., whether to shift Apple's emphasis away from Wozniak's Apple II computer and toward Jobs' Lisa computer) and symbolic ones (e.g., who would get the lower employee number) before Wozniak left the company in 1984.

7. I collaborated on this analysis with Dr. Matt Marx of MIT Sloan.

8. Hellmann, T., & Wasserman, N. 2016. The first deal: The division of founder equity in new ventures. *Management Science* forthcoming (2017).

9. Each of those solutions can also introduce their own challenges. For more on the issues introduced by time-based vesting or milestone-based vesting and which types of teams should adopt each type, please see Chapter 6 of *The Founder's Dilemmas.*

10. Kirkpatrick, D. 2011. "Twitter was Act One," *Vanity Fair.* http://www.vanityfair.com/business/features/2011/04/jack-dorsey-201104.

11. Wasserman, N. 2003. Founder-CEO succession and the paradox of entrepreneurial success. *Organization Science,* 14(2): 149–172.

12. For more on the best practices of managing this key inflection point, see Chapter 10 of *The Founder's Dilemmas.*

13. Wasserman, N. 2015. The throne vs. the kingdom: founder control and value creation in startups. *Strategic Management Journal,* 38(2): 255–277.

# 4

# KEY CONCERNS IN DRAFTING ORGANIZATIONAL DOCUMENTS

**Carney Badley Spellman, P.S.**

Joseph M. Wallin, Attorney

Susan Schalla, Attorney

Congratulations. You have decided to start a business.

You will now want to think about:

- <u>when</u> to form an entity through which to conduct the business;
- <u>what type</u> of business entity to form;
- <u>where</u> to form it;
- what to <u>name</u> it; and
- perhaps most importantly, <u>how</u> to document the economic and control agreements you have reached with your cofounders.

In this chapter we share the conventional wisdom on how to proceed if you are building a company that you expect:

- to grow fast;
- will raise capital from angels and venture capitalists; and
- will grant traditional equity awards to its employees and service providers (i.e., stock options and restricted stock awards).

## <u>WHY</u> FORM A BUSINESS ENTITY?

First, you might wonder, why form a business entity at all? Certainly it is possible to conduct a business through a sole proprietorship or an unincorporated general partnership, but these are not the best approaches for a number of reasons.

- First, you have to form a business entity if you want to protect yourself and your personal assets from liabilities created by the business. If you form a limited liability entity, you can generally protect your personal assets from the liabilities of the business, as long as you observe some simple operating procedures.
- It is hard to issue equity interests to cofounders and service providers if you haven't formed a business entity.
- If you are forming a tech business, you will want an entity to own the intellectual property created by people working for the company.

- Finally, if you expect to grow fast, raise capital from angels and venture capitalists, and grant stock options to service providers—none of these are easy to do in a sole proprietorship or unincorporated general partnership. You will want to form a legal entity that is set up to facilitate all of these goals.

## **WHEN** TO INCORPORATE OR ORGANIZE YOUR ENTITY

In general, you should form a business entity to conduct your business as soon as there is any risk of liability to third parties. For example, if you are tinkering in your garage by yourself, you probably don't need to worry about protecting yourself from liability to third parties. But as soon as you start to hire third parties to do work for you (to code, for example) or test the software with third parties (e.g., through a beta-user license agreement), you will want to do that through a business entity. If you are uncertain about whether you need to incorporate yet or not, ask yourself—am I doing anything right now that could cause a third party to sue me as a result of my business activities? If the answer is yes, then it is time to protect yourself.

## **WHAT TYPE** OF ENTITY TO FORM?

Entity formation involves both state law (you will form your entity under the laws of a particular state) and federal and state income tax law.

In general, there are two types of entities you can form under state law: a corporation or a limited liability company. (There are myriad other types of entities as well, such as cooperatives, nonprofit organizations, limited liability partnerships, etc. But for purposes of starting a high-growth venture that expects to take in capital, grant equity to workers, and grow fast to be sold or go public, these unusual entity choices are rarely the right choice.)

There are in general three types of entities available under the federal income tax law: (1) C corporations; (2) S corporations; and (3) entities taxed as partnerships (frequently LLCs). [For purposes of this book chapter, when

we refer to LLCs we are referring to entities taxed as partnerships for federal income tax purposes.]

## FEDERAL INCOME TAX ENTITY CLASSIFICATION

- *C corporations:* A C corporation is an entity that pays its own taxes. A C corporation's income does not pass through to its shareholders. First, the C corporation pays tax on its income. Then, if it distributes cash or property to its owners, its owners will usually pay tax on the amount of these distributions as well. This is what is referred to as the "double taxation" of C corporations. This double tax also occurs if the C corporation sells its assets in an asset sale. In that instance, the C corporation would pay tax on the gain from the sale of its assets. Then, when it distributed the remaining amounts after taxes to its shareholders, its shareholders would pay tax on what they received.

- *LLCs:* An LLC is a pass-through company, meaning its income is taxed at the owner level, not at the LLC level (while it is possible for an LLC to elect to be taxed as a corporation, in this chapter we assume LLCs are taxed as partnerships under the federal income tax law). Each year, the LLC files an information tax return with the IRS and also usually each state in which it does business. The LLC then issues a Form K-1 to each of its owners. The Form K-1 notifies the owners how much of the LLC's income, loss, credit, and other tax items must be reported on the investor's tax return.

- *S corporations:* An S corporation is also a pass-through company, meaning the S corporation itself doesn't pay tax. Its shareholders pay tax on the entity's income. The S corporation files an information return each year and sends its stockholders Form K-1. S corporations are different from LLCs in a couple of significant ways: (1) S corporations typically cannot have nonindividual shareholders; (2) S corporations can have only one class of stock with the same economic rights, preferences, and privileges; and (3) S corporations have to allocate income, loss, deductions, credits, and other taxes in proportion to stock ownership (they cannot "specially allocate" tax attributes).

With both LLCs and S Corporations, losses allocated to owners <u>may</u> be deductible by the owners on their tax returns.

Almost all early stage tech companies are formed as C corporations.

There are many reasons C corporations are so popular:

- C corporations are usually the entity of choice for angel and venture capital investors. Most angel and venture capital investors do not want to be taxed on the income of entities they have invested in. Investing in a pass-through company can subject you to tax in other jurisdictions. Further, some venture capital funds are prohibited from investing in LLCs by their organizational documents. This can happen, for example, when one of the limited partners in the venture fund is a tax-exempt entity and cannot receive allocations of trade or business income because it would threaten the entity's tax-exempt status.

- C corporations can grant traditional forms of equity compensation, such as stock options. Granting the equivalent of stock options in an LLC taxed as a partnership can be extraordinarily complex and costly.

- C corporations can issue "qualified small business stock" to founders and investors.

- C corporations can go public. For the most part, a pass-through company cannot go public.

- C corporations can engage in tax-free stock swaps with acquirer companies.

## WHAT IS QUALIFIED SMALL BUSINESS STOCK?

The Internal Revenue Code provides a significant tax break for investments in qualified small business stock (QSBS). QSBS is stock that if held for 5 years can be sold entirely free from federal income tax (up to a $10 million cap).

To issue QSBS, the entity issuing the stock has to be a C corporation with less than $50 million in assets both before and after the investment and engaged in a qualified trade or business. In general, services businesses cannot issue QSBS, but most tech companies can qualify to issue QSBS. Founder stock can qualify as QSBS.

## WHAT ABOUT B CORPS, PUBLIC BENEFIT, OR SOCIAL PURPOSE CORPORATIONS?

A B corp is not a type of state law corporation. A B corp is a business entity that has applied for and received certification as a B corp from B Lab, a nonprofit corporation.

Many states also allow you to form a type of corporation known as a public benefit or social purpose corporation. These are entities that have a mix of for-profit and nonprofit purposes or goals.

If you plan to pursue angel or venture capital investment or you desire to grant traditional forms of equity incentive compensation, you will typically want to form a traditional for-profit corporation. Many investors are leery of investing in public benefit or social purpose corporations.

## SHOULD YOU FORM YOUR BUSINESS AS AN LLC?

Many founders get advice to form their business as an LLC. LLCs are easier to form than corporations. (You can file a one-page form over the Internet to form an LLC in most states. You can also make an election for an LLC to be taxed as an S corporation.) For this reason, many tax accountants will advise startup founders to form as LLCs (and perhaps make S elections). Unfortunately, for most high-growth startup businesses an LLC is a poor choice as a form of entity. The reasons are many, but here are the highlights:

- LLCs cause their investors to owe tax on the LLC's annual taxable income, even if the LLC doesn't distribute any cash to its investors. Many venture funds can't invest in LLCs because they have tax-exempt limited partners who cannot be allocated income from a partnership conducting an active business.

- Granting stock options or the equivalent thereof in an LLC is extraordinarily complex.

- LLCs cannot participate in tax-free stock swaps with acquirer companies. This means that if your startup is going to be acquired by a big public company in exchange for that public company's stock, you will have to pay tax on your receipt of those shares even if they are contractually restricted from being sold for a year. If you operate your company through a corporation, you can do a stock exchange and not have to pay tax until you sell the stock.

- LLCs cannot issue qualified small business stock (QSBS). Only C corporations can issue QSBS.

- If an investor invests in an LLC, that investor will have to pay state income taxes in the states in which the LLC does business.

- If a foreign person invests in your LLC, that foreign investor will have to pay tax in the United States on the investor's allocable share of income from the LLC. The LLC will also have to remit to the IRS a substantial portion of the income allocated to the foreign partner (even if the income is not distributed).

- If you issue equity to your LLC employees, they won't be able to be "employees" for federal income tax purposes; they will be K-1 partners and have to file quarterly estimated tax payments. You would not be able to issue them a Form W-2 and withhold taxes from their wages.

## WHEN IS AN LLC A GOOD CHOICE?

An LLC is a good choice of entity in the following limited situations:

- You are forming a venture capital or a real estate investment fund.

- You are forming a company with a limited number of owners and you do not expect

the ownership to change over the life of the company.

- You will be the sole owner of the company.

- The company won't raise money from investors or grant stock options or similar equity awards to service providers.

## WHAT ABOUT AN S CORPORATION?

If you want to have the losses of your business flow through to your individual tax return, you have two choices: an LLC or an S corporation. Of these two choices, for a high-growth tech venture an S corporation is usually a better choice than an LLC for the following reasons: (1) an S corporation is more easily converted to a C corporation than is an LLC; (2) if you accept a venture capital investment as an S corporation by issuing preferred stock, your S-corporation status immediately terminates; (3) S corporations can grant traditional types of equity compensation, such as incentive and nonqualified stock options; and (4) S corporations can engage in tax-free stock swap acquisition transactions (LLCs cannot).

Be advised though—if you form as an S corporation, your founder stock cannot qualify as qualified small business stock.

## WHERE TO FORM YOUR ENTITY

The most commonly used form of entity by startup ventures that expect to take on angel or venture capital investment is a Delaware corporation.

The benefits of Delaware corporations include:

- Widespread familiarity with Delaware law. If you incorporate your business in Washington, California, Nevada, etc., prospective investors may very well ask you, Why didn't you incorporate in Delaware?

- Widespread availability of lawyers able to assist with Delaware corporations (one of the troubles of incorporating in a lesser-utilized jurisdiction, such as Nevada, is that you cannot easily find a Nevada corporate lawyer in major cities in America).

A well-developed set of case law interpreting the fiduciary duties of the directors and officers.

A special set of courts that handle only corporate disputes.

Widespread availability of template document sets frequently used in startup land. Almost all of the really good template documents that various organizations have published are designed for Delaware corporations; for example, the Series Seed documents or the document set the National Venture Capital Association publishes.

Depending on where you are doing business, your home state's corporate laws may be completely suitable. For example, in Washington state, local angels and venture capitalists are comfortable with Washington corporations. Microsoft is a Washington corporation. But even if you are headquartered in Washington, incorporating in Delaware is a good choice. Avoiding potential questions about not incorporating in Delaware is a good idea. In general, you don't want to create any questions for your prospective investors about your legal structure.

## WHAT ABOUT OTHER STATES, SUCH AS CALIFORNIA OR NEVADA?

California is a review state, meaning if you file articles of amendment or another similar type of filing with the Secretary of State, the Secretary of State has lawyers on staff who will review and potentially repeal your filing if in the opinion of state counsel it is not correct. This can slow down the closing of transactions. Delaware is not a review state.

Sometimes founders will read about Nevada and how it provides more privacy protections and better tax provisions than Delaware. Be wary of claims of greater privacy protections. Also know that your income tax considerations are not driven at all by where you incorporate but where you do business.

Finally, incorporate in a well-known jurisdiction so you can find a lawyer to help you. If you incorporate in Nevada, you will need a Nevada corporate lawyer. You can find a good Delaware corporate lawyer in any American city, but you cannot find a good Nevada corporate lawyer as easily.

## WHAT TO NAME YOUR COMPANY

Taking time to research your contemplated name for your company makes sense. If you are going to invest funds in branding, hire a trademark attorney to help you make sure someone else can't stop you from using your name later.

## YOUR COMPANY'S ARTICLES AND BYLAWS

You will want to make sure of several things: (1) that your charter or applicable law allows the shareholders to act by less than unanimous written consent; (2) that cumulative voting does not exist; and (3) that statutory preemptive rights are not included.

## COFOUNDER ARRANGEMENTS

If your company is going to have cofounders, you will need to think through what type of cofounder arrangements to put in place. In general, you will want to impose vesting conditions on all shares issued to founders. You will also want to think through how control arrangements work.

Vesting means that the shares issued can be repurchased by the company at the lower of fair market value or the price paid by the founders; repurchase rights lapse over the service-based vesting period.

Vesting is critical because your company will become unfundable if a significant percentage of the equity is held by someone no longer working for the company. This is what is referred to as "dead equity."

In the corporate context, holders of a majority of the outstanding shares of stock elect the board of directors. This means that if your company has three equal founders, any two can vote to throw the third out of the company at any time, unless the parties enter into an agreement to the contrary.

Sometimes founders enter into a voting agreement to assure each founder a spot on the board. But you will want to be careful if you do this because you will hamstring your company if you can't remove a nonperforming founder.

## EQUITY INCENTIVE PLANS

You will typically want to put an equity incentive plan in place at the same time that you organize the company and issue the founder shares. You want to do this at the outset so that you have a plan in place and ready to use when you decide to grant your first stock options to advisory board members or new hires.

## DO YOU NEED A SHAREHOLDER AGREEMENT?

Founders usually sign stock-purchase agreements with their companies that give the company the right to repurchase their unvested shares. It is also typical for those agreements to include a right of first refusal in favor of the company, meaning if the founder wants to sell his or her shares, the company has the right to buy them first. Finally, sometimes those agreements allow the company to repurchase vested shares at fair market value.

In general, you do not need a shareholder agreement for buy-sell purposes. The modern practice is to include company repurchase rights in an agreement with each shareholder separately. The exception is a voting agreement you are trying to establish control arrangements that are unique.

# WHY STARTUPS SHOULD SPEND ON BRAND

Moving Brands

## WHY DOES BRAND MATTER FOR STARTUPS?

There are many things that startups must consider in the early stages of development: where the next funding round is coming from, what the next product release will be, whom to hire, and how to scale. Understandably, brand might seem like something to consider downstream. But in a crowded marketplace, brand might be the difference between one startup receiving funding over another. A strong brand can secure higher valuations from venture capital firms, attract the attention of otherwise apathetic influencers, and most importantly, for a business that is finding its way, it can become a valuable decision-making tool.

A strong brand can also help create a better product experience for the user. It can grow awareness, which in turn creates brand loyalty. A powerful brand exemplifies a startup's unique company culture, one that attracts great talent while reinvigorating existing employees. Your brand is your identity. Brand is not just a value-add to a business; it is at the epicenter of the business.

For several decades, the world's leading companies have realized the value of their brands in terms of customer loyalty and have attributed a real economic value to them. By actively defining and shaping your brand, you are starting on the path of being able to realize this value too. The reality is, the decisions you make every day are already forming your brand, whether you realize it or not. Read on to understand how you can take control of your brand and ensure it's pointing your business on the path to success.

## FIVE PRINCIPLES THAT MAKE GREAT BRANDS

What is a great brand? It is a simple term that has huge implications for a growing business.

### 1. GREAT BRANDS ARE DRIVEN BY PURPOSE.

Your brand equals your purpose. Capture that purpose and ensure it's the driver behind all your decisions. This will become your brand story. The best brand stories provide a cornerstone for business decision making, a mirror that shows if you are staying true to your intent.

## Case study: Virgin

Restless entrepreneurialism has always driven Virgin to challenge the rules. The business disrupts each new industry it enters, challenging the status quo to deliver better, more ethical service than its competitors. By distilling the inputs of over 150 global Virgin employees to get to a common truth as well as the characteristics of Virgin founder, Richard Branson, the brand story was crafted: "Don't just play the game, change it for good." The phrase so perfectly encompasses the vision of the founder, it has become established as a Branson quote. It is an authentic, credible story in the language of Richard Branson, but accessible to every employee.

## 2. GREAT BRANDS ARE BUILT THROUGH COHERENT INTERACTIONS.

When a brand finally comes to life, you need to consider how it will be recognized across all touchpoints regardless of whether these interactions are experienced digitally or physically.

## Case study: Housing

Housing was born out of its founders' own struggle to find a home. In revolutionizing the local real estate market, Housing has grown, in under three years, from a small team in Mumbai to 1,500 employees in 45 cities across India. The idea of "look up" became inherent in the brand story of Housing. It also manifested into a unique design signature that brought the Housing brand to life. The mark, the communications, the social campaign, and the site experience all projected idea of looking up. At launch of the new brand, there were over 2 million views of the journey film within two days, and the hashtag *lookup* was trending sixth in India on Twitter.

## 3. GREAT BRANDS ARE CLEAR AND SIMPLE TO UNDERSTAND.

In a world that is ambiguous and volatile, your brand can bring instant clarity about your place and value amidst the complexity.

## Case study: Bluewolf

Bluewolf is a global consulting agency and a cloud-consulting pioneer. Already established as the leading business consultancy in the Salesforce ecosystem, Bluewolf wanted to communicate its strengths beyond the customer relationship management (CRM) platform. It needed help to position the business, create a brand system, and craft a communications language to reflect this new, broader offer. Through interviews and workshops with key stakeholders and customers, two prevalent themes arose—a passion for providing customers with the most value from future-facing technologies and the instinct to begin problem-solving and customizing solutions on the spot. These core themes became the heart of the Bluewolf story: "It's always now." The story was brought to life through a punchy visual system and action-driven messaging. The "get it done" vigor of working with Bluewolf is immediately clear to those who come in contact with the brand, setting the tone for the relationship from the very first interaction.

## 4. GREAT BRANDS ARE UNIQUELY IDENTIFIABLE AND RECOGNIZABLE IN THEIR SIMPLEST FORM.

Logos are powerful symbols but cannot carry a brand on their own. The entire system should work together to ensure your brand is identifiable whether you're viewing it as an app icon on an Apple Watch screen or seeing it projected larger than life in an immersive environment.

## Case study: Asana

Asana is anything but an average Silicon Valley startup. By imagining how people could manage their work the way they manage their lives—socially openly and efficiently—Asana has grown into a cult SaaS business. Asana needed to clearly redefine its brand and positioning, from a provider of shared task lists and engineering bug trackers to an enterprise-grade collaboration software company. Asana is about the power of collaboration, so it was important this was captured in the redesign and optimization of the brand system. Three vertical dots symbolize alignment and naturally form an abstract "A" in a mark that symbolizes the limitless potential of human collaboration. Every aspect of the mark, typography, and color palette is designed to communicate a sense of balance, clarity, and purpose-driven design. "When I see this on my phone's home screen, it's obvious: that's the teamwork app," according to Justin Rosenstein, Cofounder, Asana.

## 5. GREAT BRANDS REFLECT THE UNIQUE CULTURE OF THE BUSINESS.

A strong brand should find a balance between reflecting your unique culture, yet still look and feel credible and competitive. It allows you to shape the conversations you will have with investors, users, and partners as well as the talent that makes your business what it is.

### Case study: Coyote

Coyote is one of the fastest-growing third-party logistics companies in North America. Coyote's story, "Powerful Momentum," was derived from both the explosive growth of the company and the spirit of its employees. Throughout the organization was a simple and powerful attitude—the desire to win. Its animal-like dynamism and competitive spirit meant it was closing the gap between the company and its competitors. But its previous do-it-yourself identity had failed to capture this powerful cultural essence. It needed a brand as powerful as the Fortune 100 companies it was targeting, giving it the conviction to communicate its spirit emphatically to both powerhouse clients and to its own internal teams.

"Tenacious" and "tribal" were words that resonated company-wide. Articulating the loud, loyal, and fiercely energetic drivers behind Coyote's superior performance would serve to differentiate it from its competition and drive success in an authentic way. These behaviors underpinned the creation of a comprehensive brand system, including the bold arrowhead logo and stenciled wordmark, strategically differentiated color palette, fierce photography style derived from a shoot with a live coyote, and a tone of voice that encapsulated the employees'

mix of in-depth professional knowledge and fraternity-style rawness. Coyote fully embraced its new brand, with employees literally wearing the new identity on their sleeves in a successful line of branded clothing and accessories.

## A THREE-PART APPROACH TO BUILDING BRANDS FOR STARTUPS

A winning brand can be broken down into three components: Story, System, and Experience. This combination poises a startup to be prepared, future-focused, and creative.

### STORY

The best brands are built on stories. A good brand story is authentic, engaging, and distinct. It builds from "what" the brand does or "how it does it" to get to the "why." Brand stories are more than well-written prose. They guide decisions that drive the business—decisions on what the offering should be, how customers should experience the product or service, and whom to partner with.

The core truths and personality at the heart of a brand can be found only in the hearts and minds of its people, and often require difficult and direct questions to uncover. That's why the process of defining a brand story should involve people from across the business, from founders who hold the vision to the sales manager at the frontline of customer service delivery. Only then will employees feel that they've played an important role in shaping the brand and compelled to live it.

### LIVING IDENTITY SYSTEM

We consider the components of a brand identity a living "system." This system includes both the building blocks for your brand (for instance, logo, color palette, tone of voice) as well as the guidance needed to create from these components. By building the system on defined characters and behaviors, it can adapt to any environment, much like a person would. This ensures your brand can face whatever the future holds. A successful system should have both fixed and flexible elements; this allows the people that use the system the space to build coherent applications within clearly defined parameters. A strong system should be a springboard, not a straightjacket.

## EXPERIENCES

A brand is built on a myriad of different "experiences": microinteractions in an app, the motion design of a webpage load, the design of meeting rooms, the tone of your chatbot's response, to the sound of your product's buttons being pressed. Great brands are recognizable by these unique experiences. It is these moments that customers may instinctively bring to mind when thinking about your product and those that can differentiate you in a sea of sameness. When creating these brand experiences, build from the brand story but for your audience. Know who they are and design with them in mind by involving them in the process through research or prototyping.

# HOW TO GET STARTED ON YOUR BRAND

## WRITE YOUR BRIEF

Sit down and work out exactly what you want to achieve, a timeline, and a budget. Then, write this up into a brief. The discipline of putting it on paper will help to focus your mind. When you do decide to share your brief, precede it with a simple nondisclosure agreement before giving away any secrets or your big idea. This shows you are serious and protects you against any loose talk.

## FIND THE PERFECT PARTNER

Ask your personal network whom they have worked with; think about which brands you admire, then find out who has worked on them. Deciding between a small or large agency will be your next step. A large agency will have rigor and process and a great track record. But you will be a small fish in a large pond. Ask who the team is that will be working with you and how they will ensure that they do not lose sight of you in their daily work for their larger clients' business.

With a smaller agency, you will be a larger fish in a small pond and very likely get to work with the founders or principals. Make sure that you have seen their creative work. Do you really like it and can they be broad or will they just give you a "house style"?

Next comes the face-to-face meeting and chemistry test. Having shared your written brief in advance, use this meeting to see if you feel that there is a good fit. Ask the agency's opinion about your ideas and expect them to ask you the same about your business. This demonstrates they are really thinking about you and not just seeing the dollar signs.

## DEFINE YOUR VISION

You can start the process by completing the following prompts:

*We believe / We will always / We will never / We love / We hate / We are different because / We will be remembered for . . .*

Be open and honest and think about the brand you aspire to be. Next, try the "Writing the Future" exercise. Your brand's future is yours to write. Uncouple yourself from the limitations of the present and imagine the future in purely aspirational terms. Setting the bar impossibly high sets your brand on a path to exceed expectations.

Imagine yourself 10 years in an ideal future. You're reading an article about your organization—the one that you're going to frame and put up in your office. What publication is it in and what's the headline?

Involve your team and stakeholders. This process is meant to be intensive, hands-on, and highly collaborative. At the end of the exercise, you should be able to explain yourself and your business with conviction. Even in its raw form, documenting the intent and vision of your key stakeholders in the early stages of your brand is invaluable.

# CONCLUSION

Those startups that fail to consider brand early on may well end up spending considerable time, effort, and money either correcting their brand or making it fit its customers. Spending money upfront may seem counterintuitive, but it is well worth it. A powerful brand will prove a springboard to sustained business success.

# 6

# DESIGN THINKING AND LEAN STARTUP: A PROCESS TO DESIGN, TEST, AND LAUNCH YOUR STARTUP

**Stanford Graduate School of Business**

Stefanos Zenios

Investment Group of Santa Barbara Professor of Entrepreneurship and Professor of Operations, Information, and Technology

Co-Director, Center for Entrepreneurial Studies, Graduate School of Business, Stanford University

Startup Garage is an experiential entrepreneurship course I teach at the Stanford University Graduate School of Business. Each year, about 50 teams go through that course and between 5 and 10 teams end up launching a venture based on the work they completed in the course. Companies such as ePocrates, Trulia, SoFi, DoorDash, and BipSync came from the course. Importantly, numerous other aspiring entrepreneurs launched their careers using the process and tools they learned in the course. In this short chapter, I want to share with you the key elements of the process— we call it the Startup Garage process—we teach in that course. This chapter begins with a description of the two key methodologies that provide the building blocks for the Startup Garage process: Lean Startup and Design Thinking. It then provides a description of the integrated Startup Garage process that combines these two building blocks and concludes with a description of the role of the team in the process.

## LEAN STARTUP

Lean Startup[1,2,3] begins with the premise that a startup is a set of hypotheses about the startup's business model. The entrepreneur's goal is to prove or disprove these hypotheses using experimental data. The methodology proceeds in a cycle as follows (see Figure 1): Formulate the key business hypothesis, identify the key risks in your business hypothesis (i.e., critical assumptions on which the viability of the business rests), design an experiment to collect data to assess these risks, collect the data, analyze and determine whether they prove or disprove the key business hypothesis, and then decide whether you will persevere (continue on the same path), pivot (make a critical change in the business hypothesis), or abandon the project.

The key principle behind this methodology is that it is impossible to know whether your hypothesis about the business is correct unless you test it and collect real data. The methodology is an antidote to a common form of bias that plagues entrepreneurs, unbridled optimism that disregards any data that contradict the

**FIGURE 1** The Lean Startup Innovation Cycle

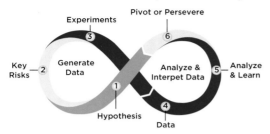

entrepreneur's hypothesis until it is too late. The methodology aims to balance that optimism with rigor and data that can guide the entrepreneur and his or her team through the process of starting a business.

The key elements of this methodology are first, the business hypothesis, which is typically framed using a versatile tool called the Business Model Canvas[4] (see Figure 2). This tool provides a common language for summarizing how the business will create and capture value, and it divides the business model into its key elements. Second is the minimal viable product: a minimal version of the product that gains customer traction. The goal of the entrepreneur is to discover this minimal viable product through a series of experiments. Third is the pivot or persevere decision, a decision to either stay the course or make a radical change, informed by the data gathered through the experiment.

*Wealthfront: A lean startup case study.* Wealthfront was cofounded by Andy Ratchleff in 2008, and it initially operated as an investment manager marketplace in which clients would find outstanding managers to manage the U.S. public equities portion of their portfolio. In early 2011, Wealthfront's managers outperformed the U.S. market by 4%. However, this was not impressing its customers and Wealthfront was not gaining adequate traction. Andy picked up the phone and spoke to some of its customers to find out what was going on. He learned that they did not want someone to manage part of their portfolio exceptionally well but rather someone to manage their complete portfolio adequately and inexpensively. Andy and his team developed a paper prototype of an automated

financial advice service that would do exactly that. They shared the paper prototype with roughly 40 potential customers and walked them through the specific advice the tool would provide to them using paper and pencil (this is referred to as the concierge minimal viable product). They received consistent and enthusiastic feedback. With that information at hand, Andy refocused the team on the development of an online financial advisor that was launched in December 2011[5]. The product was exceptionally well received, and the startup is now growing and thriving.

This short case demonstrates how Andy tried to understand why the first generation of its service was not gaining traction. He used the data to propose a new service and value proposition which he tested using low-resolution concierge minimal viable product. Armed with that information, Andy led the company through a successful pivot.

This methodology brings a much needed rigor into the process of starting a new venture, but it is not without its limitations. First, it is unclear how the original hypothesis is to be generated. And second, there is a lot of ambiguity in how the pivot-or-persevere decision is to be made. Design thinking, the second methodology we will introduce, provides a process for generating the original hypothesis and also a high-level vision that can guide the pivot or persevere decision.

## Design Thinking

Design thinking is a process developed by the design firm IDEO[6,7] and taught extensively at the Stanford design school (affectionately referred to as "d.school"[8]). It focuses on understanding the customer deeply through meaningful empathetic interactions and using low-resolution, rapid prototyping to develop and test solutions. The visual representation of the process in Figure 3 (and description below) outlines its key steps[9].

This process relies on the following principles:

1. Do not solve your own problems—solve someone else's problems. To be able to do that,

**FIGURE 2** The Business Model Canvas

| Designed for: | Designed by: | On: Day | Month | Year |
| --- | --- | --- | --- | --- |
| | | Iteration: No. | | |

### Key Partners

Who are our Key Partners?
Who are our key suppliers?
Which Key Resources are we acquiring from partners?
Which Key Activities do partners perform?

**MOTIVATIONS FOR PARTNERSHIPS:**
*Optimization and economy*
*Reduction of risk and uncertainty*
*Acquisition of particular resources and activities*

### Key Activities

What Key Activities do our Value Propositions require?
Our Distribution Channels?
Customer Relationships?
Revenue Streams?

**CATEGORIES**
*Production*
*Problem Solving*
*Platform/Network*

### Key Resources

What Key Resources do our Value Propositions require?
Our Distribution Channels?
Customer Relationships?
Revenue Streams?

**Types of resources**
*Physical*
*Intellectual (brand patents, copyrights, data)*
*Human*
*Financial*

### Value Propositions

What value do we deliver to the customer?
Which one of our customer's problems are we helping to solve?
What bundles of products and services are we offering to each customer segment?
Which customer needs are we satisfying?

**CHARACTERISTICS**
*Newness*
*Performance*
*Customization*
*"Getting the Job Done"*
*Design*
*Brand/Status*
*Price*
*Cost Reduction*
*Risk Reduction*
*Accessibility*
*Convenience/Usability*

### Customer Relationships

What type of relationship does each of our Customer Segments expect us to establish and maintain with them?
Which ones have we established?
How are they integrated with the rest of our business model?
How costly are they?

**EXAMPLES**
*Personal assistance*
*Dedicated Personal Assistance*
*Self-Service*
*Automated Services*
*Communities*
*Co-creation*

### Channels

Through which Channels do our Customer Segments want to be reached?
How are we reaching them now?
How are our Channels integrated?
Which ones work best?
Which ones are most cost-efficient?
How are we integrating them with customer routines?

**CHANNEL PHASES:**
*1. Awareness*
*How do we raise awareness about our company's products and services?*
*2. Evaluation*
*How do we help customers evaluate our organization's Value Proposition?*
*3. Purchase*
*How do we allow customers to purchase specific products and services?*
*4. Delivery*
*How do we deliver a Value Proposition to customers?*
*5. After sales*
*How do we provide post-purchase customer support?*

### Customer Segments

For whom are we creating value?
Who are our most important customers?

*Mass Market*
*Niche Market*
*Segmented*
*Diversified*
*Multi-sided Platform*

### Cost Structure

What are the most important costs inherent in our business model?
Which Key Resources are most expensive?
Which Key Activities are most expensive?

**is your business more:**
*Cost Driven (leanest cost structure, low price value proposition, maximum automation, extensive outsourcing)*
*Value Driven (focused on value creation, premium value proposition)*

**Sample characteristics:**
*Fixed Costs (salaries, rents, utilities)*
*Variable costs*
*Economies of scale*
*Economies of scope*

### Revenue Streams

For what value are our customers really willing to pay?
For what do they currently pay?
How are they currently paying?
How would they prefer to pay?
How much does each Revenue Stream contribute to overall revenues?

**TYPES:**
*Asset sale*
*Usage fee*
*Subscription Fees*
*Lending/Renting/Leasing*
*Licensing*
*Brokerage fees*
*Advertising*

**FIXED PRICING**
*List Price*
*Product feature dependent*
*Customer segment dependent*
*Volume dependent*

**DYNAMIC PRICING**
*Negotiation (bargaining)*
*Yield Management*
*Real-time-Market*

**FIGURE 3** The Design Thinking Process

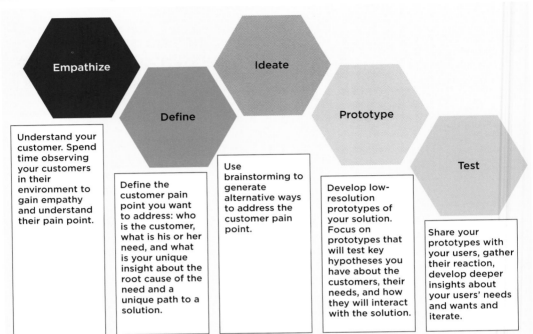

**Empathize**

Understand your customer. Spend time observing your customers in their environment to gain empathy and understand their pain point.

**Define**

Define the customer pain point you want to address: who is the customer, what is his or her need, and what is your unique insight about the root cause of the need and a unique path to a solution.

**Ideate**

Use brainstorming to generate alternative ways to address the customer pain point.

**Prototype**

Develop low-resolution prototypes of your solution. Focus on prototypes that will test key hypotheses you have about the customers, their needs, and how they will interact with the solution.

**Test**

Share your prototypes with your users, gather their reaction, develop deeper insights about your users' needs and wants and iterate.

you need to spend time with your potential customers and understand their day and their workflow and their experience from their perspective, not yours.

2. Do not jump into solutions before you can define the problem. Be clear what is the problem you want to address and maniacally focus on solving it.

3. Do not let the perfect be the enemy of good enough. At early stages of the development of a new solution, you do not know enough about the problem you are trying to solve. Low-resolution prototypes can help you quickly discover the problem and the solution.

4. Bias for action. You want to maximize your learning by accelerating the time to a prototype and testing multiple prototypes rapidly.

5. Divergent thinking—encourage wild, even crazy, solutions to open up the space of possible solutions and thus create unique and unpredictable approaches to the problem.

This process can be viewed simultaneously as a problem-definition/problem-solving methodology and a toolbox for stimulating creativity. Specifically, the empathize and define steps in the process focus on problem definition and the ideate and prototyping steps focus on problem solving. And the test step simply tests to see whether the solution solves the problem. In this last step, you can discover that the solution works but needs changes or it doesn't. The testing stage may highlight the need to change the solution completely, but oftentimes it leads to rethinking the problem statement. As a toolbox for stimulating creativity, design thinking relies on an approach that considers multiple alternatives in both defining the problem statement and generating solutions. This is known as divergent thinking and is central to the design thinking process.

Design thinking relies on intuition, insights, and small scale qualitative interactions between the "designers" and their "customers" to uncover unmet customer needs and explore new ways to solve them. It allows rapid progress and provides the basis for gaining deep customer insights. However, it also has its limitations: it does not provide clear guidance to determine when a solution is good enough, and it does not provide tools to consider the business aspects of the solution. Questions like what is the business model, or is the solution economically viable, cannot be addressed effectively with design thinking.

### The Startup Garage Innovation Process: Integrating Design Thinking and Lean Startup

At Startup Garage, the course I teach at Stanford, we have merged the two processes into an integrated process, called the Startup Garage Innovation Process, in which the students begin with design thinking to identify an unmet customer need and develop low-resolution prototypes and then progress into lean startup, in which they translate those needs and prototypes into business model canvases, minimal viable products, and experiments that supplement qualitative responses to few prototype tests followed by quantitative responses in more extensive tests. Our intention is to use the best of both worlds and develop an approach that leverages the strengths of the two foundational processes (design thinking, lean startup) and use each one to address the limitations of the other.

A visual representation of the process is provided below in Figure 4.

We will now provide more details about the steps of this integrated process.

## EXPLORE AND DEEPEN OUR UNDERSTANDING OF THE NEED

The purpose of this stage in the process is to develop an understanding of the customer, his or her needs, and develop a range of possible solutions with associated business models. The entrepreneur and his or her team spends the first month learning about the customer through direct observations, interviews, and immersion in the customer's environment. Teams spend time with customers at their place of business or at their homes, they ask questions, make observations, gather data. At the end they summarize the information they have gathered into a list of pain points and a description of customers and their behaviors. This culminates in multiple points of view describing the customer's problems. These points of view include a description of the customer, his or her pain point, and why this pain point is compelling. An example of a point of view is as follows:

George, a conscientious knowledge worker with average computing skills, **needs** an easy and seamless way to share electronic documents with his coworkers, **because** existing methods are becoming increasingly cumbersome and frustrating in accommodating the proliferation of computing platforms and are making him feel inadequate.

**FIGURE 4** The Startup Garage Innovation Process

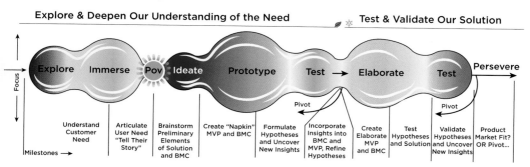

This point of view represents the customer problem solved by cloud-based document sharing and storage solutions such as DropBox and Box. It can serve as the starting point for understanding the underlying customer pain and generate possible solutions.

Teams usually generate multiple points of view, and then they focus on one based on their subjective assessment of how actionable the point of view is and how big the pain point is. No consideration for market size is made at this point.

The teams then use brainstorming to generate tens of different ways to address the selected pain point and then select one or two approaches based on team excitement, how well the approach fits the need, and team ability to develop a solution. Low-resolution prototypes of the solution are then developed in the form of storyboards, mock-ups, or videos. The team also develops a business model for each of the two solutions using the business model canvas and then performs a very rudimentary market size calculation using a top down market size formula:

Total # of Customers × Market Penetration × Revenue per Customer per Year

This calculation helps the team determine the magnitude of the opportunity.

The team then shares prototypes and basic pricing information with potential customers. Engaging in open-ended discussions, the team aims to understand whether the proposed solution resonates with the customer. At the first iteration, the most likely outcome is that the team discovers that it did not fully understand the customer need. This can send the team back to the drawing board to refine its points of view. Two or three iterations are typically needed until the team starts receiving consistent responses from the users that the need they are addressing is compelling and the solution is promising. Positive customer response takes the form of consistent willingness from the customer to engage in meaningful value exchanges with

the team: sign up to be a beta tester, commit to codevelop the product, pay a small fee to reserve a fully developed product, or join a customer waiting list. In the absence of evidence of strong positive response, the team keeps iterating but is encouraged to stop after the third iteration and pivot to a different opportunity identified in the early interviews.

When a positive response is obtained, the team now moves to the **Test and Validate the Solution** phase. The first step is to develop a more elaborate model of the business unit economics: the lifetime value of each customer minus the customer acquisition costs. By comparing this calculation to comparable metrics in the industry and customer segments the team is targeting, the team is able to determine key assumptions that would lead into attractive and positive unit economics, and they then design experiments to gather data to support these assumptions. Common assumptions have to do with attrition rates in the customer funnel, customer repeat purchase decisions, etc. The team's goal is to identify the two to three tipping point assumptions, assumptions that can tip the profitability equation with the least change in the underlying assumption. And then the team runs experiments to test these assumptions. These experiments usually take the form of engaging in meaningful value exchanges with customers using a more elaborate prototype, now referred to as the minimal viable product.

As an example, one of our teams wished to develop a turnkey forecasting tool, powered by artificial intelligence tools, to help container transportation companies better match supply and demand. Their minimal viable product took the form of consulting engagement: identify a client and work closely to analyze the client's data and provide a manual solution that demonstrates the potential financial benefits in the context of the client's operations for a given month. The team managed to secure such a client and demonstrated the potential benefits before engaging into the development of the actual tool. This enabled them to launch their sales effort to other potential customers.

Teams are also encouraged to be clear ahead of time what response will be considered affirmative for their assumptions and support that target response using a statement that "if we get X positive responses we know this will lead to a profitable business because it would support the following unit economics." One of our teams that ended up launching as the company Doordash used a spreadsheet to model their profitability, and they then designed experiments to test assumptions in the spreadsheet. Their target was getting responses that were compatible with the assumptions in their profitability spreadsheet.

*The pivot decision:* Nothing illustrates the process more succinctly than the pivot decision. Once data from experiments are collected, the team meets to decide whether it is time to change directions—make a pivot. The team summarizes all the data supporting the current hypothesis as well as risks to the business model identified either previously or as a result of new data gathered. The team then also considers one or more pivots: changes in key elements of the Business Model Canvas that would address the risks uncovered so far and possibly open up opportunities for more rapid growth. The pivot decision also highlights the iterative nature of the process; the gray arrows in the process diagram in Figure 4 are points where the process can move back to earlier steps. It is common to see 10 teams that started at the same point to be at very different steps of the process 2 months later, based on the data they have collected and pivots they have made.

*The team:* Building a venture and running the Startup Garage process is a team sport. As part of the process we are encouraging our teams to spend time on basic team activities: discussing and deciding on team norms and processes, spending time to understand each other's values and beliefs and what motivates each team member, and revisiting team norms and processes and their relationships to each other in periodic intervals. Failure to make progress in the process is sometimes due to the opportunity that

the team explores but other times is the result of team dysfunction. Teams should be mindful of the process but also of their team dynamics and pay attention to both.

## CONCLUSION

It is becoming increasingly recognized that startups that succeed follow a systematic, rigorous process of customer need identification, business model hypothesis generation, testing, learning, and iteration. This short chapter has summarized the key steps of the process as used at Stanford's Startup Garage and as practiced by several startups that were successfully launched from that program.

## REFERENCES

1. Eric Ries, *The Lean Startup: How Today's Entrepreneurs Use Continuous Innovation to Create Radically Successful Businesses,* Crown Business, 2011.

2. Steve Blank, *The Four Steps to the Epiphany,* K&S Ranch, 2nd Edition, 2013.

3. Steve Blank, Why the Lean Start-Up Changes Everything, May 2013 issue of *Harvard Business Review.*

4. Alexander Osterwalder and Yves Pigneur, *Business Model Generation: A Handbook for Visionaries, Game Changers, and Challengers,* Wiley, Jul 13, 2010.

5. https://blog.wealthfront.com/introducing-online-financial-advisor-built-silicon-valley-silicon-valley/

6. Design Kit: The Human-Centered Design Toolkit. Accessed at https://www.ideo.com/post/design-kit

7. Jon Kolko, Design Thinking Comes of Age, September 2015 issue of *Harvard Business Review.*

8. http://dschool.stanford.edu/

9. Design Thinking: A Unified Framework For Innovation. http://www.forbes.com/sites/reuvencohen/2014/03/31/design-thinking-a-unified-framework-for-innovation/#7e244dcc56fc

# WHAT'S THE PLAN? HOW TO COMMUNICATE A COMPELLING VISION

**FirstMark Capital**

Rick Heitzmann, Founder and Managing Director

Caitlin Strandberg, Vice President

## OVERVIEW

Now more than ever, the ability to communicate a clear, simple, and persuasive vision is critical in building momentum for your business and developing an effective fundraising strategy. Gone are the days of the traditional "business plan"—a thick, phonebook-like tome detailing every minute detail and hypothetical of a business operation. Building a business today means accepting uncertainty and ambiguity and yet one thing is certain—change. The business, industry, and environment will surely change. Communicating how your business fits into this ever-changing world and how you expect to navigate the ups-and-downs of entrepreneurship is a key differentiator that investors look for when evaluating a business. In this chapter, we will introduce different ways to communicate an effective narrative and present a compelling view of your business, which is not only important to potential investors but also to future customers and employees.

Today's "business plan" equivalent is a combination of materials based on varying stages of an investor conversation—getting an introduction, the first meeting, a meeting with the broader investment team, and diligence process. Knowing that a highly-detailed plan is guaranteed to change in the early stages of a business, investors often focus on the specifics around a company's team, product, and market. Investors look for signals that show how an entrepreneur thinks about the future and expects to grapple with anticipated challenges. Strong materials make it easier to distinguish the signal from the noise and serve as an opportunity to guide investors to the most important aspects of the business. Done well, great materials can generate sufficient interest in a business, turning a ~5-minute email into a ~45-minute meeting and a long-term relationship.

As with any effective communication strategy, it's not only important to present your message but also important to be thoughtful regarding your intended audience. Keep in mind that any information you present is the beginning of a relationship with your audience and the materials on the page are merely a facilitator. Effective materials should elicit deeper questions from an investor that forms the basis of a meaningful conversation. You should anticipate the questions investors will ask and use the content and discussion as an opportunity to not only tell a high-level story but also showcase depth of understanding. Anything that you do not share or convey, you allow someone else to interpret and imply on your behalf. So know your business and control the narrative, or you may risk a VC firm's analyst, a competitor, or even a customer doing it for you. At the same time, a healthy degree of self-awareness around where the business is today and what hypotheses are left to prove will also go a long way in communicating your strategy.

While investors have a finite set of criteria and signals they look for, keep in mind that every investor is different. Depending on size, scope, and traction of your business, as well as the investor's own style, their questions and expectations will vary. To oversimplify, consider a meeting as a mutual first impression, with the goal to learn more about one another and test for personality fit. It goes both ways—investors should be thoughtful, interested, and engaged in your business. And investors are looking for an athlete—someone who can set a thoughtful strategy, navigate unexpected situations, and get the business across the finish line to an IPO or acquisition.

It can be physically taxing and mentally exhausting—traveling across time zones, being away from home, running the business while also running a process. In my own experience at the end of 2001 in starting a business, I met over 87 investors and travelled over 30,000 miles to barely make payroll. So prepare and be ready for everything. Spend the time upfront to create an efficient and effective process and try to minimize stress on your body, mind, and business. And it's not all for nothing. In fact, many high-quality materials are often repurposed for other uses. Fundraising is a way to sharpen, refine, and practice business communication (for future investors, recruiting candidates, and potential customers).

As outlined below, the materials needed for successful fundraising should focus on communicating the most important information, anticipating common questions, and minimizing back-and-forth logistics to get to the final answer (yes, no, or the ever often "not right now"). From

the investor perspective, there are four key questions:

- Do we want to learn more?
- What do we have to believe about this business for it to be successful?
- Do we want to invest in this space?
- Is this a deal that fits in terms of size and stage?

The following chapter focuses on specific content and a process to design materials so that you can respond quickly to inbound requests and remain in control of fundraising at a pace that fits your business needs.

## MATERIALS PRIMER

As you embark on the fundraising process, there is a common set of materials that an investor might inquire about or expect, depending on the phase of the investment cycle.

The first step of fundraising includes generating interest and excitement about your business, often through either a cold email or preferably a warm referral. After the initial introduction, someone within the firm will determine investment fit and next steps. The decision is usually based on the information provided as well as the relevance of the referrer to a firm. A VC firm is more likely to prioritize an email from a portfolio founder or coinvestor over an inbound email from an unknown contact. Warm referrals create credibility and demonstrate an ability to build relationships within the community, and so they will typically be more compelling. A cold email is not necessarily a nonstarter; however, you have a single opportunity to grab attention so plan accordingly.

For initial outbound communication, we recommend creating brief and concise "teaser" materials. A well written 100-word description and a basic high-level pitch deck can be used to facilitate the warm introduction and spark interest. The full pitch deck is typically used later in the investment cycle during the formal investor presentation and provides the most comprehensive information for an investor to make a decision. For reference, materials we don't see any more and do not recommend spending time on developing include long-form investor business plans (e.g., Word documents), private placement memos, and nondisclosure agreements.

*100-Word Description*: This is your opportunity to answer Toyota's favorite question—why? Why should the recipient pay attention? Communicate your vision clearly and concisely to grab an investor's attention and get a prompt response. You can dual purpose this piece as an "elevator pitch"—a brief voiceover that can be articulated in 60 seconds or less. You'll be asked often—at dinner parties, networking events, press mentions, customer introductions—so be thoughtful and intentional about the way you describe your business. And consider evolving it over time as you grow and garner feedback. An elevator pitch should include a brief personal introduction, the company vision, description of the product, and one or two pieces of traction points. Keep it simple. Be memorable, be specific, and use examples.

*"Teaser Deck"*: Today's entrepreneurs and investors live and die by "the deck"—a well-designed presentation (often Windows PowerPoint, Google Slides, or Apple Keynote) that can be reviewed quickly to get a full picture of the business. It is helpful to produce two types of decks, the short teaser deck for email distribution and the full pitch deck for a formal presentation. The short teaser deck is a five- to six-page presentation intended to be shared with a broader audience. It provides enough information for an investor to determine if the business is interesting and can be a starting point before an in-person meeting, but it does not have sensitive and confidential information. The teaser deck is often a condensed version of the full pitch deck with select slides removed (think: metrics that you wouldn't want to get into the wrong hands) and is sent in advance of an initial meeting.

*"Pitch Deck"*: The full pitch deck is a 15-20-page presentation used in conjunction with a meeting, with additional backup material in the appendix. It should represent your business visually and stylistically and serve as the document to facilitate your voiceover in a pitch meeting.

Today, there is a commonly used framework to tell the story and facilitate the pitch. In fact, Google's presentation product includes a "pitch" template that provides a step-by-step process for communicating the vision of your business. The following outline provides a framework for a typical pitch meeting discussion. But most importantly, consider the intended audience, take a step back, and constantly sanity check yourself. Pitch decks that tell a cohesive story that is true to a founder's vision end-to-end will stand apart.

## CONTENTS OF THE PITCH DECK

*Company purpose*: Develop a simple one-liner that summarizes your business and makes it real, using simple language. Articulate the problem and a relevant solution to that problem. The first tell for investors is whether you are addressing a real need, or just a "nice to have." Be clear and thoughtful about the problem and your company's value proposition to relieve the pain point.

*Market size and analysis*: Investors like to see large, growing markets that are poised for change. We want to believe that you're going after a big problem in a big market that will only grow over time. That said, there are multiple stages to your plan of attack. Your market today will hopefully evolve, so showing the near and far term can be helpful. We recommend coming prepared with thinking around the total addressable market (TAM), the Serviceable Addressable Market (SAM), and the Serviceable Obtainable Market (SOM). From there, investors can consider not only how you think about the market, but also how you plan to enter and sell to that market and how the strategy shifts over time.

In many cases, timing is just as important as size of market. Be sure to describe any recent favorable trends or why the timing of technology deployment is right for right now. Is now the tipping point for smart-phone penetration? Is there a demographic shift? Companies can be too soon to market or get derailed because consumer behavior is not quite ready for a particular innovation. Are you a first-mover and is that an advantage? Have others come before you

**FIGURE 1** Pinterest: Competitive Landscape

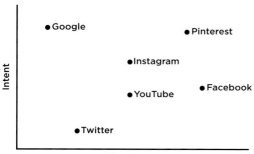

and failed? Be prepared to discuss why the right time is now.

*Competition*: While a large and well-timed market are both important, a company's positioning and competitive dynamics are also relevant. Be prepared with a list of competitors and your differentiation within the field. Do be upfront about competition and if there are obvious competitors missing from this section, expect to be asked about it in the meeting. If you do not volunteer a competitive set in the meeting you miss another opportunity to control the narrative, and you can expect a firm's analyst or associate to find them in diligence. A simple 2x2 matrix or an xy-axis chart with relevant labels is sufficient in providing a landscape. As an investor in Pinterest, we view the competitive landscape from the lens of consumer intent as well as time spent. In Figure 1, you'll see Pinterest's competitive differentiation as compared to Google, YouTube, Instagram, Facebook, and Twitter.

*Product*: Above all, product demonstration (product demos) speak louder than pitch decks. Investors like to see or touch a product or service to bring it to life. The more information you can provide here, the better. If you're early in the cycle, a detailed product roadmap, wireframes, or renderings are helpful. A product demo is preferred when a product is beyond the alpha or beta stage of development. Keep in mind, investors will understand prototype, demo phase, and anticipated development cycles. We don't need it to be perfect, we just need to see it work. At FirstMark, we've seen an on-demand

delivery company place an order at the start of a pitch and we enjoyed the delicious cookies that arrived from a nearby bakery just minutes later into the meeting. We've also experienced a new virtual reality software through a headset that took us to the sandy beaches of San Diego. These are powerful moments when you can let a product speak for itself, ideally leaving an ever-opinionated investor speechless!

*Business model*: The specifics of the business model are a key way that investors can understand how you think about positioning, growing, and scaling your business. Investors want to understand who the customer is, how do you reach that customer, how much they'll pay for a product, and how long they will use the product or service. We want to learn about your customers and revenue and how you plan on growing both. Most importantly, be prepared to discuss your assumptions and thought process. Investors will often ask how you determined a metric like customer acquisition cost: Is it blended? By channel? An estimate or actual? You should expect questions surrounding revenue, pricing, unit economics (including customer lifetime value and acquisition cost), customer pipeline, and sales and distribution model. Have the fundamentals down pat but also be open-minded to differing perspectives and views from an investor or industry expert. A handful of key metrics for technology include:

| Consumer | Enterprise |
| --- | --- |
| Users: sign-ups, downloads, registrations | Monthly, annual recurring revenue |
| Daily, weekly, monthly active users | Annual contract value, payment terms |
| Retention | Customer acquisition cost/customer lifetime value |
| Time on site/app | Sales pipeline, cycle and duration |
| Behavior of customer | Customer concentration |
| Monetization strategy | Gross churn, net churn, logo churn |

Beyond the pitch deck, investors may ask for detailed financials as interest evolves. More important than the actual numbers is the thinking about the complexity of the business as well as expectations for future growth. Investors will be looking for assumptions on growth, expense management, and burn rate. You can expect requests for the following materials: financial model, income statement, balance sheet, and capitalization table.

*Team*: The team that you've assembled to execute the business vision is just as important as the business itself. Highlight the founders and management team with relevant expertise and complementary skillsets through short bios and photos. Tell us why this is the best team to execute the vision. Expect investors to reference the team as well. It's helpful to prep a few relevant contacts for diligence calls and be willing to make introductions if asked.

*Financials*: At the end of the day, the pitch is a deal. Don't be shy about outlining the deal terms, specifically the amount you intend to raise, a clear perspective on use of proceeds to get to the next fundraise, and ultimately the anticipated cash-out timing.

*Appendix*: A pitch deck should strike a good balance around level of detail. Share enough information to move the conversation along and hit the key points without bogging investors down with details that detract from the story. Over the course of the fundraising process, you can and should expect common questions to emerge as investors engage with you and your business. It's helpful to have an appendix with relevant backup slides to reference if needed.

## DEVELOPING MATERIALS

The process to develop these materials is time consuming and requires an ability to synthesize large amounts of information into digestible insights. Throughout the process, stay organized with sourcing and citing research. It is also helpful to include calculations and assumptions in a footnote or an appendix slide. In recent years, we've seen some entrepreneurs work with a designer to polish the deck and extend brand continuity. There are mixed opinions about using a designer for a deck, but a helpful rule of thumb is that if brand and design are key components of your business, any presentation materials should reflect that focus and attention to detail.

## CONCLUSION

The goal of the materials is to communicate and generate interest in your vision. The best presentations show thoughtfulness and preparedness, making it easy to understand the business and why you are the best person to execute this vision. Additionally, being responsive and quick to provide requested information makes the process go smoothly and accelerates the ability to make a decision. While this chapter outlined the materials that you can prepare, do expect the venture firm to run some diligence of their own. It's very likely they'll be looking for market indicators, running analysis on your materials, and even calculating some of your metrics themselves. Investors want to know what they are buying when they agree to finance the business, so it's not unusual to be on the receiving end of requests for additional information. It can be very beneficial to have all anticipated materials ready to send out quickly so both parties can get to an important decision point. Ideally, the materials produced can be used for several different purposes, and they serve as a vehicle to get to know potential investors. Every conversation is an interview from both sides of the table, so do not be afraid to ask your own questions and conduct your own due diligence to find the right partner for your business.

# 8

# PERSPECTIVES ON DIFFERENT TYPES OF FINANCING

Foundry Group

Brad Feld, Managing Director

Early in the life of a company, the idea of a financing arises. While many companies are bootstrapped and rely on sales to fund the business, a wide variety of companies choose to raise a financing, or a series of financings, to help build a product, enter a market, or scale the company.

These financings can take many forms. In 2010, when my partner Jason Mendelson and I wrote the first edition of our book, *Venture Deals: Be Smarter Than Your Lawyer and VC* (Wiley), the terms and approaches to venture capital financings were a mystery to many entrepreneurs. Since then, there has been an explosion of startups around the world where financings of early stage, private companies have become pervasive.

In this section, I'll talk about a variety of different financings along with common terminology used by the various players. I'll lead you through the different stages of financings, discuss several types of venture capital funds, describe how syndicates work, and then finish with a brief discussion of equity and product crowdfunding.

## FRIENDS AND FAMILY

The first financing a company often does is called a *friends and family round*, where the investors are either friends or family of the founders. For some, this gets called the 3F round, or *friends, family, and fools*, as a common joke is that only a fool would invest so early in the life of a company.

While this is a very risky round to invest in, when companies are successful, these three F's can receive enormous financial rewards. These early rounds are typically small, often less than $250,000 in total. If the founders are unsophisticated, the documentation for these rounds is often sloppy and informal, which can come back to haunt either the investors or the founders.

You should treat a friends and family round with the same level of seriousness as any other financing, even though the money may be coming from your mother. Realize that these friends and family are betting on you and, by structuring the round as a formal financing, you are setting the right tone and expectations for all investors from the beginning.

## ANGELS

The next investor type that a founder typically encounters is an angel investor. These angels are often a key source of early-stage investment and are very active in pre-seed and seed stage financings. Angels can be professional investors or successful entrepreneurs and often invest alongside friends and family members.

While angel investors are usually high net-worth individuals, with the passage of the JOBS Act in 2012 they no longer have to be. However, the rules around these financings, especially if done with nonaccredited investors, can be complex, so make sure you have advice from a good corporate lawyer who knows how to do these types of investments.

Some angel investors, known as *super angels*, make many small investments. Super angels are often experienced entrepreneurs who have had multiple exits and have decided to invest their own money in new startups. These super angels are often well known throughout startup communities and can be a huge help to the founders of early-stage companies.

Angel investors are called *angels* specifically because they are expected to help the companies, both with capital and advice. Some angels end up forgetting their role and become devils. Reputation matters, and as an entrepreneur make sure you do your diligence on any potential angels to make sure their goals and values are aligned with you.

Many angels invest together and some end up forming *angel groups*. The level of formality varies widely from dinner groups of angels that meet with entrepreneurs but make their own individual investment decisions, to formalized funds that look like small venture capital firms.

## VENTURE CAPITAL

Once you've raised an angel round, your next round will often be done with a venture capital (VC) firm. In some cases, the angels and VCs will invest side by side, just like angels do with friends and family. It's important to realize that while there are distinctions, there are no rigid boundaries.

Firms used to define themselves by the stage of financing they invested in. You'd hear about seed-stage firms that invested very early. Or series A firms that invested once a company had a product in the market. Or series B/C firms that were mid-stage investors. Then, firms wanted to be positioned earlier in the financing timeline, so the idea of pre-seed firms appeared. In some cases, firms want to position the investment as early, even though there have been several rounds, so you'll end up with series A-1 rounds following a series A round.

There is no magic to or legal definition in naming rounds. The key is that there is a way to discuss how early or late stage a company is when determining which VC might be right for you. Generally, pre-seed, seed, and series A are early-stage companies, series B and C are mid-stage companies, and series D or later is a late-stage company.

## TYPES OF VENTURE CAPITAL FUNDS

The smallest type of VC firm is often referred to as a *micro VC fund*. These are firms with one general partner who often started out as angel investor and created a VC fund after having some successful angel investments. While the size of a micro VC fund will vary, most are from $2 million to $15 million. Micro VCs invest almost exclusively at the seed and early stages.

Seed-stage funds are the next step up and can scale up to $100 million per fund. They are often the first institutional money into a company but rarely invest in later rounds past a series A. Seed-stage funds often provide your first noncompany board member.

Early-stage funds are in the $100 million to $300 million size and invest in seed stage and series A companies but occasionally lead a series B round. These firms also often continue to invest later in the life of a company.

Midstage funds are those that invest in series B and later rounds. The funds are often called growth investors, because they invest in companies that are succeeding but need capital to grow to the next level. These funds tend to be much larger, usually ranging from $200 million to $1 billion in size.

Late-stage funds enter the picture when the company is now a significant stand-alone business, doing its last financing before a prospective initial public offering (IPO). While late-stage funds can be VCs, some other financial investors, such as hedge funds, crossover investors that invest primarily in the public markets, funds associated with large banks, and sovereign wealth funds also show up in this category.

Firms do not tightly adhere to only one of these definitions. Some firms with billion-dollar funds have early-stage programs that invest in young companies. Others have multiple funds that invest in different stages of a company. Firms can have dedicated programs or partners per stage while others invest along the company life cycle with no special delineations. Ultimately, make sure that you are targeting the types of firms that invest in your stage of company.

## THE SYNDICATE

While some VCs invest alone, many invest with other VCs. A collection of investors is called a syndicate. Syndicates can also include any investor, whether a VC, angel, super angel, strategic investor, corporation, law firm, or anyone else that ends up participating in a financing.

Most syndicates have a lead investor. Usually, but not always, this is one of the VC investors. Two VCs will often co-lead a syndicate, and occasionally you'll see three co-leads. Having a lead investor makes it easier for entrepreneurs to focus their energy around the negotiation by negotiating with the lead, rather than each investor. Even though the lead investor may manage the other investors through the process,

it's still your responsibility as the entrepreneur to communicate with everyone and drive the financing process.

## EQUITY CROWDFUNDING

*Equity crowdfunding* is a new approach that appeared in 2012 around the creation of the JOBS Act (the Jumpstart Our Business Startups Act). AngelList popularized this approach, although there are now a number of companies providing crowdfunding platforms.

In an equity crowdfunding, the funding platform, such as AngelList, is an intermediary between the company and investors. The platforms allow companies to advertise their funding or use the power of a social network to attract other investors. In some cases, such as AngelList Syndicates, individual investors can aggregate other investors to participate in their syndicate, acting like a small version of a venture capital fund.

While crowdfunding has expanded to cover several situations, there are tight legal definitions surrounding each approach. As a result, some of the aspects of fundraising on platforms like AngelList are referred to as crowdfunding but are really not anything new, other than the use of an online platform to connect companies with potential investors.

In the United States, if you are selling a security, you need to register the security with the Securities and Exchange Commission (SEC) based on rules negotiated more than 80 years ago as part of the Securities Act of 1933. Fortunately, there are a number of exemptions that allow you to avoid an SEC registration. In general, unless you are taking a company public via initial public offering (IPO), you won't have to worry about registering your offering with the SEC. However, there are important guidelines that you must follow in order to rely on an exemption. The two most important are the concept of an accredited investor and the process of general solicitation.

## PRODUCT CROWDFUNDING

Another type of crowdfunding, popularized by Kickstarter and Indiegogo, is *product crowdfunding*. This approach is often used for physical products. In the product crowdfunding scenario, a company puts its product idea up on Kickstarter with content showing what the product will do and a series of rewards for backers. In most cases, the product is at an early design stage and months to years away from shipping. The rewards vary by dollar amount and often include things that, while linked to the product, are tangential to the product, such as T-shirts, sponsorship, or events to celebrate the launch of the product.

Many campaigns have a 30-day funding target that, if not achieved, results in the campaign failing. In this case, the funding doesn't occur and the backers keep their money. But, if the campaign gets funded, it acts as a giant pre-order campaign and validation for the product. In this case, the company has raised nondilutive financing similar to bootstrapping a company by selling products to customers.

The real downside of product crowdfunding is when a campaign is successful but the company doesn't finish building the product. While some companies can raise equity to finish and ship the product, others simply shut down and fail to fulfill the preorders. In this situation, the backers are out their money, in the same way investors lose their money in a failed company.

# 9

# INITIAL FINANCING

## SoftTech VC

Jeff Clavier, Managing Partner

*"Dear Sir/Madam, To whom it may concern:*

*I read on the Internet that you were an investor in unicorn startups. I am a visionary whose ideas will generate billions of dollars in returns for you, so let's discuss how you can work with me. I will share my ideas with you once you have returned the enclosed NDA."*

I get emails like these several times a week. It's full of buzzword mumbo-jumbo, shows a lack of understanding of the VC process (VCs never sign NDAs), and a total randomness in picking an investor to pitch ("Dear Sir/Madam"). Use this kind of email and your pitch will likely go straight to the bin.

Building a startup is hard, and there are so many factors that lead to failure. One of these factors is not understanding the basics of the "VC game," or more precisely, the basics of VC math around pitch volumes and investment performance.

The probability of receiving VC funding can increase if you understand the basics. Here are some pointers to help get you started.

- Most firms will receive a few thousand to tens of thousands of pitches per year, the vast majority by email. At this point, I would strongly recommend against sending paper business plans by snail mail.

- Investment staff, ranging from associates to partners of the firm, will read through the proposal and either reject it outright, ask for more information and still pass, or schedule a meeting.

- I can't speak for every firm, but here are the numbers at SoftTech:

  - Less than 20% of the companies reaching out to us will be invited to a meeting because of a mix of actual time capacity and fit with the investment strategy (stage, size, sectors, portfolio conflicts).

  - The first meeting, if successful, will yield additional meetings with other members of the firm, until due diligence starts. Less than 5% of companies reaching out to us will get to this point.

  - The due diligence phase is when we reach out to founder references, early customers, experts that will help us validate the technology, science, or market, etc. Only a small portion of companies will successfully pass that phase (less than 1% of our deal flow).

○ Finally, we'll make an offer to invest and 85% of the time, we'll close an investment; less than 0.5% that reached out to us will actually get funded.

Not only is the probability of raising capital pretty low, it takes time too. We coach our companies that they have to assume raising capital will take six months, so you start six months before you run out of cash at the very least. The key point that founders often forget is that fundraising is close to being a full-time job, so they need to plan accordingly. Don't try to close key accounts, lead the development of a major release, and hope to fundraise at the same time.

The most critical thing to understand about VC funds is that performance is extremely uneven. In a portfolio of any size, less than 10% of companies will produce a multiple on capital invested that allows a fund to be returned multiple times. A winner for us returns 50% to 100% of a fund, which means a 20- to 30-times return on the company—implying an outcome of several hundred million dollars or more. That's what we mean by *VC scale returns*.

As you think about the parameters of your company, you need to be honest about your prospects of building such a company that can scale to tens of millions of dollars in revenue, hundreds of millions of users, etc. Most startups will not have those characteristics, which is why you hear so often that a company is not "VC scale." Other euphemisms for this include "It's a feature, not a company" or "That's a lifestyle business." So what are the implications?

1. Raising capital from VCs is predicated on proving that your company has the potential of getting to "massive" scale *and*

2. You need to end up in the 1% of some fund's deal flow to get an investment.

Out of the universe of hundreds of funds and thousands of angels or angel groups, there *is* a subset that is the right one for your company.

You just need to identify them, get the right introduction, and make the right pitch. It's not easy, but it is feasible. In the last 12 years at SoftTech, 188 startups have succeeded at getting an investment from us.

As entrepreneurs, you'll be spending a lot of your time raising capital. At every stage, you'll present a set of achievements and represent a set of risks. Over time, achievements and milestones will increase and risks will decrease. That process will allow you to continue to raise larger amounts of capital at higher valuations from different sets of investors (seed, early, scale, growth).

Let's walk through a real-life example: Fitbit.

We were the first institutional investors, alongside our friends at True Ventures, and remained active investors through the company's public offering in June 2015. Here is Fitbit's funding history:

- $400K seed round in 2007 to research and build the initial prototype

- $2M Series A round from True Ventures and SoftTech in 2008 to launch the product

- $9M Series B round led by Foundry Group in 2010 to scale distribution in the United States

- $12M Series C round led by insiders in 2011 to build new products and scale in the United States

- $30M Series D round led by Softbank, Qualcomm, and SAP Ventures in 2013 to scale internationally

The whole funding ecosystem is important to understand, whether your initial round will typically come from the pre-seed or seed part of the market. See Figure 1 to make this easier to understand.

So how much should you be raising for your initial financing?

The very first round (the pre-seed round) will typically range from a few tens to a few hundreds of thousands of dollars, at a low, single-digit million valuation (e.g., $750 thousand

**FIGURE 1** The 2016 Funding Ecosystem

| Pre-Seed <$1M | • Bootstrapping/Friends and family<br>• Pre-Seed Funds and preorder/crowdfunded campaigns<br>• Incubators and Accelerators (YC, Techstars, AngelPad, 500 Startups, SeedCamp) |
|---|---|
| Seed $1.5 to $3M | • 350+ Micro-VC Firms having raised $4B+<br>• Syndicates of micro-VC firms, angels and (potentially) traditional VCs<br>• AngelList and Crowdfunding services as alternative or "fill up" opportunity |
| Seed Prime $2M to $3M | • Companies that cannot raise a Series A will raise a bridge from existing investors<br>• Some funds have positioned themselves as go-to leads for Seed Prime rounds |
| Series A $5M to $15M | • One traditional VC, with micro VCs investing pro-rata and adding strategic angels<br>• Syndicates of micro-VCs leading smaller series A rounds<br>• Family Offices, Strategics, Micro-VCs + Crowdfunding pools as alternative |
| Series B $10M to $30M+ | • Another traditional VC (or two), with insiders coming in pro-rata. Corporate VCs start showing up.<br>• Same mix as Series A for alternatives plus the YC Continuity Fund and Strategics<br>• Family offices and growth investors coming into Series B rounds of top performing companies |
| Growth $20M to $100M+ | • Mix of traditional/growth VCs, PE firms, hedge funds. In parallel, secondary transactions.<br>• Alternative: direct co-investments from LPs, hedge/mutual funds, cash rich corporates<br>• SPVs (Special Purpose Vehicles) coming in all over the place |

t $3 million pre-money). This should give the company a runway of 12 to 18 months, enough to build an initial version of the product, hire a small team, get feedback from initial users, and raise the seed round. That seed round will have a range of a few thousand to a few million dollars t a valuation reflecting the amount of progress made ($2 million on $8 million pre-money is a very common round for software companies in our portfolio). It will also be used to launch our product and develop the traction that will llow you to raise your next round, the Series A, something like 18 to 24 months after the close of the seed round.

There is clear tension here: the more you raise, the longer your runway, giving you more time to it the milestones of the next round. But if you raise too much too early, you as founders will be diluted so much that it will make raising the next financing difficult or impossible.

Old school VCs may tell you: *"We're partners in this venture: you contribute the company, team, and product, we'll contribute capital. How's $500 thousand for 50% of the company—that way* *we'd be 50/50 partners!"* Do not say yes to this proposition!

The other day, a company presented to me and mentioned they had given 25% of their company to an early investor for $75 thousand. That makes you question the judgment of the founders if they accept terms like this. The good news is that this investment was redeemed, and the company has a clean cap table as a result (where no investor has an unjustifiably high portion of the equity).

Here are examples of "normal" dilutions:

• Equity given to accelerators/incubators should be in the 5% to 10% range, or less.

• Early rounds should be limited to 10% to 15% for pre-seed, and 20% to 25% for seed.

What may be counterintuitive though is that investors do look at founders' ownership levels before they make an investment decision, and they want to make sure there is "enough" for founders to be motivated; obviously "enough" varies based on the maturity of the company.

Who decides on your round's valuation?

Wrong answer:

*Entrepreneur: "We're raising $1 million for 10% of the company."*

*VC: "Oh, you have signed a term sheet with a lead investor?"*

*Entrepreneur: "No, why?"*

*VC: "Well, who set the valuation of the round?"*

*Entrepreneur: "We did, based on what we read on TechCrunch about company XYZ."*

*VC: "Yes, but this company had an experienced team, a product in market, and some early revenue."*

*Entrepreneur: "And?"*

Right answer:

*The market, i.e., people who will actually commit to write a check and help you build the company, not your buddies or advisors, unless they write a check too.*

Let experienced investors, preferably institutional ones, offer a valuation for your round. If you end up in a competitive situation, with multiple term sheets, you may be able to play investors against each other (a bit) and leverage the situation to your advantage. But even in that case, my advice is to choose the investor who will deliver the highest value-add, the best brand value as opposed to just the highest valuation. Brand value is linked to the credibility a company gets by being associated with you. Value-add is all the support you'll get from investors: strategy, execution advice, help raising the next round, hiring, marketing and sales, etc.

## HOW TO PREPARE FOR YOUR ROUND

Would you ever run a marathon unprepared, untrained, without advice from fellow athletes? And still expect to successfully cross the line? Your first financing is similar.

The ideal situation is to have anticipated the moves of the other side (investors) and feed them all the information they may need, both in the first pitch meetings, subsequent ones, and the due diligence phase (the steps we highlighted at the beginning of this chapter).

To get financing ready, you need to figure out what, how, and whom to pitch.

## WHAT TO PITCH

VCs will analyze opportunities through different lenses, but most commonly they use the mix "Founders, Product, Market Opportunity."[1] They'll assess why the team in front of them is uniquely positioned because of founders' personal interest, story, and challenges in tackling this opportunity. Then they'll dissect why the product/service is unique, understanding that teams rarely come up with radically new ideas in a completely white space. Finally, they'll ask the "scale" question: Can the company truly create a large outcome if it scales to massive revenue?

As already discussed, you'll ask investors for a certain amount of capital (e.g., a $2 million seed round), and you will present a plan for using this capital over a certain period of time (typically 12 months+ for pre-seed, 18 to 24 months for seed) that will allow you to hit the milestones of the next fundraising round.

## HOW TO PITCH

You are going to put together a pitch presentation for the initial meeting, 10 to 12 slides, that will address VCs' key questions:

- What is the opportunity?
- What was the genesis of the idea?
- Why is it interesting, how big can it become? Provide some proxy number for the market size.
- Who are the founders, and why are they uniquely positioned to succeed in this market (the "founder/market fit" question)? Who else is on the team; engineers with relevant

---

[1] At SoftTech, we call it the "Three Asses Rule": A smart ass team, building a kickass product in a big ass market.

experience can be listed, along with one or two key advisors, if they are truly engaged.

- Why now? What are the technology, regulatory, societal, consumption changes that make this opportunity feasible (e.g., more than one billion smartphones in use, or FAA regulations on drone usage)?

- Milestones hit to date? Think of them as elements of risk that you have already addressed or validated at least partially: parts of the product already built, key hires, or proving customers' willingness to pay through early revenue returns or targeted surveys. Limited product/prototype demos will help validate the technical feasibility of your project.

- What is your go-to-market strategy? State either what has been accomplished to date or the strategies that you plan to test or adopt post financing.

- Who else is out there in your primary and adjacent market? Who is in your competition matrix, and how well are these companies funded? It is vital that you research your market, especially if it is an already established one.

- Financing and revenues? Mention how much you have raised to date and from whom, your revenue traction if you have any, and how much you are looking to raise. Finally you'll present a summary of the use of funds (how many hires, when, in which function), your targeted runway, and the milestones you plan to hit before the next round. For example, software as a service (SaaS) companies are expected to hit $1 million to $2 million in annual recurring revenue (ARR) before they can raise a Series A.

- You can have a number of additional slides as backup materials, but don't pack too many in the front of the deck so you have ample time for discussion during the meeting.

There is no specific order in which these slides should be presented; it just has to be logical, and narratives that flow as a story tend to work better. I personally like pitches that set the scene: "For the last couple of years, we have been building a product focused on addressing this need. The founders have this background, met that way, and have decided to work on this because of 'X.' We now have a prototype in the hands of 10 alpha customers." This provides enough information to paint a broad picture of what you do, who you are, and why you do it. Then the pitch deck can be presented to dig into all the topics we discussed.

Other tips for successful pitching:

- Practice, practice, practice the narrative of your deck so it flows well. If more than one founder is in the meeting, it is advisable to have one main presenter and bring in other people into the conversation only a few times (personal introduction, specific area of expertise, pointed questions). "Passing the mic" too many times becomes distracting.

- It is vitally important that you practice your pitch, a lot. Practice in front of investors or entrepreneurs who have experience giving or receiving pitches. Listen to their feedback, summarize the key points, iterate on the deck, and pitch again until you feel that "it works." And prepare for the disappointing realization that you weren't ready once you started pitching VCs for real. It happens all the time. Don't give up.

- VCs respond to pitches very differently. Some will listen to your presentation and ask all their questions at the end. Others will ask questions at every slide or every sentence. If they ask questions about upcoming slides, it's fine to ask them to hold onto the question or show that slide's content and come back.

- Some entrepreneurs like to have a conversation with no slide in the background. It's fine, but makes it more challenging to have an engaged dialogue because you need to take more notes since there is no backup material (the deck) for you to rely on after the meeting. My strong personal preference is to go through the deck and take questions along the way, and I'll state that at the beginning of the meeting.

- Understand that the goal of the first meeting is to get to more meetings, then enter due diligence, then get to a funding offer, followed by more due diligence, leading to a close of the financing and a wire transfer. This can take days, weeks, or months, so pace yourself accordingly.

## WHOM TO PITCH

There are hundreds of VC funds and thousands of angels, all with capital to invest in startups. However it is critical to figure out which firms or individuals are the most likely to invest in your startups based on their filters:

- Stage
- Sectors
- Geography
- Round size
- Have they invested in startups that are similar but that are not competitive or overlapping?

Most startups end up being listed on AngelList and Crunchbase, and these two databases are essential resources for a comprehensive list of firms and individuals who are investing in your space. CBInsights also publishes useful market maps that highlight all the companies in a given sector, as well as top VCs investing in it. Then each firm's website or blog will give you hints about how, where, and when they invest. Yes, there is a lot of work involved in parsing all this information but it's worth the effort.

Like every CEO in our portfolio does when she or he raises capital, you'll create a spreadsheet listing firms, partners, relevant investments, typical investment size, whether they lead or not, etc. Then you will share it with existing investors, fellow entrepreneurs, and friends and ask for their input on which firms to add (or remove) and most importantly, who they can introduce you to.

## THE TRUSTED REFERRAL

VCs rely very heavily on the trusted referral as an early indicator of potential quality of a startup, essentially using the credibility of the person who makes the referral as a key element in deciding

whether they'll take a meeting or not. Why? Because we typically get way too much deal flow not to use arbitrary filters. That's unfortunate, but it's the way this industry works. It does not mean that you won't get meetings without that "magic wand," but you'll greatly increase your odds of success by "working the network" and figuring out these introductions. Just to give you a sense of numbers, over the last 12 years, we have been pitched tens of thousands of times, we've taken thousands of meetings, and have closed 191 investments. None of these investments came "cold": all were either brought from the network or found through an accelerator (less than 10%).

Who is a trusted referrer? It is someone who knows our firm well and/or has a "nose" for good opportunities: typically, our founders (especially the alumni group), coinvestors (both upstream and downstream), or executives whose function leads them to see a large number of opportunities. How do you find these connections? LinkedIn, Crunchbase, and AngelList!

How do you make these trusted introductions happen? Assuming you have built your network (and LinkedIn connections), you ask someone who knows us for an introduction. You send an email introduction that can easily be forwarded, since no one but you should pitch your concept, on top of which the referrer will provide some context and if she or he is inclined, will add an endorsement. When I receive a strong endorsement from someone I trust, I pretty much automatically take the meeting, unless I already have an investment in the space.

Know your competitors' investors. All too often I receive an email from a startup aspiring to displace one of our (fully disclosed) portfolio companies—and this is not something we want you to do:

*Dear Jeff,*

*I am very excited to share with you this investment opportunity in the on-demand space, which will directly compete with Postmates and other delivery. We'll crush them because of . . .*

It could be Postmates or any of our well-known investments. For some reason, founders don't seem to check their main competitors' Crunchbase record before blasting investors. Make sure you do that!

Often founders reach out complaining that they don't have a network allowing them to get an introduction and therefore take a chance with a cold email. That's ok, I can accept that, but the law of large numbers is against you. That's why accelerators like YC, TechStars, and 500 Startups are so useful in this case: they'll become your trusted referral to the investor community. This is especially true for founders who don't work in Silicon Valley or a core innovation ecosystem.

## A FEW MORE PREP STEPS

Once you have a target list of potential investors and connections who can introduce you to them, you need to define your priorities: P1 for the most likely to resonate with your opportunity taking the strength of the introduction into account, P2 for the next group, and P3 for the less likely. To be candid, if you have to dig into P3 VCs (the ones representing the least adequate fit on paper), it's not a good sign for your raise.

We advise our founders to have no more than six to ten open conversations at any point in time—you'll need to book meetings, more meetings, follow-up calls, make due diligence introductions, provide spreadsheets and memos in response to questions, etc. All this takes time, even if a lot of materials can be reused. So get your trusted referrers to offer these six to ten introductions using the material you provided; we always recommend doing this on a double-blind basis (referrer sends email introducing the opportunity and asking investor if she or he wants to connect, then cc's you once the offer has been accepted). Once declines start arriving, open more new conversations.

What do you need besides your pitch deck? For a seed round, we typically ask a simple financial model showing how you will use the funds you are raising, a list of founders and customer/user references (if you have any), and any material you can share to justify the size of the market (such as industry reports, link to expert blog posts, etc.). As you raise additional rounds of financing, the list of due diligence materials will become much longer.

How long does fundraising take from start to finish? It depends.

Some founders get it done in a couple of weeks. They're lucky to be the exception, the company that all VCs dream to invest in, and ends up getting showered with term sheets. That's not the standard, even if these are the companies VCs always love to talk about.

Prep time (getting materials ready, refining the pitch, going through a few rehearsal pitches, developing your target list) may take two to three weeks. Getting your trusted referrals going and the first meetings in the busy investors' calendars can take a couple of weeks too. So before you know it, more than a month is gone. You may pitch a few VCs and get a term sheet, or you may have to pitch 50; it's never certain how the market will respond to an opportunity. It typically takes us two weeks from the second meeting to issue a term sheet; we've done it in a few days, and in a few rare cases requiring a lot of due diligence, a couple of months. Once the term sheet is signed, legal due diligence and document drafting should take no more than three weeks before cash is wired.

I'd like to conclude with a Top 10 list of things that will undermine your raise, based on what I have seen happen. Note that there is no specific order in this list.

*(continued)*

| 1 | Send "To Whom It May Concern" mass emails | As noted, they ended up in investors' trash or junk mail. |
|---|---|---|
| 2 | Saying "I am either selling to Google or raising a round" | Shows you are interested in a short-term exit. Nothing wrong with that, but VCs are interested only in long-term commitments that yield a big, interesting company. |
| 3 | Not knowing your competition | This is especially true if you claim being the only ones building something, and we've met three similar companies in the last month. |
| 4 | They don't know what they don't know | That's an expression we sometimes use about founding teams who try to operate in complex environments (science, tech, regulatory, etc.) and don't understand the need for a specific expertise to be represented on the team. |
| 5 | Using too many buzzwords | That's one of my pet peeves. I have a hard time dealing with more than a handful per pitch. |
| 6 | Having a massive advisory board of "brand names" who barely know you, would not really vouch for you, or are irrelevant | "What would you say to a pitch from entrepreneurs who have two Nobel Prize winners on their advisory board?" <br><br> Me: "I pass?" <br><br> We're all about getting help and support, but often a board of advisors that is larger than five people is rarely engaged and relevant. |
| 7 | Trying to hide things | Early-stage founders very commonly make some mistakes in the initial phases of their startup life. They may also start the journey with more cofounders, and one or two of them end up leaving because they were not the right fit. We deal with these issues all the time, and the consequences are mostly benign if they are fixed early. But *never* assume that they can be hidden under the rug—we'll likely find out during the due diligence phase and may lose faith in the team outright if anything important is not disclosed. |

| | | |
|---|---|---|
| 8 | Raising too little, raising too much, and getting a valuation that is too aggressive | *"I am raising $2M to $5M."*<br><br>One side of the range is a seed round, the other is almost a Series A. Understand the typical ranges that firms you pitch attribute to the stage you are raising for. And if you can raise a $5M seed round at a high valuation, more power to you. But understand the implications for the next round's expectations in terms of milestones. |
| 9 | Acting strange, not following up on due diligence items, not showing interest | Unless you have worked with the team in the past, a financing process will give both sides, entrepreneurs and investors, a glimpse of their future relationship. If anything feels "wrong," whether it's lack of transparency, ethics, or being truthful, either party will feel the enthusiasm decline and the deal might eventually not be consummated. |
| 10 | Get your tech ready, have backup solutions | *The CEO came into the conference room, opened his Mac, connected the HDMI cable through the connector we provided, and within seconds the computer crashed. It took 10 minutes to reboot, relog, reconnect, and get going with the presentation. During that time, the CEO would not start, stood up flustered, and lost composure for the rest of the pitch.*<br><br>The good news is that we still invested, but that episode could have derailed the whole thing.<br><br>Have all types of connectors (HDMI, VGA) in your bag; standard cables typically work better than Apple TV. Try to have all the decks, videos, and if possible your demo on your laptop; you never know if Wi-Fi is going to work properly. |

# 10

# HOW TO SECURE ANGEL FINANCING

**Pioneer Square Labs**

Geoff Entress, Cofounder and Managing Director

So, you have come up with a great business idea, found lawyers and incorporated your company, started development in your basement or garage (or located physical space if your business is a restaurant or storefront), maybe have hired some first employees or sold them on a compelling enough vision that they have been working for free and, most importantly, you have burnt through all of the money that you can afford to lose, and maybe even more. Some entrepreneurs have enough cash from prior wins, inheritance, or a quickly cash-flow-positive business model to never have to take money from others. But most are not that lucky. And to whom do most entrepreneurs turn for their next infusion of capital? Angel investors.

## WHAT IS AN ANGEL INVESTOR?

Angel investors are wealthy individuals who are willing to invest in private companies. Angel investors need to be wealthy because private companies are extremely risky investments and as many as nine out of 10 private companies will fail before providing any return to the angel investors. Furthermore, the one out of 10 that does succeed, hopefully in a large way, may take several years to get to an acquisition or an initial public offering stage, and there really aren't any liquid secondary markets for most private company shares (the shares of so-called "unicorns" such as Uber and Airbnb being notable exceptions). Angel investors are in it for the long haul and need to have the financial ability to take a complete loss on most, if not all, of their private company investments.

Angel investors also need to be wealthy from a regulatory standpoint. The United States government in the 1930s enacted most of the securities laws that we still have today. Those laws require heavy regulatory reporting by companies that sell shares to the public, which is time-consuming and expensive. Small companies can't afford this reporting and, fortunately, Congress allowed an exemption to this reporting if you sell only to "accredited investors," that is, wealthy individuals. The current "accredited investor" requirement for an individual is that the individual has a net worth of $1,000,000 or more, excluding the value of the investor's primary residence, or has had income of at $200,000 in each of the last two years and reasonably expects to have income of at least $200,000 in the current year. This income requirement is increased to $300,000 for joint-tax filers. If you are raising money from angels, make certain that they are accredited investors because it will minimize headaches down the road.

## WHY DO ANGEL INVESTORS INVEST?

As discussed in the last section, most angel investments fail and most angel investors lose money. So why do angel investors invest? In contrast to venture capitalists, who need to make money because being a venture capitalist is their full-time job and the institutional investors who provide them with capital expect to make a reasonable return, angel investors want to make money but don't necessarily need to. Angel investors invest for several reasons, including the desire to advance technologies and industries for which they have passion and where they might have initially made their money, the general desire to "give back" to the entrepreneurial community that might have helped them earlier in their own career, or simply because angel investing is fun. Of course, if angel investors lose money on every deal they do, they probably will not find it fun and will eventually give up, but as long as they occasionally get a win and it doesn't hurt them too badly financially, angel investors will usually keep coming back. It is very similar to my golf game; I may play horribly for 17 holes, but if I hit one good shot on 18, I will keep coming back. In angel investing, as in golf, one winning shot can offset a lot of losers.

## WHICH TYPE OF ANGEL INVESTOR IS RIGHT FOR YOUR BUSINESS?

Angel investors come in several flavors, and which type you will be able to attract will depend on a number of factors including how far along your business is, its "stage," and how inherently credible you are as an entrepreneur. If you are a serially successful entrepreneur who has built and exited many businesses, you might be able to jump right to well-known, professional angels or even to venture capitalists. But most entrepreneurs will probably need to work their way up the angel investor food chain.

## ANGELS YOU KNOW—FRIENDS AND FAMILY

I often like to separate angel investors into two groups, those you already know and those you don't know. Odds are, angels whom you know are more likely to make a "team bet" on you than angels whom you don't know (if people that you know won't bet on you, you might not want to start a business). Angels whom you know are often referred to as "friends and family," and friends and family are usually the first outside investors in most businesses. When I had my first business during the first Internet boom of the 1990s, my mother invested in it. She didn't do it because she believed that the world needed a new hip-hop music site (it didn't), she did it because she loved me (and despite my losing her money on that one, I think she still does). Always remember that friends and family are betting on you, so make sure you treat them fairly.

The advantage of raising money from friends and family is that because they are generally investing solely because of their relationship with you, they are willing to invest earlier in the company's lifecycle and before you have hit many milestones, such as actual customers or even a built product. The disadvantage of friends and family is that they usually aren't high "value-add" in that your average person doesn't have substantial experience in either private company investing or running early-stage businesses. Which brings us to angels you don't know.

## ANGELS YOU DON'T KNOW— THE BENEFITS OF VALUE-ADD INVESTORS

So, now that you have gotten past the friends and family stage and have generated some traction on your business plan, whether that is having customers, signed business deals with partners, advanced product development or patents, or whatever constitutes real milestones in your type of business, it is time to approach investors you don't know.

Given a choice, at every stage of your company's development, you want to select investors who are extremely "value-add." What I mean by value-add is that they will provide not just money but also advice, introductions to customers, acquirers, service providers, and other investors, whether these are other angels, venture capitalists, or private equity firms. Over the years, I have helped my companies negotiate licensing deals with patent trolls, raise hundreds of millions of dollars in venture funding, sell to larger companies for anywhere from a few million dollars to a billion dollars, and go public through initial public offerings. Value-add investors are willing to roll up their sleeves and help you get what you need to get done, done.

The best thing about investors you don't know is that they are more likely to be value-add than your friends and family. That is because there are a lot more of them and you can be more selective in which ones you approach regarding your business. As mentioned earlier, one of the reasons angel investors invest is to advance technologies and businesses that are important to them. This also tends to lead them to invest in businesses and industries that they understand. Which is good news for you because that aligns with what you want in an investor: someone who understands the space and customers that you are targeting and can be value-add.

Of course, when you are assembling your angel investor syndicate, you want to make certain that you have a diverse group of investors/advisers in your corner. Having 10 experts in social media marketing may be very helpful for your social media marketing, but having 10 diverse experts would be even better. A great angel investor syndicate brings more than money; they become free advisers for you and the business and they even pay for the opportunity!

## THE DEAL LEAD—THE MOST IMPORTANT PERSON IN YOUR ANGEL FINANCING WORLD

Raising money from angels whom you don't personally know can be very difficult or it can be very easy. How difficult is often determined by the credibility of your "deal lead." Being a

deal lead is somewhat of an informal role, but it is a very important one. A deal lead might be an angel that is investing a substantial amount of money in your financing round, so other investors view them as highly "bought-in." However, they also can be influential to other potential investors, even if not highly bought-in, because of their reputation as successful investors in similar deals or based on their expertise in the type of business that you are building.

Deal leads have several tasks. They conduct due diligence on the company, including the management team, the market opportunity, the competitive environment, the go-to-market strategy, the viability of the business model, and the potential for a successful financial outcome. They negotiate the term sheet with you, including the financial and control terms of the deal, they shepherd the deal through the closing process, and most importantly, they help sell other investors on the deal. A great deal lead can make the entire financing process extremely easy for you. Poor deal leads may actually make it more difficult to raise your round, especially if they require unusual deal terms (either favorable or unfavorable to you, a topic for another chapter but a red flag either way) or if they are viewed as not credible because of a poor reputation from other deals.

Most angel rounds, beyond friends and family rounds, usually also require that the angel investor group has the right to a seat on your board of directors. Because the board of directors is responsible for the long-term strategy of the company, including having the ability to fire you, you want to make sure you assemble as strong and helpful a board of directors as possible. Since the deal lead will usually end up filling this role, you want to make certain that you choose them wisely.

## WHERE DO YOU FIND ANGEL INVESTORS?

Now that you know that you are looking for value-add investors and a strong deal lead to shepherd them, where do you begin to look for them? The good news is that they generally are not that difficult to find and the best ones want to be found. For example, here in Seattle, our local technology blog, Geekwire (www.geekwire.com), writes articles about all of the local financings and the angels who have invested. The most active and influential Seattle angels number only about 15 or 20 or so, and from the deal news in Geekwire and other publications like the business section of *The Seattle Times*, all of them can be easily identified. But, because the most active angels are often inundated with deals, you generally don't want to reach out cold to them but rather want to be referred by someone that the angel already knows and trusts.

Some of the best referrals I receive are from the securities lawyers in town. My assumption is that if you were impressive and convincing enough to have a lawyer whom I respect sign you on as a client, you are worth my taking a meeting with you. The best lawyers recognize that they are making an investment by taking you on rather than another client, so I can effectively piggyback on their due diligence. You still are going to have to convince me that it is worth my digging in further, but at least you will have gotten through the door. Referrals from other professionals such as accountants, bankers, and of course other angels, particularly ones with whom I have invested before, also carry a lot of weight.

Another good target for finding angel investors are the local angel investor groups in your area. In Seattle, these include the Alliance of Angels (www.allianceofangels.com) and the Puget Sound Venture Club (www.pugetsoundvc.com), but pretty much every part of the country now has some local or regional angel investor group. Although most angel investor groups, similar to most angels, invest primarily or exclusively in their own geographic region, some of the groups have more industry-specific focuses and may even invest nationally or internationally. A good resource to locate these groups is the Angel Capital Association (www.angelcapitalassociation.org), which is the official industry alliance of the 100 largest angel groups in the United States.

Angel "newbies" can be good targets if they are experts in something that other angels lack. For example, if I am creating a new restaurant concept and there is a very successful restaurateur in town whose advice would be beneficial, it would be great to get this person into the investor syndicate rather than on an advisory board. People tend to value things they pay for more than things that they receive for free, so getting someone bought-in to your success will usually yield better results than handing out free equity or options to advisers. And it costs you less.

Finally, there are websites like AngelList (www.angel.co) that, if you meet their criteria, can help you connect with relevant angel investors. AngelList focuses solely on technology and technology-enabled businesses, but is worth taking a look if you qualify.

## NOW THAT YOU HAVE YOUR ANGEL INVESTORS IDENTIFIED, WHAT'S NEXT?

This chapter has focused primarily on the process of identifying the best angel investors for your business. Once these investors have been identified, you will need to sell them on why this venture is one that warrants their capital and their time. Most angels will require an in-person meeting where you will walk them through a pitch deck that shows a large market opportunity, a product offering that solves a real customer problem, a sustainable competitive advantage, an impressive team, a go-to-market strategy that is believable, and a revenue model that makes sense. But some might invest primarily because of the quality of your lead investor and their due diligence and not require any meetings at all. Fundraising efforts can be very easy or very difficult, but by carefully targeting the right angel investors for your business early in the process, particularly your deal lead, you will make the fundraising process more efficient and should find the best investors and advisers to take your business to the next level.

# 11

# LEGAL ISSUES IN RAISING CAPITAL

**Gunderson Dettmer Stough Villeneuve Franklin & Hachigian, LLP**

Andrew Bradley, Corporate Partner

In this chapter, we'll review the three most important legal provisions that a company should consider as it raises venture capital. But before we dig into these provisions, we should quickly review the overall structure of a venture capital financing.

In general, the legal terms from one venture financing to the next are more similar than they are different, reflecting the venture capital community's status as a body with more or less common norms and guidelines. Since 2005, this commonality has been further enhanced through the availability of model legal investment documents on the website of the National Venture Capital Association (NVCA). The NVCA forms are influential in venture capital investing today and are often helpful for resolving points in an individual transaction among parties trying to find compromise language. Although an individual venture capital financing almost invariably includes legal provisions customized to meet the needs of the company and its investors, the NVCA forms provide a window into what is typical and what is possible in private company investing today.

As helpful as these documents are, they are also impenetrably dense to the entrepreneur or investor encountering them for the first time. Taken together, the NVCA model agreements contain 247 explanatory footnotes and span 199 single-spaced pages. Few entrepreneurs or investors have the time or the inclination to pore over the legal fine print in these financing documents. Instead, in connection with a financing they will typically agree to a summary-level term sheet and then will rely upon their attorneys to reduce those key terms to formal legal agreements.

There are typically five core documents in connection with a venture capital financing:

*Certificate of Incorporation* (often called the Charter): The Charter is a publicly filed (and publicly available) document setting forth the fundamental rights of the stock-holders of a company and is generally the foundation of a company from a legal perspective.

*Stock Purchase Agreement* (often called the SPA): The SPA is the primary sale and purchase contract between the investors and the company and includes various representations and warranties from the company to the investors in connection with the sale of the stock.

*Voting Agreement:* The voting agreement describes the specific procedures concerning the election of the company's board of directors and, occasionally, certain procedures that need to be observed in connection with a sale of the company.

*Investors Rights Agreement* (often called the IRA): The IRA is a bit of a catch-all agreement, describing a host of rights that the investors may hold in connection with their stock purchase. Some of these rights may influence the company's day-to-day operations; other rights come into play only in the event that the company eventually conducts an IPO.

*Right of First Refusal and Co-Sale Agreement*: This agreement (typically shortened to the Co-Sale Agreement) describes the processes that apply in the event that an employee stockholder receives an offer by a third party to purchase his or her shares outside of the context of a sale of the company.

Before going through the most important terms in these agreements, three final explanatory notes are required.

- First, venture capital financings typically involve the sale of "preferred" stock. The difference between the preferred stock purchased by investors and the "common" stock held by founders and employees is that preferred stock contains control, governance, and economic rights not granted to the common stock.

  Preferred stock is typically divided into different series, and as a company increases in value, it will issue multiple, different series of preferred stock. A company's first series of preferred stock is often called "Series Seed" or "Series A," and then as a company matures it will issue Series B preferred stock, Series C preferred stock, and so on. The Series Seed preferred stock is often the least expensive on a per-share basis, and one of the company's goals is to sell preferred stock at progressively higher prices as the company becomes more successful and

valuable. In addition to having a different price per share, each series of preferred stock can have governance and control rights that differ from the other series, and these rights will vary depending on the leverage held by the company or the investors at the time of each investment.

- Second, although the majority of venture capital financings raising at least $1 million involve the sale of preferred stock, this method is not the only way to finance a startup company. Emerging companies in the venture capital economy also raise capital through the sale of convertible promissory notes or other convertible or exchangeable financial instruments, as well as through growth capital loans from commercial banks or other lenders.

- Finally, this chapter was written from the perspective of a startup attorney practicing in Silicon Valley, and this list reflects a view of the venture capital world from that perspective.

The chapter could rightly be accused of having a Delaware corporation focus (or bias), as nearly all the companies aspiring to obtain conventional venture capital investment are Delaware corporations. We don't have the space here to discuss at length the reasons for Delaware's dominance in this arena; however, the primary reason for Delaware's dominant position in venture capital is that Delaware has long maintained a highly specialized court to hear corporate governance disputes and to interpret its corporate law, the Delaware Court of Chancery. This structure means that the outcome of governance disputes in Delaware corporations may be more predictable than governance disputes involving companies formed in other jurisdictions. This predictability permits entrepreneurs and investors, advised by attorneys familiar with Delaware corporate law, to move forward with greater certainty and confidence.

# THE MOST IMPORTANT TERMS IN A VENTURE CAPITAL FINANCING

1. *Understand the protective provisions held by the investors.* Entrepreneurs often focus intently on the imputed valuation of their company in connection with a venture capital financing. That's understandable. Generating a high "pre-money" valuation feels a bit like a scorecard, confirming success. But a company's valuation is far from the most important term, especially for a first-time entrepreneur who has never before navigated the process of collaborating with venture capital investors to build a private company.

We start with the protective provisions because these provisions are a stark reminder to an entrepreneur that choosing a venture capital investor means choosing a business partner. To put a finer point on it, after a venture capital financing, it is no longer "your" company. After a venture capital financing, control of the company is shared, and an entrepreneur ignores this sharing of control at his or her own peril.

The protective provisions (also frequently called the "voting rights") are set forth in the charter. These provisions address a set of corporate actions for which a company needs the consent of a large percentage of the preferred stock in order to take such action. The list of actions requiring approval varies from deal to deal, but this list almost always includes getting preferred stock approval before the company can (a) sell a new series of preferred stock or (b) conduct a merger or a sale of the company.

Read that last sentence again. By selling his or her first series of preferred stock, an entrepreneur agrees that he or she will not sell the company without the approval of the holders of the bulk of the shares held by the investors, nor will he or she conduct another financing. You don't need to use too much imagination to see how this structure could create problems in the future.

The shared control structure created by the protective provisions means they are more important than getting the highest possible valuation when selling stock in a financing. Getting a high valuation might be a superficial gain for the preexisting stockholders, since the sale of preferred stock at a higher price per share means the existing stockholders suffer less overall dilution of their ownership position, but a high valuation can come at a terrible cost if it means that company management will then need to deal with a difficult or uncooperative business partner in the future.

Just as an investor is choosy in the companies in which it invests, it's important that an entrepreneur be selective and thoughtful when choosing to accept investment. Have you spoken to others who have worked with this investor, and would those entrepreneurs do the same again? Do the investor's expectations and goals for the company align with your own?

2. *Understand what level of investor approval is required for key actions.* So we've discussed that a company's management needs to work with the company's investors to approve future financings or a sale of the company. But among the investors, who needs to approve an action in order to satisfy a protective provision?

After the company's first venture capital financing, the answer to this question is straightforward. It's usually the case that one investor will either fund 100 percent of the company's Series Seed financing or that a lead investor will set the terms for the financing and will end up holding a supermajority of the preferred stock following the closing of the transaction. In such a situation, this investor will typically call the shots wherever the financing documents call for the approval of the preferred stock, including the protective provisions discussed above.

As the company grows and issues new series of preferred stock, it is often the case that, over time, the set of investors whose approval is required will change. For example, if a company were to complete a Series Seed financing and then a Series A financing (where, in this example, a different investor leads each round), it wouldn't be at all unusual for a company to need the approval of both the lead investors for key matters going forward.

The specific percentage of preferred stock approval required to take an action covered by a protective provision is often set to a majority of the preferred stock shares then outstanding; however, it doesn't have to be at that level. For example, if a company had two large investors, each holding 33⅓ percent of the preferred stock, and also had a number of investors holding smaller percentages, you could see a situation where the financing documents might provide that 66 percent or 60 percent of the preferred stock would be required to approve a matter. This higher threshold would ensure that a matter up for investor approval was either (a) supported by both of the company's major investors or (b) was approved by one of the major investors with substantial support from the rest of the company's investor community.

Although it's generally a good idea from the company's perspective to stay as close as possible to a simple-majority preferred stock approval standard (instead of a higher and harder to reach supermajority standard), the approval threshold itself is less important than understanding whose approval is needed in order to conduct business, since losing the support of the requisite stockholders for important amendments can grind things to a halt. There are 25 places in the NVCA forms where the documents require the approval of the relevant majority of the preferred stock in order for the company to take some action. It is imperative that a company understand the relevant approval threshold before proceeding down a particular path.

In addition to the above approvals, which require the preferred stock to vote together as a single class, investors will occasionally request "series-specific" protective provisions, especially in later-stage financings as a company approaches an IPO or a potential acquisition.

A company should be especially cautious when considering these provisions, since such terms can give a single investor a degree of leverage and control that is far greater than that investor's overall ownership percentage of the company.

Sometimes series-specific provisions are very targeted to address as a specific investor concern (for example, requiring that the company get the separate approval of the Series D preferred stock in the event of a sale of the company where the Series D preferred stock doesn't at least get its money back). In other situations, series-specific approvals and protections can be quite broad (for example, requiring that the company get the separate approval of the Series D preferred stock in the event of *any* sale of the company). In either case, entrepreneurs should be cautious and think of potential speedbumps down the road before accepting such terms.

3. *Understand the investors' economic rights*: A fundamental theory underlying the preferred stock structure of venture capital investing is that in connection with a sale of the company, the investors will receive their money back prior to common stockholders receiving anything in exchange for their shares. This concept is referred to as a "liquidation preference" held by the preferred stock.

Although the early stage venture capital investment community has largely settled on a standard form of liquidation preference, investors can and do propose investments to companies with varying liquidation preference terms. Understanding the economic impact of these modified terms will help you see that two deals that otherwise are at the same pre-money valuation can have very different exit economics for the founders and employees holding common stock and stock options.

The standard liquidation preference in venture capital investing is called a "nonparticipating liquidation preference." The "nonparticipating" reference describes what happens to the preferred stock after its liquidation preference is fully paid out. If preferred stock is "nonparticipating," in the event of a sale of the company the preferred stock will not "participate" in payments to stockholders in excess of its liquidation preference. For example, in a company that has taken $10 million in venture capital investment and is later acquired for $15 million, the first $10 million in the acquisition would go back to the venture capitalists, then (generally speaking) the common stockholders would split the rest.

"But wait," you say. "In this example, the investors are simply getting their money back, without interest." And you'd be right. No venture capitalist is trying to simply get an investment's liquidation preference returned to his or her fund. By holding preferred stock with a nonparticipating liquidation preference, a venture capitalist has a choice in a sale of the company: It can either (a) receive its liquidation preference back (or, in a downside scenario, a fraction of that liquidation preference) or (b) it can convert its preferred stock into common stock and can share in the upside as the dollars paid to the company begin to greatly exceed the aggregate liquidation preferences of the preferred stock investors.

When an investor holds nonparticipating preferred stock, that investor will convert its preferred stock shares to common stock shares if that would yield a higher price per share than just the return of the preferred stock's liquidation preference. In my example company with $10 million in outstanding venture capital investment, should the company later be acquired for $50 million it would be quite likely that the preferred stock would receive a greater per-share payout were it to convert to common stock. Upon conversion, the liquidation preference associated with the converting preferred stock would evaporate, which would in turn increase the proceeds distributable to the common stockholders.

Now compare the above economics with "participating" preferred stock. A participating preferred stock structure is less common in venture capital transactions today, but it is

still present. The presence of a participating liquidation preference in a deal may be a signal that the investor was concerned about certain risks in the deal, or that the investor had to increase its upside in order to get comfortable with the transaction. Or it simply may be a part of the investor's overall investment thesis and is a standard term that it includes in deals to drive returns to its limited partners.

If an investor holds participating preferred stock, the investor will first receive its liquidation preference and thereafter will participate alongside the common stock in the payment of any additional stockholder proceeds. Let's look again at my example company with $10 million of investment, later acquired for $15 million where the preferred stock (in this example) is all participating preferred stock. In this sale, the first $10 million would still go to the investors, but—assuming in this example that the preferred stockholders own 50 percent of the overall stock of the company—$2.5 million of remainder would be split among the preferred stockholders and $2.5 million would be split among the common stockholders, reducing the common stock payout by 50 percent relative to my earlier nonparticipating example. There would never be an inflection point where the preferred stock would convert to common stock, because participating preferred stock does not need to convert to common stock to receive an upside benefit at a sale of the company.

In addition to participating preferred stock, there is also "partially participating" preferred stock of several types, all of which yield the same fundamental result, which is to raise the inflection point at which the preferred stock will be incentivized to convert into common stock. Whether participating or partially participating, if an entrepreneur is considering a deal with a participating liquidation preference deal component, it will be important for the entrepreneur to understand the impact of this feature at the sale of the company so that he or she isn't later stuck with a nasty surprise regarding the common stockholders' exit economics.

From the perspective of this author, the three above terms are the three most important terms in a venture capital financing. Other investors, entrepreneurs, attorneys, and advisors may look at the NVCA forms, with their 247 explanatory footnotes and 199 single-space pages, and see other terms that they believe to be more crucial. But what is certain is that any entrepreneur or investor would benefit from slowing down and better understanding the meaning of the terms governing a venture capital investment. At times, these terms read like so much legalese, but these are the provisions that ultimately determine how investment returns will be shared among investors, founders, and employees.

# 12

# UNDERSTANDING TERM SHEETS

**Foundry Group**

Jason Mendelson, Managing Director

Every entrepreneur who raises money seeks one thing in common: a term sheet. Term sheets come in all shapes and sizes and can be used for equity or debt investments. Some lucky companies get more than one term sheet, which enables them to have leverage in a negotiation. With these different permutations, there are many things to consider. In this chapter I will present all the major issues around term sheets and provide some pragmatic guidance.

## WHAT IS A TERM SHEET?

A term sheet is a *nonbinding* document that summarizes the major deal points of a contemplated transaction. In other words, it's an informal agreement between two parties who are thinking about doing a deal, in this case a financing between an investor and a company. Getting a term sheet, while exciting, is only the first step to getting money in your bank account, but it is a very important step because it spells out each party's intentions. In most cases, once a term sheet is issued, an actual binding contract is consummated. Only when one party acts badly do deals not close.

## WHAT REALLY MATTERS?

Valuation. Liquidation preferences. Protective provisions. Antidilution. Board seats. Option pools. Registration rights. Attorney fees. Conditions to closing . . .

Take a deep breath. It's okay. We'll get to all of this, but there are only three things that matter when negotiating a term sheet:

1. Understanding the agreement you accepted;

2. Making sure that incentives between you and your investors are aligned; and

3. Making sure the relationship with your investor (and most likely future board member) was enhanced through the process of negotiating the term sheet, not harmed.

It's amazing to me how many times I meet entrepreneurs who don't understand the ramifications of the term sheet they just signed. Sure, money is coming in the door, but has the value of the company shifted to the investors? No matter how much entrepreneurs study this, they'll never be as experienced as a seasoned venture capitalist (VC). For this reason, it's imperative that good legal counsel be consulted.

I would also recommend, regardless of who the lawyers are, that every entrepreneur should have an experienced mentor who can provide feedback.

For every term in the term sheet, consider whether that term aligns or misaligns incentives between the parties. For instance, if an investor asked for the ability to veto a sale of the company for a purchase price under $30 million, what misalignments could exist? Perhaps at a $25 million sale you'd be wealthy beyond your imagination while the VC would hold out and block the deal. When you find a provision in a term sheet that bothers you, consider whether or not alignment is an issue. If you push back and argue alignment of incentives, you have a much stronger position than "it's not market" or "I don't like it." If your VC isn't interested in incentive alignment, that should tell you something important about the person who you are dealing with.

Lastly, consider the long-term dynamics around relationships. If I were to offer you a term sheet and you were to stick your aggressive and overbearing lawyer on me, that is going to negatively affect our relationship. Every person whom you introduce me to (regardless if they are your cofounder or a service provider) is a reflection on you. Given that I'm going to be working closely with you for the next several years (it's not uncommon that I'll work a decade with an entrepreneur), it's wise for us to both start out on the right foot. Strongly consider whom you choose to represent you when negotiating with an investor.

Ultimately, keep it simple. Term sheets pale in significance to building a company and the working relationship you will want with your investors. This goes both ways, too. If your future investors aren't behaving well, consider other options.

## THE TERMS THAT MATTER

While there are many terms to understand, there are only two types of terms that matter. They are 1) economics and 2) control.

When considering any provision in a term sheet, ask yourself the question, *"Does this provision affect either who controls the company or how the economics (returns) are divided up by the parties on a sale of the business?"* If the answer to either of these is *"yes,"* then the provision matters and you should focus on it. If the answer is *"no,"* then you are dealing with a much less important issue.

## ECONOMIC TERMS

The most important economic term is *valuation*. This is also usually the toughest term to negotiate. Some people don't want to negotiate a valuation and choose to use instruments other than equity, such as convertible debt. We'll talk about those later. For now, let's assume that you are going the most common route, which is selling preferred stock in your company to an investor.

Valuation is a simple concept to understand. There are only three things to keep in mind:

1. *Pre-money valuation*: This is the value that is agreed upon as what the company is worth before the investor puts money into your bank account;

2. *The investment amount*: This is the amount of money the investor is offering you; and

3. *Post-money valuation*: This is the pre-money valuation plus the investment amount.

For example, if I offered you $4 million at a $6 million pre-money valuation, then the post-money valuation would be $10 million. Since I put in $4 million and the post-money valuation is $10 million, I would own 40 percent of the company after the financing.

Note that if I changed my offer to an $8 million pre-money valuation, then the post-money valuation would be $12 million and I would own 33 percent of the company post financing. Valuation is the factor that most directly impacts the entrepreneur's return because it defines who owns what piece of the pie.

Be careful when you are discussing valuation with an investor. Often you will hear an investor say, "I'll give you $4 million at a $10 million valuation." It's likely that she is thinking post-money, not pre-money as the entrepreneur often thinks. Make sure that you are speaking the same language.

The next economic term to consider is *liquidation preferences*. This term comes into play when a company is liquidated. In English, this means the company is sold (whether the outcome is good or bad), shut down, or sells off all its assets. Liquidation preferences allow for the investors (who normally buy preferred stock) to get their money back before money goes to the common stockholders, which normally includes founders and employees. There are several types of preferences.

First up is the simple "1x preference" which stands for "one times back your money." In our example where I put $4 million into a company and own 40 percent of the company, I have a choice of getting from the proceeds either the percentage I own or the first $4 million of proceeds in a liquidation event. If the company sells for $4 million or less, I would take all the proceeds. If the company sells for $6 million, I would take $4 million, leaving $2 million left over for the common holders. If the company sells for $50 million, I would take 40 percent of the proceeds, or $20 million, leaving $30 million for the common holders.

There are other situations (usually when a company is in dire straits or having a very difficult time raising money) where one will see a 2x or higher multiples. In a 2x preference situation, I would have the choice to take the first $8 million off the table from a liquidity event. Thankfully for entrepreneurs, it's typical in the VC industry to see a 1x preference.

After looking for what type of liquidation preference is being offered by an investor, check to see if there is also *participation* as well. If the preferred stock is participating, then after the liquidation preference is received, the investors will continue to receive proceeds based on their ownership. Let's go back to our example of an

investment amount of $4 million and pre-money valuation of $6 million. Assuming I'm the only investor, I own 40 percent of the capital stock of the company. If I have a 1x preference and my stock is also participating, then in any liquidity event, I'll take the first $4 million of proceeds, then 40 percent of whatever is left.

If this sounds like a lot of money flying out the door to your investors, realize that the participation right has even greater impact as you raise more money. Try to negotiate your way out of giving a participation right, even if it means trading for a lower valuation. If you can't negotiate the participation away, try to put a *cap* on the participation so that investors stop participating once they hit 2x or 3x their investment amount. This is called *capped participation*.

Next on our list to address is the role of the *option pool*. The option pool is the amount of stock set aside to grant to current and future employees of the company. While you may think that this is something that founders and CEOs should decide, investors will want to make sure that the option pool is large enough to hire all your new employees with the proceeds from the financing. In most cases, this isn't a contentious argument, but beware that whatever option pool is agreed upon comes out of your ownership, not the investors'.

For instance, if you and I agree to a 10 percent option pool being available post my investment, the option pool is created before I put my money in the company. This 10 percent option pool comes out of your ownership (and any other founders, employees, or period investors as well), so you are immediately diluted 10 percent just from the option pool itself. Be very careful if you are judging two term sheets that you have. One may have a higher pre-money valuation, but if the option pool is twice the size of the other term sheet, you could end up owning less of your company despite the higher valuation.

*Antidilution protection* is a provision in almost every VC deal. Antidilution protection gives a benefit to current investors if, in the future, stock of the company is sold at a lower price than previous rounds. In other words, if you sell me stock at $2.00 a share and then the next round is priced at $1.00, I will have my effective price adjusted downward. In the most extreme cases, called *full ratchet protection*, my price would be lowered to $1.00. This results in my doubling my ownership at the expense of the founders and employees. More typically, VCs ask for *weighted average protection,* which looks at how many shares were sold, not just the price, in order to determine how significant the financing actually was. In this case the effect of the dilution is muted but can still be large. There are complicated math equations that determine all of this that are beyond the scope of this chapter. Ultimately, try to never agree to full ratchet anti-dilution and make sure that your lawyer is paying attention to this term.

*Dividends* look a lot like an interest payment on your credit card debt or mortgage. You agree to pay a certain percentage automatically while your debt is outstanding. In a VC deal, an 8 percent dividend would mean you would pay out in cash or stock 8 percent of the investment amount every year (in our case $320,000). While dividends are common in hedge fund and private equity deals, they are very rare in the VC world. Normally one would expect to see a dividend provision that was contingent on the board approving the actual payment. No reasonable investor, in my opinion, would want to take money out of the company this way nor deserve an 8 percent free stock grant every year.

## CONTROL TERMS

Now that we've addressed some of the economic terms, let's look to the other important type of terms: ones that affect the control of the company. The two most important ones are *board of directors* and *protective provisions.*

Pay attention to who sits on your board of directors and who controls the ability to elect members. Among the powers and legal responsibilities that a board has is the power to hire and fire the CEO. When negotiating a term sheet, expect that the lead investor in your round will request a board seat. (This may not be the case if you are raising a smaller seed-type round.) Assuming the CEO/founder takes a seat, what does that say about the remaining seats? Here are some suggestions:

1. Keep the board small. A well-functioning board should be strategic and nimble. The more people in the room, the less functional the board will be; and

2. In the early stages of your company, expect to have a balanced board. This means the investor(s) will get one seat, the CEO will have a seat, and then an *outside board member* (a person who is a noninvestor and nonemployee) will make up the other seat. In the case of a five-person board, there will usually be two company board members (CEO plus one), two investors, and an outsider.

The concept of a balanced board scares some entrepreneurs, but if you are working with a reputable investor, it's rarely an issue. The key is creating a board that is your true inner sanctum. This is the group that you trust with your biggest issues and look to for guidance.

While there are other terms that affect control, the second most important one is which *protective provisions* exist. Normally, the protective provisions allow the preferred stockholders to have a veto right over certain actions the company could take, including issuing new stock, changing the terms of the existing stock, selling the company, and taking on debt. You can try to fight these, but over the past decade these have become standard terms. Rather than fight each term, you should try to keep all of your preferred stockholders voting together as a single class. If you give every new investor in each round a separate set of protective provisions, it's much harder to get things done.

## OTHER TERMS—THE ONES THAT MATTER LESS

There are many other terms that we could discuss, but this chapter would soon become a book (more on that later). We've discussed the most important ones but be prepared to deal with things like *attorney fees* where you negotiate how much you'll pay to your investor's counsel to get the deal done. You'll see arcane terms like *registration rights,* which will talk about a whole bunch of stuff concerned with going public one day. Don't worry, none of this is complicated, nor does it all matter that much. If you find the other side arguing strongly about these terms, you should be concerned about their focus and priorities.

## CAVEATS

In generalizing a lot of information, be wary of certain caveats. Not all investors are the same, and as you deal with later-stage investors, terms tend to diverge more than at the early stages.

Furthermore, this is a discussion about equity term sheets only. If you find yourself negotiating a convertible debt deal, things are quite different. You'll likely be negotiating fewer terms, including the amount of the financing, the interest rate (as low as possible is the norm), terms regarding how the debt converts into equity at the next financing, and what happens if the company is acquired while the convertible debt is outstanding. In these cases, it's possible for debt to convert at a moderate (10 to 30 percent) discount to the next round and even potentially have a valuation cap, which puts an upper limit to the valuation at which the debt can convert.

## WHERE TO GET MORE HELP

Remember that regardless of how well you think you understand these terms, most VCs will have a lot more experience than you. They've likely negotiated tens or hundreds of deals before, so make sure that you have competent legal counsel to help you. Keep in mind that this chapter is a very high-level summary of some of the important issues. If you are looking to dive deeper into all things about term sheets (for equity, debt, and acquisitions), raising money, negotiating, and learning about what really motivates VCs, I encourage you to get a copy of the book *Venture Deals, How to Be Smarter Than Your Lawyer and VC,* coauthored by myself and my Foundry Group partner Brad Feld.

# 13

# DEVELOPING A PATENT STRATEGY FOR STARTUPS

Schox Patent Group

Jeffrey Schox, Founding Member and Patent Attorney

## INTRODUCTION

There are six questions to ask when considering patent strategy for startups: (1) Why should we build a patent portfolio? (2) Which inventions should we file as patent applications? (3) How often should we file? (4) When should we file? (5) Where should we file? and (6) Who should we engage for our patent work?

## WHY DO STARTUPS BUILD A PATENT PORTFOLIO?

Fortune 500 companies build a patent portfolio to enforce against a competitor, to generate licensing revenue, and to market technical and creative ability. None of these reasons, however, applies to startups. Enforcement against a competitor is too expensive, the return on investment in generating licensing revenue is too low relative to the time and effort required, and there are better alternatives to marketing technical and creative ability. In the short term, a more valuable approach is to file a few pending patent applications that can help a startup reinforce a technology narrative to an investor, create a hurdle for smaller competitors, and establish "background IP" for technology partners. The significant impact of building a patent portfolio, however, comes in the long term. A portfolio of issued patents can deter patent infringement lawsuits from larger competitors and can increase valuation during an acquisition or an IPO. Our patent strategy has deterred patent infringement lawsuits for Twilio (which competes against AT&T) and Farmlogs (which competes against Monsanto) and has created significant value for Cruise (acquired by GM for $1 billion) and Accuri Cytometers (acquired by Becton Dickinson for $200 million). When a startup first stops to truly understand the reasons to build a patent portfolio, it can then focus on the appropriate goals and budgets for its patent work.

## WHAT INVENTIONS SHOULD STARTUPS FILE AS PATENT APPLICATIONS?

In an ideal situation, patent applications are pursued if they are both highly patentable and highly valuable. Identifying and prioritizing inventions that are highly valuable can be a daunting task for large companies, especially if they have multiple divisions and product lines. For this reason, as shown in Figure 1, larger companies often optimize for identifying highly patentable inventions and then filing hundreds to thousands of

**FIGURE 1** Valuable and Patentable
Applications

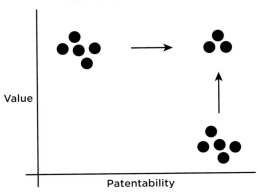

**FIGURE 2** Avoiding Waste and Lost
Opportunity

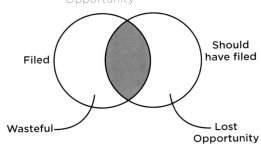

patent applications with the hope that some are also highly valuable.

The system that larger companies use to accomplish this can be considered a bottom-up approach, which includes incentivizing engineers and scientists to identify their own inventions and submit an invention disclosure form to a patent committee that evaluates and selects the inventions that are highly patentable. The fact that the low-level engineers (and sometimes even the patent committee!) do not understand the bigger picture and do not know what inventions are the most valuable to the company does not matter, because the larger company will simply file patent applications with a "quantity over quality" approach. Filing hundreds to thousands of patent applications on an annual basis is really expensive in terms of both dollars (in the range of $10 million) and time (in range of decades of people-power).

Startups do not have the luxury of either resource, but are often misguided to institute a version of the bottom-up approach when building their own patent portfolio. This is not only wasteful but also dangerous.

Failing to file patent applications on the inventions that are both highly patentable and highly valuable is clearly problematic in relation to a startup's ability to deter patent infringement lawsuits and increase valuation. But, as shown in Figure 2, filing patent applications on the wrong

inventions is potentially worse, because this additionally wastes precious resources of time and money and, because patent applications are automatically published by the patent office 18 months after the filing date, teaches competitors how to make and use their (unprotected) inventions.

Why does the bottom-up approach fail for startups? Startups, which are often not large enough to harness the wisdom of a crowd, struggle to correctly identify inventions that are highly patentable.

Because patent applications are not published for 18 months, there is no way to conduct an accurate patentability search. There is another problem with the bottom-up approach: I have encountered an inverse proportionality between the brilliance of inventors and their ability to identify their inventions and evaluate the patentability of their inventions. Average people think that all of their ideas are brilliant, while brilliant people think all of their ideas are average. In other words, a brilliant startup chief technology officer (CTO) cannot accurately identify the inventions that are highly patentable.

So, what approach should a startup use to identify inventions? We recommend a top-down approach. In a top-down approach, we first start with the two to three core differentiators that articulate the reasons the startup will succeed in the marketplace. This could be as simple as the REST application programming interface (API) and multitenancy attributes of Twilio or the low cost and compact features of Accuri cytometers.

Next, we help our clients identify the technologies that enable the core differentiators. And finally, we interview the engineers and scientists to capture and select the inventions that support these technologies. Instead of a "quantity over quality" approach to the patent application, we recommend the opposite. Patent applications with better claims and with more embodiments and variations in the specification will overcome the rejections from the patent office.

While Fortune 500 companies identify patentable inventions and then use quantity to get great patents, startups should identify valuable inventions and then use quality to get great patents.

## HOW MANY PATENTS SHOULD WE FILE?

In my experience, the ability of a patent portfolio to deter a patent infringement lawsuit from a competitor has a value that can be graphed as an "S" curve based on the number of issued patents. The reason is based on the power of exponential numbers. A defendant in an infringement lawsuit of one patent can expect to invalidate the patent or avoid infringement roughly 50 percent of the time. But to escape the lawsuit, the defendant must try to invalidate or avoid *every* patent in the portfolio. If every issued patent in the portfolio offers a 50 percent chance, then, as the number of patents in the portfolio increases, the chance for the defendants to escape the lawsuit decreases at an exponential rate. While escaping one issued patent might be easy, escaping a hundred issued patents is close to impossible. In my experience, the sweet spot is around 15 issued patents as the "S-curve" rapidly climbs from five issued patents to 25 issued patents and tends to increase only marginally thereafter.

On the other hand, the value of the patent portfolio is more linear. Large companies that sell hundreds or thousands of issued patents in bulk tend to fetch $500,000 to $1 million per issued patent. For instance, when Facebook bought 500 issued patents from IBM, it paid $1 million each. There is probably, however, a limit to how many

valuable and patentable inventions that a startup can produce in a given year.

With an understanding that we have the S-curve for the ability to have a patent portfolio to deter an infringement lawsuit and a linear relationship for the value of the patent portfolio, we can now consider the timing for future events for the startup. A startup is not likely to be sued by a competitor until the startup has reached $100 million per year in annual revenue. Depending on the startup, this revenue milestone takes many years to reach, but can often be predicted with enough accuracy within a two- to three-year range. Similarly, most startups can predict an acquisition or an IPO with enough accuracy within a two- to three-year range. In years past, the expected four- to five-year life cycle of a patent application would make it impossible to hit a moving target that is two to three years away. But now we now have the ability to "fast-track" patent applications (for only $2,000 in government fees) and quickly move from filing to issuance in less than one year. Thus we can set a goal to have 12 issued patents in five years and 25 issued patents in seven years, and work backwards to determine how many patent applications should be filed on an annual basis between now and then.

The actual pace of patent application filings often mimics the valuation and engineering headcount of the startup. It is typical for our clients to file 2 to 3 patent applications in the first year to cover the core differentiators, 4 to 6 applications in the next couple years to cover the improvements, and then 6 to 12 patent applications on an annual basis to pursue the features enabled by the core technologies. These patent filings, however, are always dictated by the goals of the patent portfolio.

## WHEN SHOULD WE FILE PATENT APPLICATIONS?

To maximize the success rate of a patent application, one should attempt to get an early filing date to beat the competitors in our first-to-file patent system, and one should include more details in the patent application to distinguish from prior inventions. These twin goals (file earlier to beat the competition and file later to discover more details) appear to be in conflict. An appropriately timed provisional application followed by a full patent application, however, solves this.

I have a motto that good ideas are simply not patentable. In my experience with over 2,000 patent applications, the inventors that have built and tested their inventions have discovered the important details that help distinguish their invention from prior inventions. This level of inventing typically does not happen during a morning jog, a shower, or any other eureka moment but rather happens with a great team that has significant funding and focused direction. Thus, as shown in Figure 3, the optimal time for a full patent application to be filed is after the invention has been built and tested. The optimal time for a provisional patent application to be filed, however, is exactly one year before this date.

In the software space, technology development is more predictable. And thus, when an invention has been conceived and it is believed that the invention will be built and tested within a year, we encourage our clients to file as soon as possible. In the hardware space, however, technology development is often less predictable. And with our clients in the hardware space, we often encourage them to delay the filing of the patent application until they

are confident that they will build and test the invention within the next 12 months.

The twin goals to file early to beat a competitor and to file later to distinguish from prior inventions do not apply equally across different technology spaces. For instance, we often encourage our startup clients in the clean tech space to delay the filing of their provisional patent applications because the space in which they are inventing is often very crowded, and the goal of distinguishing from prior inventions is more important than the goal of beating competitors. In contrast, we often encourage our startup clients in the software space to speed up the filing of their provisional patent applications because the goal of beating competitors is more important than the goal of distinguishing from prior inventions.

## WHERE SHOULD WE FILE PATENT APPLICATIONS?

The question of whether or not to pursue foreign patent protection is, by far, the one area of patent strategy that produces the most anxiety and, unfortunately, the most regret. Our most successful startups often regret not filing more foreign patent applications, while our less successful startup clients often regret spending so much money in the pursuit of patent protection in faraway lands. For this reason, we spent a significant amount of time analyzing the historical data of our more than 250 startup clients, and we found that spending roughly 30 percent of the patent budget in the pursuit of foreign protection was ideal.

Pursuing patent protection in the United States is expensive, and pursuing patent protection in foreign countries is no different. One can expect to spend approximately $30,000 in the pursuit of issued patents per foreign country. When considering the 70:30 ideal split within the patent budget, and knowing that the foreign patent applications (approximately $30,000 each) are almost as expensive as the domestic patent application (approximately $40,000), one can

**FIGURE 3** Timing the Provisional Application

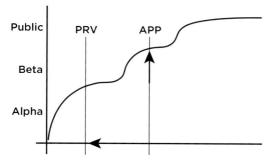

uickly calculate that the ideal pattern is to file
wo foreign patent applications for every five U.S.
atent applications.

here are three factors to consider when choosing
which countries to select for your foreign patent
pplications: (1) where might you make and sell
our product in the next three to five years,
2) where might you have competitors that make
nd sell an infringement product in the next three
o five years, and (3) where might a potential
cquirer of your startup be located? Keep in mind
hat while there are over 200 countries with patent
ystems, one can cover a very large portion of the
lobal market by filing patent applications in the
Inited States, the European region, and China.
Vhen our clients choose to pursue foreign patent
rotection, we often recommend filing in Europe
nd China. There are, of course, many exceptions.
Dur medical device startups, which often have
maller but more valuable portfolios, often
ursue patent applications in Canada, Australia,
nd Japan as well as Europe and China. And,
ur manufacturing startups often pursue patent
pplications in Japan and Mexico as well as Europe
nd China.

## WHO SHOULD WE ENGAGE FOR OUR PATENT WORK?

here are several different roles in building
 highly functioning patent portfolio: (1) the
atent strategist who determines the why,
vhat, how often, when, and where of the patent
ortfolio, (2) the patent agent or attorney
"patent associate") who interviews the
nventor and crafts the patent application, and
3) the technologist who reviews the patent
pplications. The CTO is almost always the
erson who assumes the role of the technologist,
ut there are a few different ways to structure
he patent strategist (who often has seven or
nore years of patent experience) and the patent
ssociate (who often has two to six years of
atent experience). One model is to hire an in-
ouse patent counsel as the strategist and use
utside patent firms for the patent associate.
he challenge with this structure is that a good

in-house patent counsel can often command a
salary in the $250,000 range. Another model
is to hire a consultant as a part-time in-house
patent counsel and use an outside patent firm
for the patent associate. While this solves the
financial challenge, it often fails because the
consultant and the associate (who are both
external to the startup) rarely communicate, and
the patent strategy is not properly implemented.
Twilio, like all of our other clients, used a third
model: engaging a patent law firm for both
the strategist and the associate. I was the
person who designed the strategy and one of
my associates was the person who crafted the
patent applications (while the Twilio CTO was the
technologist who reviewed each of the patent
applications along with the inventors).

If a decision to use a patent law firm is made,
the next question is to determine the best
fit for the startup. I recommend optimizing
for four factors: (1) experience, (2) technical
background, (3) startup focus, and (4) proximity.
The Supreme Court has stated that patent
applications are the most challenging of all
legal documents. It pays to work with someone
who has traversed the steep learning curve of
developing patent portfolios and writing patent
applications. It is also important to work with
someone who is fluent in your technology.
Patent applications stand and fall based on the
words that are chosen in the claim section of
the patent application. The patent associate
must be fluent in your technology to be able to
choose the right words. For instance, while I am
fluent in mechanical, electrical, and software
technologies, I could not write a high quality
patent application on a pharmaceutical invention.
I simply do not know the right words. As I
hope it is abundantly clear, patent strategy for
startups is wildly different than patent strategy
for Fortune 500 companies and, for this reason,
I strongly recommend that startups work with
someone that has extensive startup experience.
Finally, I recommend that startups choose
someone that they can meet with and brainstorm
in a face-to-face manner on a regular basis.

## CONCLUSION

By answering why should we build a patent portfolio, which inventions should we file as patent applications, how often should we file, when should we file, where should we file, and who should we engage for our patent work, startups can build a patent portfolio that deters patent infringement lawsuits from their competitors and increases the value of their startup.

# INTELLECTUAL PROPERTY ENFORCEMENT 101

**Kasowitz Benson Torres LLP**

Steven C. Carlson, Managing Partner, Silicon Valley Office

Intellectual property (IP) disputes are the badge of honor that most successful companies have to bear. As success has many fathers, so too do successful companies face many IP claims. Common disputes include:

- competitor-versus-competitor suits to block market access;
- "patent troll" suits, whereby a nonpracticing patentee will sue one or more companies, often an entire industry, usually for a payoff; and
- employment-related disputes, often alleging trade secrets.

To maximize your leverage on the offense and protect yourself on defense, here are some strategic considerations for these IP disputes that are likely to impact your company.

## OFFENSIVE ENFORCEMENT CONSIDERATIONS

*Patents:* Developing a strong patent portfolio is a "quality not quantity" requirement. A single patent, with a single good claim, can do the job. The best patent claims cover your competitor's product as it exists when it is shipped or sold or housed on their servers. Proving infringement becomes difficult if it is necessary to determine how customers ultimately use the product.

Worldwide protection is costly, so prioritize the United States, Europe (designating at least Germany and the Netherlands), and China, among other jurisdictions that may be important for your particular market. Consider getting patents issued by the German Patent Office, as opposed to the European Patent Office (EPO), because upcoming rule changes may strip the benefit of the German court system for patents issued from the EPO. Also consider getting "utility model" protection in Germany and China, which is a form of "baby patent" that can be obtained in weeks at low cost.

*Enforcing in the United States:* Protecting your U.S. market may be your top goal. Patent suits in the United States typically cost $2 million to $5 million, and may take two to four years to fully resolve, depending on the course of proceedings. Enforcement in the United States has become increasingly challenging with the advent of the Patent Trial and Appeal Board (PTAB), discussed below, which is a Patent Office tribunal for invalidating patents.

PTAB challenges create the likelihood that your enforcement case may be shelved for 18 months, which may be an intolerable delay. Although a risky strategy, seeking a preliminary injunction in court may be your best leverage. If you sue within three months of patent issuance, then district courts cannot stay a preliminary injunction request pending a PTAB challenge (for Post Grant Reviews, discussed below). If you are confident in your patent, this "guns blazing" approach may be your best option for keeping a competitor off the shelf. Otherwise, the delay of 18 months while the Patent Office reexamines the validity of your patent may be insufferable in the market.

*Enforcing overseas*: Enforcement options outside the United States should be part of every company's toolkit. The "biggest bang for your IP buck" may be Germany. Winning in Germany is tantamount to winning in Europe, and most companies cannot afford to lose access to the European market. The time to trial in Germany is around a year, often as short as nine months. The cost is on the order of $500,000, often less. The German court system has unique procedural rules that generally favor plaintiffs by limiting the enforcement trial to infringement questions and resolving validity in a separate trial, which usually lags behind. Essentially the first day in court is the trial itself, with none of the procedural exit points that are characteristic of U.S. proceedings, such as motions to dismiss, claim construction proceedings, or summary judgment. German courts that find infringement generally award injunctions, unlike the United States, which may simply award royalties. There are options for swift customs actions for seizing goods within days or weeks, including at trade shows. For cash-strapped companies that need maximum leverage over their opponents, Germany may be the best strategic option. Thus prioritize obtaining patent protection in Germany.

The Netherlands is also a key jurisdiction— get patents there. The port of Rotterdam is Europe's shipping hub, so locking the doors on your competitor in the Netherlands may effectively shut down your competitor's access to Europe.

Europe is on track to finally establish the Unified Patent Court (UPC), which will provide a single forum to enforce patents across most European jurisdictions. While this takes shape, preserve your options by obtaining patents through the national patent offices of particular countries (particularly Germany). The court systems of those individual countries may be more advantageous than the UPC. The consequence of losing in the UPC is a loss of all your rights across Europe in one fell swoop.

China is another important forum. It is a "wild card," with the system generally more opaque and uncertain. Procuring and enforcing your IP in China can be extremely powerful, particularly if your adversary manufactures its products in China—in that situation, getting an injunction in China effectively gives you worldwide exclusivity. Trials are also swift (about a year), and low cost.

*Threat letters*: Be careful making IP infringement threats. An allegation with any particularity can expose you to "declaratory judgment jurisdiction," meaning the recipient can sue you in its home court for casting a cloud over its business.

## TRADE SECRETS

If you don't have patents yet, trade secret protection may be sufficient. In some cases, trade secret protection may surpass patent protection, particularly in software fields where patent protection is difficult to obtain. Companies should make a deliberate decision on whether to rely on trade secret protection instead of patent protection, because filing a patent on your technology will undercut its trade secret status. Trade secret cases require an act of misappropriation, typically an employee taking secrets, or some kind of espionage. Documentation is key for establishing your possession of particular trade secrets, for showing access to and misappropriation of the secret, and for demonstrating that you maintained reasonable safeguards against disclosure.

## NONDISCLOSURE AGREEMENTS (NDAS)

Often overlooked as a form of IP protection, NDAs can provide the cheapest and most effective form of protection if done correctly. If you are heading into a critical negotiation where your key technology is being disclosed, customize the NDA and conduct yourself accordingly:

Document the items being disclosed, preferably with numbered pages, marked confidential;

Keep a duplicate copy of whatever is being given to the other side;

If you disclose things orally, document the conversation with a follow-up email, describing what you conveyed;

Specify the people who have access;

Require the receiving party to document evidence of independent invention in the event of a dispute;

State in the NDA that you will be irreparably harmed by breach, and state that injunctive relief would appropriate in the event of a breach;

Specify your home court as the venue for disputes;

Keep the things confidential that you say are confidential.

If you get these terms agreed to (and you may be pleasantly surprised what other people don't read or push back on!), you may have superlative options for IP enforcement. The action can be brought as a breach of contract, so no patent is necessary. The contract may provide for injunctive relief, which patent protection might not even support. And the action can be brought without the delays and procedural hurdles of patent cases (such as PTAB challenges). So if you have an especially important negotiation where there is a credible risk of misappropriation, don't just reach for the standard form NDA—customizing it to fit the situation may be your cheapest and most effective form of IP protection.

## DEFENSIVE IP DISPUTE STRATEGY

### PATENT COMPETITOR SUITS

Competitor patents suits are the highest risk, because the patentee has a credible injunction threat. Evaluating PTAB challenges is a top priority. If you foresee the dispute, prepare your invalidity arguments in advance. This is particularly true in the medical devices and life sciences sector, where there is often a small and known universe of players. You cannot afford to rush a PTAB filing, and so conducting the prior art investigation and at least outlining the arguments is worthwhile to do prior to conflict.

Note that you may be paying for two proceedings at once. Filing a PTAB petition will cost on the order of $200,000 (explained below). The district court proceeding will likely continue at least until the PTAB issues an order to institute the proceeding, typically six months after filing the petition. Thus you must budget for both tracks, which may easily total $500,000 to $1 million before the court may decide to stay the litigation. Depending on how far along the litigation has progressed, the court may decline to put its work on hold pending the outcome of the PTAB proceeding, another reason to proactively prepare.

### "PATENT TROLL" SUITS

Suits from nonpracticing entities are a costly annoyance. Establish a policy about how to handle them, particularly whether to pay out early or to fight to the end. Companies will develop a reputation for settling or fighting, so an early settlement may invite future litigation.

Be wary of joint defense groups. It is attractive to sign onto a larger group to defray costs across multiple defendants. However, if a codefendant botches a PTAB challenge, the estoppel (see below) will likely apply to you, as being "in privity" with the petitioner. And if the defendant who has been taking the lead in the litigation decides to settle, you may be left in a scramble.

## PTAB CHALLENGES

The PTAB has become a major player in patent litigation since its creation in 2011. The PTAB resolves only patent validity and does not hear infringement disputes. These proceedings were enacted under the basic belief that it makes more sense to have a panel of specialists at the Patent Office, rather than a lay jury, hear disputes about whether prior art invalidates a patent. The PTAB has strict deadlines for resolving these disputes; from the filing of a petition to ultimate disposition takes about 18 months (i.e., roughly half the time of court trials). Costs through disposition typically run about $200,000 to $500,000. These Patent Office challenges are far less intrusive on a company's operations because of the limited scope of discovery.

PTAB trials are popular with defendants. Parties to patent disputes now routinely consider:

- Is a PTAB challenge appropriate for the case, considering the limitations on the scope of the Patent Office's review?

- Which among the PTAB proceedings (Covered Business Method, Inter Partes Review, and Post-Grant Review, each with their idiosyncrasies) is the appropriate procedural vehicle?

- What is the best timing for filing a PTAB petition?

- Whether to move to stay the district court litigation pending the PTAB proceedings; and

- How to harmonize positions in the PTAB and district court, where divergent goals may apply.

Filing a PTAB challenge is a risky move. It is essential to "look before you leap." Prominent considerations include:

*Cost:* PTAB litigation is immediately costly. As opposed to district court litigation, where costs are low initially and steadily crescendo, PTAB litigation is the inverse. For the petitioner, most of the costs are incurred immediately. These costs include conducting a thorough prior art search (do NOT skimp on this!), paying an expert

to prepare an invalidity declaration, paying the lawyers to draft the petition, and paying a stiff PTO filing fee (typically $25,000 to $40,000 per patent). Thus immediate expenses are typically on the order of $200,000 to file a petition. Sinking this much money into litigation on Day 1 may harden you for battle rather than facilitate settlement.

*Noninstitution:* The Patent Office declines to hear about 25 percent of cases filed. This decision will occur about six months after the petition is filed. Although formal "estoppel" (discussed below) does not result from a noninstitution decision, significant negative consequences follow. The patent owner will certainly tell the district court judge that the specialists at the Patent Office found no reasonable likelihood that the patent is invalid. The judge may allow this argument to be made to the jury, which is highly prejudicial but sometimes allowed. Defendants will not know until the eve of trial if the patentee will be allowed to make this argument.

*Estoppel*: Challengers are "estopped" from having two bites at the apple, by trying to invalidate patents in the Patent Office and then if unsuccessful, reasserting these arguments in court. This rule differs from that in Europe, where challengers may file an "opposition" in the European Patent Office and if unsuccessful, relitigate these same issues in court. The U.S. rule of estoppel forces accused infringers to pick the forum where they are going to make their invalidity arguments—often the instinct is to give this authority to the specialists at the PTAB rather than a lay jury. However, given the limited scope of PTAB proceedings, certain arguments (such as prior use, for example), may play better in district court where live witnesses have a bigger role. The different PTAB proceedings have different levels of estoppel, with Covered Business Method (CBM) being a low-risk option and Post Grant Review (PGR) the highest risk; in the latter, you will have almost no validity case preserved in court if you lose at the PTAB (or if you are found to be "in privity" with a losing petitioner).

*Inflexible positions:* Challengers at the PTAB have to make all their arguments in the initial petition. This is a handicap relative to district court. At the time of the initial petition, the claim construction will be unresolved, so it may be uncertain what prior art applies. Furthermore, the priority date of the patent being challenged may be unknown, meaning that certain prior art may be later disqualified. Generally these fundamental issues remain unresolved until the merits hearing. If the PTAB "moves the goalposts" unexpectedly, then the entire basis of the petition may be undercut. By contrast, in court parties have more latitude to adapt to changes in claim construction, priority dates, etc.

Thus, PTAB challenges should only be launched after careful considerations of potential pitfalls, and after determining if your defense would be better presented in court.

## EMPLOYMENT AND TRADE SECRET DISPUTES

Some of the ugliest litigation arises from trade secrets. Preventive measures include:

- Establish a screening process for new employees, particularly those who just departed from competitors.

- Require employees to scrub their computers, Dropbox accounts, Gmail accounts, memory sticks, etc., of any and all competitor information and to sign an attestation documenting their efforts to do so.

- If you receive confidential materials through an NDA, keep that information sequestered and destroy it (assuming this is permissible) after conclusion of the collaboration.

- If competitor confidences do make it into your system, act aggressively to sequester that information, including the tainted individuals. Consider excluding them from certain product teams.

- Ensure your development documentation is preserved, so that if accused of misappropriation you can establish independent development. Generate archive copies of your inventive work, and lock it away.

Trade secret cases are often more intrusive, costly, and vitriolic than patent cases because discovery may properly extend to dozens of computers, email collections, texts, and even the slack space on hard drives, etc., with overtones of theft. Thus reasonable preventive measures should be structured into your organization.

## CONCLUSION

IP disputes can make or break companies. Before litigation, have a litigation plan. From both an offensive and defensive posture, preparing for likely disputes will give you the advantage for defusing, avoiding, or flat-out winning the fight of your company's life.

# 15

# INSURING YOUR BUSINESS

**Woodruff-Sawyer & Co.**

Priya Cherian Huskins, Partner and Senior Vice President

Wade Pederson, Partner and Senior Vice President

You've just started your business . . . or you've grown it to a point where you have something worth protecting. In any case, sooner than later, the issue of "what makes sense to insure" will come up. This chapter is intended to help you answer this question.

## GROWTH STAGE: RISK MANAGEMENT FOR PRIVATE COMPANIES

Once a growing private company determines that it wants to recruit and retain excellent directors, it's time to think about acquiring directors and officers (D&O) liability insurance. D&O insurance covers directors and officers of companies when they are sued in this capacity. Placing this insurance sooner than later gives directors and officers the comfort of knowing that there is more than just the company's balance sheet standing behind them should they be sued.

Some of the reasons private companies purchase D&O insurance include:

- Attracting new directors
- Venture capital requirements
- Emerging risks
- Regulatory exposures
- Bankruptcy
- Mergers and acquisitions
- Shareholder lawsuits
- IPO considerations

Let's take a closer look at the details of private company D&O insurance, including how it works and what to watch for.

### THE INS AND OUTS OF D&O INSURANCE

It's helpful to understand how D&O insurance is structured and responds. There are typically three insuring agreements in a private company D&O insurance policy: Side A, Side B, and Side C (Figure 1).

**FIGURE 1** Traditional ABC Policy for Private Companies

| | Personal Protection | Balance Sheet Protection | |
|---|---|---|---|
| • Traditional ABC policy strikes a balance between personal asset protection and corporate balance sheet protection | **TRIGGER** Actions of D&Os that aren't indemnifiable | **TRIGGER** Actions of D&Os that are indemnifiable | **TRIGGER** Actions of entity for securities, EPL & limited other claims |
| • Vast majority of companies incorporate primary ABC coverage as a means of risk transfer | **PAYS** On behalf of D&Os | **PAYS** On behalf of entity (Funds indemnification of D&Os) | **PAYS** On behalf of entity |
| | **RETENTION** None | **RETENTION** Applies | **RETENTION** Applies |
| | A | B | C |

©Woodruff-Sawyer & Co. 2017 (used with permission)

Side A responds when a company is unable to indemnify its directors and officers. Side B reimburses a company for its indemnification obligations to its directors and officers. Side C provides corporate coverage whenever the company is sued alongside directors and officers.

Private companies can purchase D&O insurance as a stand-alone product or combined with other policies for cost savings. See Figure 2.

## Negotiating Exclusions

A policy exclusion removes a particular claim from the policy's coverage. The scope of these exclusions can sometimes be negotiated. Some areas of negotiation include:

*Intentional fraud:* Insurance carriers will not insure intentional fraud, but companies can negotiate the point at which the conduct is excluded. If the fraud exclusion can be triggered

only after a final judgment, insurance can cover defense costs until then.

*Insured versus insured:* Private company D&O insurance carriers will not cover claims in which directors and officers (former or current) of the same company sue each other. However, companies can negotiate limited exceptions to the exclusions (also known as "carve-backs" that give back coverage), for example, limiting the number of years a director must be separated from the company before the exclusion no longer applies.

## Duty to Defend vs. Duty to Indemnify

Defense costs are a big part of what's covered in a D&O insurance policy and are always part of the total limit that will be paid for this type of insurance. Private companies can purchase either a duty to defend or a duty to indemnify policy.

**FIGURE 2** Menu Driven Approach

- Carriers provide a single policy with options to add multiple coverage lines.

- Creates a customized comprehensive coverage program under one policy with one carrier.

- Buyers have the option to combine limits for premium savings or purchase separate limits for each coverage.

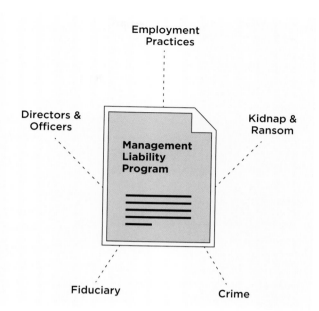

©Woodruff-Sawyer & Co. 2017 (used with permission)

'Duty to indemnify' means a company selects its own counsel. However, the carrier will only pay "reasonable" defense fees. The difference between what a company thinks is reasonable and what an insurer thinks is reasonable can be significant.

'Duty to defend' means the insurer chooses the defense counsel, who may or may not be the company's first choice. However, the upside to a duty to defend policy is that the insurer is typically responsible for paying the defense fees for all allegations brought in the litigation and not just the allegations that are covered under the policy.

**Choosing Policy Limits**

How much coverage does a company need? Two common ways for a company to identify a prudent limit for its D&O insurance policy are to:

Benchmark against similar companies; and/or

Work through common private company litigation scenarios and then contact outside counsel to understand the costs associated with them.

Younger and smaller private companies will typically buy only $1 million to $3 million in limits. As private companies mature, they start to look at $5 million to $10 million in limits. Amounts may be higher for companies in highly regulated industries.

The next question is usually: How much will the insurance cost? The answer depends on many factors, including the overall state of the D&O insurance market.

In purchasing D&O insurance, pricing should not be the end of the analysis. D&O insurance is highly customized—in other words, policy contracts are not standardized. The same carrier has the discretion to offer many different versions of policy terms to different companies.

At the end of the day, money spent on an insurance program with broad coverage terms offered by a quality insurance carrier will provide a better value for a company than a less-expensive program with poor contractual terms offered by a carrier that has no intention of paying future claims.

## Choosing a Broker

Because D&O insurance is a highly customized financial product, partnering with the right insurance broker is critical. Here are five key questions you might ask when looking for an expert partner.

*What can you tell me about your firm and its culture?* This question allows interviewees to give an overview of their brokerage firm, including their culture. Listen for things like team cohesion and stability. This matters because in difficult situations companies need brokerage teams to row hard in the same direction on their behalf.

*In your view, what are the key exposures my company faces?* This question is a chance to get free advice from the experts as well as gain insight into how the brokerage teams are thinking about a company's risk. In the best case, the answer to this question will also tell if you like the broker's style of communication.

*What do I need to know about the insurance policies you would recommend and your process for placing them?* An insurance program needs to be customized for a company's specific risk profile. This question will give good brokers the chance to identify critical insurance policies and share their process for placing them.

*What additional services do you provide?* This question is about client resources. Some brokers have invested more than others in client resources such as access to databases, secure online platforms, claims advocacy, and other client services. Some of these services will be more useful to you than others. In general, most sophisticated brokerages provide more support than just placing insurance.

*What will all of this cost?* Cost is important, and a good broker will break down the costs in an understandable way. Remember that the cost of insurance has two elements: the premiums paid to insurance carriers and the amount paid to the broker. In this part of the interview, look for how the broker thinks about premiums and how the broker manages premiums over time. This is also where a company learns if the broker wants to work on commission or fee. Finally, a company can find out if its prospective broker is planning to charge separately for certain services, for example, claims handling.

## International D&O Considerations

If a company has foreign subsidiaries, it will want to consider how to optimize its global D&O insurance program. The issue is that while your D&O insurance policy probably says that it provides coverage on a worldwide basis, whether or not insurance can legally respond in a local jurisdiction depends on the laws of that jurisdiction.

In many countries, the stakes may be quite low because advancing legal fees from the local subsidiary to an individual director or officer is easy and straightforward. Where this is not the case, however, there is a lot more pressure to have local insurance that complies with all local regulations.

Depending on a company's situation, there are options. Some companies will rely on the worldwide coverage provided by a master program and call it a day. Others will decide to take advantage of certain features that some European-based D&O policies can provide when it comes to international coverage.

Many companies will decide to purchase a few local policies in some of the countries where the company does business. Some conservative companies will decide to purchase D&O insurance in every country where they do business. A few companies may even build a tower of insurance for the "rest of the world" that is separate from the insurance program they use for their U.S.-based exposure.

In all cases, decisions about international D&O insurance coverage are rarely static. Part of the risk management process is to routinely review the international program with an eye on the changing business, political, and regulatory environment.

## OTHER INSURANCE PRODUCTS TO MANAGE RISK

D&O insurance is not, of course, the only insurance that growing companies need to buy. Consider the following guidelines when putting together your company's entire insurance risk management program:

### 1. Invest in Insurance When it's the Law

Certain insurance coverages such as workers' compensation or auto liability for owned vehicles are statutorily required in nearly every state. Other insurance requirements will vary by industry, for example, clinical trial insurance for life science companies. Companies will want to work with trusted advisors such as their attorney and insurance broker to understand the insurance requirements in each state or country where a company does business or has an office.

### 2. Invest in Insurance to Fulfill Contractual Requirements

Signing a lease, entering into an agreement with a prospective customer, and signing up with a preferred employer organization are all examples of contracts that require a company to maintain basic commercial insurance. Along with legal review, have an insurance broker review the details of the insurance and indemnification provisions in all your contracts.

### 3. Invest in Insurance to Transfer Catastrophic Risk

A catastrophic, multimillion-dollar claim can quickly strangle a growing private company, for example, an auto accident involving an employee on work assignment with major injuries to third parties or a class action lawsuit related to a defective consumer product. For these scenarios, products such as a general liability policy and auto insurance are key. It usually makes sense to supplement these with an umbrella policy that provides an additional layer of protection.

### 4. Invest in Insurance for Operational Risks

Companies with unique operational exposures, such as those that use hazardous chemicals or companies in the life sciences sector, will want tailored insurance for these exposures. Most businesses will also accumulate some quantity of sensitive information they have an obligation to protect, even if only on the company's own employees. Cyber liability insurance has come onto the scene to address risks associated with the financial impact of a data breach.

## EXIT STAGE: RISK MANAGEMENT STRATEGIES FOR PRIVATE COMPANIES

At some point, your growing private company might be interested in a liquidity event, be it a merger and acquisition (M&A) or IPO. Insurance can help you optimize these outcomes.

### THE M&A ROUTE

*Reps and warranties insurance:* A merger or acquisition is a common exit for many fast-growing private companies. During M&A, representations and warranties insurance can be a powerful bargaining chip for both buyers and sellers. This insurance protects against breaches of the representations and warranties made in a purchase and sale agreement. This insurance is typically used to reduce the total size of the escrow in the deal.

Buyers in the M&A transaction are the ones who most frequently purchase this insurance (because buyers can insure against a seller's fraud), but it is available to the seller as well.

If a buyer agrees to purchase a company based on the reps and warranties given and those reps and warranties turn out to be false, the buyer has the right to submit this claim to the insurance carrier. Similarly, should the seller purchase the insurance and the buyer file a dispute, the seller can expect the insurance to cover the claim.

*D&O insurance tail policy:* When a company is acquired, its existing D&O policy will terminate at the end of the policy year—not ideal if you are worried about claims that may arise against your directors and officers in the future. A tail policy, also known as a run-off policy, is the solution. Because D&O insurance is a claims-made type of policy, the D&O insurance policy that responds to a claim is the policy that is in place *at the time* the claim is made. So, for example, if in 2016 a set of actions took place that is later challenged in 2017, it's the 2017 policy that would respond.

This is where a D&O tail policy is crucial. After companies sell themselves, they stop renewing their D&O insurance. A tail policy covers what would otherwise be a gap in coverage for directors and officers after the sale of a company.

The gap exists because the D&O policy of the acquiring company will typically not respond on behalf of the selling company's directors and officers for claims that arise post-closing that relate to pre-closing activities.

It is completely standard for a buyer to allow a seller to purchase a six-year tail policy. The policy should be placed and serviced by the seller's broker. This arrangement gives the seller confidence that, even when the company is gone, someone loyal to the seller's directors and officers will be in charge of the insurance program that protects them.

## THE IPO ROUTE

An IPO is an exciting time for any private company. But with it come risks—especially for directors and officers.

When it comes to D&O insurance and an IPO, it's best to ramp up the D&O program during the renewal cycle the year prior to the IPO. This allows companies to make a few simple—but strategic—moves. For example, increasing limits early on gets the all-important warranty statement out of the way. Whenever a company purchases a higher limit of insurance, the company has to tell the insurer selling the new layer of insurance that the directors and officers

of the company know of nothing that's likely to give rise to a claim (a "warranty statement").

When contemplating an IPO, consider the five key steps to building a D&O insurance program that run parallel to the IPO milestones that a company must achieve (Figure 3):

- Prepare
- Launch
- Broker
- Implement
- Support

Let's look at those five steps in closer detail.

The first step is to **prepare**, which includes developing a risk-management strategy. This process takes place while the company is drafting its S-1. Some of the key questions that need to be answered in this stage are:

- What is the timing of the IPO and is the company on a dual track?
- What is the size of the IPO and will there be selling shareholders?
- What is the company's philosophy on risk transfer and buying D&O insurance limits?
- Which insurers best fit the company's needs?
- Does the company face any unusual risks?
- Who are the key executives and who will be involved in the insurance process?
- How involved does the board of directors want to be in the insurance decisions?

In addition to its D&O insurance, a pre-IPO company will want to upgrade all of its other lines of insurance as well.

The next stage in the D&O insurance process ahead of the IPO is **launch**. This process typically takes place after a company files its first S-1 registration statement with the SEC. During this time, companies want to make sure their insurance broker is modeling policy limits based on their unique needs and negotiating with the insurance markets on the company's behalf.

**FIGURE 3** D&O Insurance Process for an IPO

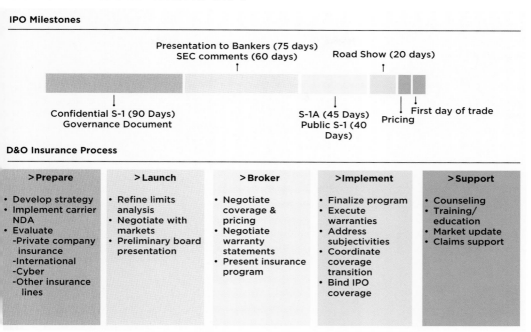

©Woodruff-Sawyer & Co. 2017 (used with permission)

Next comes the **brokering** phase. This is where all the negotiation happens around insurance coverage, pricing, and higher limits warranties. The proposed D&O insurance program will be presented to and discussed with the board of directors, who will no doubt want to ask your broker questions about the program. After all, like the officers of the company, directors face the possibility of personal liability should the company fail to perform post-IPO.

The final stage is **implementation**. This is where the program is finalized, the warranties are executed, and subjectivities (carrier-imposed conditions) are addressed. When the Securities and Exchange Commission declares a company's registration statement effective and a company prices its IPO, it's time to contact the company's

insurance broker to bind the D&O insurance program.

Finally, expect ongoing **support** from your insurance broker. Keeping directors and officers up to date with training and advisory services helps to mitigate risk all year long. Of course, should the need arise, companies will also want the benefit of robust claims handling and advocacy as well.

When done well, insurance can be extraordinarily useful to a growing company, serving to support and protect a company's growth over time. Sometimes insurance can seem both opaque and expensive. However, when you work with an experienced and technically skilled insurance broker, insurance can be straightforward, fairly predictable, and very helpful.

# PART II

# THE GROWTH STAGE: SCALING THE BUSINESS

**THE GROWTH STAGE: OPERATIONAL PROGRESS AND PITFALLS**

**THE GROWTH STAGE: FINANCING THE GROWING BUSINESS**

# 16

# PRODUCT DEVELOPMENT AND DISTRIBUTION (OPERATIONS)

Sphero

Paul Berberian, CEO

Product is where passion and an experience intersect. Either can come first, but both need to be there.

How you sell is different. The "how" can often make or break a product. How involves the distribution of your product or service as well as the customer service element and the supporting components of your product. Collectively I call this "operations."

In building a business you need to focus on two elements—building the right product and nailing the operations. Having a great product can make up for a lot of bad operations. But if your product isn't the absolute must-have item of the year, bad operations can really hurt your bottom line.

## MAKING PRODUCT

In the case of Sphero, we started with an experience: controlling objects in the real world from a phone. Cofounders Ian Bernstein and Adam Wilson entered startup accelerator Techstars armed with this idea and made a series of app-controlled items from lights to robots to garage door openers. Eventually it was time to focus on one thing, and a mentor asked them what they'd like to do. They debated a bit, thinking a door lock might be the easiest to monetize. Their mentor said OK, but is that what you are passionate about? "What do you actually *want* to make?" Their immediate answer was robots.

Three 'bots, a wearable, and one Droid from a galaxy far, far away later, and here we are.

What started as an app-enabled ball from Boulder has become a line of products sold in over 18,000 locations all over the globe!

### MAKING VERSION 1.0 (V1)

Making V1 is cake. Not really, it's actually hard, really hard. But V1 will also likely be the easiest product that you will ever make. Here's why.

V1 is all about passion. It is the reason the company was founded. The initial team is like-minded and just as passionate as the founder(s), and everything you do every day is about getting V1 out the door. If you have outside investors, that's all they care about—shipping V1. All early customers from a Kickstarter campaign want is the product you promised to build. The entire world is all about you shipping V1. No one cares about revenue, costs will naturally contain themselves as you can only spend what you have, and you will pace yourself to spend just the right amount of money to ship V1.

For V1, the product development process is chaotic but extremely focused. It is like water running downhill—it can gush a bit to the left or right, but it will always flow downhill. So if you're at this stage my advice is don't fight it. It works— it's not efficient or without frustration—but it generally gives you a great product. Embrace the chaos and be maniacal about driving the focus towards shipping product.

## AFTER V1

Once V1 is shipped you now have customers. You also have revenue and can develop sales targets if you haven't done so already.

V1 customers will be vocal but generally supportive. You will get a few trolls that will go out of their way to say how crappy your product is, but mostly you'll get some great feedback if you hit the market's expectations for your idea. Regardless, if the feedback is a bunch of angry people or criticism of the product's capabilities, you must develop a thick skin—no product receives perfect reviews 100 percent of the time. You should look at the instant feedback as a wonderful gift. Within days of launching your product you will know if your vision for V1 has met the expectations of your consumer. Most likely you fell short somewhere. That is OK and you need to allow yourself a pass— things will get better with V2.

As soon as V1 is shipped, start on V2. Knowing that this is what you are going to do at the onset will allow you to push a lot of "scope creep" into V2, which will help you get V1 out the door. But now that V1 is out, what should go into V2?

With V1 in customers' hands, gather all feedback and match that to the backlog of features that you wanted to put in but didn't have the time or money to complete. When looking at the list of what needs to be done, something will become very clear: there is either enough positive

momentum to continue moving forward with this product or the response is so poor you need to kill it.

At Sphero we made the mistake of building a V1.5 vs. going straight for V2. At the time we thought we were being smart to fix the few things we didn't get right as the product went out the door, such as packaging and some minor cost reductions. What we realized too late into the process (this may be more true for hardware products vs. software) is that V1.5 took just as much time and energy as V2 would have, which ended up being a greatly improved product at a much lower cost.

## KILLING A PRODUCT

If the feedback is overly negative or the sales well below your expectation, you may decide to kill the product altogether. So how do you know when the news is too bad? For me there are three indicators that say the product is done:

1. Your investors won't put in more money.

2. The sales are dramatically off expectations, like 10 percent of plan (not 10 percent off plan).

3. The team is so demotivated that no one wants to work on V2.

If you have all three, then it is time to move on to something else. Two out of three, you need to do some soul searching because clearly several things aren't working. If you only have one of the three, you should forge ahead if YOU believe in the product (remember, it was that passion that got you here in the first place).

## A THOUGHT ABOUT REVIEWS

If you have the type of product or service where you can get unsolicited feedback from customers (such as Amazon or app store reviews), value them for trends and insights but do not hang on every word. Just because you have a 4.8 star rating on Amazon does not mean your sales will rocket forward. High ratings just mean you made a good product—congrats!

A low rating, on the other hand, can definitely hurt your sales (below 3.5 stars). Negative reviews can come from many places and many of them may not be your fault. At Sphero we received poor reviews for all kinds of crazy reasons, like Amazon was out of stock, or a competitor's product didn't work with our app, or the product didn't work on a device that we clearly said we did not support. Somehow you have to make sure these low reviews do not overwhelm the good ones. The best way to combat that is to build a rating function into your app or encourage your registered users to rate you. That said, you need to use caution; paying for positive reviews, even by offering a discount on future products, is a dangerous game and dilutes the value of the feedback.

Buried in all the reviews will be "votes" for future product features and bugs to be fixed. Use them to define V2.

## MAKING V2 AND BEYOND

If you get to make V2, something is going right. Now things get really hard; you must deliver a product that grows to meet the expectations of your investors and your future customers—V1's success is the bar you must clear by a big margin with V2.

Your organization is stressed at this point because part of your team is spending time supporting your current customers, while the other part is working on the New Thing that will be so much better than what is out in the market. You may even have people complaining that you have to support the folks that gave you money vs. betting on some future new version. This is normal. The best you can do is try to divide and conquer. You cannot leave one side to starve; you must split the baby and take care of those customers using your current product while driving focus towards version 2.

You will realize that a chaotic, water running downhill approach to building product no longer works at this stage, and you will need to put some structure in place. Things like scope definition, schedules, sales forecasts, release dates, marketing support, and budgets all start to come into play. This is a good time to read a

book on product development; winging it from this point forward gets pretty risky (trust me, I know from experience).

One thing I wish we did at this stage was to really focus on developing product managers (PMs). In the beginning, the founder or CEO typically serves as the PM but once V1 is out the door this function needs to be delegated in order for the company to grow. If you develop a culture where the PMs rule the product and get to act like mini-CEOs for the product—that is, they own the profit and loss, the development costs, and the features—then you build a foundation for the next stage, which is making multiple products simultaneously.

Product managers are worth their weight in gold. They are hard to find, difficult to develop, and generally require a larger salary than you budgeted. Great PMs have a true passion for the product—they love it, they care about it, and most importantly they care about your customers. They talk to your customers, read every review, and understand the costs and opportunities of improving or making a product. The best ones run their product like they are the CEO—they are concerned about all aspects of the product, not just the features and software, but also the sales, marketing, and support. They are generally well liked but most importantly they are well respected and are viewed as being very fair. When you find a great one you will know it, and you will try to duplicate this PM over and over again.

## MAKING MORE THAN ONE PRODUCT

If your first product is a success, at some point you will need to make something else in order to grow your business. You may choose something that leverages the same customer base but maybe not, depending on your business model. You may have a product for men and then choose to make a product for women. Or you have a product for men and you choose to upsell them on something else.

Whatever your choice on what new product/ service to make, you should start to become more disciplined about using the numbers to decide your investment. Chances are you got V1 and V2 out the door before you started to think about product #2. The first product was the basis of founding the company, the promise, but the next product is delivering on that promise. Sphero 1.0 was the app-enabled ball that started it all, but now that we have a suite of products, they all focus on connecting the digital and physical worlds of play.

It is typically at this time where investors start looking at the economics of the business and how it scales. A key driver to building a scalable company is making sure the economics work for each product. This is where having a robust product management function in place will help you pick the right idea for product #2 as the numbers will point the way.

We use four criteria to choose what product to work on:

1. Does it align with our strategic vision?
2. Does it make economic sense?
3. Does it leverage our existing assets (tech or distribution)?
4. Does some group of people have a deep passion to bring this product to market?

While these criteria work for us, you need to find the right questions to ask when selecting product #2 and beyond.

## OPERATIONS

Making product is one thing but getting it into a customer's hands is another. Regardless what you make, be it a physical product or perform a service, you have think about the entire customer purchase lifecycle.

### DISTRIBUTION

Distribution is really the "where can customers get your product." If it is a physical product, it refers to where consumers can buy it, what stores or online sites. If it is a service, it may refer to what geographic area, language, or applications you support. The focus in this section will be physical products, but I'm sure there are some lessons for service companies as well.

Distribution can really make or break a product. Unless your product is so phenomenal that folks will seek it out no matter where it is sold, having a poor distribution model can really hurt your sales. While great distribution seldom creates demand for your product, it will certainly ease the friction of buying your product if the demand exists.

The best practice is to benchmark yourself against a top-notch competitor or top-performing company you wish to emulate. For example, at Sphero we are in 18,000 stores worldwide. To benchmark we looked at major toy and consumer electronics companies; they are in well over 30,000 stores—so we have a way to go but we are off to a good start.

Not all distribution points are equal. Make sure the places you sell target your consumer and reflect well on your brand. For us, we sell to a premium toy buyer. That means deep discount stores are not where we launch our newest products. We launch our newest products in premium stores like Apple, Brookstone, and Best Buy. We launch our licensed products in stores such as Toys R Us, Target, or Walmart.

If you are selling a new product or trying to redefine an old category, you may want to choose a select few distributors/retailers to launch your product, brands that share common values or have a common customer base that you would like to reach. For our first entry into retail distribution we chose two key partners to launch our first product (Apple and Brookstone) and then gradually expanded out from there.

The only exception to this thinking is Amazon—virtually everyone sells on Amazon. Amazon should be part of your physical launch plans for every product if you goal is to reach a broad customer base.

"No" is never no in retail and a "yes" is never forever. If you sell a physical product through retail channels, remember their motivation: retailers want to move products that are staples or new to the market, that turn over at a high rate, and have a good margin for the category.

No one cares that you have the hottest new gizmo if it doesn't sell off the shelf in the store. Buyers will look for products that they think will move, and if they get it wrong because they passed on your hot item, they will bring it in next year. If it doesn't move, they will move you out.

Retail is all about what is new, so before you go into retail channels make sure you can feed the product development beast with new updates on a consistent basis. How often you should update your product is a function of what category you are selling in. If you sell into floor cleaners, maybe once every five years works, but toys need new products every year.

A successful product sells at a rate faster than the other products on the shelf. For us, makers of a physical consumer electronic/premium toy, our goal is to sell on average one unit per store per week per year. Obviously our business is oriented towards the holidays so that is the metric we want to hit on an annualized basis with the bulk coming in Q4.

## CUSTOMER SERVICE

Customers are going to have questions and problems, and your response will determine how happy they are with the product.

Having excellent customer service isn't free. It requires people to answer questions and policies to make customers happy when things go wrong. You have to determine the level of customer service you want to provide. That being said, a little bit of love from customer care can go a long way.

Some companies barely have any support because the expectations are easily matched. For example, for a box of nails, it's unlikely many customers will have any issues, so it is safe to say customer support needs are low. Other products are sold largely based on the level of support, like a complex piece of machinery for a factory. Where does your product live on that spectrum and can you use it to your advantage?

For Sphero, selling high tech toys, we opted for a high level of customer support because we knew some folks may have issues with their software or hardware. It is unusual for toy or similarly priced consumer electronic companies to operate with such a high level of support, but we want to make sure we maintain high ratings and deliver a premium experience.

While customer service costs money, it can also make money if it elevates your sales or makes consumers more confident when they are making their purchase decision. At Sphero, we have employees who applied to work at our company because of the level of service they received as customers. I think selling premium product requires a premium level of service, but that is just my philosophy.

Ultimately customer service needs to reflect how the organization thinks about the customer and the value they are delivering. We promise to deliver joy and fun—we don't want any child to be unhappy playing with our products—so we invest in service to ensure we make good on that promise, and if we can't, we give them their money back.

# 17

# WINNING STRATEGIES FOR ACHIEVING GROWTH AND SCALE

**First Round Capital**

Chris Fralic, Partner

Having spent the last decade investing in seed stage companies at First Round Capital, I've seen the entire arc of company growth play out again and again. I've seen dozens of startups move into their growth phase and take on the unique and varied challenges of scaling. I've also seen many that never made it that far. While there are numerous paths to and through the growth and scaling phase, there are multiple strategies for survival that aren't shared widely enough. When asked to contribute a chapter to this book, I thought one of the most helpful things I could do would be to share some of these observations about strategies that I've seen have an impact.

## CUSTOMER HAPPINESS IS THE METRIC THAT MATTERS MOST

Early in your company's life, it's all about product-market fit. According to Marc Andreessen, that means "you're in a good market with a product that can satisfy that market." That's a solid definition, but I've also heard founders say, "I have a product-market fit problem on the market side." Of course, that's impossible. The market is always right whether you like it or not. In my experience, there's a simple metric that's more telling than this concept of "fit"—and that's "happy customers."

Yes, you'll have to worry about customer acquisition costs and lifetime values, but you want to do everything you can to understand and maximize customer happiness to start. It's a simple and powerful lens to view how people perceive your product and company. To get that information, you can start with three simple questions:

1. Would your customers be upset if your product or service went away?

2. Would they be willing to recommend you to other users?

3. How often are people engaging with what you've built?

Other related questions you can add over time: Ask customers if they'd be willing to pay for your product if they haven't already. And, would they be willing to talk to your investors? Having a good sense of these answers is an important sanity check for whether you're ready to scale with more resources, processes, and capital.

These questions will also help you hone a crisp, clear definition of what a happy customer is for your company. Perhaps you track your net promoter score (NPS) or

99

focus on just one metric to get a snapshot of how you're doing. Using too many metrics can give you false precision in drawing big conclusions. At First Round, we keep tabs on how many of our existing founders refer us to new ones. So far in our current fund, over 50% of new investments were referred to us by executives at companies already in the portfolio, which for us is an important measure of customer happiness.

Engagement is another good one. If your product requires a login, how often are customers signing on? If email is a core part of your strategy, what are the open and click rates? If you're selling an enterprise product, how fast does usage spread inside companies using it? Does it stop at one person? Are you getting repeat customers? Simple analytics tools or short, low-lift surveys can help gather this data.

If your customers are lukewarm or ambivalent, then get back to the customer development cycle to discover what they really want and need. Consider picking a representative handful of customers and ask them to be on an advisory council to help you with development. People love having their voice heard—and it gets them more invested in your success. Don't involve just your fans either. Have customers who are loudly or constantly complaining? Go see them in person. Make it clear you care enough and want to do better for them. That's how you can get a handle on your happiness metric and closer to your early customers.

## THERE'S NO SUCH THING AS SELF-SERVICE

This is a bit of an exaggeration, but not much for many "software as a service" companies. There's a dream that enterprise founders tend to share: their product will be so straightforward and easy to use that their customers will be able to just sit down, log in, and immediately know how to use it. This doesn't happen very often. Sure, they all want to offer a self-serve product because it's cheaper and simpler, and they can sell it at a lower, more appealing price—and maybe that will be possible in the long run—but to get started,

they need to be prepared to show customers how to use what they've built.

If this describes your company, you're going to have to hire some people. And they'll need to spend time with customers to get your product used the way it's intended. Customers will say they want a self-service product too, but what they actually want is to get a lot for their money.

At First Round, I worked with a company called Invite Media, which was one of the first demand side platforms for online advertising. Their customers wanted the platform to be self-serve over time, but Invite also offered it as a managed service—and charged them more to do it. It worked, the company's reputation in the industry grew, and Google acquired it in 2010.

When you're introducing a new concept or breaking into a new market, it's vital that your product works well. It's okay to have your people run the software for your customers if it gets you there. Let it shape your hiring and pricing. You're much more likely to have happy customers who get value from the product, and they're much less likely to get frustrated and cancel their contracts.

## GET SMART ABOUT INORGANIC GROWTH

One way to grow is organically on your own. Another is to grow via mergers and acquisitions. This is something most startups don't think about much in their earlier stages—and it's not surprising why. My friend Alan Patricof at Greycroft Partners says that private-to-private transactions are like "me trading my dogs for your cats," and the biggest discussions tend to be around relative valuations. I recommend approaching these opportunities from a different angle.

If you're thinking about any type of merger, the first thought experiment to run is: "Would you take it if it were free?" Too often, I've seen a whole bunch of discussion and argument about price and structure and who reports to whom before that simple question gets answered. If you can't answer it, then you should stop right there. But if the answer is yes, then you can start thinking about strategic fit, strengths, and benefits the combination could have.

One good example of a private-to-private acquisition was our company Pinch Media merging with Flurry. These companies complemented each other really well, leading to their ultimate acquisition by Yahoo!. One was really good at pure analytics, the other at monetization and advertising. Their existing investors actually found new capital to put into the combined, re-energized entity. This type of symbiosis is not something people think about as often as they should. More companies should consider this type of inorganic growth before they need to merge or sell out of necessity.

## DON'T WAIT TO THINK ABOUT STRATEGIC PARTNERSHIPS

I tell every company I work with to add a slide to their board deck called "STRATEGICS." On it, I want to see a list of the five companies most likely to acquire the business over time. And I want to hear what they've done to further those relationships since the last board meeting. The goal is to build strong ties—the kind that can only be truly built over the long term. Start with creating awareness, get to know the people involved, and aim for familiarity with the most important strategic players in your industry.

The last thing you want is to find yourself in a position where you desperately need to get to someone inside a company for an investment or partnership or to sell. One of our past founders was looking for a buyer for his social media company. He eventually ended up selling to one of the largest Internet companies in the Valley but had eight identical conversations going with other companies at the same time. That's what you want. You *don't* want to be scrambling to figure out who runs corporate development at a likely buyer when you're a month away from running out of cash.

Nurturing these relationships can have another positive byproduct—a commercial relationship. In fact, you should aim to focus conversations on the commercial side and let the strategic

side be a natural evolution. When you start early, commercial relationships can expand into strategic investments. A few years back, I helped introduce one of our companies, Percolate, a rapidly growing marketing startup, to one of the biggest consumer goods companies in the world, Unilever. When there is an enormous player like that involved, it's not unusual to see them try to throw their weight around to get the startup to do everything for nothing. They'll often ask for big discounts or product customizations without doing much in return. It doesn't have to go that way, and Unilever was a visionary partner that ultimately combined a commercial and strategic partnership with Percolate, its product got rolled out globally, and Unilever is still one of their largest customers. You do need to be aware that if a commercial relationship is structured incorrectly, it can send a negative signal to others in the market or have a dampening effect on future financings, but when it works you can have real strategic alignment.

What's in it for the big company, you ask? They have a lot to gain in terms of optics and energy. Partnering with a startup gets them closer to the innovation and the hottest new developments and talent in their industry. They can learn to move faster and get more done with less. And it reserves their first place in line if and when the newer company wants to sell.

## CREATE SCARCITY AND EXCLUSIVITY

Scarcity and exclusivity are your friends—and can be important tools, if not weapons, as a forcing function to get a deal done. Let's say you're looking to do a big deal with American Express. You know it'll take everything you have—all your product, sales, and customer support bandwidth—to serve that one customer. There's no way you could work with another partner even if you wanted to. Exclusivity can become an extremely handy tool. You can tell AmEx, "Hey, if you sign this deal by the end of the month at this level, we'll commit that you'll be our exclusive credit card partner for the next year." Companies love these opportunities to block their competitors. In a way, you're selling the sleeves off your vest, in that you couldn't do multiple deals if you wanted to—but the value and commitment is still there.

There are several variations on this theme: give clients the chance to be the first to do something—like eBay offering 20th Century Fox to be the first customer to do a homepage takeover and get some major press out of it. When Steve Jobs was launching Apple's iAds product, he made it clear there would only be a limited number of launch partners. To get access, they'd have to pay millions and sign immediately. Similarly, Facebook promoted its new video product by saying each spot would have the same audience and value of a Super Bowl ad. Creating scarcity and exclusivity arms you with desirable forcing function to get things done sooner than later.

## HOST A CONFERENCE (AND MAYBE START A MOVEMENT)

I've seen several companies do an incredible job creating events that bring together customers, press, and even competitors to accelerate their brand and leadership in their industry. Of course there are the big ones like Dreamforce, Oracle World, and Oculus Connect. But the ones I'm talking about are put on by growing startups, like Mashery's Business of APIs conference, Percolate's Transition Conference, and Performline's annual COMPLY event.

How can smaller companies throw events with this kind of impact? The key is that they don't just make it their own conference. Yes, they host it, but they're not afraid to bring in voices from across their industry. In doing so, they take things up a level. Their events don't seem like sales pitches. They tackle the broader issues and challenges that impact everyone in their ecosystem. Done right, this can fill a room with the most important people in your business, especially if you're the first one to bring this specific cross section of leaders together.

When Mashery launched its conference, APIs were not a major topic of conversation and

definitely not from a business perspective. The company gave sales leaders a platform to talk about how APIs could be used strategically in a way that wasn't purely technical for the first time. It became a signature experience to offer their customers and prospective partners. Think bigger and more broadly about the types of conversations people want to have about your business. If there isn't already a venue, that's your opportunity to reach out to the luminaries in your field. Asking people to keynote at your conference is very different from asking them to buy your software, and it's much more likely to get you into a conversation and relationship with them.

## GAMIFY YOUR BOARD OF DIRECTORS

Your board is one of your most powerful tools for achieving all of the above. Every board deck you make and every email update you send should include an "HTBCH" section—How the Board Can Help. Be specific. Ask directly for introductions to customers, help closing candidates, and referrals to investors. Be sure to thank the ones who do pitch in and say exactly how big of an impact they've made for you. That's where gamification comes in. All of your investors, advisors, and board members want to be the most helpful *and* get recognized for it. If one is going above and beyond for you, seeing that will galvanize the others.

It's not just about networking or contacts either. You also want to reward use of your product. It'll win you more support and valuable feedback. I work with growth startup Hotel Tonight, and one of the first pages in their board deck is always a leaderboard showing how many nights each member has booked using the app. Believe me, it's influenced my behavior and gets those competitive juices flowing.

## BUILD A ROBUST SALES CULTURE

Another powerful acronym is "HTDWW"—How the Deal Was Won. Several companies we've worked with at First Round send out regular emails chronicling and celebrating how they closed deals. The first time I saw this was at BazaarVoice, which ended up going public, largely on the strength of their sales culture. Not only does it reward high-performing employees, it is an invaluable knowledge share and a training tool that shows how deals can move from suspect to prospect to client. It also gives you a chance to recognize everyone who helped and showcase plans for expanding the business going forward.

I can't stress enough how important it is to celebrate these types of wins. Too often, deeply technical founders don't fully grasp the value of acknowledging sales triumphs. It's a remarkably effective way to balance your company so that salespeople feel invested and not expendable. It doesn't have to be a big display, just consistent. For example, one of the companies in our portfolio, Troops, has a tool that can celebrate every closed deal with a victorious GIF on Slack, and people love it. Other CEOs make sure to spend plenty of time with their sales people and going on sales calls. Their presence alone shows how valuable the team is to the company. Don't let sales be an afterthought when it's this easy to build a positive culture where people want to win for more than the money.

## THE TAKEAWAY

Entering the growth stage can be daunting. It's surprising how different and distinct it can feel from the early days—like everything has sped up as the decisions and challenges get more layered and complex. But that doesn't mean that the same scrappiness that made you successful in the first stage won't be useful. If anything, I hope you take away from this that it's the small actions, being thoughtful, starting early, and paying close attention to your relationships and messaging that can still go a long way, and maybe even get you to that next level up.

# 18

# CREATING YOUR DREAM TEAM

**Korn Ferry Hay Group**

Debra A. Nunes, Senior Client Partner

*Who's on your team?* For CEOs, it's one of the most important questions to consider. The strength of the team determines how well the organization can respond decisively and swiftly to opportunities as well as to challenges. It's the team's responsibility to help the CEO formulate and execute a coherent strategy to achieve the company's objectives. But not all teams are created equal. In our study of the effectiveness of leadership teams, we found that only 25 percent were outstanding, as determined by their ability to serve all their constituencies superbly, while growing in capabilities as a team over time. The remaining 75 percent rated only mediocre to poor.

While our research focused on well-established companies, the findings and lessons learned are highly applicable for startups and other new companies. For these organizations, creating a real team—beyond the core nucleus of the founder(s)—is key to future success. In this chapter, we will discuss the highlights that can help startup companies establish great teams and foster their success over time. We will draw from the lessons and examples of the outstanding teams—what do they have going for them; and examine the struggling ones—what got in their way.

Before launching into the structure and elements necessary for creating a top team, it's helpful to look at some of the common themes among organizational success stories. One is getting individual team members to move out of their silos and to function as an interdependent team. These teams are able to advance the leader's agenda quickly and switch gears when market changes require it. As one CEO noted, his team traditionally had worked very independently. However, the leader recognized that if they had continued in that vein, the company could not have accomplished a turnaround that led to significantly increased revenues, which was due in part to capitalizing on more opportunities once products and services were combined. In effect this transformed the company from a product and services company to a solutions company whose offerings commanded a premium price.

For all companies—large and small, startup and mature—collaboration within the top team is a necessity, not a luxury. "The world is too complex today," said one executive. "Executive teams, especially in global companies, can't afford to allow a silo mentality. To think a company can achieve its objectives with individual team members acting in isolation is naïve."

Even within startups, in which teams are lean, people can become territorial. Therefore, it's imperative for teams to strike the right balance to achieve interdependence as they work together toward a common purpose. There are individual leadership roles, but accountability is shared in the work they do together as a team. Interdependence can be compromised when teams get too big. While that may not be a problem for startups at first, it is a lesson to learn early and remember as the company grows.

Creating effective teams is neither instant nor easy. It takes time and hard work, and most important, the leader's full commitment. For startups that are investing so much time and energy in the priorities of early-stage development—meeting and courting investors, product development/improvement, acquiring customers, expanding into new markets, and so forth—putting adequate focus on a creating a dream team can be a challenge. But even amidst these challenges, startups can create and sustain highly effective executive teams.

Our research shows there are five conditions that promote top-team success: Direction, Structure, People, Support, and Development. By addressing each component that distinguishes top teams, startups will be on their way to ensuring they have the leadership team talent necessary to support their current and future success.

## DIRECTION—CLEAR AND COMPELLING

A competent leader typically is able to communicate a clear, compelling mission and get employees to buy into the company's goals. But when it comes to leading their *executive teams*, many of these same leaders assume there is no need to provide direction. In fact, one leader was taken aback when asked if all his team members could identify the team's purpose. "Of course they can," the leader said. "These are smart people. I don't want to insult their intelligence." That attitude, unfortunately, is widespread.

The challenge for leaders is identifying the unique added value that his or her leadership

team brings in advancing the company's strategy. Among outstanding teams, the leader has answered this question. Clarity is paramount. Where clarity does not exist, a leadership vacuum is created. Then, one of two things happens: members rush to fill the vacuum by advocating priorities and goals that benefit their agenda, or members see the team (and leader) as ineffective and set out on their own path. When there is no unifying team purpose, irresolvable conflicts can erupt. Ultimately, the top team can self-destruct, often with considerable collateral damage, including personality clashes and deep cynicism about the value of teams.

As leaders discover, even high-level people who are leaders themselves really want leadership to guide them. They need a framework of ground rules in which to operate and clarity that promotes common purpose.

## STRUCTURE—APPROPRIATE AND SUPPORTIVE

With direction firmly established, the CEO who hopes to create a successful team must also put in place an appropriate structure for the team. To do so, the CEO must set team size and boundaries, establish its procedures, and spell out the norms of conduct for the team to follow.

A successful decision-making team is normally composed of no more than six to nine members. More members than that often means more competing interests, more personality clashes, and greater risk that competing factions will form. While this problem is likely more common among well-established companies, it's worth addressing in startups (if for nothing else than as a cautionary tale for the future). Teams can grow too large when the CEO and other top executives include too many people on the leadership team. They are fearful of leaving star individual players off the team or offending others who are valued players within the organization. For example, some leaders believe all their direct reports need to be on the leadership team—an assumption that does not serve them well. The est leaders understand that they need to have comprehensive view of the enterprise, and this an be achieved without having a representative rom each component of the organization on heir team.

he appropriate question is which individuals ring the expertise to contribute to the team's urpose? Anyone who lacks the expertise or the bility to work should not be on the team.

s part of structure, CEOs also must periodically eview procedures followed by their executive eams and continually ask whether the rocedures impede or advance the team's fforts. For example, one executive team began s meetings with tactical items and ended ith strategic ones. It was no surprise that heetings often got bogged down on the early ems, while making decisions that advance the trategy—the team's real purpose—almost always ot short shrift. When the leader recognized he unintended consequence of following his particular procedure, it was changed nmediately.

n addition, leaders must address norms—the round rules for determining what is acceptable ehavior by team members both inside and utside of meetings. Too often, establishing orms is overlooked. Typically, norms speak o expected meeting behavior, i.e., not doing mails during the meeting. However, norms in utstanding teams also address how members re expected to carry out their role as one of the ompany's most senior leaders. For example, uch teams often make it explicit that it is not cceptable for a team member to publicly riticize another member.

ne word of advice: CEOs should never assume hat just because the team is composed of right, successful individuals, there is no need o establish clear norms. Research suggests the pposite is actually true: Because top teams are omposed of strong personalities, clear norms re even more important—and only the leader an establish the norms and must enforce them ffectively in order for team members to hold ach other accountable.

# PEOPLE—SELECTING THE RIGHT TALENT FOR THE TEAM

When it comes to top teams, this finding might surprise you: People on outstanding teams are often not brighter, more driven, or more committed than those on less-accomplished teams. Rather, people on the best teams are distinguished by their ability to work well with others. In other words, they bring their emotional intelligence to the table.

Emotionally intelligent people are capable of self-control, are adaptable, and exude self-confidence and self-awareness. Among outstanding executive teams, two attributes in particular distinguish the members—empathy and integrity.

Empathy is the ability to understand others' concerns and goals. Empathy is important because team members will only buy into the team process if they feel they are both heard and understood. Furthermore, it is critical that CEOs select emotionally intelligent team members capable of empathy—people who are capable of mutual respect who can listen to others' views in order to understand what is underlying a person's resistance or advocacy regarding an issue. Equally important, team leaders must be willing to remove anyone not willing to demonstrate this important attribute.

Integrity is generally associated with honesty and strict adherence to an ethical code. For top teams, integrity also means behaving consistently with the organization's (and the team's) values—even when there might be personal sacrifice involved. Consider the example of the executive team debating whether to shut down a factory that was not productive. Many team members took a hard line and advocated closing the factory immediately. But one team member had the courage to speak up and ask how closing the factory in this way was consistent with the company's core value of respecting people. On some executive teams, such candor could be professional suicide. But the leader of this team had created conditions of trust; therefore, the team member felt she could safely present an opposing point of view. High-performing teams also understand conflict is good as long as it involves ideas, not personalities.

Getting the right people on the team and the wrong ones off means making sure the team is composed of people who can take an enterprise perspective—that is, their view is not limited to seeing only their own function. Rather, they take a company-wide perspective. This is particularly important with a startup, in which "all hands on deck" means ensuring that everything the company does—from financing to branding, production to market—advances the company's goals. Having the right people also means choosing those who are willing and able to put things on the table that affect the whole business, rather than making those decisions on their own. They are able to hear others' concerns and have the integrity to stand by the decisions the team makes.

One note about derailers: they must be taken off the team. A derailer is a person who brings out the worst in others. That said, the derailer label should never be applied lightly. There may be organizational issues at fault: unclear purpose, trivial tasks, no norms, and unclear boundaries that lead to bad behavior. Fix those first. In addition, top teams are often composed of strong personalities. Discussions should be robust, passionate, and even heated at times, especially around important issues affecting the enterprise. But the debates should not get personal; that's out of bounds.

## SUPPORT—CRUCIAL FOR THE TOP TEAM

CEOs who want outstanding teams must ensure they are supported—for example, provided with sound information and forecasts. Often, leadership teams are plagued by inadequate information systems. As a result, leadership has too much data but not enough usable information for making decisions.

In addition, CEOs must see to it that team members get training and that their efforts are adequately rewarded. Within startups, compensation may take many forms; for example, equity to encourage buy-in and nonfinancial perks to encourage loyalty. Whatever form it takes, compensation can be a powerful tool for accomplishing the top team's goals. Within a more established company, that tool can be variable compensation of bonuses and long-term incentives for helping the company as a whole attain its corporate goals.

One last word on compensation: Rewards will not bring a team together and get them to collaborate, but they can break them apart if the compensation scheme rewards individual efforts over those of the team.

## DEVELOPMENT—LEARNING AND LEADING

CEOs who are outstanding team leaders periodically review team performance. They hold meetings to discuss how the team is doing, what it is doing best, what it is doing poorly, and what the team and its members have learned. Consider the example of a leadership team that went through a very rocky acquisition together. When it came time to undertake another, the CEO gathered the team together to discuss candidly what had gone well in the past and should be applied this time, in addition to seeing what went wrong the first time around and should be avoided. As a result, the second acquisition went smoothly, and the team felt a strong sense of accomplishment. While a startup probably isn't in the position to make an acquisition, nonetheless, the lesson still applies. Candid discussions about any undertaking—what when well, what did not—lead to team learning and improved results over time.

It's not surprising, perhaps, but leaders often spend little time coaching individuals or teams. For startups, in particular, most of the effort is spent on growing the company. The irony is that when leaders spend more time coaching their teams, the result is more positive relationships—and greater team effectiveness.

# TOP TEAMS CAN WORK

When organizations, large and small, put in the effort to create and foster top teams, there can be significant payoffs, from faster execution of the business agenda to improved responsiveness as the market changes. Higher perceived valuations from investors may also result, which is good news for startups seeking additional capital.

Creating and sustaining effective top teams is hard work. Top teams are organic units. Effective leaders will take care to nourish and renew their teams, as they would any valued living organism. For startups that often have ambitious growth goals, there is always another mountain to climb. As successes are achieved, the team celebrates and becomes motivated to tackle the next challenges. Yes, leaders should take pride when their efforts result in members' willingness to put divergent point of views on the table in service of finding a new and viable way forward. But external conditions, as well as the complexities of interpersonal relationships on top teams, can conspire to erode the team's effectiveness unless the CEO continues to give his or her team the attention it deserves.

For senior executives who have never run a top team (which may be common among startups) or for those whose past experience has made them cynical about teamwork at the executive level, the five conditions outlined in this chapter offer a roadmap for creating successful top teams. It takes Direction, Structure, People, Support, and Development. The reward is a team that encourages and challenges members to be more and achieve more than any individual could do on his/her own.

A CEO of a well-established company shared his view, which is aspirational advice for the road ahead for startups. "On top teams you have very talented individuals who demand a lot of themselves but who also have the team demanding more and more of them," the CEO said. "People feel tremendous pressure from the group. So you get results that you wouldn't get from individuals only acting for themselves. That's the real richness of teams."

# 19

# RETAINING KEY TALENT FOR THE NEXT STAGE OF GROWTH

**Korn Ferry Hay Group**

Mark Royal, Senior Principal

As your startup has grown, so has your team, with the right people in place to help scale the business and expand its competitive edge. At some point, though, turnover is bound to happen. Some may be due to people moving on because of life events or to pursue other opportunities, or the firm may require a somewhat different skill set as it matures. What companies need to avoid, however, is the unexpected loss of key talent—those employees who are the strongest performers, have high potential, and/or are in critical jobs.

Retaining key talent is a major concern for both large mature companies and for newer firms and startups. Across the board, the war for talent in critical areas, such as digital technology, is becoming fierce. Looking ahead, the outlook for the labor market will keep talent retention on the workforce radar. The widespread prediction is that talent shortages will likely increase well into the next decade, which could limit the ability of some companies to expand. Where talent shortages become acute, companies' very survival could be jeopardized in the face of intensifying global competition. According to the Bureau of Labor Statistics, longer-term labor shortages may result from slower population growth, increasing specialization and technical demands of jobs, Baby Boomers retiring, a lack of experience among Millennials to advance into more responsible and demanding jobs, and increasing global competition for talent.

Individuals with scarce and mission-critical skill sets and expertise increasingly will be in demand as organizations compete for talent just as they do for market share. Key talent disproportionately contributes to organizations' current performance, and these individuals are also likely to assume future leadership positions. Thus, losing them has a major impact. Consider the estimates that suggest the cost of employee turnover ranges from 50 percent to 200 percent of the employee's annual salary, depending on the type and level of job. When highly valued key employees are lost, costs escalate considerably since their contributions are greater than those of typical employees, and they are more difficult to replace.

Not only is competition for key talent increasing, but opinion surveys indicate about 20 percent of employees plan to look for a new job in the next two years and another 20 percent plan to leave their employers within the next five years. Some movement might be the result of discontent in the wake of years of downsizing, doing more with less, and limited base salary increases and incentive payouts. But the trend may also reflect changes in the social contract surrounding the employment relationship. As individuals and organizations become more tenuously attached to each other, turnover has become a more prominent and accepted aspect of organizational life.

Advances in technology also make it more difficult to retain talent. In today's world, a company cannot hide its top talent. Social media outlets such as LinkedIn allow people to promote their capabilities and accomplishments. Plus, top talent can compare the compensation they receive with that of other companies through multiple online resources.

Given all these factors, it's no surprise that one of the foremost management challenges is retaining key talent. Startups and other new firms are not immune to this problem. While the core team may be highly motivated by the challenges inherent in a startup, these motivations may not be enough to keep key talent going forward. As the company advances from the launch phase through stages of growth, it must pay attention to its culture. Whether because of current talent pressures or with an eye toward the future, leaders in startups and other new organizations must ask themselves: how can we keep our key talent?

## FOCUSING ON TOP TALENT

In our work with clients, we frequently investigate gaps in workplace perception between employees most committed to remaining with their current employers and those considering exiting in the near future. The lessons learned from larger, more mature firms hold key insights for startups and emerging organizations as well. Here are five retention factors that can make all the difference between whether key talent stays or leaves.

- *Playing for a winner*: Employees are unlikely to bind their futures to organizations unless they view them as well led and headed in a

positive direction. As employee surveys have shown, a far greater percentage of those who stay report having trust and confidence in senior management versus those who leave. Considerably more "stayers" also report having faith that their company's direction and goals are the right ones at the present time.

- *Somewhere to go if I stay*: Employees today are increasingly aware that they are responsible for managing their own careers. As opportunities for career development are among the most consistent predictors of employee engagement, it should not be surprising that "stayers" are much more optimistic about their ability to achieve their career objectives with their current employers. Likewise, the majority of "stayers" report that their supervisors provide ongoing coaching for development, compared to a minority of "leavers."

- *A fair exchange:* If organizations want employees to do and deliver more, it's essential that talented people know they're valued—that their extra efforts are recognized and appreciated, and that there's a reasonable balance between rewards (tangible and intangible) and contributions. Not surprisingly, the "stayers" give much higher ratings to the care and concern for employees displayed by their companies compared to the "leavers." The "stayers" also report greater levels of satisfaction with the fairness of their pay in relation to the work they do.

- *Support for success:* Because many employees have been asked to do more with less, they need to feel that they are working smart as well as hard. Of particular concern are efficient work processes and collaborative support from coworkers to allow employees to perform at their best. "Stayers" give their companies higher marks for being effectively managed and well run and are considerably more favorable regarding cross-work unit working relationships.

- *A sense of control and influence:* Critical to optimizing work processes, especially in dynamic environments where goals and objectives change frequently, is leveraging the ideas and input of employees at all levels. Far more "stayers" indicate that they have the authority necessary to do their jobs well as compared to "leavers." The "stayers" are also more positive about the support their companies provide for employee creativity and innovation.

Taken together, these findings provide organizations with a roadmap for reducing turnover. Leaders who are successful in keeping their best people recognize the need to foster a positive view of the company's prospects in the future as well as opportunities for individual growth and development. These leaders also focus on structuring work environments to support employees' success in their roles. They leverage employee input to promote high levels of effectiveness and reinforce the balance between what employees contribute and what they get back from the organization in return.

## SUPPORTING EMPLOYEES TO GET THE JOB DONE

It's a well-known fact of life in the workplace: organizations around the world are asking employees to do more with less. While this dynamic has been seen in large companies, particularly in the wake of the 2008-2009 global financial crisis, it is also very common in startups in which people wear "multiple hats." In larger, more mature organizations as well as newer and nimbler ones, perception matters—especially about compensation and rewards. It's all about equity. If work demands force employees to routinely miss social or family events, they will ask themselves whether what they're getting matches what they're giving up and putting in.

While work/life balance issues may seem particularly tricky in the early stages of a startup, with its notoriously long hours and intense demands, they also raise questions about the kind of culture that's being created. To create sustainable work patterns for employees, companies need to look beyond traditional solutions (like telecommuting and flexible

schedules) and help employees with work productivity. Since the work isn't going away, the real recipe for success is allowing people to be as efficient as possible while at work.

To succeed in doing more with less, many leaders are heavily focused on employee engagement. While motivation is important, it is only one piece of the puzzle. Equally essential is enabling employees to get things done. In other words, to foster long-term success in high workload environments, organizations have to create the "want to" but also add the "can do."

## EMPLOYEE ENGAGEMENT DRIVES PERFORMANCE

Employee engagement is a powerful tool for driving performance. Employees who are highly engaged, well prepared, and equipped for the work they have to do are better able to deliver more. From the leanest startup to the biggest global companies, organizations that earn reputations for high employee engagement become magnets that attract—and retain—valuable talent.

It's important to understand that employee engagement is not about making people happier, per se. Rather, engagement seeks to help employees improve performance and increase their productivity by creating conditions that foster commitment to the organization as well as a willingness to go the "extra mile" to do what needs to be done. That said, engagement leads to the greatest impact on business outcomes when work environments also enable and empower employees. Otherwise, even when people are engaged by the goals of the organization and enthusiastic about making a difference—two attributes that distinguish the best startups—if the work environment impedes them (barriers and obstacles to getting things done) or they feel held back in their jobs, motivation and performance will suffer.

Korn Ferry Hay Group's partnership with *Fortune* magazine to identify the World's Most Admired Companies highlights the factors that contribute to making these organizations successful. Recent

113

findings showed 94% of executives in the World's Most Admired Companies say their efforts to engage employees are a significant source of competitive advantage. What's more, these efforts have reduced employee turnover and strengthened customer service.

Equally important—and a lesson best learned early, as startups and other new organizations scale and mature—engaged employees can help their organizations navigate more successfully through change. Engaged employees are better able to cope with new and unanticipated situations, especially when the leaders are not there to guide them to the answers. In these scenarios, leaders are counting on agile and engaged employees to determine the right courses of action and make the best decisions.

So how can organizations help employees become more engaged and deliver more? One way is with compensation that is fair and that recognizes the employee's contribution. But rewards are not monetary alone. Increasingly, employees are seeking development opportunities that will prepare them for future challenges and further their careers. Communicating the career possibilities available to employees in the organization is critical, along with providing ongoing coaching support.

The best and most effective leaders also do a good job of providing clear directions on organizational priorities. Aligning the organization around a sense of shared purpose creates a common goal bigger than functional silos, quarterly results, or geographic differences. And as people increasingly are choosing firms that provide meaningful work, companies that lead with a shared sense of purpose attract top talent.

If employees' to-do lists are longer than the workday can accommodate, leading organizations give guidance on where and how to prioritize. These companies also rate well for creating higher levels of teamwork and managing collective relationships. Today's leaders need to act more as facilitators than as managers. Connecting people enables them to solve complex problems together.

As companies grow and mature, employee engagement becomes a lens through which to look at everything an organization does, from developing leaders to community involvement (corporate social responsibility). The holistic nature of engagement means organizations cannot rely on annual employee engagement surveys alone to ascertain effectiveness and gather feedback. Evidence of employee engagement can be found everywhere, from social media comments to pulse surveys and polls. By listening to and observing employees, leaders will be able to ascertain the level of engagement among their employees—especially the key people who must be aligned with the organization's objectives, priorities, and goals in order to achieve mutual success.

## TALENT RETENTION GAME PLAN

For employers of all types and sizes there is concern about retaining key employees. (In a recent survey of rewards professionals, more than 50 percent indicated concerns that key talent retention will be challenging in the future.) However, there is considerable variation in how organizations define key talent—and how far down into the organization they actively manage this group. Those that identify, define, and manage key talent the deepest into the organization express the greatest confidence in being able to retain these individuals.

Lessons learned from more mature organizations can be helpful for startups and other new companies in their growth phases and as they mature. (After all, while it's important to learn from your own mistakes, real wisdom comes from learning from the experiences of others.) Here are some tips for making sure the key talent that has come together to launch the company stays together to propel it forward:

- Develop clarity around what defines "key employees" or "top talent." If this definition includes "high potential," it begs the question: high potential for what? Specific criteria to distinguish "top talent" from other employees must be carefully developed and applied consistently throughout the organization.

- Determine how key talent will be managed and developed. What extra resources should be invested in top talent? Should the organization communicate to these people that they are "top talent"? What about the employees who are not on that list? How and under what circumstances are employees added to the "top talent" pool?

- Establish a rewards system that is perceived as relevant, differentiated, and fair to lessen the chances that competitors can lure valuable employees away. Careful monitoring of the external labor market for key talent is advisable. Employees must understand why they are paid what they're being paid. Reward systems that differentiate key talent from other employees are more likely to be perceived as equitable.

- Put talent development and succession planning processes in place for each employee.

Key employees should be kept apprised of their development and advancement opportunities. Although it may be tempting to keep a key employee in his or her current position, that may create retention problems if advancement is perceived as slow.

- Monitor voluntary turnover among key employees to find out why they are leaving. This information will help guide strategies and policies, including when it is advisable to make counteroffers.

If companies truly believe that "people are their greatest assets," as is so frequently said, then retention must be a priority. Managing turnover will be increasingly important as key talent is becoming even scarcer. In a competitive global economy, organizations large and small will need to develop strategies for attracting, developing, and retaining the employees who will be key to their success.

# 20

# RE-ARCHITECTING GROWTH-STAGE COMPANIES ON THE ROAD TO IPO

**Sapphire Ventures**

Jai Das, Managing Director

People think that once a startup is successful early on, growth follows in a straight line. Once you have money raised in the bank and market validation, it's just a matter of not screwing up. In reality, companies flatten out at every stage on the growth curve, from $25 million in annual revenue to $50 million, to $100 million. On the path to IPO, nearly all companies experience turbulence and are forced to give up ground. In our experience, the companies that survive are the ones that can take a step back and constantly re-architect every aspect of the business.

## HOW TO SCALE YOUR BUSINESS AND YOURSELF

In the early stages of your company, you've successfully built something out of nothing, and you likely feel invincible. But without the ability to shift gears, you might be setting yourself up for a hard landing. CEOs who know only how to push harder and faster won't scale. In the growth stage, you need to know when to step on the brakes and fix the parts of your business that are breaking.

We believe there are two key characteristics to scaling well:

- *Self-awareness*: Entrepreneurs who scale well constantly evaluate their businesses and themselves in a realistic way. They're always trying to figure out what they do well and what they could do better.

- *Advice-seeking*: Entrepreneurs in the growth stage need to get out of their own heads by getting counsel from leaders of other companies as well as trusted advisors within their own. Being receptive to a variety of inputs allows them to synthesize a broad spectrum of advice into what works for their business.

Scaling the business means not being satisfied with the strategy that led you to success. That's the kind of complacency that leads to stagnation and decline. To thrive you need to continually reinvent every stage of the business, and that means starting with yourself, the CEO. You have to re-architect the way you organize your people, the way you configure your tech stack, and the kind of product you're building.

## REINVENT THE COMPANY CULTURE

As Zynga CEO Mark Pinkus says, when you're still small "you can manage 50 people through the strength of your personality and lack of sleep. You can touch them all in a week and make sure they're all pointed in the right direction." As you scale, this shifts dramatically. You can't be the single architect of your company's culture and values any longer.

Bringing in veterans to fulfill senior roles is one way to help with this. Having seasoned leaders at the helm helps you reinforce your culture from the top down and cut down on organizational overhead.

At the same time, this doesn't mean anything if your regular employees don't feel a sense of ownership of the company. As your company continues to grow, we believe that building autonomy throughout the ranks is the most efficient way to maintain focus.

- *Bring on senior execs:* For founders who haven't grown a big company before, hiring a senior Chief Operating Officer (COO) and VPs is a proven way of filling the experience gap.

- *Promote athletes to build from the bottom up:* Focus on empowering athletes within your workforce. These are the well-rounded team players who might not be the best within their individual fields but can work across many fields. Athletes have the potential to be CEOs and help you build a tightly knit team.

- *Part with employees who don't scale:* Some people excel during the early stages but falter later on. Growing means that you have to part ways with people who have been with you since day one, even if they've helped you get to where you are.

It's not always productive to force a senior engineer with no interest in management to take charge of a team just because that's the traditional path to promotion. Scaling your culture and your organization is about how you build flexibility into management.

## CASE STUDY: BOX

Founded by Aaron Levie in 2004, Box followed a proven formula for scaling: recruiting a senior COO. His pick was an experienced operator named Dan Levin, who was already a Box board member and had spent years before that working as a VP and General Manager at Intuit.

Bringing on an experienced COO helped compensate for Levie's inexperience at management while also allowing him to focus on building out a vision for the product. Levin had already seen a company scale to making hundreds of millions in revenue, and at Box he took over a lot of the day-to-day operations and responsibility through the organizational chart. Nearly everyone reported to the COO, which allowed the CEO to focus on building out his vision for Box's product.

But even after implementing a more efficient management structure, what allowed Box to excel was its continued focus on people and culture. As CEO, Levie still made time to interview almost every new hire who came to Box. This helped him make sure that everyone fit the culture. It also sent a crystal clear message to all prospective hires, emphasizing the importance of culture all the way to the very top.

## RE-ENGINEER THE TECH STACK

When you're a startup, using the latest technology is what allows you to move fast. Once you've been around for five years and are earning $25 million in revenue, getting bogged down by technology is how you slow down. Young companies can build their architecture completely on top of the cloud. They can use the latest offerings from Amazon Web Services or Google Cloud Platform with minimal infrastructure and maintenance overhead.

As your company matures, you have to deal with technical debt, buggy code, and a mix of cloud and on-premise servers. Maybe you still sell software on a licensing model, and you need to figure out how to deliver it over the cloud to stay relevant. Until you re-engineer your stack, you're just putting Band-Aids on a much larger roblem. You have to choose whether to try to eep grinding on a creaky stack or take the time o fix it.

*Technical debt:* Products break under scale as they accumulate bugs and unwieldy code. Small bugs that don't matter that much in the beginning compound into huge problems down the line.

*Aging tech:* If you don't reengineer your technical stack every five to six years, you cripple your ability to offer the best product and user experience to your customers.

ou'll never find the perfect time to rebuild your rchitecture. Rebuilding means simultaneously guring out to deliver your software as a service. ou'll need to cut from sales and marketing pend as you divert resources to engineering.

hoosing to rebuild your stack means that you ill miss sales goals and revenue targets—which ou're under pressure from your board to meet o secure your next round of funding. It's a hoice that might not be popular with your team, our board, or your stakeholders, but one you ave to make sooner rather than later.

## CASE STUDY: COMPANY A

ompany A is an example of an organization hat had to decide whether to re-architect their tack. They knew that their tech stack needed ome serious maintenance under the hood but hought it could wait another year. They focused n hiring more salespeople to ramp up growth efore revamping their infrastructure.

n our observation this just exacerbated the roblem. The new salespeople had a hard time elling the product because it didn't have a eature set that was competitive in the market. Vhat had been cutting-edge five years earlier no onger cut it.

## REFRESH THE PRODUCT

ven in enterprise software, products win by eing easier to use. Maintaining discipline around uilding a product that people want to use is nother big challenge of scale.

When you start off, you have a rough roadmap for where your product is going. You leave room in the design to add new features and functionality. But after a certain point, you find that there isn't space in your navigation panel to add anything else. Your original roadmap no longer fits, and you have to refresh your product to stay competitive.

- *User interface and ease of use*: Design grows stale rapidly and if you don't refresh your product, it will look dated very quickly.

- *Feature creep*: As your product grows over time, you add on a lot of extra features. This eventually bloats your product and makes it unusable. Growing your product means knowing what to cut.

Everyone pays lip service to building a customer-facing product. But it's hard to stay focused on this as you grow. Your engineering team is larger, which means there is more communication overhead and lengthier development cycles. Your product is also bigger, because it has evolved to serve a bigger customer base.

To keep focused on product, you have to think through the user experience and the entire workflow of what your customers are trying to achieve. These are all things that constantly change over time.

## CASE STUDY: NUTANIX

Dheeraj Pandey, CEO and founder of Nutanix, likes to say that "the most transformative technologies are the ones we don't think about. They work all the time, scale on demand and self-heal. In other words, they are invisible."

As Nutanix has scaled, it's tackled increasingly difficult technical problems around the datacenter, hyperconverged infrastructure, and the hybrid cloud. The beauty of Nutanix's products is that they have evolved over time to make this complexity disappear for the customer.

For Nutanix, this meant launching "one-click" technology that allows for instant software upgrades, analytics, planning, and efficient maintenance. Where overworked system admins were once responsible for provisioning and maintaining hundreds of servers, with Nutanix's products, they can do it on their phones. Nutanix's focus on product revolves around delivering enterprise-grade scalable infrastructure—and making it easy to access and manage from anywhere.

## MANAGE YOUR BOARD, DON'T LET YOUR BOARD MANAGE YOU

All of these problems around scale are challenging because they force you to face the realities of your business and share bad news when it comes. To surmount them, you can't just present a united front internally. You need to get your board on board.

Many first-time CEOs are caught off guard by the necessity of managing the board of a large company. They're used to calling the shots and executing them. But when you're in your Series C and making $100 million in revenue, you're no longer the primary stakeholder in the outfit. Your board is. Asking your board to spend $2 million dollars to rebuild your data warehousing isn't something that can be done on the fly. You have to figure out who on the board is in your corner and who you need to win over.

In order to get support behind hard decisions, you have to actively manage your board.

- *Be careful who you take money from:* Bringing on a board member is a marriage without the option of divorce. If your interests aren't aligned, it can fracture your company as you scale. You don't always have a choice about who you take money from, but you should always enter the relationship with your eyes wide open.

- *Build alliances within the board:* Know to whom on the board you can go for sales issues and

to whom you can turn when you need advice on building your cloud infrastructure and your marketing funnel. These board members not only provide you with valuable operational advice but also can help you build consensus among the larger board.

Different stakeholders will have different motivations—as well as different areas where they can guide and help you. Familiarizing yourself with your board and its dynamics is a condition of survival.

When you build up trust with your board and work in sync, it's much easier to steer the decision-making process that will shape the future of your company.

## SLOW DOWN TO SCALE FAST

As you scale, the amount of inputs you receive skyrockets. Your inputs aren't just from your employees. They're from your customers, your partners, your suppliers, and the board. You have to constantly synthesize vast quantities of information that pull your attention across hiring, marketing, sales and product.

The best thing to do in this situation is something that a lot of entrepreneurs are really bad at: slowing down and taking a breather. You might just need time to validate that you are in fact doing the right thing at the right time. You might have to dismantle the company to build it back up

Ultimately slowing down and making sure you have the right processes and people in place are what allow big organizations to move fast. As one McKinsey consultant said it best, scaling well is about "moving a thousand people forward a foot at a time, rather than moving one person forward a thousand feet."

# 21

# PUBLIC RELATIONS AND THE AGE OF CONTEXT

**104 West Partners**

Patrick Ward, CEO

Public relations has long been heralded as a cost-effective marketing tool to gain customer mindshare and industry awareness, even if some people's murky understanding of PR was just a "trophy" article from the *New York Times* or *Fortune Magazine*—the kind of piece that executives were convinced resulted in an apparent rise in sales and growth. A connection between press and sales may have been true in an era when media outlets were as authoritative as their circulation reach was impressive. A story from the venerable *Wall Street Journal* columnist Walter S. Mossberg could make or break a product. But once the Internet started disrupting traditional media models about 15 years ago and then social media upped the ante five years later, the connection between PR successes and business achievements grew more opaque.

In this chapter, we will examine how PR programs are successful today and, using the technology industry as a proxy for other contemporary industries, we will examine how PR has evolved and why. We will offer some insight into how developments in the news media and media technologies have shaped PR practices, how those practices are productive and in some cases unproductive, and how those practices may offer some productive approaches to PR in most growing businesses.

Thomas R. Friedman, the *New York Times* columnist and author, suggests in his newest book, *Thanks for Being Late*, that the volume of developments in the technology field in 2007 dwarfed any other period in recent history. The advent of powerful mobile phones, information platforms like Twitter and Facebook, and infrastructural developments in creating, storing, and delivering data forever changed how we author, distribute, and share information. No other industry has felt the seismic disruption those developments created more than the news industry and therefore, by extension, public relations.

## THE INFLUENCER'S GUIDE TO BRAND AWARENESS

But, before examining that shift, it's probably worth investigating why PR had become so critical to so many young companies. Public relations had always served the tech industry well, simply because it was hard to explain complex concepts in ads, so PR was a natural alternative marketing medium.

Out of the ashes of the dot com boom and bust, one of the consistent technology categories that had moved almost effortlessly from corporate to consumer users was computer security. From the first notable virus, dubbed *Melissa*, companies like Network Associates (now McAfee) and others had seized on the opportunity to protect consumers from the growing scourge that could paralyze personal computers. By 2002, Symantec's Norton AntiVirus software was a massive seller.

But viruses were essentially pieces of digital graffiti created by attention-seekers, modern versions of "Kilroy Was Here." Then, along came spyware.

Spyware was a very different animal. It was distributed differently, requiring users to click on something to acquire it, but it also had a much more malicious intent. Viruses were after recognition, seeking the limelight. Spyware was after your money and it wanted to be well under the radar.

A small Boulder-based company called Webroot Software had identified the problem and an opportunity. With a new product called SpySweeper, the company embarked on an aggressive PR campaign to educate consumers about the peril of spyware. Its message was simple: viruses are graffiti; spyware is criminal. And they talked to anyone who would listen. The idea was to articulate the difference and create a new security category beyond viruses and spam, the two most popular problems.

The company's savvy CEO, a Kellogg-School-educated first-time chief executive, recognized that PR could help catalyze the category and the company and initiated a year-long effort of courting influencers through a series of product announcements and face-to-face meetings. He was knowledgeable and charming and within a year, three critical events coincided, all in the span of one month. A comprehensive cover story appeared in *PC Magazine*, the most influential consumer computer magazine in the world. The *New York Times* editorial board called for Congressional investigations into spyware. And the United States Federal Trade Commission announced an "open-house" discussion on the commercial impact of spyware.

Within five years of launching SpySweeper, Webroot had gone from a company that fit in one conference room to a company with 500 employees in offices around the globe. A significant contributor to that growth was PR.

This is a familiar pattern: find a compelling issue, create a differentiating message, convince media to share it in a network effect, and then use that attention to disrupt market leadership. And companies like Webroot have used it very effectively.

But the most critical point is the ability to get the media to create the network effect necessary to spread the word.

## THE RISE OF SOCIAL, THE DEMISE OF MEDIA

It's no coincidence that Webroot's success occurred before Friedman's seminal year of 2007. In today's world of PR, Webroot's game plan might not work. The reason has little to do with execution or strategy and more with institutional changes in the media landscape. And that comes back to 2007.

Between 2007 and 2010, both Twitter and Facebook changed irrevocably. At the South by Southwest (SXSW) Conference in 2007, Twitter experienced its first inflection point when it surged to 60,000 daily messages. By 2010, people were sending 50 million messages a day on the platform. The period was just as important to Facebook. At the beginning of 2007, Facebook had about 12 million active users. Within three years, by 2010, it had over 600 million active users.

The impact of social media on the news business—and therefore PR—cannot be overstated. Combined with the inexorable shift from analog media to digital, the result is a shrinking newsroom at most major media organizations. The trend is well documented. So is its impact on PR.

At the end of this critical 2007–2010 period, the Pew Research Center conducted an important examination of the technology media world. In the study, Pew sought to understand the kind

FIGURE 1 Accelerating Awareness

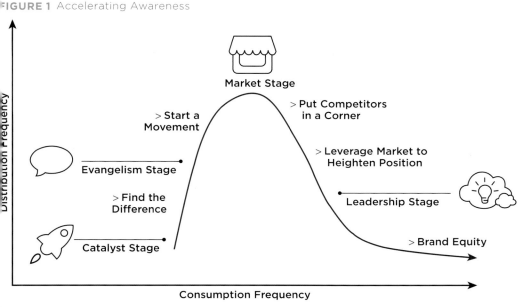

© 104West Partners, 2017

of coverage in the tech industry by looking at every article written in one year (from June 2009 to May 2010) and then examining what those articles were about. They intended to how which firms received the most coverage. But inadvertently they determined that a group of about five companies (Apple, Google, Twitter, Facebook and Microsoft) constituted close to 40 percent of all the coverage; one out of every 2.5 articles in an entire year was about just five companies. That is a stunning finding.

There's no reason to think that situation has changed today and if you toss in a few contemporary companies, like Amazon, Verizon, and Samsung, and that number probably gets closer to 50 percent. Call those companies the Media Oligarchs.

Two other categories then emerge, the Media Upstarts and the Media Middlers. The Upstarts are those companies that flare up quickly and gain a lot of media attention. Think Uber or Square or SnapChat. They collectively garner, by estimates, about 25 percent of the media's attention. The Media Middlers are therefore the

remaining 25 percent and represent every other company. In the case of technology companies, that is a massive group that includes large and important companies like Adobe, Oracle, SAP, Cisco, Salesforce, and on and on. It's a point worth emphasizing: if a company is not Facebook or Apple or Google, and it's not Uber or SnapChat, then it is competing for media attention along a very long and powerful tail of companies.

The impact of that environment on PR efforts is enormous. Any young company, unless it has the rare and mostly alchemic good fortune to become an Upstart, is going to have a very hard time solely relying on PR and the media to catalyze its company into a market position that challenges legacy leaders. There is simply an institutional bias.

## CONTENT, CONTENT EVERYWHERE

As the last decade closed, this evolution in media relations became even more tenuous for PR groups, as the macroeconomic conditions of 2008–2010 further pressured the industry. Many PR agencies and departments scrambled

**FIGURE 2** Reaching the Audience

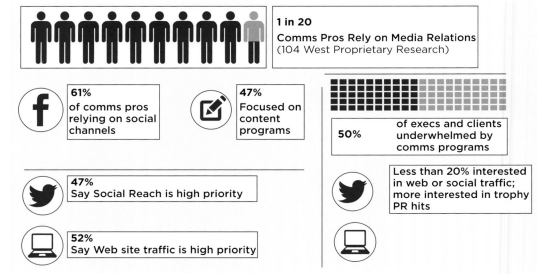

© 104West Partners, 2017

to develop programs that justified their fees and jobs, and many of them turned to "content distribution" as a fix. The idea was simple: if the media opportunities were shrinking, create proprietary content and distribute it through any number of emerging channels, like social media and direct media or direct mail.

Most companies soon embarked on programs that leveraged original content, like tweets and other social posts on blogs or sites like LinkedIn, as well as content that acted like direct mail but was subtler than typical marketing material. Many companies called that "owned" and/or "paid media."

They also still used traditional indirect channels, or "earned media," that reflected legacy PR tactics. Call that "engineered content" (because they have to *engineer* the result by persuading someone to write an article or an analyst report or offer a speaking slot). Some companies also used another category of media, call it "curated content," taking beneficial or complementary content from third-party sources and distributing it through their own channels.

The problem for many clients and companies, however, was the content fell flat. Traditional earned media (or engineered content) had branded validation from media companies like newspapers and online blogs and TV networks, as well as built-in distribution networks. But original content struggled for both relevance and reach. And there was the thorny topic of return on the investment. Business leaders generally accepted the sort of black box of legacy PR efforts. If they couldn't put their finger on a return, they certainly knew that the article framed on their wall was a respectable trophy.

Some recent research shows a continuing disconnect between business executives and communications pros on this issue. PR and communications pros, when asked where their current program focus is, predominantly point to social media, citing among other factors the ever-increasing difficulty in attracting sustained and quality media attention. But, their bosses and clients, according to the same communications pros, still regard major articles as their goal and differ with their comms colleagues on strategy.

These execs don't see the efficacy of the social programs their PR teams are advocating. Presumably, the execs do want a sustained and measurable dialogue with their markets, and social content certainly provides a platform for both. But they don't seem convinced.

## IT'S THE MESSAGE, NOT THE MEDIUM

There might be two issues worth investigating to find the solution: the medium or the message. The medium or media are certainly becoming increasingly sophisticated. Social media and direct channels have become easy to track and measure, both highly appealing attributes for senior leadership as they look to generate return on every marketing dollar, including communications.

So, if the medium with its increased sophistication and measurability is not the problem, then what about the message? One consideration is the role of context. In other words, is the content providing its audience with a message to which they can relate? The connection between the content and the audience has taken on new importance in recent years as social media platforms became ubiquitous. Social media created a new and almost instantaneous platform for news distribution, often providing highly targeted content since people can refine their feeds according to their own preferences.

**FIGURE 3** Developing Contextual Content

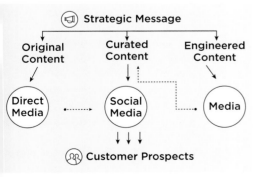

© 104West Partners, 2017

But the more significant shift is in what people do with the news when they consume it on sites like Facebook or Twitter: They share it. Facebook reaches over two thirds of U.S adults, and two thirds of U.S. adults say they get news from social sites, either from Facebook or Twitter. The implication of this data is that the age of serendipitous discovery of news is over. Fewer and fewer people are going to news sites to find news. Instead, they are relying on social feeds to provide news for them.

That behavior evidences new willingness to consume news that is shared. If someone reads a story that a friend has shared, the credibility of that article increases. That trust extends to professional experiences as well. Content produced by professional news organizations or by companies is more engaging than content that lacks requisite context.

But context can be elusive. Many companies have turned to data as a way to have content reflect a marketplace and therefore become more engaging. It's a simple concept: if someone sees that XX percent of people believe something and they believe that too, then they are naturally more engaged. That is highly effective, but it also requires some specialized expertise. Not all engagement is created equal. PR as a function has moved beyond the concept of publicity, something that is particularly true for business-to-business communicators who are especially keen on ROI and shy away from publicity for publicity's sake. It's no longer about relationships and publicity; it's about seeing the whole field and developing programs that have greater applicability across traditional and emerging communications functions.

Even so, for years marketers and business leaders alike thought that the mere appearance of positive press would send floods of leads to their sales funnels. That is a myth. It doesn't happen. What does happen is those articles become powerful tools that sales and marketing professionals use to engage customers and prospects directly.

## THE FALL OF THE BLACK BOX, THE RISE OF MEASUREMENT

If anything has changed in PR in the last decade or so, it is that PR is no longer a black box. Instead, it is a fully realized communications function that translates messages into ideas and infuses those ideas with context to engage audiences and turns it into content.

Then that content needs to be filtered through as many channels as possible, because one of the other truths about contemporary communications is that the audience is fickle and defused. No single program element is assured an audience. But when the chorus of efforts is orchestrated right, it will resonate. And if it's all done right, the audiences are hearing the same messages multiple times from multiple channels. When that happens, that's truly a modern and effective communications effort.

Take the example of Rapt Media, a young company in Boulder, CO, that offers an interactive video platform. For all its popularity, video is a notorious medium for marketers and business executives because it's very hard to gauge its marketing efficacy. People start a video and they stop a video and that action is registered. But there is really no other data, so marketers have no sense of engagement.

Rapt developed a platform that invited interactivity, thus offering behavioral data and insights. And in order to demonstrate that increased efficacy to its market, it needed to present the problem with video. In a three-part series of surveys and accompanying reports, the company asked three primary questions about greater creativity and engagement, greater funding for better performing videos, and audience reactions to these newer videos.

The resulting content was beneficial to Rapt: it said that with greater interactive technology (like Rapt's) creative departments would develop more engaging videos that audiences would eagerly watch and react to, and therefore business leaders would fund more of them.

So, the message was on point. Next came the distribution. Of course, since PR drove the

campaign, media relations was a significant component, garnering over 100 million impressions in over 100 articles over about four months. That alone would have been successful. But Rapt also pushed the campaign through various marketing and communications (marcom) channels, like SEO, direct mail, sales communications, etc. The result was impressive. Tens of thousands of website visitors were directly attributed to the campaign, representing a 65 percent increase over previous efforts, and the conversion rate of those visitors was more than 300 percent over goal. The campaign was by far the most productive marketing and communications effort the company undertook in 2016.

Because the campaign had a strong message that translated into a compelling narrative that was infused with data to provide context and the company leveraged every distribution channel at its disposal, it created a new kind of communications that was unlike any other PR program the company had attempted in the past. The media loved it because it wasn't some product announcement or self-serving press release. The customers loved it because it offered insight into an issue they were looking to understand better. And the company's marketing and sales teams loved it because it offered them a string of opportunities to engage with clients and prospects and sustain that dialogue over a relatively long period.

That's contemporary PR. The objective of most communications efforts is to maintain a productive dialogue with a company's market over time. That is how companies change minds, create persistent brand positions, and ultimately gain market share and succeed. But the recent developments in how we consume media have changed the traditional channels. So, PR pros are looking for new ones, but they need to do that thoughtfully and with an eye toward the businesses they serve. Long gone is the era when a leading article could satisfy a client or an executive team for months. Like most of marketing and communications, business results are paramount, and so new strategies are emerging to accommodate the changing notion of what communications is and what it must be.

# 22

# HOW TO RAISE VENTURE CAPITAL

Flybridge Capital Partners

Jeffrey J. Bussgang, Cofounder and General Partner, and Senior
Lecturer, Harvard Business School

## INTRODUCTION

Among potential financing sources for new companies, venture capital (VC) occupies a unique position. Venture capitalists (VCs) are the only class of professional investors whose sole occupation is to study, finance, and support startups. They generally invest $1 million to $10 million in an early-stage venture in exchange for a significant equity stake—10 percent to 30 percent. The significance of the investment typically gives the VC firm a seat on the board of directors, which allows for direct influence on strategic decisions. VC investors are richly rewarded for backing winners, including the professional reputation that comes with success. That reputation enables them to continue raising funds and to attract "deal flow"—the next wave of talented entrepreneurs and their startups.

Although VCs invest in only a small fraction of all startups, many of the most successful startups in recent decades have relied on VC funding (e.g., Amazon, Apple, Facebook, Genentech, and Google). As a result, VCs have a unique perspective on opportunity evaluation, deal structure, new venture support, and exit. Indeed, their work at all stages of the entrepreneurial life cycle offers many lessons to company founders, even those whose ventures are not backed by VC.

Because VCs are paid, full-time investors with a strong incentive and a duty to represent the needs of the investors (known as limited partners) who contribute to the VC funds, VCs' motivations and incentives can sometimes conflict with those of entrepreneurs and their startups' stakeholders. Conflicts are generally outweighed—at least in successful deals—by the alignment of interest between the entrepreneur and the VC. Everyone wants the company to be successful, and everyone wants to make money. But an important part of building a successful partnership is being aware of potential conflicts and dealing with them openly and professionally.

There is certainly a subset of entrepreneurs who, in their heart of hearts, would love to get a check from VCs and never see them again (until perhaps the dinner celebrating the big sale or the Initial Public Offering [IPO]). And there's a subset of VCs who would love nothing more than to be on the other side of that deal—to write the check and get a big payday with little or no work in between. But experienced

VCs and entrepreneurs know that there is much to be gained from a true partnership. VCs as individuals and VC firms as institutions are pattern recognition machines—they have seen how various choices and strategies play out time and time again. They can't be as close to the day-to-day operations of the business as the entrepreneur, which has its benefits and drawbacks—objectivity and distance can provide valuable perspective. Hanging over the whole relationship is the fact that, on average, VCs replace company founders about half the time. So entrepreneurs are understandably nervous about giving VCs too much power and the interactions have high stakes, requiring a healthy give-and-take as well as an open and respectful relationship.

## WHAT ARE VENTURE CAPITALISTS LOOKING FOR?

The venture capital deal-evaluation process is sometimes described as a three-legged stool, in which the legs are the market, the technology, and the team. There is a perpetual argument about which leg is the most important. Indeed, it can be seen as a kind of a "rock-paper-scissors" problem in which each option can be overcome by another:

- The market is the most important, because a good market will make up for a mediocre team.

- The team is the most important, because the market is unpredictable and a good team will find the good market opportunity.

- The technology is the most important, because without a defensible, competitive advantage, it is impossible to sustainably hold on to the value created, even in an attractive market with a good team.

A robust business model with solid margins, high rates of recurring revenue, and long- lived customer relationships will add another positive dimension to the argument the entrepreneur is making for funding.

Finally, it is worth remembering that the funding decision plays out not like a snapshot but like a movie. As the VCs get to know the entrepreneur, the team, and the idea, they have the opportunity to judge how the founders develop and execute their plans (or experiments) and respond to new information and setbacks. VCs know that the early speed bumps a startup faces are generally minor compared with the issues that arise once they have more employees and invested capital on the line. But watching an early stage startup make progress, achieve important milestones, and make adjustments in the face of setbacks provides a great deal of valuable data for a VC trying to make an investment decision.

VCs are looking for passion and commitment, traits that will be required to sustain the venture across the many obstacles and hurdles it will face. But they also want to see a team with intellectual honesty, analytical rigor, and the ability to learn from experience. Most businesses—especially successful ones—don't succeed with their original business plan. Early contact with customers and with the market generates new information and insights that must be digested and incorporated into the venture's plan. The courtship that plays out during the search for funding is an opportunity for VCs to evaluate the team's ability to pivot when it needs to. Moreover, good VCs can demonstrate their value by serving as useful sounding boards and can provide insights based on their own varied and extensive experiences.

Of course, throughout their relationship with a startup company, VCs are paid to be focused on one and only one thing: a financially successful exit. VCs know that even an ideal arrangement of all these variables and ingredients can nonetheless end in failure, and, conversely, a less-than-perfect set of circumstances can still yield great success. There is a lot of luck and good timing involved.

Again, this all points to the advantages of a true partnership, in contrast to a more transactional relationship, which has as its only objective the procuring of a check from VCs and the generating of high returns. The partnership model offers a greater upside for both parties.

## THE VENTURE CAPITALIST'S DECISION-MAKING PROCESS

VCs evaluate deals through a complex process that serves as a funnel: The number of deals under active consideration decreases as the VC does more investigatory work, known as due diligence. (See Figure 1 for an example of the way one VC firm thinks about the decision process.) As the exhibit suggests, VCs invest more time as the number of deals they are investigating shrinks. An initial meeting or phone call will, if successful, lead to a longer, more in-depth meeting and, potentially, meetings with a broader set of the startup's team members. The VC will call the new venture's customers (if they exist) and try to learn about what competitors are doing. At some point, if things continue on a positive track, VCs will have their partners meet the entrepreneur and possibly the team.

The VC wants to get a look at every interesting startup, particularly those led by proven entrepreneurs. The more deals VCs see, the more likely it is that they will find a high-quality deal in which to invest. Moreover, VCs become smarter as they look at more deals, learning from the wide variety of potential investments. Note

that although individual VCs do much of this work on their own, the decision-making process is collaborative. Many firms are large enough to have several professionals who invest in the same area—say, software, biotech, Internet, or cloud services. One will generally be the lead (and will serve on the portfolio company's board if the investment is made), but investment decisions are usually made by the group as a whole. Some firms require unanimity among partners before a positive decision is made; others have a lower hurdle, such as a majority or supermajority. Often a designated devil's advocate will try to make a case against investing to be sure the risks are fully fleshed out.

The volume of potential deals—each partner may see between 300 and 500 per year—poses a challenge. VCs struggle to sift through all the plans, people, and data to select the startups they wish to fund. Active VCs—who join the boards of the companies in which they invest— typically have the capacity to do just one or two deals a year. Passive VCs—who often invest at a later stage in a company's life, take a smaller ownership stake, and don't join the board—can typically invest in only three or four deals a year.

**FIGURE 1** Venture Capital Decision Tree

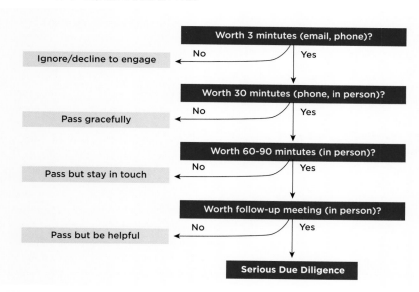

Source: Flybridge Capital Partners

So the volume of proposals is large, and the number that gets funded is small. How can an entrepreneur improve the chances of being one of the chosen few? It's crucial to keep in mind that the process of building a partnership with a potential VC investor begins before the first meeting even takes place. The nature of the introduction, the emails, and the material sent in hopes of gaining a meeting all establish the identity and credibility of the entrepreneur. Several steps will help.

**Find a trusted source to make an introduction.**
The source of the introduction can send a powerful signal to the VC. Instead of making a cold call or sending an unsolicited plan in "over the transom," the entrepreneur should get as "warm" an introduction as she can. The odds of a follow-on conversation are much higher if someone who knows the entrepreneur and is known and trusted by the VC makes an introduction. The best introductions to VCs come from people VCs have reason to trust: entrepreneurs who have made them money or the entrepreneurs in their current portfolio companies. The next tier down would include the wider pool of executives in the VC's portfolio companies, as well as lawyers, bankers, and other service providers who work with the VC firm. Of course, the more someone has to lose by making a bad introduction, the more the VC will tend to take it seriously. And the more the VC trusts the judgment of the person making the referral—by having seen that judgment play out over time—the more time and energy the VC will invest in understanding the new venture. This means that entrepreneurs with a broad network of relevant contacts may find it easier to be introduced to VCs. Indeed, research shows that the depth and breadth of an entrepreneur's social network can have a positive effect on the search for funding. Because new ventures are inherently risky, anything that reduces that perceived risk—such as information about the entrepreneur's character and abilities, gleaned through a network of relationships—can help the entrepreneur secure financing.

**Build a strong reputation.** Entrepreneurs should work on building their reputations long before attempting to raise funding. Entrepreneurs naturally establish their reputations by behaving in a trustworthy and honorable way and by being known to others. Today, being known is accomplished by means of both face-to-face and virtual interactions. Blogging, tweeting, appearing at conferences, speaking, making an effort to become acquainted with key players in the industry, and having something to add to the conversation—all help build an entrepreneur's reputation and network. Research has shown that the extent of an entrepreneur's "reputational network" (i.e., the range of people who know an entrepreneur by reputation, even if not personally) can have a positive effect on the success of the venture. This reputational network is based on the entrepreneur's relationships with market-leading firms, such as well-known technology or distribution partners, and customers.

**Conduct due diligence on VCs.** Entrepreneurs need to perform due diligence on their potential investors. VCs all have reputations that are based on their earlier work with companies. Entrepreneurs must figure out which startups their prospective VCs have financed and worked with (they will usually list their portfolio companies on their website) and talk to entrepreneurs at those companies. Were the VCs available? Helpful? Did they have a wide network of relevant contacts, and did they open up that network to the entrepreneurs? Were they supportive of management and work as part of the team, or were they more likely to be critical observers? How quickly did they pull the trigger in changing out management when things were not going according to plan? These are important dimensions of the way a VC works with portfolio companies, and entrepreneurs should understand them before entering into this important partnership. Note that there is no perfect VC for every startup. It is a question of fit between the particular kinds of help the startup needs and the specific value an individual VC can add. Style and personal chemistry are important, as well in working together in a productive, trusting relationship.

An entrepreneur should consider the "sweet spots" of individual VC firms—each has its own experience and expertise. This requires an understanding of the areas in which VCs invest and the way in which markets are segmented, for example, big data analytics, medical devices, mobile advertising. It is not smart to go to a VC who has invested in a direct competitor, but it is helpful to pitch to someone who has invested in and knows the industry, and it is even better if the VC has had a successful investment in that space or an adjacent one. Many VCs also specialize by deal size and stage. But perhaps more importantly, individual venture capitalists within a firm often have their own areas of focus. An entrepreneur's chances of success in approaching a particular VC firm may be maximized by getting on the radar of a particular VC partner at the firm.

Getting to know VCs and their reputations has never been easier. Many VCs and their firms blog and tweet, providing transparency into their areas of investment interest and how they work with startups. There are numerous specialized media properties that focus on the world of startups and VCs, from the mainstream (e.g., *Fortune, Wall Street Journal, Forbes*) to the niche (e.g., TechCrunch, Re/Code, StrictlyVC, Axios). Most VCs use LinkedIn or their website bios to provide a comprehensive list of investments; speaking with entrepreneurs at those companies, both the successful and unsuccessful ones, can be invaluable. Finally, service providers who specialize in the startup world, such as attorneys, search firms, and accounting firms, have behind-the-scenes knowledge of VCs that cuts across many startups. Any and all sources of information to gain a perspective on what it will be like to partner with a particular VC individual and firm should be utilized.

**Develop a good pitch.** The entrepreneur also needs to hone the pitch she will present to VCs.

Once due diligence and analysis—by both VC and the entrepreneur—are completed and the VC has signaled intent to invest in a startup, the VC will bring the investment proposal to the firm's partners for a formal vote. They will discuss the pros and cons, the risks and the upside, as well as other VC firms that might be involved (if any), investment amounts, and the specifics of the security the firm will get for its investment.

- **Hit the sweet spot**. Gail Goodman served as president, CEO, and chairman of the email marketing firm Constant Contact. Gail estimates that she was rejected by more than 40 VCs before securing her first round of VC money and by over 60 before securing her second. Although there was some overlap between the two rounds, this means nearly 100 VCs were wrong to turn her down—the company went public and later sold for over $1 billion. Gail's experience would suggest that the biggest lessons are to be tenacious and work hard to find the right firm as well as the right person at the firm and, as in a general sales process, determine that they are a fit for what you are doing.

- **Get the right people on the team.** You need to be the right person, and have the right team, to pursue this compelling vision and bring it to life. Ideas are a dime a dozen. Having a world-class team that can uniquely execute on the ideas is golden. All venture capitalists worry, "What happens if a 'fast follower' comes up with the same idea, raises more money, and recruits a better team?" The entrepreneur who has a clear, unassailable competitive advantage—an "unfair advantage"—is the most compelling entrepreneur when it comes to the pitch, and the team may very well make the difference.

- **Have a compelling vision.** You need a vision, an idea, an approach that gets the venture capitalist excited. LinkedIn cofounder and chairman Reid Hoffman's idea about how the Internet might be harnessed to bring professional people together caught the imagination of several venture capitalists. The more dramatic and unrealized the vision, however, the more the experience and expertise of the entrepreneur come under scrutiny by the venture capitalist. That's why people are perhaps the most important attribute required in order to attract VC money.

- **Demonstrate momentum**. As discussed, venture capitalists like to invest in movies, not still photos. In other words, they like to see how a story evolves over time so that they can extrapolate what will happen over the next few years. If you can show momentum in your business—across any metrics or strategic objectives—you can build momentum in the investment process. If the story gets better with time, you pique VC interest and give the impression of being a "hot" company and therefore a "hot" deal.

So, venture capitalists are looking to back entrepreneurial teams that can effectively execute the big vision and make it a reality. As Fred Wilson of Union Square puts it, "We venture capitalists love to invest in the serial entrepreneur who's done it before, knows the playbook, and won't make any of the rookie mistakes. And when those people come back, if they still have the fire in their belly to do it again, we're likely to say 'yes' almost every single time."

But experience cuts both ways. Entrepreneurs who know physics don't believe they can defy gravity. Many venture capitalists prefer young founders who are incredibly brilliant and gifted even though they are inexperienced and naïve. Look at the case studies of the successful startups begun by college dropouts, such as Microsoft (Bill Gates), Dell (Michael Dell), and Facebook (Mark Zuckerberg). Fred Wilson's observation about Facebook in the early days was that the singular focus of the young entrepreneur is very powerful. "You have this twenty-five-year-old founder, Mark Zuckerberg, who doesn't have a wife, doesn't have kids, doesn't have anything in his life that's distracting him from what he's trying to do. And there's nobody saying to him, 'God damn it, take the money off the table. You should sell it now.' Instead, he's going for a hundred billion!"

The combination of these three forces—finding the right VC match, having a compelling vision, and assembling a uniquely strong team—is very powerful and attractive to venture capital firms.

Without question, the odds are stacked against the entrepreneur. It can seem hard to get access to a member of the VC club and convince its members that your story is a compelling one and that you have the right team to execute against it. But with good preparation and thoughtful planning, a warm introduction, and a set of well-defined experiments and milestones, you can improve your odds considerably.

# 23

# BEYOND VC: ALTERNATIVE FINANCING FOR STARTUPS THAT WANT TO GROW WITHOUT GIVING UP CONTROL

Lighter Capital

It's exceedingly rare for a startup to succeed without at least *some* outside funding. Building a company is an incredibly challenging and costly endeavor, and founders almost always need a boost—even if only from friends and family. More often than not, they want to raise venture capital.

The VC industry, for its part, has done a tremendous job of encouraging this aspirational narrative. Hollywood productions including *The Social Network, Jobs,* and HBO's *Silicon Valley* have taken this narrative out of finance industry obscurity and into popular culture. And what entrepreneur doesn't romanticize following in the footsteps of Musk or Bezos?

Yet here's the reality: in the world today, there are approximately 200 unicorns (startups worth $1 billion or more) and more than 900,000 tech startups in the U.S., according to census data. That means that less than 1/50th of 1 percent of startups ever reach the upper echelons of success. For fun contrast, your chances of founding a unicorn are just slightly better than your chances of being struck by lightning.

Worse, most founders of those unicorns give up huge chunks of equity to achieve that scale. For example, the founder equity stakes of Yelp, Trulia, and Hubspot were worth only about $10 million each at IPO and founder equity stakes in TrueCar, Box, and ZenDesk were only worth about $9 million each at IPO. That's a collective $57 million in founder equity for a collective market cap of $5.9 billion at the time of IPO, or less than 1 percent of total. A wonderful reward for all of that hard work, no?

There *are* ways to achieve your growth goals without giving away half (or more) of your company. You *can* control your destiny, achieve financial independence, and build something wonderful for your employees and customers. You *can* build a great business, on your own terms and at your own pace. Over the next few sections, we'll discuss alternative funding methods to help you achieve your dream and keep the fruits of your labor.

## IS VC ALL IT'S CRACKED UP TO BE?

Let's examine VCs for a moment. When you agree to take that hefty, multimillion-dollar check, you also agree give up a heart-stopping 20 to 50 percent of your business, form an official board, and cede a lot of control. After all, they can now fire you from your own company.

Venture capital does make sense for businesses that are on track to become the next AirBnB or Uber. However, if you sympathize with any of the following considerations, then VC may not be the right fit for you:

- You don't want to give up 20 to 50 percent of your business.

- You don't want to manage a board of directors.

- You don't want to have others voting on how you should run your business.

- You don't want the pressure to reach certain milestones or exit by a certain year.

- You don't want to take six to nine months of time to fundraise every other year.

- You're okay with your startup not becoming a multi-billion dollar business

## WHAT YOUR FINANCING OPTIONS LOOK LIKE

There's been a lot of talk about the "bubble," but it's more like the dust settling. There have been some very high valuations in recent years, and now it's becoming even harder for startups to attract and earn VC. VCs are becoming more risk averse and are sticking to safer deals with tried-and-true models, which leaves a lot of great ideas unfunded. VC aside, here are a few alternative financing options to fund your venture.

> **Important note:** Double check the *moonlighting clause* in your employment contract before you do any work on your new business on the side. Many companies have strict rules and can end up owning the intellectual property in your new venture if you do side work on company time or using company resources such as a work laptop, for example. You should always talk to a lawyer before getting started, just to be safe.

## REVENUE

Most startups fail because they don't make revenue a priority or they can't earn revenue. Your idea doesn't make the leap to a real business until you have paying customers. Before that, it's still just an idea.

While there are certainly many valid reasons for why you might need to raise investment at the onset of the startup journey—engineering or physical manufacturing for example—you should still be able to find at least one paying customer for your idea *before* you write the first line of code or build the first prototype. Find the people who have such a burning need for your solution that they're willing to prepay for the product, sight unseen.

You should spend most of your time in the first 6 to 12 months of your startup journey talking to potential customers—which can often be done before you quit your current job, saving you critical cash resources until you're absolutely sure you're ready to quit and launch a new business. This effort will strengthen your understanding of the market dynamics, competitors, critical customer needs, and sales and marketing costs—all critical factors in business success.

Remember, a business exists to deliver value to people in exchange for money. If you can't find at least one customer to prepay, that's a big red flag. It means that you haven't yet identified the key set of features needed to be competitive in the market, or you haven't found the right customers or the right market.

If you have revenue, you've successfully solved a problem for someone, and revenue is the best kind of investment for a startup. That's the whole point of the game.

## FRIENDS AND FAMILY MONEY

Nearly every business in America—from restaurants, to dry cleaners, to many tech startups—got some of their early funding from a friend or family member. This source of funding is the bedrock of what makes American entrepreneurialism possible. From Donald Trump to Bill Gates, American business is filled with entrepreneurs who took a check from their parents and then took a chance on building something great.

The upside of friends and family funding is that it's easily accessible in a safe and welcoming environment. When Aunt Jane cuts you a check, you know she wants to see you succeed.

Yet, there are three major downsides to taking money from Aunt Jane. First, she likely doesn't have enough money to give you all the resources you need. Which means you also need to get checks from Uncle Joe, neighbor Bob, and your college buddies Jennifer and Shameek to fill out the round. While not immediately apparent, you've just taken on more work than you realize. Each of these friends and family members— correction: *new investors*—will want to be kept in the loop. They may want to know how you're spending your money, the ins and outs of your go-to-market strategy, who you're hiring first. They may ask you to justify your use of funds. It doesn't matter whether one has put in $50,000 and another just $2,000. These friends and family are betting their savings on you and you owe it to them to claw your way to the top. Along the way, you'll likely be hearing quite a bit of advice from these new investors, regardless of their business background or industry expertise. This always ends up being a major distraction for startup operators and it adds stress to an already incredibly stressful experience.

Second, there's the legal framework of accredited versus unaccredited investors. Friends and family rounds often unknowingly get entangled in Securities and Exchange Commission (SEC) regulations. These rules are there to protect people from losing it all—which is a very real risk in a startup investment. If you see your company being acquired in the future or going for a VC round, obtaining money from friends and family could throw a wrench in your gears. It will come up in the audit phase of the process; there's no way around it.

Third and most important is the potential for irreparable damage to relationships. Friends and family are more than just potential investors. Mixing personal relationships with business is a road fraught with danger. If the thought of losing Aunt Jane's $20,000 investment and having to face her at Thanksgiving makes you sick to your stomach, it might make sense to skip this option and look for capital elsewhere.

## BANK LOANS

Getting a small business bank loan is a challenging endeavor made especially difficult since the 2008 financial crisis and the ensuing credit crunch. Today, it is virtually impossible to get a new business loan. To understand why, consider how banks handle risk.

Banks make loans—not investments—and they need their money back paid back with interest. Lenders will want to see a financial track record that demonstrates your ability to repay the loan. Without that business history, lenders can't determine if your venture will succeed and they'll have to default to the next best source of financial history: your personal credit based on your FICO score. As a result, most loans for new businesses require you to personally guarantee your loan. If the business fails, the bank will come for your personal resources. If you're not comfortable with betting your family's house, retirement funds, and resources against your business's success, you might want to look for alternatives to a bank loan.

And personal guarantees aren't the only downside. Most loans have financial or use-of-funds restrictions called covenants. These are specific clauses that must be met for you to stay in good standing with your loan. Unfortunately, the language of covenants—and their implications—is often murky.

We recently met with a startup founder in the Seattle area who agreed to a 50 percent growth covenant at his last startup, meaning the bank required him to grow 50 percent year over year to stay in good standing with the loan. One year, he missed the growth covenant goal (growing

48 percent instead of 50 percent) and the bank called the loan. The founder had to scramble to repay hundreds of thousands of dollars.

There are also cash-on-hand covenants, where a founder is required to keep a large portion of the loan balance on hand at all times—say $500 thousand of a $1 million loan—yet the company has to pay interest on the total principal, which is incredibly frustrating for entrepreneurs trying to allocate resources and grow their businesses.

Banks tempt entrepreneurs with interest rates low enough to distract from the dangers of a personal guarantee or a list of restrictive financial covenants. Don't ignore that fine print. For most early-stage tech entrepreneurs, bank loans aren't the safe option they seem to be.

## CROWDFUNDING

Crowdfunding has taken off in recent years, mostly due to its accessibility. Most startups can get a campaign up and running on a crowdfunding platform in a few days, and everybody has social networks they can leverage for capital.

This ease of access is also one of crowdfunding's downsides. Easy entry means there's a lot of competition and noise out there—it's a very crowded space. The startups that succeed with crowdfunding are the ones that spend countless hours fine-tuning their messaging, marketing their product, filming a compelling video, and

enlisting the help of early supporters. Yet the crowdfunding campaign itself can become very much like another job.

Think about this in terms of opportunity cost. The effort to promote a crowdfunding campaign is often equal to the effort of promoting your product to your first customers. One clear winning use case is if you have a physical product and you take preorders to fund the design and manufacturing costs of producing thousands of units at scale. In these scenarios, Kickstarter campaigns are often extraordinary proving grounds for you to get dozens—or sometimes thousands—of preorders and prepayments from future customers. This is especially useful for companies that target consumers (B2C) rather than serving other businesses (B2B).

## REVENUE-BASED FINANCING

Revenue-based financing offers a hybrid option, taking the best features of debt and equity. With revenue-based financing, there is almost always no personal guarantee required and no equity surrendered. It works, and it's quickly gaining traction in the startup industry.

This type of funding is over 100 years old. It's used in Hollywood: when films are financed, investors give money in return for a cut of ticket sales. It's also used by the oil, gas, and solar industries. It's a proven method of financing, with no distractions and near total autonomy for the project owner. The best part? It is often much faster to get this funding—weeks as opposed to months.

**FIGURE 1** Revenue-Based Financing 4-Year Loan Example

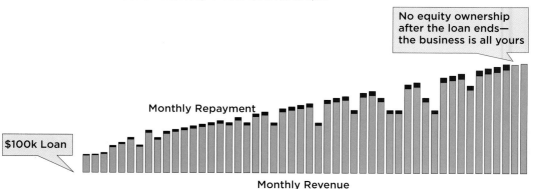

No equity ownership after the loan ends— the business is all yours

Monthly Repayment

$100k Loan

Monthly Revenue

Here's how it works. You take a loan—let's say $100,000—and agree to repay it over a set time frame, generally three to five years. During that time, you pay back a percentage of your monthly revenues each month— generally between two to eight percent. The amount you repay is capped at a specific amount (referred to as the repayment cap). If your repayment cap is 1.6x, in the end you repay $160,000 total ($60,000 in interest and $100,000 in principal) over the course of the loan. Simple as that.

This model works well for two kinds of founders. The first are founders who never want to raise VC. These entrepreneurs are okay with running successful businesses that afford them financial security. They probably will never hit $1 billion in revenue, and they're totally okay with that. Selling their business for $5 million and owning 100 percent works really well for them. Revenue-based financing allows them to get the resources they need to expand and

grow without giving up any ownership in the company.

The second bucket of startups is those who want to delay VC fundraising. Maybe they need just a little more cash to close out their next big customer. Maybe they need capital to hire that sales or marketing leader. Or maybe they want to wait until they hit revenue goals or market traction before they speak with VCs so that they can negotiate a better deal. Revenue-based financing helps them improve their metrics without giving up ownership in the interim and eventually allows them raise a VC round at much better terms down the road.

In either case, revenue-based financing provides extraordinary optionality. Bootstrappers can later change their mind and go raise VC at much better terms. Or, founders who are on a VC track might decide to get off that train and preserve the remaining equity for themselves.

**FIGURE 2** Revenue-Based Financing Breakdown

| | | | |
|---|---|---|---|
| **Example Terms** | Example Amount: | $100,000 | *You borrow $100,000* |
| | Royalty Rate: | 5% | *You pay back 5% of monthly revenue, flexing up or down with net cash receipts (no fixed payments)* |
| | Repayment Cap: | 1.6x | *Interest is capped at a specific amount, which is the max upside as RBF doesn't take equity or warrants* |
| | Total Repayment: | $160,000 | *Simple total amount repaid over four years* |

**FIGURE 3** Sample Company Growth Journey

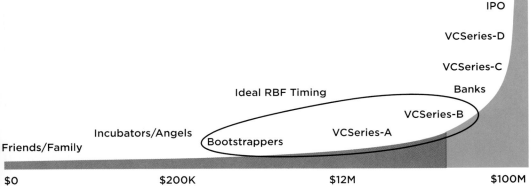

IPO

VCSeries-D

VCSeries-C

Banks

Ideal RBF Timing

VCSeries-B

Incubators/Angels

VCSeries-A

Bootstrappers

Friends/Family

$0    $200K    $12M    $100M

## REMEMBER, YOU'RE IN CHARGE

There is a multitude of funding options available to today's founders. Which one is right for you depends on just that—you.

It may be that VC is the right path for your startup. It also might be that you just need a runway of fast cash to take your company to the next level. It's all a matter of where you see your startup going and what you need to get there.

# 24

# KEY CONCERNS IN FOLLOW-ON FINANCING ROUNDS

**Gunderson Dettmer Stough Villeneuve Franklin & Hachigian, LLP**
Jeffrey Engerman, Corporate Partner

In taking on growth capital in a follow-on financing round, an emerging company must address the maturation of its capital structure beyond the relative simplicity found in early-stage companies. Investing larger amounts at higher valuations, later-stage venture or growth firms will have incentives that diverge from those of the company's early-stage investors, particularly with respect to growth and exit strategies. This divergence requires a careful balancing of economic and governance rights among the company's stockholders: new investors need to protect their economic interests and existing stockholders are wary of ceding flexibility on key strategic decisions.

The costs of getting this balance wrong can be steep: an emerging company can find itself, post follow-on financing, in need of unanimous approval from multiple constituencies with conflicting incentives to set and act on its strategic goals.

## STRUCTURE—PRIMARY AND SECONDARY TRANSACTIONS

The threshold issue in a growth-stage investment is how the capital will be used: whether funds are added to the company's balance sheet to fund corporate growth or paid to existing stockholders in purchase of their holdings in the company. Growth-stage investment firms are significantly larger than early-stage venture funds and require a certain minimum "check size" to take on a new portfolio company, which minimum may exceed the company's need for operating capital. The specifics of the situation will dictate whether the financing is primary only (all cash is going to the balance sheet), secondary only (all cash to existing stockholders), or a combination of the two.

The primary portion of a typical growth transaction involves the sale of a newly authorized series of preferred stock, with the company providing customary representations concerning its business, financial results, and assets (including intellectual property). The preferred stock also will carry standard economic rights, such as a right to preferential payment in a liquidation.

For the secondary portion, investors will purchase either additional preferred stock, with the company using proceeds to repurchase shares from existing holders, or outstanding shares directly from existing stockholders. In this latter structure, referred to here as a "cross-purchase," the purchasing investor will receive only the economic rights already present in the shares being purchased (which, if common stock, will be minimal). Accordingly, the cross-purchase structure often occurs at a slightly discounted price per share compared to primary shares.

Regardless of the form, the following issues must be addressed in any secondary transaction:

*Tax and accounting concerns*: It is critical that the company's financial advisors are consulted to ensure proper tax and accounting treatment. Depending on the participants and structure, a portion of the proceeds may be treated as employment income under tax or accounting rules for sellers that are (or were) employees.

*Impact on option grants*: For a secondary transaction involving common stock, the company must consider the relationship of the transaction price to prior determinations of fair market value, as well as the impact on any future valuations undertaken to support the granting of stock options.

*Participants*: Generally, most secondary transactions involve either a limited number of sellers (typically founders or senior management) or a broader group of stockholders, potentially segregated by type of shares held or employment status (e.g., participation may be limited to current employees as an incentive tool). An offer to purchase shares from a broad group of shareholders (whether by company repurchase or a cross-purchase) may be subject to the tender offer rules of Section 14(e) of the Securities Exchange Act of 1934. Failure to comply with such rules could result in sellers have a right to unwind the transaction

after the company's value has significantly increased.

*Disclosure*: If stockholders other than the company's management team and investors represented on the board of directors are eligible to participate, potential sellers should be given sufficient information about the company (including financial reports) to enable a fully informed investment decision.

*Liability issues*. In a typical primary transaction, the company makes representations concerning its business and operations, and investors will be able to bring a breach claim if those representations prove untrue (although it practice, such claims are rare). While selling stockholders will be required to represent to ownership of their shares and right to sell, whether they should additionally be liable in the event of a breach of commercially focused representations is open to negotiation. Recent market trends have generally exempted sellers from such liability in transactions where the secondary portion represents only a small fraction of the total investment.

*Other concerns:* Other items to consider include: exemptions from the Securities Act of 1933, compliance with the state and federal antifraud protections, and the applicability of transfer restrictions (and other contractual rights and obligations) to the secondary sale and, in the case of a cross-purchase, afterwards.

## ECONOMICS AND PATHS TO LIQUIDITY

The economic terms of a growth-stage financing are typically consistent with earlier stage financings; in fact, those earlier terms generally will serve as the baseline for the negotiation of the new round. However, despite the similarity of terms, differing investment valuations and amounts create the potential for misalignment of interests between earlier-stage and later-stage investors with regard to the various paths to liquidity.

## MERGERS AND ACQUISITIONS
### The Liquidation Waterfall

The liquidation preferences of preferred stock result in a waterfall governing the allocation of proceeds of a sale of the company among the company's stockholders. As shown in the example below, conventional "non-participating" preferred stock will have a right to be repaid its purchase price at lower relative valuations or participate on the basis of overall ownership percentage at higher relative valuations.

A simplified example is below, assuming a $6,000,000 Series A round shared by two venture capital firms at a $15,000,000 post-money valuation and a $25,000,000 Series B round at a $100,000,000 post-money valuation. The Series B round is primary only, with a $20,000,000 investment from the new investor and each of the Series A investors adding $2,500,000.

**TABLE 1A**  Base Example

|  | Series B Preferred ($5/share) | Series A Preferred ($1/share) | Common Stock | Fully Diluted Ownership |
|---|---|---|---|---|
| Founder |  |  | 4,500,000 | 22.5% |
| CEO |  |  | 2,000,000 | 10% |
| VC1 | 500,000 | 3,000,000 |  | 17.5% |
| VC2 | 500,000 | 3,000,000 |  | 17.5% |
| New investor | 4,000,000 |  |  | 20% |
| Employee option pool |  |  | 2,500,000 | 12.5% |
| Total shares | 5,000,000 | 6,000,000 | 9,000,000 | 100% |

Post-financing, the Series A Preferred and the Series B Preferred have a total liquidation preference of $31,000,000, meaning that no payments will be made on the common stock unless the sale price for the company exceeds that amount. At sale prices between $40,000,000 and $100,000,000, the Series A will act as if converted to common stock and share in the remainder after the Series B preference is paid, and at sale prices above $100,000,000, the Series B will act as

if converted to common as well, and all shareholders will be paid based on their fully diluted ownership.

### Flat Exits

One key concern for new investors in a follow-on round is a sale of the company at a price at or close to the valuation of their investment, as this would result in a return of their capital without increase but a significant gain for the existing stockholders. The new

TABLE 1B

| | B Preference | A Preference | As-Converted | Total |
|---|---|---|---|---|
| Founder | | | $22,500,000 | $22,500,000 |
| CEO | | | $10,000,000 | $10,000,000 |
| VC1 | $2,500,000 | $0 | $15,000,000 | $17,500,000 |
| VC2 | $2,500,000 | $0 | $15,000,000 | $17,500,000 |
| New investor | $20,000,000 | | | $20,000,000 |
| Employee option pool | | | $12,500,000 | $12,500,000 |

investor will have effectively provided an interest-free loan, giving the company time and funds to locate a sale opportunity without increasing the company's valuation above the follow-on round.

In the example above, if the company were sold for $100,000,000 after the Series B investment, the proceeds would be distributed per Table 1B.

The new Series B investor receives their $20,000,000 investment back with no gain, while each of the Series A investors has realized $17,500,000 on an aggregate investment of $5,500,000.

To address this concern, the new investor may push for an approval right over any sale of the company. However, a blanket approval would allow the new investor to reject future sales even where the concern regarding a flat exit did not apply—the new investors' higher valuation creates a risk/reward misalignment with the new investor seeking continued growth beyond what may satisfy the existing stockholders in order to generate returns.

One conventional compromise is for the new investor to have approval rights over a sale only if the investor fails to receive a negotiated minimum return, for example 1.5x or 2x the investment amount (typically in liquid consideration, such as cash or publicly traded securities). This blocking right may also be time-limited, possibly applying only for two to three years after the investment, preserving longer term flexibility for the company.

## Protecting the Liquidation Preference

The mechanics of preferred stock can create further misalignment among early and later investors. Preferred stock will be convertible into common stock on an initial public offering (as discussed below) or on the voluntary election of the preferred stockholders. The terms of the financing round will determine whether such an election can be made by the holders of all preferred stock voting together, or only on a series by series basis (e.g., the Series B holders must elect to convert the Series B preferred stock).

In the context of the example, should the preferred stock convert to common stock upon the election of the Series A Preferred and Series B Preferred shares voting together, or should the Series B Preferred shares only be converted on election of the holders of such Series B shares? Analyzing a low-value sale demonstrates the issue.

The tables below compare the results of a company sale at $40,000,000 if liquidation preferences were paid on the Series A Preferred and the Series B Preferred (top table) and if all preferred was first converted to common (bottom table).

Note that the as-converted distribution results in the early investors (whose 7,000,000 shares constitute the majority of 11,000,000 shares

of preferred stock) increasing their payouts substantially at the expense of the new investor. Accordingly, the two early investors will have the incentive to trigger the conversion of all preferred stock into common, and the new investor will seek protection by requiring its approval for any such conversion of the Series B Preferred.

Running counter to the new investor's desire to avoid circumvention of their liquidation preference (whether by conversion to common or through exploitation of other

**TABLE 2A** Proceeds Distribution if Preferences Paid

|  | B Preference | A Preference | As-Converted | Total |
|---|---|---|---|---|
| Founder |  |  | $4,500,000 | $4,500,000 |
| CEO |  |  | $2,000,000 | $2,000,000 |
|  |  |  |  |  |
| VC1 | $2,500,000 | $3,000,000 | $0 | $5,500,000 |
| VC2 | $2,500,000 | $3,000,000 | $0 | $5,500,000 |
| New investor | $20,000,000 |  | $0 | $20,000,000 |
|  |  |  |  |  |
| Employee option pool |  |  | $2,500,000 | $2,500,000 |

At a $100,000,000 sale, the Series B shares will receive the amount as preference or if treated as converting to common. For the purposes of the example, they are shown as receiving preference.

**TABLE 2B** Proceeds Distributions if all Preferred Converted to Common

|  | B Preference | A Preference | As-Converted | Total |
|---|---|---|---|---|
| Founder |  |  | $9,000,000 | $9,000,000 |
| CEO |  |  | $4,000,000 | $4,000,000 |
|  |  |  |  |  |
| VC1 | $0 | $0 | $7,000,000 | $7,000,000 |
| VC2 | $0 | $0 | $7,000,000 | $7,000,000 |
|  |  |  |  |  |
| New investor | $0 | $0 | $8,000,000 | $8,000,000 |
|  |  |  |  |  |
| Employee option pool |  |  | $5,000,000 | $5,000,000 |

provisions of venture financing documents) is the company's wish for flexibility in a future recapitalization transaction, where modifications to the preferred's economic rights may be a precondition to additional investment. Needing each investor to separately approve such changes could vastly increase the difficulty in completing such a transaction

## INITIAL PUBLIC OFFERING

When an emerging company completes an IPO, all preferred stock will convert to common stock; a general prerequisite for listing is that only common stock be outstanding. The company's governing agreements will provide for this conversion to occur without any need for stockholder approval, subject to certain negotiated minimum requirements: characteristics of the offering (e.g., a firm commitment underwritten offering on specified exchanges) and a minimum offering size and a per-share price (usually expressed as a multiple of the price paid by the new investor). A proposed offering that fails to satisfy such criteria would require the holders of preferred stock to voluntarily elect such a conversion, meaning that new investors who have negotiated for an approval right on conversion of their preferred stock can effectively block an IPO that doesn't satisfy the specified requirements.

The specifics of these minimum requirements are typically heavily negotiated, particularly in later stage rounds where an IPO at a lower valuation than the financing is feasible. Without any such requirements, the new investor could see preferred stock with $100,000,000 in liquidation preference converted into $80,000,000 worth of common stock at the closing of the IPO. The company will seek to preserve flexibility in the event that the board of directors determines an IPO at such lower price is the best path for the company.

A conventional solution to such competing demands is an "IPO ratchet," allowing for the preferred stock to be converted into common upon the closing of an IPO even in the absence of achieving a minimum offering price, with

an adjustment made to the number of shares of common stock issued in such conversion to ensure a minimum value for the investors. In the example from the prior paragraph, the holders of preferred stock with $100,000,000 in liquidation preference would receive additional shares of common stock so that the total value of the shares received by the investor, based on the IPO price, would be at least $100,000,000 (or potentially more in the event that a premium, such as 1.5x or 2x, had been agreed upon).

## OTHER LIQUIDITY TRANSACTIONS
### Secondary Sales

Investors in emerging companies have historically been permitted to engage in secondary sales of their shares, although only companies for which an IPO was seen as a near-term inevitability will trigger genuine demand for private shares. However, such companies have recently begun to take dramatic steps to prohibit trading in private shares, including blanket prohibitions of secondary sales without board approval.

### Redemption Rights

A final path to liquidity is the right of investors to require the company to redeem their shares after a fixed period. Although the actual exercise of redemption rights is exceedingly rare (and subject to a number of limitations imposed by corporate law), such rights can be used as leverage to encourage a sale of the company in circumstances where management might otherwise prefer the status quo. Seniority of redemption must be addressed in a follow-on round, and it is typical to require the new investors' approval for any redemption of earlier issued preferred stock so long as the new investors' shares remain outstanding.

## GOVERNANCE AND CONTROL TERMS
### BOARD COMPOSITION

New investors will typically desire a seat on the company's board, which may require a balancing of investor, management, and independent representation on the board, and may cause a hift from a founder controlled board to one controlled by the investors.

## BLOCKING RIGHTS

In all but the most unusual cases, emerging companies with significant investor capital will be subject to an investor consent requirement prior to undertaking a specified set of actions (such as new rounds of financing, sale of the company, etc.), with the particular actions (and exceptions) varying by situation. Typically, the key issues in a follow-on round are less about which actions require such approval than which particular investors are required to satisfy such approval, and whether there will be a subset of actions that require the approval of the new investor separately from the earlier investors.

Best practice for an emerging company is that the general set of preferred stockholder approval items requires a nonunanimous pooled investor vote to prevent any single investor from exercising exclusive control over key strategic decisions. Such pooled voting, at a minimum, requires the approval of the holders of a majority of all preferred stock, voting together. In the example above, each of VC1 and VC2 hold 5.5 million shares of preferred stock and the new investor holds 4 million shares; a majority of the 11 million preferred shares could be achieved by any two of these three investors. What threshold is ultimately implemented will depend on the specifics of the company's capitalization and the relative leverage of the parties.

### Series-Specific Votes

Because of the potential for a growth round to misalign investor incentives, new investors typically seek some exceptions to general pooled voting. In the example above, allowing VC1 and VC2 to vote their majority of preferred stock to benefit the holders of Series A Preferred at the expense of the holders of Series B Preferred is unlikely to be acceptable to the new investor. The following are a few areas where new investors might seek voting rights under their exclusive control.

*Senior capital*: To protect their liquidation preference, new investors may negotiate for a right to block the company from incurring significant payment obligations that would be senior or of equal priority to their rights, whether in the form of debt or a new series of preferred stock.

*Adverse/disparate treatment*: Pooled voting leaves open the possibility that one series of preferred stock could be subject to adverse treatment as a result of changes to terms approved by a pooled vote of the preferred shares. Delaware corporate law affords some protections against adverse changes that "single out" a series of preferred stock, but such a provision may not adequately protect the new investor's rights in all circumstances. New investors will seek to require their approval for changes that adversely impact their shares, regardless of whether the other shares of preferred stock are affected. The specific language to address this concern is typically highly negotiated.

*Affiliate transactions*: A new investor may wish to ensure that a transaction between the company and its officers, directors, or major existing stockholders not be subject solely to a pooled vote. The risks presented by such a transaction are mitigated by the fiduciary duties of the members of the company's board, but investors often prefer an explicit approval right.

*Increasing shares*: To ensure continued benefit from the aforementioned Delaware law protections, new investors will usually seek to maintain the majority of the shares of their series of preferred stock by prohibiting the company from authorizing more shares of such series without the new investors' approval.

*Dividends/repurchases*: New investors may seek a separate approval right over transactions that would cause the company's cash to be paid to stockholders, as dividends, repurchases, or otherwise.

## OTHER TERMS AND CONSIDERATIONS

Emerging companies can also anticipate that the level of legal due diligence performed in a follow-on financing will be substantially more involved than earlier rounds, given the larger investment amount. As a follow-on round is generally correlated with the company's evolution from an idea to a successfully scaling business, new investors will be carefully reviewing corporate files to ensure that the company has been properly documenting its employment and commercial relationships to ensure ownership and control of intellectual property rights, that strategic relationships and customer contracts pass close examination, and that there are no ambiguities with respect to equity ownership. International operations and regulatory matters will come under scrutiny as well.

As required in all private financing transactions, care must be taken to comply with federal and state securities laws. Additionally, the federal antitrust provisions of the Hart-Scott-Rodino (HSR) Act may affect larger financing transactions. Significant foreign operations could likewise result in the need for analogous consideration by foreign governments.

## CONCLUSION

Managed properly, growth financing rounds can be key building blocks for an emerging company's future success. If executed poorly, the company can be left subject to conflicting interests and overlapping blocking rights that impair its flexibility. Such flexibility is critical when decisions about a sale of the business are under consideration or in the event the company hits the proverbial "bump in the road" and needs to act quickly to get back on track.

A final reminder: this article was written to outline the key concerns and present issues for consideration. Ultimately, the "right" solutions to the legal and economic issues that can arise in a follow-on financing round will be heavily influenced by the specifics of the situation. Emerging companies are advised to engage and seek strategic advice from experienced counsel.

# 25

# ACCESSING THE DEBT MARKETS FOR THE FIRST TIME

KeyBanc Capital Markets Inc.

Pacific Crest Securities, Technology Specialists of KeyBanc
Capital Markets Inc.

John Brock, Managing Director

Sarah Hill, Director

Gabriella Blunk, Analyst

When a company transitions from early- to late-stage growth, capital sources beyond equity and venture debt become viable alternatives. Business owners, management teams, and boards of late-stage growth companies may be able to access structures that will better scale with the business over time, namely, recurring revenue or cash-flow-based facilities. Importantly, just as entrepreneurs take care in assessing shareholder dilution and future funding capacity in their equity partners, companies should take equal care in choosing the right lender and debt structure.

When a company is considering debt as its next capital source, management is wise to look well beyond a year or two, because lending relationships typically last for many years. Finding the best terms for an initial loan is less valuable than finding a trusted partner that will best serve the company for the foreseeable future. Determining which lending partner can successfully execute not just the immediate transaction but also the next several is important.

A lending partner who understands your business and industry will provide agility and scale as the business continues to execute on its growth strategy. In this chapter, we will walk through the optimal process for raising debt capital, as well as the final step of choosing the best financing partner.

## STEP 1: GETTING READY

Once a company decides to seek debt capital, it is essential to assemble the right information ahead of any conversations with potential lenders. Required information will include a recent management presentation, historical financial statements, financial forecasts, a sales pipeline, as well as customer data that together will illustrate the risk profile of the company and drive the size, structure, and pricing of the debt facility.

### MANAGEMENT PRESENTATION

Management presentations that are used to educate and update shareholders can provide lenders with a better understanding of the business and assist in the underwriting process. The presentation should include the Key Performance

Indicators (KPIs) that drive your business. Ongoing financial management presentations should be shared regularly with the lender to ensure plans are aligned with expectations and supported.

## HISTORICAL FINANCIALS

Lenders look for historical financial statements comprised of income statements, balance sheets, and cash-flow statements, preferably audited and presented on a generally accepted accounting principles (GAAP) basis. Additionally, interim year-to-date statements presented on a monthly basis, including the preceding year's corresponding statements, will allow a lender to calculate the most recent trailing 12-month performance. This helps a lender see the trajectory of the business and understand the growth patterns. You should be prepared to answer questions about trends, margin shifts, working capital, capital spending, and cash-flow generation. The ability to show detailed cost of goods sold (COGS) and operating expenses (e.g., selling and general and administrative expenses, R&D, sales and marketing) will speed up the initial due diligence process.

## FORECASTS

A financial forecast model is crucial to providing potential lending partners a view of projected revenue growth, gross margin trends, capital expenditures, and cash uses. Lenders would prefer to see this presented on a quarterly basis, including income statement, balance sheet, and cash-flow statement. A forecast helps to illustrate a path towards positive cash-flow generation, with earnings before interest, tax, depreciation, and amortization (EBITDA) often serving as the proxy and the measurement to which lenders will apply a leverage multiple to determine overall debt capacity. Often lenders will make adjustments to EBITDA to reflect the cash generation of the business, such as adding changes in deferred revenue, which is referred to as cash EBITDA. Forecasts are also instrumental in setting financial covenant levels for liquidity and leverage, since they provide insight into

growth and the impact it will have on the company's cash position.

## CUSTOMER DATA

Lenders will also want to see a detailed sales pipeline report. The pipeline provides insight into the sales cycle and gives credibility to the company's overall revenue forecast. A good pipeline report will include potential revenue by prospective customers, existing customer renewals, and upselling wins. It should also illustrate the sales stage and probability of closure for each opportunity. To further bolster forecast credibility, companies should provide lenders with a historical look at the pipeline and actual sales conversions.

In terms of customer data, lenders will want to understand the components of revenue growth, including revenue derived from existing customers versus new customers as well as concentration of total revenue by the top 10 or 20 customers organized by geography and industry. Contract terms, including commitment length and payment terms, will help determine the predictability of revenue from any single customer. Diversification in the customer base is important. While having blue-chip customers is an attractive attribute for any company, high concentration among a few customers is a potential risk. Retention rates and length of relationship are also important data elements, because they demonstrate market acceptance of the company's products as well as the likelihood of strong future cash flows from a recurring revenue base.

Once this information is provided, the lender will focus on recurring revenue, revenue growth, gross margin strength, healthy customer retention, trends in adjusted cash flow and EBITDA, liquidity, leverage, and the company's ability to repay debt.

## STEP 2: VETTING LENDERS

Often a board member, equity partner, or even a large customer or vendor will provide initial introductions to lenders. You should also include regional and national lenders who are active in the ndustry on your list. There are four main areas to onsider: industry knowledge, product breadth, eople, and focus on emerging growth companies.

## INDUSTRY KNOWLEDGE

: is critical for your lending partner to have xperience and expertise in your industry, as his will ease every part of the capital-raising rocess. With this experience, lending partners vill be more supportive of market "add-backs" or mergers and acquisitions (M&A), EBITDA djustments common within an industry, and ndustry-driven one-time events. Asking lenders or credentials and references in your industry is a ood way to determine their industry knowledge.

## PRODUCT BREADTH

here are various types of debt and related roducts that lenders may offer their clients. enders should have the ability to support acility sizes from $20 million to $500 million so hat they can support the growth of the company ver a long period of time. In addition to size, ompanies should assess lenders based on the readth of the structures they can offer. Ideally, a ender will offer revenue- and cash-flow-oriented ebt facilities in addition to asset-based facilities. sset-based loans, where availability of funds governed by the size of the company's liquid ssets, can be useful structures for companies rith low to no growth. However, they are dministratively burdensome and much less calable over time for growing businesses.

nother consideration is whether or not the ender can support and underwrite transformative vents such as acquisitions, large "leveraged" ividends, or management buyouts. Further, ompanies should also assess not only the ability f lenders to offer risk-management products uch as foreign exchange or interest rate hedges ut also whether the lender understands how hose products are best utilized in your industry.

ompanies should also consider a lender's ncillary operating products, such as payment utomation or other cash management services,

which can simplify a company's treasury functions and accounting practices. A robust treasury platform could be highly beneficial to your company over time and should be able to support your growth, whether that includes adding international capabilities or integrating corporate investment services.

Some of the best debt providers also offer integrated investment banking solutions. This allows management to work with a single team, providing greater strategic leverage of that relationship over time.

## PEOPLE

A common mistake is to limit conversations only to those lenders you're already familiar with. While vetting existing relationships is a fine practice, it is important to broaden your alternatives beyond these firms to identify the best long-term partner. Companies should expect potential lenders to field a broad team of senior-level professionals throughout the process. That team should include a relationship manager and experts focused on underwriting, syndicating, and investment banking. Having access to a broader team will demonstrate a lender's expertise in your industry as well as a commitment to building a strong strategic partnership for your company.

## EMERGING GROWTH FOCUS

A final consideration in selecting a lender is to find one that focuses on emerging growth companies that are or have been at a stage similar to your own. While the biggest firms may count your largest competitor as a client, their banking needs may be in stark contrast to your own. Are the majority of a firm's clients and transactions comparable to those of your company? Will your business be a focus for them? Finding lenders that can speak to their experience and focus on companies similar to yours will ensure a stronger execution on the company's behalf.

## STEP 3: PICKING A PARTNER

After identifying, contacting, and providing the information assembled, the company should conduct a face-to-face meeting at its headquarters between interested lenders and the senior management team. Within two weeks, lenders will respond with financing views or term sheets for your evaluation.

Term sheets can vary from institution to institution. Some lenders will provide term sheets only after thoroughly vetting internally with necessary approvers of both credit and pricing. The benefit of this approach is that you know that the terms presented have a "soft approval" and if you choose to work with that lender, you will not be surprised by any major shifts during final negotiations.

Other lenders allow their teams to provide terms before conducting diligence, working through structural points with the company after the terms sheet is signed. While this can feel slightly more efficient in the short term, it can also prolong negotiations down the line if the approving team members cannot get comfortable with the company, industry, or other aspects of the transaction.

### GREATEST CAPACITY

In order to achieve the desired capacity for growth, it is best to focus on lenders who provide recurring revenue and cash-flow structures. This will allow the scalability that an emerging growth company needs over time. A typical structure would be lending on a multiple of cash flow based on adjusted EBITDA with capacity set against certain leverage points. If your company generates a material amount of recurring revenue, a structure lending against this revenue base may be appealing until cash flow generation is achieved.

### LOWEST RISK

Two components in reducing risk are flexibility and diversification. Flexibility refers to financial covenants, such as liquidity, leverage, and coverage of fixed charges. The number and

threshold levels of these covenants can affect growth initiatives if they are set too conservatively and likewise lose their risk management effectiveness for lenders if they are set too wide. Other considerations include the ability to sell assets, make distributions, and acquire businesses, all of which can be negotiated with the lender during the initial phases of diligence.

As the size of your debt facility grows over time, managing diversification risk becomes more of a focus. Diversification refers to using more than a single lender to provide your debt facilities. As the company continues to grow and utilize debt as a funding mechanism, it will be important to consider broadening your banking relationship. Most lenders realize this and as facilities grow larger they can market your facility to other lenders, creating a "syndicate," while still maintaining control over the day-to-day relationship. Typically, once a facility size exceeds $35 million, your company should consider adding other lenders to the relationship. Even if a lender emphasizes its ability to provide larger commitments during the marketing phase, companies should be wary of the power a single lender can have over a company under stressed conditions. It is therefore important to understand whether a lender has a strong syndicated debt capital markets capability, even if the use of one of those facilities is several years away.

### LOWEST COST

Building a relationship with a lead lender requires time and education on both ends. Savvy lenders will seek to educate their new clients on the holistic banking relationship, including the syndication process, cash management systems and options, the importance of a scalable loan document, and important financial attributes that may improve a company's risk profile to lenders. Many first-time borrowers will overlook this relationship building and focus on rates and fees as the primary factors in choosing a lender. However, this could hurt a borrower in the longer term. While consideration of rates and fees is important and relatively easy to understand, the addition of warrants, equity kickers, and conversion features can make comparison of term sheets difficult.

Other factors can be much more important than interest rates and fees. Our research shows the average life of a loan is approximately one-half of the time to maturity, because most transactions are refinanced for some material reason. Refinancing can be caused by many factors, including:

*IPO:* How will future public equity investors view the lender and structure?

*M&A:* What is a lender's ability to finance material acquisitions?

*Adverse performance:* How will a lender behave if a company has failed to achieve its financial forecast?

Identifying a lender that can help navigate through all these potential scenarios holds tremendous value for a borrower over the long term.

The upfront investment into the development of a thoughtful, fully negotiated set of legal agreements will not only increase flexibility for your company in the immediate deal, but it will also provide a document that should live with the company for several years and multiple debt transactions. Playing a bigger role in the early

documentation will ensure your ability to operate your company effectively within the confines of the agreement.

## REFERENCES

Ascertaining the experience and expertise of your potential lending partner in working with companies like yours is crucial for your success. Ask to speak with a lender's clients in comparable industries and with similar loan sizes. Lenders will typically show a company all of the transactions that their firm has recently completed. It is important to consider only those references that are from the same team that your company will be working with, because these individuals will ultimately drive your relationship.

## FINAL THOUGHTS

Maintaining a healthy relationship with your lending partner requires an ongoing investment of time. Monthly and quarterly financial information demonstrating compliance with the loan terms will be required, and quarterly business update meetings are recommended. As the relationship progresses, a good lending partner will proactively provide additional capital, ideas, and services. Choosing a lender with the best combination of people, industry knowledge, product breadth, and the ability to grow with your company will make the most of your investment of time and money.

# PART III

## PREPARING FOR THE NEXT CHAPTER

# 26

# GOING GLOBAL IN HIGH GROWTH MARKETS

**KPMG**

Brian Hughes, National Partner in Charge of Private Markets
   Group & National Venture Capital Co-leader

Mark Barnes, Partner in Charge of International Corridors

Phil Isom, Global Head of M&A

Businesses, including startups, are always looking for opportunities to grow. In many cases, that means expanding abroad. If your firm is considering this international option, you have some choices. Some firms may prefer establishing operations in one of the developed foreign countries (e.g., France, Germany, Ireland, Italy, Japan, the Nordic countries, United Kingdom, and Spain). These countries typically have stable governments, well-developed infrastructures, and an established business culture. Or they can look to one of the many developing countries located in Africa, Asia, South and Central America, and parts of Europe with rapidly growing economies and potential high growth markets (HGMs). This article focuses on business opportunities in these HGM countries, the challenges you may encounter, and some examples of companies that have faced and overcome these challenges.

## $600 BILLION IN INVESTMENTS

A recent KPMG LLP survey of 200 senior executives in the United States found that 86 percent view developing overseas HGMs as important to their company's strategy and growth. In fact, U.S. businesses invest over $600 billion annually in these markets. Yet more than half of this amount goes to just five countries: Mexico, Brazil, Chile, India, and South Korea. That's because, despite their enormous potential, U.S. companies consider many of these developing countries to be too risky, too unstable, and/or too corrupt. So they are skittish about investing in them.

We believe that this perception can get in the way of real opportunity. Unquestionably, many developing countries present challenges for multinational companies (MNCs) and startups alike. But there are ways to minimize these risks. This article takes a look at several developing HGM countries that the KPMG survey identified as having particular promise. {For more detailed information about these and other promising overseas markets that have been overlooked by U.S. companies, read KPMG's white paper, *Don't miss out: Recognizing opportunity in high growth markets.)*

## CHINA

China is trying to shift from a high-growth, manufacturing-based economy to one powered by consumer spending. That means MNCs should focus on what the government needs to meet domestic demand: quality and affordable healthcare and housing, improved transportation, and environmental cleanup. Many U.S. technology startups have the know-how to help China achieve its ambitious goals, but they face significant competition from Chinese domestic companies, which have been quick to embrace e-commerce and are increasingly globalizing. Currently, partnering with domestic companies may be the only way in, depending on the industry, but the results can be very lucrative.

*Case in point*: While Ford Motor Company isn't a startup, its success in the highly restricted automotive industry provides a blueprint on how both large and mid-market companies can succeed.

The Chinese government requires foreign automakers to operate through 50-50 joint ventures with domestic partners. Large, state-controlled companies typically provide the labor and government connections for the joint ventures, while MNCs provide most of the designs, engineering, and marketing. Ford entered a 50-50 joint venture in 2001 with China's largest domestic automaker. Between 2003 and the first quarter of 2015, Ford increased market share among both domestic and joint venture automakers by more than 563 percent, and it continues to grow.

## INDIA

India offers extremes of opportunity and challenge. On one hand, it's the fastest-growing major economy, with strong forex reserves, a rising middle class, and a young, educated English-speaking workforce. On the other hand, India ranks low for ease of doing business because of its bureaucratic regulatory environment.

However, over the past few years, a new pro-business government has taken steps to transform the business landscape, including increasing transparency, liberalizing industry sectors, and launching manufacturing initiatives. All of this has helped make India the # 1 U.S. foreign direct investment destination in the world.

Still, before a business makes a direct investment in India, it should understand ground-level

impediments—such as red tape, lack of infrastructure, and changing tax and regulatory rules—and formulate a long-term strategy for dealing with them.

*Case in point:* One foreign online retail company recognized that it would need to radically revise its strategy to accommodate the wild-west chaos of India. Management realized that its methodical and precise playbook wouldn't work in a country with inadequate infrastructure, opaque rules, and a primitive retailing structure.

Leadership understood that it didn't need computer scientists as much as personnel who weren't afraid to take risks. So they built smaller warehouses near customers, established informal drop-off locations, navigated clogged motorways with motorcycles, and perfected backpacks for delivery personnel. They also figured out how to deliver packages to addresses that were only vaguely defined. These improvisations allowed the company to succeed in the growing online retail market.

## INDONESIA

This historically protectionist country recently removed 45 business lines from the Negative Investment List and began allowing foreign companies to operate in those areas without restriction. Indonesia also launched a massive infrastructure program to speed up commerce among the country's 13,500 islands. While Indonesia can be one of the most rewarding and profitable countries in which to operate in Southeast Asia, there still can be regulatory hurdles that need to be overcome and a risk that local businesses could demand the government reinstate some restrictions.

*Case in point:* A North American manufacturer of infrastructure had a significant business relationship with a large U.S. natural resources company located in Indonesia. But because of Indonesian regulations, the manufacturer needed to have its product manufactured in Indonesia (rather than in North America). This requirement could have been a roadblock to the manufacturer's ability to do business in Indonesia. But by working with its U.S. customer and drawing on the many business relationships that the customer had developed during its years of operating in Indonesia, the North American manufacturer was able to quickly identify and secure a local partner. As result, it was able to begin manufacturing product in Indonesia, meeting the regulatory requirements, satisfying the needs of its customer, and keeping the government happy by generating local job and tax revenues.

The lesson here is that you sometimes need to think outside the box, and work with people or companies that have already developed contacts in the developing country to comply with government requirements.

## NIGERIA

Nigeria has the largest economy in Africa and is the key driver of international trade in West Africa. In 2014–2015, it was the third fastest growing economy in the world. But with oil representing 70 percent of government revenue and 90 percent of export revenue, the fall in crude oil prices resulted in the projected growth rate dropping to 2.3 percent in 2016, the lowest rate in 15 years.[6] Still, the government is committed to going ahead with plans to increase capital spending by 30 percent this year to build up its infrastructure. It's also cracking down on corruption and moving ahead with plans to make the country less dependent on oil. Foreign companies planning on investing in Nigeria stand to benefit from these moves.

*Case in point:* In 2014, the Coca-Cola Company faced sluggish sales due, in part, to concerns that its sugary drinks were contributing to obesity and diabetes. It felt the need to expand beyond its core soda bands. At the same time, Coke was increasingly targeting Africa for growth, announcing that it would invest $17 billion between 2010 and 2020 and singled out Nigeria as a country with great growth potential. Despite a history of political and government instability, Nigeria is one of the

most culturally diverse societies in the world. So in 2016, Coke bought a 40 percent stake in Nigeria's largest juice maker, Chi Ltd., which also sells evaporated milk, drinkable yogurt, and snacks. (It plans to buy the remaining 60 percent within three years.) Coke is now well positioned for a post-oil-boom market. And partnering with Chi Ltd. also means that Coke can broaden its portfolio and introduce new products to market. By doing its due diligence and weighing the pros and cons of investing in Nigeria, Coke found that risks of political and government instability were outweighed by the potential rewards.

## SAUDI ARABIA

The fall in oil prices has forced Saudi Arabia to confront two big issues: the country's over-dependence on oil and its massive public spending. The government is encouraging foreign investment in nearly all economic sectors, with priority given to transportation, education, health, information and communications technology, life sciences, and energy.[7] Still, the kingdom's fundamentalist Islamic culture and Sharia-based judicial system present obstacles to even modest reforms. On the other hand, the country has an ample local talent pipeline that foreign companies can train and employ to staff their operations.

*Case in point:* Honeywell has been delivering technology solutions to Saudi Arabian industries and consumers since the 1970s. One challenge has been recruiting workers with the necessary advanced technical skills to staff its systems, electrical, computer, and chemical engineering areas. This is due, in part, to Saudi restrictions on the number of "foreign" workers a company can employ. The other factor is the lack of properly trained Saudi workers. Only about 20 percent of college graduates major in technical and scientific fields; the vast majority major in humanities and social sciences.[8] In 2009, Honeywell began offering enhanced technical support, regional training services, and research and development collaboration with Saudi universities. As a result, by the end of 2015, Honeywell was able to employ more than 600 Saudi workers. And it's continuing to recruit and develop Saudi talent in engineering and technical roles. Honeywell found that the investment in education for the native Saudi workforce has paid off in multiple ways. It's allowed Honeywell to (1) meet the government's employment restrictions, (2) acquire qualified and loyal talent, and (3) engender good will with the government.

## SOUTH AFRICA

South Africa has plenty of challenges: political uncertainty, electricity shortages, skills gaps, labor unrest, and economic and social disparities. Yet the county also provides lucrative opportunities for foreign companies. Despite the global commodity price crunch, the country still has a wealth of natural resources. And the struggling economy makes the government more receptive to granting favorable investment conditions to foreign companies. Still, South Africa has a host of complex laws and regulatory measures that must be accounted for.

*Case in point:* In 2011, Walmart acquired Massmart, one of the largest wholesalers and retailers on the African continent. The acquisition needed to be approved by South Africa's antitrust authorities, which Walmart anticipated. But it didn't anticipate the onerous tax compliance requirements that impacted the non-South African workers it brought into the country on a temporary basis to help manage the transition. Under South Africa's tax rules, temporary workers who spent even a few days in the country were required to file complete tax returns. But with the help of KPMG's High Growth Markets practice, Walmart was able to arrange things so that only a dozen or so employees out of the hundreds of assignees each year were required to file full South African tax returns. According to Walmart, these efforts, while costly, were important and necessary ones. As the Walmart example illustrates, there are times it makes sense to bring in a third party to help advise you on how to comply with complex tax and regulatory requirements in the most cost-effective and time-efficient manner.

## VIETNAM

With Vietnam's participation in recent trade agreements, the country is tilting decisively toward the United States. Vietnam is eager to welcome U.S. investors, but companies have been slow to take advantage of the opportunities. As China's economy slows and labor becomes more expensive, Vietnam is becoming the go-to place for manufacturing, particularly in textiles and electronics. However, there's a need to educate and develop skills among its labor force, particularly skills for modern industry and innovation.[9] This can be a challenge to potential U.S investors that are considering opening operations in Vietnam.

*Case in point:* Intel, headquartered in Santa Clara, California, was one of the first high-tech companies to build a factory in Vietnam. Intel understood from the outset that it needed to help develop a workforce with appropriate technology skills. To date, it has invested over $22 million for education, notably in the Higher-Engineering Education Alliance Program (HEEAP), the first-ever public-private partnership in education and in the Intel Vietnam Study Abroad Program. As with Honeywell in Saudi Arabia, Intel found that the investment in education and training of the native workforce has resulted in multiple benefits. It's helped Vietnamese students achieve higher education degrees and employment opportunities. What's more, in 2014, Intel announced the first ever "made-in-Vietnam" central processing unit (CPU), and the company is on track to produce 80 percent of its CPUs for the world market in Vietnam.

## 12 TIPS FOR INVESTMENT SUCCESS

Before a company makes an investment in a potentially high growth market, there are a number of factors to consider and steps to take that can increase the likelihood of success.

The following are 12 guidelines for spotting—and overcoming—challenges that companies may encounter along the way. Keep in mind that these guidelines apply regardless of whether the HGM is a developed or developing country. However, they are particularly critical with respect to expanding into developing countries.

*See the local country through HGM eyes:* The lack of cultural understanding is a top reason for failure in HGMs. This is especially relevant now as executives are looking to a broader range of emerging and frontier markets than ever before. Consider establishing a long-term local community presence and have local talent help guide important initiatives.

*Blend local and U.S. leadership:* Ensure that you have strong local HGM leaders. Also, leverage local managers and market experience while still maintaining U.S. leadership. Develop strong communication between local country employees and host countries, and develop strong mentor-mentee relationships. Train local talent in core business operations so they can take higher positions as soon as possible.

*Be patient:* Take a long-term view when considering the profitability of your investment. This includes taking the time to understand potential partners and the overall business environment.

*Build a flexible business model:* Make sure your business model can respond quickly to emerging competitive threats and the unique needs of individual HGMs. Observe how local HGM companies adapt to changes so you'll know how to react appropriately when the time comes.

*Develop a strong employee retention program:* Provide competitive compensation and benefits, opportunities for advancement, training, and programs that create optimism and a desire to stay at the company. This applies both to workers native to the HGM as well as to "foreign" workers you need to bring in. If available, hire employees who are already comfortable working in a U.S. company and pay them a premium.

*Raise capital for the long term:* Assemble enough capital to support your long-term view. Adequate

capital can also help you develop an adaptable business model as well as attract and retain the right talent.

*Understand the business environment:* Audit the business environment prior to risking technology and capital. Make sure that management and the board have the proper experience to provide international oversight.

*Retain a local trusted adviser:* A local trusted adviser can offer invaluable knowledge on a variety of issues. This includes regulatory and tax advice as well as help in dealing with local government officials. Work closely with your adviser to develop a thorough understanding of the political, cultural, legal, and business environments.

*Learn how to deal with government:* It's essential to learn and understand what a specific HGM government needs. Build relationships through the help of a local adviser. Retain local or market experts to help manage the different government relationships and the bureaucracy.

*Establish a robust anticorruption policy:* Maintain a non-negotiable set of global ethical standards and provide compliance training throughout all levels of your organization. Partner with a local adviser who has longtime operations in the HGM and who shares your company's values. Clearly communicate to local operations that there is to be no compromise on these rules, and reinforce this message with periodic follow ups.

*Spend time observing foreign operations:* Take the time to visit foreign operations. Experience the culture, meet the people, study the operations, and understand what management is struggling with. This can provide you and your executives with invaluable insight into your HGM operations and what you need to do.

*Establish an exit strategy up front:* Develop an exit strategy to leave a country if a certain level of net profits is not achieved by a certain time. It is sometimes more difficult to exit a country once you've "broken ground" than it is to establish operations there in the first place. Companies must be clear eyed about market entry or foreign acquisitions and know when and how to walk away.

## CONCLUSION

Expanding your business into high-growth markets has its risks but also can hold great potential for growth and profit. What's more, as we've explored in this section, there are great opportunities for success in some lesser known and less developed countries considered to be HGMs. While some of these countries may, at first glance, appear too risky, too unstable, and/or too corrupt, there are steps you can take that minimize these potential hazards. We've included examples illustrating challenges that multinational firms have encountered while expanding into HGMs, and how they've successfully addressed these issues.

Granted, the companies in our examples are international giants. However, the challenges they face typically are the same or similar to the ones that large and mid-market entrepreneurial firms would encounter. So before you expand into a HGM, consider partnering with one of the established companies with experience in

that space, or at least consult with them to get a better idea of what to expect. Doing so can greatly increase your chances of success in both the short and long term.

## REFERENCES

1. *The Economic Times,* Dec 24, 2015.

2. *The Indian Express,* Apr 4, 2016.

3. "Ease of doing business in India." World Bank Group, August 30, 2016.

4. makeinindia.com.

5. Rapoza, Kenneth. "U.S. leads top 15 countries investing in India." *Forbes,* November 15, 2014.

6. Giokos, Eleni. "Africa's top 4 economies are in trouble," *CNN Money US,* June 9, 2016.

7. "2015 Investment Climate Statement - Saudi Arabia," Bureau of Economic and Business Affairs, May 2015.

8. House, Karen Elliott (2012). *On Saudi Arabia: Its People, Past, Religion, Fault Lines and Future.* Knopf. p. 111.

9. "Vietnam overview." Worldbank.org, August 31, 2016.

# 27

# ENTREPRENEURSHIP IN LARGER COMPANIES

**Harvard Business School**

William R. Kerr, Professor of Business Administration

Entrepreneurship in large and established companies is vital for their long-term success. Incumbent firms face many challenges ranging from global competition to digitization. In times past, being caught flat-footed might have set a company back several years, but it could recover. Today, the threats are existential in nature, and competition can emerge quickly and from the places one least expects. Successful incumbents must ensure that they do not become self-complacent but instead look to renew themselves through corporate entrepreneurship (sometimes also called intrapreneurship).

Many books and articles document the overall importance of corporate entrepreneurship and associated business renewal, and many advisors consider the important perspective of the CEO looking across the whole company. An example is *Leading Breakthrough Innovation in Established Companies* (Harvard Business School Press #5272) by Lynda Applegate and William Kerr, which provides a longer reference set for the CEO and corporate-wide perspective.

This chapter uses a different lens—it focuses instead on the perspective of a middle-to-upper-level manager contemplating a potential assignment to lead an internal venture in a large company. Befitting this series, we build lists of important considerations that this manager should evaluate. These lists are not exhaustive, but they offer corporate leaders a starting point for a careful due diligence and action plan around new ventures.

## 1. ASSESSING THE IMPORTANCE OF THE OPPORTUNITY AND FIT

Leading a new venture in a large corporation is not for everyone, and decisions to pursue these opportunities require careful consideration by managers and executives.

There are potential advantages to leading a new venture in a larger company:

- *Excitement*: Many venture opportunities provide cutting-edge exposure to an industry's trends and latest business models. This can be an exciting change of pace from a career focused on operational efficiencies, and it can be a very good experience for executives who think that they may want to start their own business one day or move to a smaller, growth-focused firm.

- *General management experience*: For executives coming from functional areas or junior roles within established business lines, these roles as leaders of new ventures can offer general management and leadership responsibilities much earlier in a large-company career than otherwise possible.

- *Visibility to senior leadership*: The CEO and executive team should be taking a guiding role in the exploration opportunities pursued by their corporation, and managers who take on the task of leading a new venture may benefit from exposure and regular contact with senior management, boosting a career substantially.

There are also potential disadvantages to leading a new venture in a larger company:

- *What happens if it does not work?*: Success is great, but the pursuit of these new opportunities often identifies that the business idea won't work out. The best companies know how to separate the quality of the leader from the results of the experiment. If, however, you are not in one of these companies, be cautious about the career risk involved if the company confuses project failure with leadership failure.

- *Turf wars and political issues*: A flip side to senior-level visibility is that you are exposed to more senior-level issues, which could include turf wars over resources and the right path for the company to take forward. If you are contemplating an assignment that could directly cannibalize the core existing business of the company, these issues may become especially acute.

Key questions to ask:

- *Is the CEO, board of directors, and senior management really really really (I mean really) behind this work?* Many senior leaders say they want corporate ventures, but their support in reality is on par with their support for world peace. This is a very dangerous misalignment. The best companies have clearly aligned

processes for new ventures, a common understanding of the entrepreneurial leader's roles and responsibilities, and unmistakable senior support. If your company is less mature with respect to these elements, you need to at least closely observe the CEO and senior leaders to make certain they truly are ready to put their money (and time) where their mouth is

- *How well do I handle uncertainty and limited resources?* Great new opportunities bring lots of uncertainty; given this uncertainty, resources tend to be quite expensive, in short supply, and must be closely managed. Make sure that you are a leader who can handle the uncertainty and also navigate a world with fewer resources than an established operation procures. Not only do you need to be okay with the fact that fewer people will be reporting to you in the new role, but you also need to be even more capable of using as few resources as possible to get the job done.

## 2. NEGOTIATING THE TERMS OF THE ASSIGNMENT

There is no one-size-fits-all format to new ventures, and the best large companies tailor the management and governance of each new venture to the venture's specific setting. It is vital to recognize that your bargaining power is at its strongest point before you agree to the job, so make sure you get the appropriate issues on the table.

Key pieces for your venture:

- *Budgets:* You need appropriate financial resources to investigate your opportunity. You need flexibility in allocating these resources because the path ahead is very uncertain, but you also need firm commitments of the resources. Recognize that it always costs much more than initially expected! Aim for a sweet spot where you have commitments that are large enough to conduct your investigation but also small enough to not be subject to objections by other executives and possible clawbacks.

- *People*: Talent is paramount. If someone is essential, get the person's name (or description) on the table from the start. On the flip side, recognize too that a large team can be quite unwieldy for a new initiative and that your goal is not to build an empire. You want a Special Operations Forces team that brings together very effective skillsets to accomplish a tightly defined mission.

- *Time to investigate*: Experimentation requires time to find the right solution. While you will want to report back regularly and run fast iterative cycles (as described further below), you need to negotiate a sufficient time horizon for your project to meaningfully investigate multiple paths. Remember, it always takes longer than expected, and most established operations of a large company are managed with short-term expectations. Negotiate for yourself sufficient runway to accomplish takeoff.

- *Access to critical resources*: Many ventures are created in large companies with a belief that they will leverage an existing asset (e.g., the corporate brand, customer database, distribution network, etc.). This synergy always looks fantastic on paper, and it really is the key advantage that ventures in large companies can have over true startups. Remember, however, that these assets are controlled by other people in the large company, not by you, and thus access is not guaranteed! Set expectations about the critical assets, including what your venture must prove to gain access to them and how access will be granted.

- *Anticipated future path of venture*: A sad (but common) outcome of the new venture development process in large companies is that the new business works (yes!) but there is misalignment about what happens next: integration or spinout, independence or cross-selling, etc. You can't nail this future path down the way you can nail down next year's budget, but it is important to understand the default early plan and to make sure that you have the resources ready to pursue that path.

Key pieces for you personally:

- *How your performance will be assessed:* Perhaps the biggest mandate for corporate entrepreneurs is to define in advance what "success" means for them. In very uncertain waters, many ventures fail even when the manager did everything right, and you want your performance measured by how well you did the job versus whether or not this particular venture happens to work.

- *Compensation structures:* Compensation programs for corporate entrepreneurs are quite varied. In some settings, there is very little difference from the pay structure of other executives, especially in settings where the company's philosophy emphasizes corporate-wide results for everyone. In other settings, corporate entrepreneurs have very high-powered incentives and compensation tied to the objectives of their venture (e.g., performance targets, shadow stock).

- *Reentry points after the assignment:* Some star employees negotiate for themselves in advance what their role will be in the large company after the venture assignment is over (especially if the venture fails).

## 3. MANAGEMENT OF THE PROJECT

Many of the chapters in this volume about entrepreneurship apply to corporate ventures, because the corporate entrepreneur needs to navigate extreme uncertainty and limited resources just like startup entrepreneurs. We do not seek to repeat all of those lessons, but instead highlight a few particular ones that are very important in corporate settings.

Key pieces for your venture:

- *Utilize lean testing methodologies:* Take advantage of the lean testing tools that are popular for startups (e.g., *The Lean Startup* by Eric Ries). Not only will these make your internal venture more effective, but they can also be powerful for corporate purposes. For example, when working with the leadership to define your performance metrics, you can directly use the business hypotheses that your venture needs to test—how rapidly and effectively can you and your team test these hypotheses? Success becomes less about whether or not the idea works but how quickly and cost effectively you deliver the key pieces of information to senior leaders.

- *Focus on biggest assumptions:* Every new opportunity brings many assumptions, and corporate entrepreneurs have the greatest impact when they can resolve the really big uncertainties, especially when they are "deal killer" risks. The problem is that managers tend to test what they know how to test—that is, leaders with marketing backgrounds tend to first test customer and sales features, while those with engineering backgrounds naturally start with technical features. Prioritize the most important pieces of information, not the ones easiest or most comfortable for you to consider.

- *Be wary of fear of failure:* Like a bad penny, the fear of failure can creep back into a team, even if all of the team members agree at the start to pursue the idea aggressively and with a focus on understanding whether the idea will work. This is especially true in large companies where there is a limited history for new ventures and a dominant culture around execution of existing proven businesses that are the company's core operations. Corporate entrepreneurs must guard against reverting in this way through team culture and task management. For example, showing the team a workflow for a new product design that allocates time and budget for four product iterations with customers helps establish the expectation that the first tests will not be perfect products but are early trials to gain feedback.

- *Respect but also minimize your parent company's requirements:* Internal ventures can be stifled by structures and processes of their parent company that are designed for large and established businesses (e.g., IT system requirements, decision-making procedures). Identify what can be minimized early on to allow faster progress. On the other hand, recognize legitimate corporate factors that need to be addressed even

though inconvenient (e.g., corporate-wide risk compliance).

- *Leverage external collaborations and partnerships:* The boundaries of innovative large companies are porous and permit you to harness the capabilities of others, ranging from university collaborations to joint-development partnerships with other large companies to accelerator programs that can grab the attention and insights of local startup entrepreneurs. Corporate entrepreneurs must harness these external resources as effectively as they harness internal ones. Avoid the mindset of making internal resources always the default, because your fiercest competitors are not doing so!

- *Search for objective advice:* If you have organized your performance evaluation to focus on successful execution of the business idea, your job will include objectively assessing whether or not the business development tests are promising and warrant continued investment. This assessment may not be easy for your team, and so consider how you can harness those outside your team, either inside your parent company or among external advisors familiar with the venture's domain, to provide unfiltered and objective advice about the venture's progress and prospects.

Corporate entrepreneurship is a vital capacity for incumbent firms to develop and master in today's turbulent business environment. If they are behind on this front, incumbents need to begin today the development of this skillset and the platform for new growth opportunities for the company in the decade ahead. For individual leaders, corporate ventures can be as rewarding and powerful as the creation of a new startup company. To realize this potential, managers need to successfully evaluate the venture concept and existing senior executive support, negotiate the terms for the venture and for their own performance assessment, and manage the venture with the best of startup tools and the power of their parent company. Managers that do this well can find these opportunities a powerful lever for career advancement.

# 28

# IS THERE A *THERE* THERE? WHAT STARTUPS AND ENTREPRENEURS NEED TO KNOW ABOUT REAL ESTATE

**CBRE Group, Inc.**

Lenny Beaudoin, Senior Managing Director

Georgia Collins, Senior Managing Director

Nina Charnotskaia, Director

Real estate can be a dynamic and flexible asset for your organization, capable of driving business performance, strengthening your brand, and bringing together a community of people. Taking the time to define the strategic role real estate will play in your business from the onset will set your organization up for success in the long run, creating a physical and experiential platform that helps you support your most important asset: your people.

The stage of growth you are in plays a huge role in how you think about your workplace and the level of investment you should be making in space. With that in mind, this chapter is based on the common stages organizations go through as they scale.

## PHASE I: THE MOVE FROM (GARAGE/HOME/ COFFEE SHOP) TO COWORKING
### POPULATION 1 TO 3, GROWING TO 10 TO 15

As your company grows from one or two employees into a small team, so will your demand for space. Suddenly, a home office or a coffee shop is no longer a viable option. While you could have everyone work remotely, the agility and pervasive collaboration required to build your business is best supported when you are together. But with growth uncertain and investments prioritized toward growing your business, the ideas of signing a long-term lease, buying furniture, and investing in equipment all seem inordinate.

### How Do You Provide an Effective Workplace While Focusing Your Investments on Growth?

Shared workspaces serve as an effective entry point into office space. The shared workspace model aggregates demand for space across multiple tenants and in turn offers flexible, short-term contracts in lieu of leases. By sharing space, tenants gain access to a broader variety of resources such as meeting rooms and spaces that support a range of work style preferences, as well as the infrastructure, technology, and services.

Coworking environments take shared workspace models a step further by placing a greater emphasis on community and experience. In these models tenants are considered members, with access to a range of services, curated events, and professional development opportunities. Community is truly a benefit, and by investing in experience, coworking provides a place where entrepreneurs build networks and leverage relationships with other members to catalyze business growth.

## What to Look for in a Coworking Experience

Experience varies broadly by coworking environment and membership level. Most coworking spaces are designed to encourage interaction and collisions, resulting in opportunities for members to network, share learnings, capabilities, and resources. When looking for space, consider the primary role an office will play for your team:

- **Will you be doing all or most of your work from the coworking space?**

  Look for environments that provide on-demand access to individual spaces and that support a range of workstyles. Consider support for quiet and focused work, availability and types of collaborative spaces, and potential added costs associated with accessing space not included in your membership.

- **Will you use the space primarily to collaborate as a team?**

  Look for membership that provides access to a private team space. Consider the flexibility of the space: look for writable surfaces, large screens that allow you to share information digitally, and the ability to arrange the space in a way that works for your team.

- **Will you be connecting with customers, teammates, or partners remotely?**

  Consider how well the environment supports virtual collaboration through video conferencing, acoustically private meeting rooms, and wireless network bandwidth.

- **Are you still building the business and could use help?**

  Many coworking memberships include access to discount or free business services and professional development opportunities targeted at entrepreneurs and startups. These can range from HR support to web development and may be supported through staff available on site.

# PHASE II: FROM COWORKING TO YOUR OWN OFFICE
## POPULATION 10 TO 15, GROWING TO 80 TO 100

You are growing. Fast. You may only be 10 or 15 people today but you've got plans to be 80 to 100 in the next year or two. Your shared office space has worked well up to this point, but now you're entering a new phase: you need more space to grow and you want more control over how you configure, operate, and brand it. It's time for an office of your own.

## Step 1: Choose a Location

Although choosing a location may seem a fairly straightforward decision, this is an important step in your long-term real estate strategy. Most organizations don't stray far from where they first put down roots. So while it may be tempting to choose an office location that minimizes your commute, it is important to also consider the following:

- *Attraction and retention of talent:* Consider whom you are looking to attract and where they will be coming from. Commute times, particularly in talent-rich markets, can and do impact the decisions people make to join particular companies.

- *The neighborhood:* Often cast as the suburbs vs. the city conundrum, it is important to consider what is around you. Does the surrounding area offer the kinds of amenities and services your people will want and need during the day and/or before or after work (restaurants, fitness centers, drugstores, etc.)? If not, you may eventually need to provide some of these amenities/services internally. Is this kind of offering (and associated expense) part of who you are or would you rather rely on other businesses to provide it?

- *Room for growth:* Once you've settled into a particular community or neighborhood and your people establish commute patterns and connections within that vicinity, it's unlikely you'll want to stray very far. Ask your broker about how likely the neighborhoods/areas you are considering will be able to accommodate you as you grow.

## Step 2: Define Your Footprint and Organize Your Space

Your first office represents the start of your real estate and workplace strategy. How you occupy, configure, and assign space, and the types of amenities and services you provide, will establish a set of baseline expectations. Getting these right in the beginning ensures that you'll be able to scale responsibly later without being in the awkward position of having to "take things away."

- **How much space you do you need?**

  Determining how much space you need isn't always easy, especially given the volatility most startups experience in hiring. The best rule of thumb is to use a rentable square feet (RSF)/person range and apply it to your three- to five-year headcount projection. (See Box 1 for common ranges by size of company.) While it is good to build a cushion into your estimates, don't be too aggressive. A lot can change in a five-year period. The hurdles that come with faster-than-anticipated growth are far easier to clear than the costs of carrying too much space and low morale associated with empty offices. Your vacancy should fall in the range of 5 percent to 8 percent on top of your three-year growth projection. For greater flexibility, talk to your broker about negotiating expansion rights into your lease.

- **What kind of space do you need?**

  The best way to determine what kind of space you need is to think about how you work and/

BOX 1 Defining Your Footprint: How Much Space Do You Need?

Most startup organizations target a range of 100–165 USF*/seat**. Smaller startups tend to be on the lower end of this range because they have fewer requirements for large conferencing spaces and/or amenities. More established startups tend to fall on the higher end of this range as they hit headcount thresholds that make it more reasonable and desirable to bring conferencing, training, and employee services and amenities in-house.

*USF (usable square feet) is the actual space you occupy from wall to wall. It does not include the common areas of a building such as lobbies, restrooms, stairwells, storage rooms, or shared hallways. RSF (rentable square feet) is calculated by adding the USF to a pro-rata share of building common areas. Pro-rata means that tenants pay for these common areas in proportion to the amount of space they lease in the building.
**For startups, it is best to consider seats rather than people because the number of seats translates to how many people can be accommodated.

or how you'd like your people to work. Do your people work alone or in teams? What is the average size of a team and how regularly does the makeup of a team change? Are people's work patterns largely similar from one day to the next or is there a high degree of variability in the work process? How do your people communicate with one another and those outside your organization? How do you gather as a community? How do you recharge?

Organize your space around the answers to these questions, starting from the perspective of the individual employee and working your way out:

- The size of your desks should be defined by what happens there. If your work is paper intensive, you may need more desk space. But if your work is mostly digital, the size of a desk will likely be defined by the size, number, and configuration of your monitors. Don't oversize individual workspace—it just means less space somewhere else.

- The amount and type of collaboration space you need will be determined by the frequency with which you meet, the size of your meetings, and the tools you need to collaborate effectively. Most meetings tend to be small and impromptu. A greater number of smaller spaces will likely provide more utility than a smaller number of large spaces. Ensure your enclosed space is truly acoustically private. Spaces that give the illusion of privacy but don't actually provide it are of little use to anyone.

- Ensure choice—individuals have different work patterns and work preferences. By providing a range of places from which work can be done, you provide employees with access to space that fits their tasks and personal work style preferences most effectively. In turn, people feel more productive and better supported by the organization.

- Plan your community space to be attractive and multifunctional. No one will spend time in a windowless breakroom. Position your community space for impact, making it a place that people will gravitate to throughout the day. By making it multifunctional, your community space can serve both as a social space and as an alternative workspace.

## Step 3: Furnish, Equip, and Brand

Furniture can be a huge cost when you make the first move into your new space. It's tempting to go the IKEA route and just as tempting to make huge investments into high-end office lines. The answer lies somewhere in between: make every dollar count and spend on the things that matter, not what will get your office photograph in a magazine. A few "do's and don'ts" to keep in mind:

- **Do** invest in the things that matter most to your day-to-day work. This likely means a super-fast and reliable Wi-Fi connection, dual monitors at your workstations, larger monitors in your meeting rooms, ergonomic chairs, and sit-stand desks.

- **Don't** build-in flexibility by putting everything on wheels. True flexibility comes with enabling people to move, not furniture. Workstations on wheels will just create fire and safety hazards (think of all the cables) and will not scale.

- **Do** experiment with the products and services that are free or come at a nominal fee. The latest videoconferencing equipment will be obsolete before your lease term is up. Instead, consider the tools you use to communicate in daily life, such as text messaging, FaceTime/Skype/Google Hangouts, and messenger apps such as Slack, and look for ways that they can scale to support your team.

- **Don't** buy too much "soft seating." Everyone likes the idea of meeting on a couch until they have to sit through a meeting on a couch. Comfortable seating is good and has a place in your office, but it shouldn't replace the functional seating you need to get real work done.

- **Do** provide good coffee and at least some free snacks. Breaks are the best times to create and foster community. Don't miss that opportunity by forcing people out of the office in pursuit of a decent cup of coffee or quick snack.

- **Don't** paint your walls in your company colors and call it branding. Instead, consider how you can display your product or service, the evolution of your thinking, and/or showcase your work in progress. These efforts will convey your brand far more effectively than a bowl of branded chocolates on the table in your reception area.

- **Do** understand that how you allocate and fit out space will speak volumes about what you value. If you say you value transparency, ensure that people are visible. If you value collaboration, invest in space that supports it.

## PHASE III: FROM ONE FLOOR TO TWO OR MORE
### POPULATION 100 TO 250, GROWING TO 200 TO 400

By the time you hit a population of 200, your people will likely be spread across two or more floors and most will have defined roles and specialties. Gone are the days when one person wore ten hats and when knowledge was transferred almost by osmosis.

While growth and expansion of this kind is certainly a sign of success, it can also create new and sometimes unwelcome changes to how work gets done:

- As people begin to specialize and departments or business units take shape to tackle core business functions, silos can more easily form. The division of people across multiple floors or buildings can exacerbate this by breaking down informal communication channels.

- As their span of control widens, leaders in the organization will begin to travel more regularly, leaving underutilized space and direct reports who require more intentional connection to business goals.

- As teams become more distributed, the number of formal meetings will likely increase to accommodate remote participants, placing greater demand on enclosed meeting rooms with audiovisual equipment.

- As authority is delegated to more people, the population of people managers will increase, thus increasing the demand for private space and decreasing the amount of "white space" in calendars across the organization.

There are a number of ways your workplace strategy can help you combat (or conversely, exacerbate) the challenges inherent with these changes. Consider the following:

- *Density is not a bad word.* Density is what makes cities vibrant, exciting places. The same can be true of your workplace. Don't be afraid to increase your density; just do it wisely. Consider how space can be shared rather than shrunk.

- *What works for 10 people doesn't necessarily work for 100 (or more).* Behaviors and relationships that happened organically will now require more intention. Consider how information is shared, mentorship is supported, and business goals are permeated throughout the organization. Define clear roles for community and business champions.

- *Invest in growing your community.* As you scale, it won't happen as naturally as it did

when you were all 15 people in the same room together. Helping people build and maintain networks within your organization is a critical part of employee engagement. Allocate, provision, and activate space that people are drawn to.

- *Establish clear norms and protocols.* These help to reinforce community and help individuals and teams come together around a common set of goals.

## PHASE IV: FROM ONE LOCATION TO MANY
### POPULATION 200 TO 400+

As your organization continues to grow, you are likely to expand geographically. New locations are an opportunity to be closer to customers, access a bigger talent pool, and expand brand presence. It is time to think of your office as a network of places, all working together as one platform for your employees. How will experience be consistent and reflect you as an organization? And how will the sites be distinct and reflect the work being done there? How will you preserve or reignite your culture as you scale?

Once again, the right location is key, but an added variable is the *purpose* of the new site. Locating a call center in a prime downtown space may give you brand presence but at a significant labor cost increase. Finding the right labor market is essential—missing the mark can lead to long-term wage inflation and significant competition for the best talent. This is a good time to leverage brokerage services that provide in-house labor and location analytics services and can help you target sites that meet strategic needs.

Depending on your business model and organizational structure, the new site may fall into one of two (or even both) categories: regional or functional.

**Regional** sites represent the business in a specific region—think United States regional HQ or San Francisco office. They serve as brand beacons in the region, providing closer access to partners and customers, and housing a variety of functions. These sites require access to a diverse talent pool that supports the broad range of roles.

**Functional** sites are home to specific business units or functions, such as R&D, sales, customer service. Where the regional site may serve as a hub, these are the spokes focused on serving a particular aspect of the business.

You may also consider a return to coworking as a way to grow and test new markets and/or incubate new products/services without significant infrastructure investment. The collisions and networking opportunities coworking provides are just as invaluable to an established brand as they are to a startup. Readily available coworking sites also mean you can grow quickly, establishing the team without waiting for the new lease and build-out of space.

While each location in your portfolio will serve its unique purpose, the overall experience should consistently reflect your values. These three strategies can help you drive a more consistent experience:

- *Service is the most flexible amenity.* You can scale it appropriately to each site and target the specific needs of the local population. By making the employee experience a central element of your strategy, you can reduce a "haves and have-nots" experience that is common as organizations scale.

- *Keep space standards and protocols flexible.* Specific site purpose and the work done there might require some adjustment, but creating guidelines for planning and space types will help the experience feel consistent.

- *Integrate brand as the common variable across all sites.* Brand can be integrated in ways that are tangible and abstract—events, interactions, even signature snacks that are available at every office. Consider how you integrate and celebrate both company culture and local culture, working with your local teams to find balance between the two.

## IN SUMMARY

Real estate is not the domain of mature companies alone. The smartest startups consider it an enabler of their business and a benefit to their people. When treated as a strategic tool, your workplace can enable your people, nurture your culture, and promote your brand. When sidelined as an inconvenient but necessary expense, your workplace can hinder your ability to attract, retain, and properly support talent. Getting the foundational elements right early on—a location people can easily access, an environment that supports the way you want people to work, branding, services and events that reflect your culture—will serve you well as you scale.

# 29

# ACT PUBLIC, STAY PRIVATE: BEST PRACTICES FOR PRIVATE COMPANIES

**Ipreo**

Charlie Young, Executive Vice President and Managing Director

## SHIFTING SENTIMENT AMONG PRIVATE COMPANY FOUNDERS

A significant disruption is occurring in today's capital markets, driven by a simple fact: private companies are staying private longer. During the height of the dot.com boom, a typical company may have stayed private for just over three years before tapping the public markets. Indeed, the initial public offering was the aspiration of the entrepreneur as the best possible outcome. That sentiment is no longer true. Today, it is not uncommon to spend 10+ years as a private institution, refining business models, taking on additional capital, and generating significant revenue before going through an IPO process. Stoking the flames of disruption, U.S. IPO proceeds in 2016 were $20.1 billion, a 54 percent decline from the average of the past 10 years (Figure 1), according to data compiled by Ipreo. Finally, through a combination of various factors, the number of listed companies has fallen to 3,700 in 2015, roughly half the record high of 7,322 in 1996 and more than 1,000 fewer than in 1975.

## WHAT IS CAUSING THE SHIFT IN SENTIMENT?

Founders and CEOs are making the decision to operate as a private company longer for two primary reasons. First, companies want to avoid the significant challenges associated with the public markets, whether it is the cost associated with IPOs, ongoing disclosure requirements the threat of activist investors, or the short-term performance focus that public markets seem to incentivize. Over the last 10 years, fees associated with an IPO have remained flat, at about 6.5 percent to 7.0 percent, which means companies would look to pay about $7 million for every $100 million raised. Included in those fees are costs associated with achieving initial regulatory compliance which, according to surveys compiled by the SEC, average $2.5 million. More importantly, the ongoing cost associated with remaining compliant is estimated to be $1.5 million per year. Beyond cost, regulation also forces a level of disclosure that, in the view of many entrepreneurs, compromises the competitive edge, which is inherent in privacy. Meanwhile, the number of activist investor campaigns against public companies has seen a drastic increase over the past 15 years, many of which have resulted in director-level turnover at the company. According to FactSet SharkRepellent (Figure 2), 2015 saw 15 activist campaigns against mega cap and large

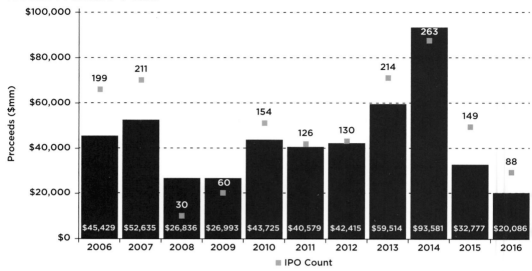

FIGURE 1 Annual IPO Stats

cap companies that were successful in attaining board seats.

Secondly, companies are staying private longer because it has never been easier. Regulation is accommodating, and while the supply of capital is increasing, the demand for that capital is decreasing. New companies, especially tech-focused companies, have a decreasing reliance on physical assets because they are able to outsource critical capital requirements into the

cloud. A significant result of this "asset-light" business model is the decreased reliance on IPOs for broad-based financing. Furthermore, although nimble, technology-enabled companies require less capital, access to capital in private markets is at an all-time high of $1.4 trillion (Figure 3). That level, which represents the amount of private capital available for investment, is a function of three dynamics: First, traditional private market investors, such

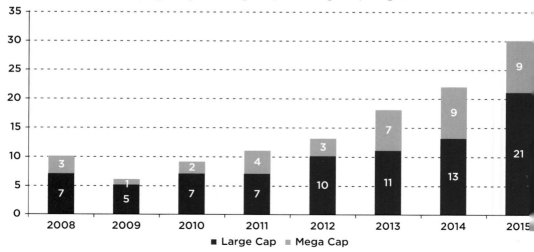

FIGURE 2 Activist Campaigns Against Mega Cap and Large Cap Targets

s private equity firms, are raising larger funds
greater quantities as they seek to diversify
vestment strategies and increase assets under
management (AUM); second, nontraditional
rivate markets investors, such as institutional
vestors, sovereign wealth funds, and high
et-worth individuals have increased allocations
private markets in pursuit of higher returns;
hird, given the interest rate environment,
rivate companies may consider a greater
ange of financing options, which intensifies
he competition to put capital to work among
vestors, and as a corollary, keeps more capital
nspent ("dry powder").

## ONE BUT NOT FORGOTTEN

Vhile the ability to stay private longer is clear,
does not mean that the "IPO is dead," as
many headlines have been quick to claim. After
he financial crisis of 2007–2008, the global
macroeconomic picture recovered, with the
ew issuance market leading the charge. The
esult of the recovery was 2014's record issuance
ear, where, according to Ipreo, 807 companies
aised $248.8 billion via IPO; in the United States
63 companies went public in 2014, raising
93.6 billion in proceeds. This record issuance,
ompounded by a slight destabilization in the
macroeconomic picture globally, caused the well
f capital to dry up as investors searched for

yield via private investments. The year 2016 may
have been a low point from an IPO perspective,
however; analysts are predicting a strong
recovery for the IPO market in 2017 and 2018. In
an interview with CNBC, Mark Hantho, Deutsche
Bank's global head of equity capital markets,
suggested that there will be 1,000 IPOs over
the next two years. The initial public offering
still remains a critical milestone in the life of a
company, because it brings in fresh shareholders,
additional capital, and, importantly, returns for
those private markets investors that have been
with the company since its formation. Indeed, as
the recent Snap IPO highlights (in which shares
sold came without any voting rights), the private
to public blur is enhanced by the fact that public
markets are increasingly accommodating novel
structures. Lastly, while sponsor-to-sponsor
deals are more common, some subset of private
companies, for which strategic exits are not
viable, will inevitably need to tap public markets.

## AN INCREASINGLY BLURRED DISTINCTION

For companies, however, a strong IPO market
or a strong private investment market is a
less relevant distinction; the critical point
is that the line between public and private
has blurred. From that blur emerges the key
conclusion, which is that as more capital pours

**IGURE 3** Global Dry Powder ($bn)

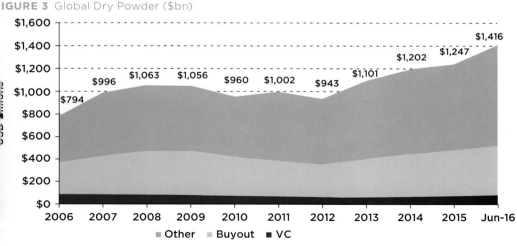

Other includes: Distressed PE, Growth Equity, Mezzanine Capital, and Real Estate

into the private markets, as shareholders demand more reporting, as companies take on more complicated capital structures and hire more employees, and as regulators add more regulation and heighten governance standards (which is inevitable), private markets will more and more closely approximate public markets. So then, the question facing many private companies will be, *How to act public, but stay private?* The answer lies in financial preparedness; effectively, the ability to more seamlessly manage critical information, track performance, and translate that data to stakeholders in a way that promotes long-term scalability (and is necessary for any company ultimately considering an IPO), and does not bring about significant back-office costs.

## ACT PUBLIC, STAY PRIVATE

Regardless of the reason a company decides to remain private, this fundamental shift in the capital markets has had a significant impact on how a company needs to operate in what is now seen as the "new normal" by investors and regulators alike. As companies continue to build shareholder value to new heights while private, investors' commitment to private capital vehicles is at an all-time high. New private capital fundraising has surpassed over $500 million in each of the past three years ending in 2015, according to Preqin, an alternative assets data and intelligence company. This heightened interest has led to a several key concerns for private companies, including but not limited to increasingly complex capital structures that come with new rounds of financing, a need for consistent investor communication, an understanding of regulatory compliance, and a need for liquidity for long-term shareholders. While nearly all private companies are busy refining business models, gaining market share, and building a brand, it is important that they consider implementing some of the best practices below to help build a strong foundation for the long term.

*Shareholder management:* Shareholder communication is an important aspect

for any company, public or private. A lack of communication can result in unhappy shareholders, difficulty raising additional capital, or even a regulatory violation. However, the specific requirements of a private company when it comes to communicating with its investors is a bit of a grey area and is dependent on the terms and agreements with investors. Many private companies opt to stay private because they wish to limit the amount of information they have to disclose; however, in most cases shareholders of private companies have just as much, if not more rights than those of public companies.

Given the industry trend of companies choosing to stay private and raise new capital in the private markets, the number of shareholders requesting information and regular updates has continued to increase. In 2004, Google exceeded the number of stakeholders, 500 at the time, that allowed for a company to continue to be private and therefore not have to disclose detailed financial information. However, the Jumpstart our Business Startups Act (JOBS Act) in 2012 increased the shareholder threshold to 2,000 "holders of record," making it easier to stay private while continuing to find new investors. As a result, many private companies have a long list of investors, including employee shareholders, yet do not have systems in place to adhere to the varied information rights afforded to investors. This can end up with bespoke processes to handle individual or group investor requests that come at significant cost, in both time and dollars.

In order to fulfill the duties to an increasing number of investors, it is important to consider implementing an efficient investor reporting process before the investor list gets too long. This process should be incorporated for all types of sensitive information that needs to be communicated securely to investors, including regular financial reporting, updated capitalization tables following a capital raise, tax documentation, etc. While it may seem as though this much communication can be overwhelming for a small company, getting a handle on this early on can create major efficiencies down the road, and be managed by software.

*Capitalization table management:* As a founder or operating executive of a private company, it is critical to properly manage the company's capitalization table, or the master ledger of ownership in the company. While it may seem like an easy exercise during the seed round of financing, cap tables can turn complex quickly when a company goes through a few more rounds of financing, issue different share classes, offer options plans to key employees, etc. If a company waits to update its cap table until its next round of financing, it may result in a prolonged fundraising process, as the company scrambles to gather relevant documentation, fix errors, and at worst, grapple with previously uncontemplated regulation.

To ensure this is done properly, it is important to engage with a lawyer around any of the aforementioned financing events; however, there are also steps that a company can take to begin managing its own cap table. While managing a cap table in a spreadsheet is one way to capture each transaction, this method can prove to be error prone the more complicated the cap table becomes. Many companies opt to use an online platform that can automate cap table management, or else enlist the help of a lawyer to assist in ensuring the accuracy of each transaction. Many of these online platforms also allow for private company executives to understand the implications of a new capital raise on their own ownership. This can help drive better decisions around how much to offer in a new round of financing and how it will impact existing shareholders during any liquidation event.

*Compliance:* SEC compliance is a daunting and costly proposition for both public and private companies. The challenge of compliance is compounded by the fact that many private companies do not have the legal experience or capital to make sure they are adhering to all the regulations that apply to them. Section 220 of the Delaware General Corporations Law, Section 1501 of California Corporations Code, Rule 701 of the Securities Act of 1933, and the Recognize, Assist, Include, Support, and Engage Family Caregivers Act (RAISE Act) of the recent Fixing America's Transportation Act (FAST Act) all apply to private companies, but it is estimated that thousands of private companies are noncompliant with at least one of these regulations, according to research done by Lowenstein Sandler. In 2016, the former head of the SEC, Mary Jo White, spoke to Silicon Valley leaders about the importance of regulation for privately held companies. She stated, "From a securities law perspective, the theory behind the private markets is that sophisticated investors do not need the protections offered by the robust mandatory disclosure provisions of the 1933 Securities Act." White followed with the statement that all market participants, public and private, look to lose if there are no regulatory guidelines in place to help standardize reporting and valuations from private companies. The complexity in solving the regulatory headache lies in the fact that it is an ongoing and evolving problem. As an executive, having a complete operational picture, whether it is an always up-to-date financial view or detailed understanding of a firm's cap table, allows a company to stay compliant and quickly adapt to new regulation.

*Employee compensation:* In order to grow, private companies need to attract and retain high-performing employees, which can be a difficult proposition, given that base salaries within public companies are generally higher than those at private companies. On average, public companies pay CEOs $244,873 more than privately held company CEOs, according to data provider CapIQ, with other positions seeing similar differences in base salary pay. Private companies look to bridge this gap by offering current and prospective employees partial compensation in the form of stock options. This method aligns employees with the success of the company, as they can see net worth grow as the company continues to hit various milestones. In order to address questions on value (i.e., "Sounds great, but what could those options be worth?"), and thereby expedite hiring processes, companies can implement systems that provide prospective hires and current employees detailed scenario analytics on how much their options will be worth upon realization of various value drivers, such as growth in revenue or earnings before interest, tax, depreciation, and amortization (EBITDA); or for earlier stage companies, achievement of key performance indicators (KPIs).

A second issue prevails as illiquid companies remain private longer: traditional modes of compensation come under pressure. For example, as companies remain private longer, employees have limited ability to exercise vested options and thereby access liquidity, which may be required for "life" events, such as mortgage payments or financing a child's college education. Increasingly, companies offer employees partial liquidity programs, which allow shareholders to sell stock, allowing them to tap some of the value that they were instrumental in generating. A central repository of data allows founders to distribute and retain important documents, inform scenario analytics, and most importantly, create confidence that the cap table of a company is not being diluted in order to retain key employees.

*Promoting scale:* "Growing pains" are a problem that afflicts all companies, regardless of industry or size. Systems and processes that worked at one stage of a company's life may be completely ineffective at another. The trouble is that at young, high-growth companies, the focus is on revenue generation and fundraising, rather than the implementation of systems that ultimately make scale sustainable. A company that manages all of its documents, financials, and reporting on one cloud-based solution will be able to handle scale quickly, because data is organized and highly extensible, allowing companies to deploy systems that meet the demands of the future.

## CONCLUSION

While there has been a significant shift in the capital markets, in that private companies are opting to remain private rather than pursue an IPO, it is important to note that there is also a notable change in how private companies need to operate in this "new normal." Facing scrutiny from limited partners, who have put record amounts of capital to work in alternative asset vehicles, and regulatory organizations, such as the SEC, many investors are requiring new levels of communication and governance from private companies that receive investment. Whether change originates from investors, regulators, or management teams themselves, one thing that is clear is that private companies need to begin "acting public" and should prepare for increasing levels of governance, regulation, and transparency. Ultimately, there will be a time when a company needs to decide the best path forward in driving growth, whether that means pursuing an IPO or raising a new round of private capital. Success for private companies will be a function of financial preparedness, which will inform smooth fundraising, optimize valuations, and streamline compliance.

# 30

# INCENTIVIZING THE EXECUTIVE TEAM BEFORE AN IPO OR SALE

**VLP Law Group LLP**

Mark D. Bradford, Partner

Achieving the business objectives that drive a company toward a successful exit event requires careful consideration of an effective executive compensation program that uses an array of incentive tools, including short- and long-term bonus opportunities, equity-based awards, severance benefits, and change in control benefits.

## BALANCING COMPETING INTERESTS WITH APPROPRIATELY CALIBRATED INCENTIVES

Realizing the business goals that result in the opportunity for an initial public offering or sale of the company requires that companies attract, retain, and motivate their executive team. Each company must determine the right balance between amounts of realizable compensation, short-term and long-term incentives, and the appropriate mix of equity incentives.

An effective executive compensation program balances the competing interests of the executive team, employees, stockholders, and other stakeholders. Insufficient rewards provide inadequate incentive and retention effects in competitive labor markets. Overly generous and poorly designed reward packages result in excessive management costs and a misallocation of resources. Misplaced incentives further constrain the board's flexibility to make personnel changes without undue cost and leave less consideration to allocate among employees, stockholders, and other stakeholders.

### SHORT-TERM INCENTIVES

A mix of short-term incentives, granted over a number of award cycles, can drive business outcomes that serve the long-term interests of the company. Multiple performance objectives tend to be superior to a single performance objective. For example, a short-term incentive program that singularly rewards either sales or profitability, to the exclusion of the other objective, will not drive sustainable long-term value creation as well as a balanced incentive program that rewards both increased sales and profitability on those sales.

Short-term incentives that provide for disparate payouts based on small differences in actual achievement risk creating incentives that reward questionable behavior. Such perverse incentives can be mitigated by setting minimum and maximum payout thresholds and applying linear interpolation between these thresholds.

## EQUITY-BASED INCENTIVES

As maturing companies build toward an initial public offering or sale, a mix of equity incentives helps drive business goals. Equity awards that derive their value from an appreciation in the value of the company, most commonly in the form of stock options, reward executives for increasing the stock price but subject executives to the risk of earning no value if the stock price decreases. Excessive appreciation equity awards may encourage excess risk-taking through "all-or-nothing" payment outcomes. Equity awards that derive their value from the whole value of the company, most commonly in the form of restricted stock and restricted stock units, encourage retention and sustainable value creation by exposing executives to downside risk. However, excessive awards of such equity awards may not encourage an appropriate level of risk-taking that is necessary to differentiate the company in a competitive field.

## COMPENSATION REVIEW

When an initial public offering or sale is being considered, the board should conduct a review of the compensation arrangements of the executive team and evaluate their compatibility with the desired business goals. A compensation consultant can assist with the effort to select a peer group for comparison and benchmarking purposes and determine the appropriate mix of incentives. After deliberation, the board often finds it necessary to adjust base salaries, establish short-term incentives that pay cash bonuses upon the achievement of performance goals in coordination with the strategic business plan, and establish long-term incentives with equity awards.

## EQUITY INCENTIVES

Equity-based awards are powerful tools that align the interests of executives and stockholders, drive business strategy and growth, and enhance stockholder value. Broad-based awards of equity incentives to employees generally fosters an "ownership culture" that motivates employees at all levels of an organization to think and act like business owners. The use of equity awards also permits companies to conserve cash that may be invested in the business.

## CONSIDERATIONS FOR EQUITY AWARDS

Tax efficiency can be achieved by qualifying more profits as long-term capital gain rather than short-term capital gain or ordinary income, both of which are generally subject to higher tax rates. In general, more favorable tax consequences involve greater investment risk. Executives may invest early for an opportunity to save on taxes but risk losing some or all of their investment, with no guarantee of a public market or liquidity for the company's shares. Deferring investment and waiting for a public market or liquidity event permits the acquisition of company shares and the payment of an exercise price (if applicable) and satisfaction of tax liabilities without cash outlay. Less investment risk tends to involve higher tax rates.

Equity-based awards are generally subject to a vesting schedule tied to continuing service or the achievement of specified performance objectives. Vesting is a mechanism by which the executive earns the right to hold shares that participate in the future success of the business should he or she depart from the company. Except in situations where severance benefits are paid, cessation of employment generally results in the forfeiture or repurchase of unvested equity

## TYPES OF EQUITY-BASED AWARDS

The value of appreciation awards, such as stock options, increases as the value of the underlying stock exceeds the exercise price of the option. Value is realized by the executive when the option is exercised. If the value of the stock is less than the exercise price, the option will not have economic value until the stock value exceeds the exercise price. Such an underwater option can be held in the hope that the underlying stock value will increase.

nfortunately, studies suggest that underwater ptions have negative (as opposed to zero or nodest) incentive and retention effects.

he value of full-value awards, such as restricted :ock and restricted stock units, persists as ong as the company's common stock retains ome value. Accordingly, economic value is elivered even if the value of underlying stock as decreased from the time when the awards 'ere granted.

## tock Options

 stock option confers the right to purchase a xed number of shares at a fixed price. Stock ptions become more valuable as the value of 1e company's stock increases. Although they ntail no ownership rights, stock options allow articipation in the growth of a company without n immediate payment of cash, taxes, or risk of 1ss until the options are exercised. If a company emains privately held and the executive must xercise the option, such as following termination f employment, the executive will need to invest inds to pay the exercise price and applicable axes in order to acquire company shares. As a ompany becomes more valuable, exercising an ption tends to require a larger cash outlay for 1e exercise price and taxes (depending on the /pe of option).

 stock option gives the optionee flexibility ) choose when to exercise and thereby when ) recognize taxable income. As long as an xecutive is not forced to exercise an option, xercise can be deferred until a liquidity event, uch as after an initial public offering or a sale of 1e company. An option allows the acquisition of ompany stock at an earlier time in the expected fe cycle of the company, when the value of the :ock is relatively inexpensive. As a result, the apital gain holding period can begin at an earlier me, and more profits may qualify as long-term apital gain, rather than as ordinary income, pon a subsequent sale of company shares.

tock options are subject to a potentially raconian tax regime under Section 409A of the iternal Revenue Code if the exercise price of the option is deemed to be less than the fair market value of the underlying stock on the date of grant. If the Internal Revenue Service determines that a stock option is "discounted," income tax is imposed on the vested portion every year the option remains outstanding (whether or not the option is exercised), plus an additional 20 percent tax and an interest penalty. Such a tax regime results in the confiscation of nearly all profits through taxation.

To reduce the risk that Section 409A applies to options, most startup companies obtain a third-party valuation. Despite the added inconvenience and expense, most early- to mid-stage startup companies find the flexibility and other advantages of stock options to outweigh their disadvantages.

## Restricted Stock

A grant of restricted stock immediately transfers shares of company stock to the recipient, generally subject to a vesting schedule. The transferred shares typically come with voting and dividend rights. If granted for services, restricted stock delivers greater value than options on a share-for-share basis because no exercise price needs to be paid to acquire the shares.

Restricted stock can be either purchased at its fair market value or granted for services, subject to compliance with state corporate law. Paying the fair market value for the stock with cash, check, or a substantially recourse promissory note generally results in no tax consequences.

Granting stock in exchange for services can result in combined federal and state income and employment withholding taxes of about 45 percent of the value of the stock under current rates. These taxes may be satisfied by an executive delivering cash or a check to the company. Alternatively, the company can pay the taxes subject to the executive entering a promissory note that is either full-recourse (upon default of note, borrower is personally liable if value of shares is less than note balance) or nonrecourse (upon default of note, borrower is not personally liable).

The advantage of restricted stock is that it starts the capital gain holding period. It also presents the opportunity to characterize more profits as capital gain, rather than ordinary income, upon a subsequent sale of the shares. In addition, it generally avoids the draconian tax regime of Section 409A. However, depending on the value of the stock, the cost of acquiring the restricted stock (whether paying the fair market value or entering a promissory note for the taxes) may be cost prohibitive for all but the wealthiest executives with risk capital.

Promissory notes are a solution to the lack of liquidity but entail real economic risks. Many executives do not appreciate that loans can be subject to collection by the company, its creditors, or a bankruptcy trustee. In addition, if the company forgives the note, the executive will recognize taxable income, and the company will have a withholding obligation. Finally, executive officers may not hold promissory notes at the time that the company commences the public offering process with the SEC (even if the IPO is withdrawn).

Because of its drawbacks, restricted stock tends to be awarded at early stages of companies when stock may be purchased at nominal cost or acquired with nominal tax consequences.

### Restricted Stock Units

Restricted stock units, or RSUs, represent the right to receive payments in the future based on the value of the company's stock when vesting conditions have been satisfied. RSUs are settled and paid by delivery of shares of company stock or their cash equivalent, with each RSU having the economic value of one share of stock at the time of settlement.

As contrasted with restricted stock, RSUs are merely a promise to deliver shares in the future rather than an immediate transfer of shares. As a result, no capital gain holding period starts until the shares are delivered. RSUs also have no voting rights and typically do not include dividend rights. However, unlike stock options, there is no need to invest funds to pay an exercise price or purchase price to receive shares, although settlement of the shares requires a source of cash to satisfy applicable withholding taxes.

Private companies can grant RSUs that vest upon the later of the satisfaction of a time-based service requirement and a liquidity event requirement. The time-based requirement is satisfied by providing continuing services for the company. The liquidity event requirement is satisfied by the occurrence of an IPO or sale of the company.

Upon termination of employment, RSUs for which the time-based requirement is not yet satisfied are forfeited. RSUs for which time-based requirement is satisfied as of termination remain outstanding and will vest should the liquidity event requirement be satisfied within some period thereafter. RSUs for which the time-based requirement is satisfied but for which the liquidity event requirement does not occur within some period of time after termination are forfeited. If RSUs vest after meeting both the time-based and liquidity event requirements, they are settled in cash or stock.

Such dual-vesting event RSUs are commonly used in later stages when the value of company stock is high and employees perceive less upside value in stock options. The RSUs postpone the tax liability until a time of liquidity but at the cost of higher taxes in general.

## SEVERANCE BENEFITS

Severance benefits are designed to mitigate executives' uncertainty about potential involuntary termination of employment. Severance benefits help attract and retain executives by permitting them to focus on performing their duties rather than their employment situation. These benefits typically include payment of some portion of base salary or bonus in cash, continued medical benefits, and partial or full acceleration of equity-based awards.

Severance benefits are usually triggered by an involuntary termination of employment without condition that justifies a termination for cause. Such conditions generally include reasons other than theft or misappropriation of real or intellectual property, failure to perform assigned duties, gross negligence, willful misconduct, and commission of serious crimes. Because severance benefits are not paid if an executive is terminated for "cause," the conditions constituting cause are carefully scrutinized, with broader definitions favoring the company and narrower definitions favoring executives.

Severance benefits may also be triggered by a voluntary termination for good reason. Such "good reason" conditions typically include adverse changes in compensation, authority, duties, responsibilities, reporting relationships, or work location.

## CHANGE IN CONTROL AND RETENTION BENEFITS

Change in control and retention benefits are a tool to reduce management anxiety and the inherent uncertainty during periods of merger and acquisition (M&A) activity. Management departures during such times can be disruptive and adversely impact the value of the business from the buyer's perspective. By assuring that executives will receive consideration upon a successful exit, retention incentives help the management team focus during uncertain transition periods that may require performing additional job duties.

Although change in control and retention benefits represent a real cost for buyers, buyers often prefer modest retention incentives because these promised benefits offer assurance that the management team will remain in place for some duration after closing of the sale transaction.

Change in control and retention benefits generally provide for the payment of cash consideration or acceleration of all or part of an equity award. They are typically structured as follows:

"**Single trigger**" benefits are paid upon the consummation of a sale of a company. Such benefits permit the executives to capture a part of the value that they have helped create, with such value measured and paid at the time of the sale. Such arrangements are disfavored as an undeserved windfall to executives.

- "**Double trigger**" benefits are paid if there is a sale of the company and an involuntary termination or resignation for good reason occurs, usually within some period of time before or thereafter.

- "**Walk right**" benefits are a blend of single- and double-trigger benefits. Such arrangements allow an executive to resign for any reason within a short period after the closing of a sale transaction and receive severance benefits. This provides executives with an opportunity for a probationary period to determine their role and compatibility with the buyer after closing.

## CARVE-OUT PLANS

Despite their best and diligent efforts, some startup companies are unable to raise money at an acceptable valuation and level of dilution, and likely exit scenarios fail to cover the liquidation preferences held by investors. In these situations, the value of common stock approaches zero, and equity awards lose their motivation and retention effects.

A carve-out plan is an incentive tool that sets aside in a pool for key employees amounts that would otherwise be payable to investors as merger consideration. This arrangement provides management with the incentives to maximize the value of the company in the sale transaction and remain engaged through the completion of the sale.

The desire for flexibility to modify allocations of the carve-out pool as business needs change needs to be balanced against the retention incentives that are served by providing certainty to the executives. Some carve-out plans set fixed allocations for each member of management. Others permit changes to allocations by board approval or majority vote of the plan participants.

# TREATMENT OF EQUITY AWARDS IN AN IPO OR SALE TRANSACTION

Following a successful initial public offering, the company's shares are usually freely tradeable, subject to securities laws restrictions and a lockup imposed by the underwriters to limit sales by company insiders and help build an orderly market in the company's shares.

The treatment of equity awards in a sale transaction depends on the interaction between the contractual terms of the equity awards and the sale agreement, and typically includes one or more of the following:

- Equity awards are converted into the right to receive their economic equivalent in stock of the buyer at the time of the sale, with the vesting schedule continuing after closing.

- Unvested equity awards that are not converted into the right to receive their economic equivalent in stock of the buyer at the time of the sale are either accelerated and paid in full at closing, or canceled without the payment of any consideration.

- The economic equivalent delivered for vested and unvested equity awards may be paid in either cash or stock.

Equity awards that are converted into buyer's equity are sometimes referred to as "rollover equity." Rollover equity benefits the buyer because it reduces the cash outlay and aligns the seller's interest with the success of the combined company. Rollover equity also benefits the seller because it allows the seller to participate in the upside of the combined company in a subsequent sale or liquidity event. In addition, rollover equity typically can be structured to defer taxes until a future liquidity event.

# 31

# LESSONS FOR ENTREPRENEURS IN THE LATE-STAGE PRIVATE MARKET

Morgan Stanley

Ted Tobiason, Managing Director and Head of Private
  Capital Markets

## OPTIMIZING YOUR LATE-STAGE PRIVATE PLACEMENT

The late-stage private market continues to develop and mature, and so do the options available to growth companies that in prior cycles would have simply executed an IPO. These options include trade-offs on deal structure, investor targeting, how much management time a company is willing to commit to the execution of a transaction, and how the company wants this financing to fit into the context of future offerings.

## GADGETS, RATCHETS, AND HATCHETS

Late-stage companies and investors have a wide variety of deal structures available to them. In a transaction, it is likely that investors who get all the way to the term-sheet stage will have a fairly narrow consensus around the true economic value of a company. However, investors and issuers alike will typically have different opinions as to how to value key features of a term sheet. As an example, we can take a high growth negative-cash-flow company with reasonable customer concentration and a typical risk profile. "True economic value" may be around $1 billion; i.e., where would an investor value the company with minimal downside protection. Investor A may offer a term sheet with *nominal value* of $1 billion with "plain vanilla" terms such as 1x downside protection in the event of an acquisition, no IPO protection, and very limited governance. Investor B may offer nominal value of $1.2 billion but a 1.5x guaranteed return on an IPO *and an acquisition* plus governance features to protect the investor. In the event that this downside protection is relevant, it will come at the expense of existing investors. Investor C may offer a convertible security, which converts to an IPO discount that increases over time. It's important that the issuing company understand precisely what they are selling and the upside and downside features of each security. Selling structure to get a higher equity value should be a calculated risk with a strong foundation of confidence in the business. The best-case scenario is to "sell structure" when the valuation environment is at a trough but business confidence is at a peak. The convertible security is similar. The convertible security defers the valuation of the company to an IPO date in the future. The best case for this is also when the valuation environment is pessimistic but the issuer's confidence in the business and its one- to two-year IPO prospects are high. This security has the added uncertainty of making a judgment on the future health of the IPO market.

The "plain vanilla" option is the easiest to understand but it also has its costs and benefits. Let's assume that similar public companies ("comparables") for a given private company are trading a 2-3x forward revenues today but typically have traded at 3-5x. And let's assume that this company is at or near an inflection point in its business where there will be a material change to the upside in its margin structure, growth rate, and/or risk profile. If that company goes the "plain vanilla" route today, it is capturing the valuation trough and monetizing the inflection in the business only to the degree it can convince investors to give it full value. It's also worth noting that the value investors are willing to pay for downside protection increases when there is market and/or business uncertainty. Finance geeks would say the arb (arbitration) value of downside protection is at its peak, so this is the time to monetize structure. Conversely, many Silicon Valley veterans would argue that entrepreneurs should focus on their businesses and not on optimizing their financial structure for current value at the risk of future value; i.e., there is more than enough risk in the execution of a high-growth business without adding undue financing risk.

All of this can play into the recruiting of top talent, which is very fundamental to the creation of value for growth companies. Adding downside protection to a preferred security transfers risk to common-equity/equity-linked securities that are so important to attracting and retaining key talent. We are at a point in the cycle where employees are pretty savvy about where they are in a capitalization structure and what it means to their value if a company executes a highly structured fundraising and the value of the company subsequently declines. Overstretching on value, even if it is not via selling structure, can also hurt an issuer's ability to attract talent. Take two late-stage private companies where company A stretched (aggressive model,

aggressive terms, aggressive multiple) on value to get to $2 billion and company B that took a more modest approach to get to only $1.5 billion in value. Company A might have the better headline, but company B may very well have the better pitch to that elusive top Caltech data scientist.

Deal structure is an important topic for issuers. It's critical that issuers take the time to map out possible scenarios and what it will mean for the company. These scenarios should include the company's microeconomic performance as well as what might happen should the macro- and/or financing environment take a turn for the worse. Issuers should also consider the possible consequences for talent acquisition and future financing within these scenarios in addition to their base case.

## WHO DO YOU LOVE?

Investor targeting is always a major component of any late-stage financing; to whom and to how many? This is a dynamic environment in a constant state of investor entry and exit. In 2014 and 2015 crossover investors were dominant. In 2016 crossover investors were very quiet while we saw substantial market-share gains from Asia, the Middle East, and strategic investors. A simple conceptual model would be probability of investing + valuation framework of the investor + the intangible value of the investor all divided by the time + work required to get those investors to close. Casting the net wide has real cost—management time is valuable. So to the extent possible it's important to weed out the "looky loos" that are unlikely to get to market terms. Secondly, it is important to think about what certain investors may bring to the table beyond simple "value x volume." This is where considering strategic investors can be very valuable. Working with bankers with a keen understating of the industry (especially the orthogonal dynamics), a strong industry rolodex and a mergers and acquisitions (M&A) mindset will change the game. Strategic investors can both find and create value; i.e., they can validate a technology and they can combine he investment with a commercial relationship. inancial investors can come with their own xpertise, rolodexes, and geographic expertise nat can also make their capital greener.

## WHAT'S YOUR NUMBER?

's been long held true that companies going ublic need to be very judicious in their rojections because missing their first and/or econd quarter post pricing will likely precipitate ne dreaded "gap down" in stock price the next rading session. And of course this comes with all ne attention on CNBC and the wrath of investors nd analysts. Perhaps it's because the private narkets don't have this overhang that the models late-stage private markets have been more ggressive and therefore have a higher rate of nissing forecasts. But this is not to say there isn't ccountability. As a substantial number of tech ompanies go public this year, they will face many uy-side analysts privy to the projections they nowed investors in prior rounds. The variance to nose rounds will have an impact on the multiple nose investors put into their financial models s well as the financial projections they use. On more immediate level for companies that are the private markets now or the near future is ne fact that deal execution is taking so long that nvestors are getting a look at one and sometimes nultiple quarters before they submit term sheets. these circumstances the accountability is nmediate as investors sometimes say, "Given ne variance to this quarter's performance, ve want to wait to see how the next quarter oes." Investors may also more heavily discount orward projections and/or begin to discount nanagement's ability to forecast and execute.

## ECH PRIVATE CAPITAL MARKETS SET TO REBOUND N 2017

*Data as of Friday, December 30, 2016)*

espite a decline in overall volumes in 2016, lobal private tech financings outpaced global PO volumes for the sixth consecutive year. Asia, ed by China, is now the largest region by volume n the back of the proliferation and massive scale

of unicorns across the Internet, e-commerce, and online finance sectors. Although the private market still recorded large volumes in 2016, down rounds, smaller deal sizes, and longer average deal execution (launch to closing) all point towards a normalization or a return to the mean in the private fundraising market.

Importantly, many of the largest and highest profile private companies have sustained or grown their private market cap with the more than $2 billion market cap companies now representing approximately $540 billion in value. Some (many) of those companies will make their way to the public markets over the next two years as the IPO market recovers. Putting the numbers into context—If we sold approximately 15% of each company at IPO, that would translate into IPO volume approaching $100 billion, a number that equates to the last nine years of U.S. IPO volume, including Facebook and Alibaba. An increase in IPOs will help replenish the depleted landscape of investable public growth companies in technology.

We believe that a once again vibrant tech IPO market offers a twofold benefit to the private markets:

- *Healthy private market financing activity:* opportunity for crossover investors (mutual and hedge funds) to deploy more capital to new private investments post the monetization of some of their current private investments in the public markets, and

- *Improvements in the overall valuation environment for private issuers:* a dynamic and higher volume IPO market to lower the illiquidity discount ascribed to private companies due to a shorter expected time horizon to liquidity (IPO)

This year's crop of tech IPOs will provide a new set of valuation benchmarks and comparables for private enterprises raising money in the private markets. Obviously, how this impacts valuations could go either way, depending on the performance of the IPOs. Given we have an optimistic view on the quality and likely performance of these IPOs, we expect that this will benefit the market.

While 2017 volumes are off to a slightly slower start than anticipated, pricing outcomes have been strong and issuer friendly, as is evidenced by the lack of structure we are seeing in the market. Deal duration has subsequently shortened, and diligence requests have become less robust—all signs pointing toward a return to normalcy for 2H2017.

## A DEEP DIVE INTO THE DATA ON THE PRIVATE TECHNOLOGY FINANCING MARKET

Global and U.S. private markets have outpaced IPO volumes for the sixth consecutive year. However, there are signs of normalization:

- Global transaction volumes peaked in 2015 and were down approximately 5 percent in 2016, despite meaningfully larger average deal sizes in 2016 (+9 percent) (Table 1).

- The decline in transaction volume (from $90.3 billion in 2015 to $85.5 billion in 2016) is even more pronounced when excluding large Chinese FinTech transactions (Ant Financial, Lufax, JD Finance, Ping An, 51credit.com, worth approximately $8 billion).

- Despite the $10 billion decline in financing volume, the private market volume numbers are still far above the 8-year average of $34 billion.

- Activity in the United States fell slightly faster than the broader market with deal volume in the United States down 16 percent year over year (YOY), with an average deal size of $90 million (-4 percent YOY and -15 percent from its peak of $105 million in 2011).

Global distribution of private deals also mirrors that of public tech markets.

- In aggregate, Internet and software companies represent 91 percent and 85 percent of the deal count in the tech private and IPO markets, respectively (Table 1).

TABLE 1

| Global Private Placements | | | | | | | | | |
|---|---|---|---|---|---|---|---|---|---|
| | **2009** | **2010** | **2011** | **2012** | **2013** | **2014** | **2015** | **2016** | **2017 YTD** |
| Deal Number | 53 | 72 | 169 | 151 | 186 | 480 | 825 | 720 | 200 |
| Deal Volume ($MM) | $3,146 | $5,897 | $17,168 | $11,939 | $14,094 | $51,957 | $90,319 | $85,502 | $25,077 |
| Average Deal Size ($MM) | $59 | $82 | $86 | $79 | $76 | $108 | $109 | $119 | $125 |
| Multiple of Global IPO Volumes | 0.4x | 0.3x | 1.0x | 1.5x | 1.4x | 2.1x | 8.9x | 11.3x | 3.3x |
| Average Global IPO Deal Size ($MM) | $144 | $148 | $156 | $103 | $170 | $173 | $118 | $88 | $180 |
| Issuance By Sector (2015–2016) | | | | | | | | | |
| Internet & Software Private Placements | | | | | | | | 91% | |
| Internet & Software IPOs | | | | | | | | 85% | |

TABLE 2

| % of Total | Issuance by Region | | | |
| --- | --- | --- | --- | --- |
| | North America | Europe | Asia/Pacific | Others |
| 2009 | 60% | 24% | 13% | 2% |
| 2010 | 57% | 22% | 19% | 2% |
| 2011 | 59% | 14% | 26% | 1% |
| 2012 | 61% | 12% | 23% | 3% |
| 2013 | 67% | 16% | 14% | 3% |
| 2014 | 51% | 17% | 29% | 3% |
| 2015 | 46% | 8% | 44% | 2% |
| 2016 | 41% | 7% | 49% | 3% |
| 2017 YTD | 39% | 6% | 54% | 1% |

- Increasingly similar average deal sizes also highlight the degree of overlap between the pool of capital in the public and private tech capital markets.

- Asian volumes, carried largely by Chinese issuers, now constitute the largest region by volume, having increased in market share during each of the last three years (Table 2).

## A DEEP DIVE INTO THE EXECUTIONS OF PRIVATE TECHNOLOGY FINANCINGS

While private market deal execution has been challenging lately, the bounceback in the tech IPO market will have positive implications for the tech private capital markets.

- Beginning in late 2015, many crossover investors (investors who are able to invest in both private and public investments) indicated that their private allocations were approaching levels where they either could not buy more private stock, or would need a very compelling investment thesis to invest.

- Participation of crossover investors (mutual and hedge funds) as lead investors have declined from 15 percent in 2014, to 12 percent in 2015, and to 5 percent in 2016.

- Similarly, the proportion of crossover investors as new investors in private rounds has fallen from a 5-year high of 10 percent in 2014 to only 6 percent in 2016.

- The previously tepid tech IPO market also impacted valuations because of the higher discount rates associated with a longer time horizon to liquidity.

- A multiple re-rating in the public tech sector will likely result in an uptick for private market valuations, which have been under pressure for most of the year.

- Amid the more challenging deal environment for private placements, investors increasingly favor "mega-deals" vs. traditional transactions.

- Over 40 percent of the private market volumes are now attributable to deals above $500 million, versus the 27 percent average from 2011 to 2015.

- Flat (round) is now the new up (round).

- Anecdotally, the number of publicly disclosed down rounds has increased from 5 in 2014 to 15 in 2016, although this number is likely underreported.

- Strategic investors have become one of the most important constituencies in private market transactions. While many companies, such as Intel, Google, Qualcomm, Salesforce. com, and Microsoft have been important private market participants for a long time, we have seen new entry from the industrial, retail, automotive, energy, and other typically "non-tech" industries. Technology can even be a crucial defining element for companies that are "non-tech." Minority transactions as well as M&A are often the most effective way to get access to leading disruptive technology.

- Deals are also taking longer to execute and have been more broadly marketed, as average deal duration lengthened to about 20 weeks in 2016 versus the approximately 12-week average for deals closed in 2015.

- The high percentage of private market issuers that have materially underperformed projections provided to investors has led to more intense diligence sessions where a company's execution and management's ability to forecast are intensely vetted.

All these directly impact a company's readiness as a public company.

*The bottom line*: Even with the recent normalization of private market financings, it is unlikely that the global IPO market will eclipse the volumes seen in the global private financing market in 2017. But with a lively tech IPO market and a large cohort of maturing private companies that have attractive growth, business model, and scale, the gap in issuance should narrow. We will need to see some of the megacap private tech companies come to the public markets in order to have a shot at eclipsing the volumes seen in the private markets, and the timing of those transactions is very hard to predict. The private financing market will remain active as private companies around the globe, especially from China, will need capital to invest heavily in building large, enduring companies. Capital will remain a strategic weapon. We may also find that access to liquidity (secondary selling for employees) becomes a key competitive tool to hire the best talent—and this liquidity could come via IPO or private deals. The uptick in tech IPO activity will help create more liquidity in the portfolios of private investors, especially for crossover investors. Funds holding private capital will finally be able to monetize their long-held private positions, creating dry powder to invest in the next class of emerging private companies. A functioning and active IPO market will restore balance to the funding cycle of private and near-public private companies.

# 32

# STRUCTURING A STRATEGIC ALLIANCE

**Frankfurt Kurnit Klein & Selz PC**

Jay S. Rand, Partner

Emerging growth companies at some point generally will need to develop strategic alliances with other businesses. Partnering with an established company can provide a wealth of benefits for a startup, not only in terms of access to the larger company's resources but also from the increased visibility that such a relationship can generate. However, studies have shown that the failure rate of strategic alliances may be as high as 60% to 70%.[1] Therefore, it is prudent to consider some of the ramifications of these relationships so that reasonable expectations are set.

## WHAT IS A STRATEGIC ALLIANCE?

Broadly speaking, a "strategic alliance" is a relationship among two or more parties who for mutual benefit desire to share resources. These resources may include money, intellectual property, distribution channels, and expertise.

Strategic alliances can be formed to achieve one or multiple objectives. Some common examples of these objectives include:

*Business development or referral*: Your company seeks out a marketing partner that has broad reach within a customer base that your company desires to penetrate, or access to an analogous customer base that offers your company an expansion opportunity. Headspace, a developer of guided meditation courses offered via an app or online, developed marketing alliances with companies such as Starwood Hotels and Virgin Atlantic, recognizing that stressed-out travelers presented an attractive market to tap. Stand-alone referral or affiliate marketing relationships, such as those offered by companies like Amazon, can be as simple as links between two companies' websites; broader marketing arrangements with stated budgets and deliverables can be more complex. If your company is pursuing such a relationship, you should be considering what the referral partner can offer you in terms of reach and support.

*Supply chain/OEM alliances*: In this type of alliance, businesses seek to create stream-lined and efficient supply chains that lead to increased sales for both parties. SiriusXM has relationships with many automobile manufacturers to supply satellite radio and telematics services, among other items. Makers of artisanal food products desire relationships with large retailers such as Whole Foods to increase sales and distribution. As with business development marketing alliances, supply chain alliances permit suppliers to leverage the broad reach and brand of the OEM to better penetrate an existing market or to enter into a vertical arrangement that may not otherwise be possible for a smaller company. However, there is a risk that a small company may become overly dependent on OEMs for its sales and marketing and does not establish its own presence and pursue other channel opportunities.

*Strategic integration:* In this type of alliance, companies collaborate with each other to offer joint products or services to their respective customers. These relationships may have features of supply chain/OEM alliances but also entail some integration of the product or service offerings. These alliances are common among technology companies—a PC manufacturer that ships its product with preloaded third party software, or two software companies or app developers that may work together to allow their products to communicate with each other, such as Google integrating its mobile mapping service with Uber. Issues may develop concerning which alliance partner actually "owns" the customer.

*Development alliances*: Development alliances feature collaboration on research and development activities among parties with shared objectives. Such relationships often entail each party bringing a specific set of resources such as know-how, expertise, or capital. Typically, the objectives include mitigating the risks and costs associated with R&D and leveraging the resources of the other participant. Sometimes a separate legal entity may be established for a development alliance so it is treated as a stand-alone entity for operational, legal, and accounting purposes. Because these relationships often last several years and entail significant contributions from the participants, monetary and/or nonmonetary, development alliances can be complicated to structure and document.

*Cobranding alliances*: Cobranding allows two or more companies to present products or services to a target audience. The purpose is to increase customer awareness of the business's brand and help shape its image by partnering

with, and leveraging the brand awareness of, another business. Examples include: high-end smartphone manufacturer Vertu partnering with Italian automaker Ferrari to create a limited-edition smartphone inspired by the automaker's design features; British Airways and Citibank offering a credit card that provides automatic membership to the British Airways' Executive Club; and Spotify and Starbucks partnering to link Starbucks retail outlets and Starbucks loyalty card holders with the Spotify music-streaming service.

## ADVANTAGES AND DISADVANTAGES OF STRATEGIC ALLIANCES

If deployed judiciously, strategic alliances can help a startup accelerate its growth by providing access to vital resources such as cash, product development, and marketing and sales support. Attention needs to be paid, however, to the appropriate timing in your company's development path for entering into a strategic alliance as well as selecting appropriate strategic partners. To make these determinations, it is helpful to consider the advantages and disadvantages of strategic alliances:

*Advantages*:

- ∘ If planned and structured properly, they can help your business grow faster and with less capital.

- ∘ Your visibility may dramatically increase from the publicity, reach, and services that your partner may offer.

- ∘ Your credibility may increase by having a recognized brand name willing to partner with you.

- ∘ You can mitigate risk by outsourcing a service or function to a strategic partner at less cost than trying to provide it yourself.

- ∘ If successful, the relationship can turn into a possible investment or M&A opportunity.

*Disadvantages*:

- ∘ Opportunity cost—does choosing a particular partner preclude you from working with that partner's competitors (even if there is no stated exclusivity, as discussed below)?

- Your business is not likely to be your partner's highest priority (or maybe it was at one time but isn't any longer), and it can be difficult to get the attention and responsiveness you may need.

- The players may change—the project leaders who initially championed your strategic alliance are no longer there, and their replacements may not share the enthusiasm or the mandate of the original team.

- Larger companies tend to be bureaucratic and slow-moving, creating communications and decision-making challenges.

- You may be locked into a contractual relationship that may last several years, with ramifications if you breach the terms.

## KEY FEATURES THAT YOU MAY EXPECT TO ENCOUNTER IN NEGOTIATING A STRATEGIC ALLIANCE

Here are some deal terms that we frequently see in strategic alliances with emerging companies:

- *Strategic investment:* Requests for equity relationships with emerging-growth companies are particularly common when venture markets are frothy and large companies to benefit from a strategic relationship not only through results from operations but also through an "investment strategy." (Note that this discussion will not focus on the types of corporate investment funds that function independently from a company's corporate decision-making and more like true venture capital funds that are primarily focused on investment returns.) The equity relationship between an emerging company and a corporate partner will typically take one or more of two forms: an actual cash investment or a warrant.

A cash investment from a strategic partner can enhance the visibility and perceived viability of a fledgling company. In addition, it may

be expected that the corporate partner will support the cash investment with valuable expertise and strategic guidance from key members of management.

A strategic investment very early in a company's development, however, may place that company "off limits" to the strategic investor's competitors. This can create challenges (both real and perceived) for an emerging company in expanding its market reach and in attracting future investors. In addition, strategic investors often require investment terms that may be unacceptable to a purely financial investor. For example, most institutional venture investors will require that the investment documents of its portfolio companies contain a "drag-along" provision, requiring all stockholders to support and approve a sale of the company that is approved by a certain threshold of the company's stockholders. The logic of such a provision is to facilitate the sale process and increase the likelihood of a successful exit. Strategic investors, however, may balk at such a provision, fearing potential embarrassment from letting a good acquisition opportunity slip away (particularly if the acquirer is a competitor of the investor/partner), or because the investor/partner wants its own opportunity to submit a bid. Strategic investors also may not have the experience (or tolerance) of VCs in working with early-stage companies or with the vagaries and cycles of the venture markets, leading to culture clashes or worse. An emerging company would thus be well-advised to consider the ramifications of accepting a strategic investment and to explore the strategic investor's track record and reputation in terms of being supportive to its investee companies.

- *Performance warrants*: A warrant is the right (but not the obligation) to purchase equity in your company for a specified price prior to an expiration date. A strategic warrant is generally a "kicker"—the warrant holder does not typically pay cash to exercise the warrant. Instead, the warrant holder will typically wait until there is a liquidity event (sale or IPO) and undertake a "cashless" exercise of the warrant, in which the warrant holder surrenders its warrant in exchange for the incremental increase in value of the warrant over its exercise price.

The metrics for performance are often measured in terms of revenue: a referral/business development partner may seek warrants based on the amount of business that it delivers; a supply-chain partner may earn equity based on the amount of purchases it makes from the emerging company. Warrants may also vest based on the duration of the relationship. The revenue goals may be set in terms of a short-term time horizon (perhaps for a single year or until an aggregate amount of revenue is achieved) or perhaps in terms of annual quotas over a longer period.

Key considerations in issuing strategic performance warrants are (a) matching the incentive to performance and (b) providing realistic incentives. Thus, both the duration of the performance period and the attainability of the performance goals need to be assessed. Warrants that are either earned too quickly or vest based on unattainable metrics may each result in a strategic partner losing its motivation to continue to provide support. Keep in mind that for purposes of calculating your fully diluted capitalization, maximum exercise of the warrants will be assumed. Therefore, when a VC prices your company, the strategic warrants that you assume will never be earned will be every bit as dilutive to your stockholders as the other types of equity (employee options, investor shares, etc.) that you issue. Naturally, the longer the period over which the warrant targets are achievable, the more likely your partner will be motivated to add value. In addition, you should expect that your company will increase in value over time and thus the targets you set should also increase over time commensurately.

- *Exclusivity:* There is no need to immediately stop discussions with a potential strategic partner because exclusivity is raised. In

fact, a request for exclusivity in a business relationship can be used to your advantage.

It is important to understand the rationale for the request for exclusivity. Sometimes there is no rationale—the larger company is simply trying to use its perceived leverage to exact a term in a negotiation. If that is the case, then you have a decision to make about the opportunity cost of granting exclusivity. If, on the other hand, your strategic partner appears to have a solid business rationale for its request for exclusivity, then it is incumbent upon you to take advantage of this desire, consider the commitments that you would want from your strategic partner to support your business, and then carefully balance the value to your business of these commitments against the risks of the specific type of exclusivity that is sought. This analysis will vary depending on your industry, the type of product or service you offer, and the type of alliance you are entering. For example, the length of exclusivity would be of great concern to a technology startup in a competitive and fast-moving industry. In any case, you should aim to be specific in terms of spelling out your expectations in the alliance agreement.

Negotiation points pertaining to exclusivity include the following:

- *Scope of exclusivity:* Be as specific as possible in granting exclusivity. Are you willing to be wedded eternally to only one ally? Such a relationship will likely limit your exit alternatives and your valuation upon exit. Can you limit the scope of restriction to a list of competitors? Can you put a time limit on exclusivity or perhaps offer a "first-mover" period during which you grant your partner exclusivity, after which you can offer your product or service to others? Can you limit exclusivity to a specific-use case? Can you tie continued exclusivity to achievement of specific metrics such as revenue targets or milestones? Would your partner be willing to agree to not work with any of your competitors? Can you unwind the exclusivity in the event that you are acquired?

- *Marketing support:* How will your strategic partner help you to expand your business beyond simply supporting its relationship with you? Will it be willing to participate in co-marketing activities to increase your visibility and customer base? If so, it is best to specify terms in the alliance agreement, such as names of project leaders and amount of spend.

- *Publicity:* Will your partner actively participate in publicity efforts regarding the strategic alliance? Will it allow a press release mentioning its participation? Will it be willing to tout you (or allow you to tout the relationship) on an ongoing basis at industry conferences? Will you be accorded some sort of "premier partner" status?

- *Technical integration*: If you are developing a joint solution or custom deployment for a strategic partner, what kinds of resources will be made available to ensure the success of the deployment? Would you have access to your partner's tech team? Is there a defined timetable for the project with specified milestones?

- *Acquisition offers*: A large strategic player may view a strategic alliance as a precursor to a possible acquisition of your company. That motivation may be obvious at the outset: your conversations with a strategic partner may have begun as a discussion about an acquisition, but one or both parties may have decided to pursue an alliance instead. In other instances, the concept of rights with respect to acquiring your company may come seemingly out of the blue. As with other terms, try to understand your partner's point of view in making the request. Your partner may feel that because of its vital role in fostering the growth and development of your company, it should be afforded some sort of special "insider" right if you decide to sell the company. Your partner may also want to prevent having your company fall into the hands of one of its competitors and thus request notification when you propose to sell and to whom.

The types of requests for special acquisition rights that you may encounter can include one or more of the following:

- *Right of first refusal:* This is a right to receive notice of an acquisition offer and a right to match its terms. This term may have a "chilling effect" on potential buyers. First, a potential third-party buyer, upon learning that another party has a right of first refusal, may not be willing to do the legwork required in exploring an acquisition opportunity. Second, if the right of first refusal has a long notice period, the third-party buyer may not want to wait for that period to elapse. And even if your strategic partner agrees not to match an offer, your potential buyer may wonder why. Is it because the potential buyer's offer is too high? Does your strategic partner know something about you that the potential buyer doesn't know?

- *Right of first offer:* A right of first offer can provide that once you have determined to sell your company, you would be required to provide your strategic partner with a first right to submit an acquisition offer. If your partner elects to submit an offer, you can decide to either accept the offer or, for a limited period, pursue a better offer from a third party. In theory, the right of first offer mitigates some of the concerns raised by rights of first refusal regarding the discouragement of third-party offers, and you may suggest this term in response to a request for a right of first refusal. In practice, however, your strategic partner may feel that it would now be the "stalking horse" and thus not be willing to accept this term.

- *Right of notification/negotiation:* This alternative provides your strategic partner only with notification that you are considering an acquisition offer, typically followed by a limited exclusive negotiation period. The right would be triggered upon receipt of a third-party offer or perhaps at your discretion if your company is considering putting itself up for sale. Unlike a right of first refusal, the terms of a third-party offer need not be revealed to your strategic partner; all your partner is told is that there is a process either under way or expected to commence. You may be required not to enter into a binding commitment until the end of the exclusive negotiation period, but that period is usually relatively short (generally 14 days or less).

## CONCLUSION

If your company is considering a strategic alliance with a larger corporate entity, consider the longer-term ramifications of partnering with the specific ally and whether your company is positioned to take advantage of the alliance.

Remember that an alliance is a two-way street: explain the value you can offer your alliance partner and not just what your alliance partner can do for you. At the same time, be mindful of your company's goals in seeking the alliance and set forth specific commitments from your ally in the alliance agreement.

## REFERENCE

1. Jonathan Hughes and Jeff Weiss, "Simple Rules for Making Alliances Work," *Harvard Business Review,* November 2007.

# PART IV

## GETTING READY FOR AN EXIT

# 33

# PREPARING FOR AN IPO

**Class V Group**

Lise Buyer, Partner

Leslie Pfrang, Partner

The ratio of myth and misinformation to reality around IPOs is enormous. Perhaps because the events are such significant milestones or perhaps because they attract more press and are more glamorous than more mundane business announcements, rumors, innuendo, and significant misunderstandings lead many a company down a rockier road than need be. In this chapter, we hope to offer just a few suggestions to get started down that yellow—or hopefully gold—brick road while minimizing flying monkey and wicked-witch visits.

Going public is a time consuming and tedious process of dotting a lot of "i's" and crossing many "t's." Before rolling eyes at that, understand that the process should be hard. If a company's management finds going public too trying, the team should contemplate that "going" public is nothing compared to being public. Operating as a public company is a whole new stair-step up in corporate responsibility.

An IPO is neither a payday nor an exit. It is a change in the ownership structure of the company in return for a change in the amount of cash in the bank. The upshot is that, after an IPO, management and the board have a responsibility not only to customers and employees but also to a large new group of owners/investors. In return for cold hard cash, a company is selling an ownership stake to these unaffiliated funds and individuals, all of whom have high expectations. Quite simply, IPO participants are buying ownership in the company today because management convinced them that as the company grows, these new investors will receive more money back for relinquishing that ownership "tomorrow."

## WHY GO PUBLIC?

Thanks to the JOBS Act, companies can increasingly raise previously unimagined sums from the aggregation of a large number of private investors. Until that Act, companies had the obligation of sharing audited financial information with investors once there were 500 of them with money at stake. Many, including Google and Facebook, used that public information-sharing requirement to launch the transition from private to public. The thinking generally was "let's use the unveiling of our financial information as the catalyst to kick off our IPO." Unfortunately, the JOBS Act removed the 500 shareholder rule, swapping in a toothless placeholder, and thus removed a legal incentive for the best of the growth companies to share the investment opportunity with public investors during what is likely to be a period of rapid growth. Prior to the change, it was not at all common for a private, venture-backed company to be valued at over $1.0 billion pre-IPO; that valuation was only for the best of the best. After the JOBS Act, "unicorns," companies valued at more than $1.0 billion in the private markets, are suddenly as common as golden retrievers, although not nearly as dependable.

Since private investment money can, for some companies, be seemingly unlimited, private company management can reasonably ask "Why go public at all?" There are four main, important reasons:

- to create a liquid market in the stock

- to enhance the profile of the company

- to provide liquidity to early investors and

- to discover the "real" valuation of the company as determined by third-party trading in the stock. Among other uses, this information is critical should a company want to use its stock as an acquisition currency.

While there are a host of other attributes accompanying public market status, those four are for many the primary drivers.

Once a board has made the decision to go, the next question to consider is timing. First and foremost, companies should know that the process is time consuming and cannot be tightly controlled. Even the most organized teams find the timing of an offering will fluctuate depending on market conditions, auditor schedules, the SEC's schedule, and sometimes competitors' plans. While there are plenty of examples of both shorter and longer processes, it is not unreasonable to expect the process from pre-banker selection through IPO to run seven to nine months, if all runs smoothly. Yes, some move more quickly but for others, more than a year can elapse between banker selection and an IPO's effective date. All who embark on the process should understand that like air travel through O'Hare in the wintertime, mapping out an expected, precise ETA is an exercise in futility.

## MINIMIZING DELAYS

Before the board says go:

The IPO process is long and involves intense scrutiny, just as is the case with the sale of any high-priced asset from a home to art to a business. Fortunately, potential issuers can reduce the intensity of the project by taking a few steps before any formal IPO process begins.

For example, the best time to gain a first-hand understanding of how public investors differ from private company investors is when the IPO is just an imaginary date on a distant calendar page. Investors in public companies make decisions differently and work on time frames completely foreign to venture investors. The sooner a management team understands the former's lens, the greater the understanding and therefore the ease of the entire process. In recent cases, crossover investors have participated in later-stage private rounds and can be one source of information for private company management teams, but for others, attending a couple of investment bank public company conferences, even just as an unidentified audience member, is a terrific way to see what kind of questions these investors ask and how they view and evaluate investment opportunities.

Even better, while still far from an IPO, invite an institutional investor or two to come visit. Do not share projections or even historical financial results but do show the most recent company presentation and ask (and watch) for feedback about what works and what baffles. The more of these early meetings a team has, the more able it will be to incorporate some of the thinking into future presentations and ultimately, into the S-1 and the roadshow. Investor thinking matters at IPO time because generally, and too often overlooked, is the fact that these people are not interested in a company's technology or patent collection. They are interested in the commercial application of those assets and how they will ultimately convert to growing revenue and profitability.

Frequently, private companies overshare their financial results and forecasts far too early, in hopes of impressing future public investors. There is no benefit and definitely a potential cost in doing so. Threading the needle between promoting financial success and forecasting financial prospects is complex. Companies that keep their numbers confidential until the time comes to unveil them thoughtfully and with appropriate talking points often end up better able to control the narrative on an ongoing basis. If the financial results are solid, companies will benefit at the time of publication of the public prospectus and IPO. If the investment proposition is more about future hopes and dreams, there is no advantage to launching that often distracting conversation too soon.

In addition to potential investors, companies that believe an IPO is on the horizon should spend some time with investment bankers. The operative word is "some." Bankers can offer solid insight into what is on investors' minds, competitive dynamics, and overall market trends. They can also chew up a significant amount of management's time. Companies need to find the optimal mix of meeting bankers, both to hear their commentary and to assess their strengths relative to one another, as well as to know that "No thank you" is a perfectly fine response to the umpteenth request for a meeting. Otherwise, the process can quickly become unproductive. When the time comes, the bankers will (of course) take management's call, regardless of how often they were turned down in the past.

However, of greater importance than meeting with bankers is meeting with investment banks' research analysts well before the process begins. As long as they hail from reputable (which is not the same as large) firms, for analyst introductions more is better. Again, the caveat applies: keep financial results confidential or at very least vague, "we generated more than $85 million top line last year and can see profitability in our future," with no further clarification. With that caution, teams will benefit from meeting with and reading the research of analysts from a wide variety of firms. Once public, the analyst community will act as a megaphone for all new issuers' messages, complemented by their own

thoughts. Time spent helping these analysts understand the nuances and differentiation of a business is almost always time well spent.

While still in the early days, ask a CEO or CFO who has recently been through the process to lunch, or perhaps preferably, a drink. Ask them what they know now that they wish then knew "then" or about their experiences with various service providers including bankers and lawyers. Ask them what they would do differently. Every transaction is different but everyone can learn from the wheel-building that has already transpired.

## HOW DOES A COMPANY KNOW IF IT IS READY? HOW BIG IS BIG ENOUGH?

Perhaps the most frequently asked question in the period before the board has hit the IPO launch button is "How big do we have to be?" Unfortunately, the answer really is "it depends." Investors understand the 0–90 mph trajectory of companies in the biosciences fields, and therefore often invest when revenue is nonexistent or microscopic. On the other hand, for companies selling more tangible products that don't require FDA approval, investors generally require evidence of an enthusiastic reception from the target customer market. Service companies often fall somewhere in between. While some of their preferences are variable, stalwart, fundamental investors always favor companies with solid financial results and a promising forward-looking profit and loss (P&L). "Solid" does not mean "currently profitable" but the stronger the financial health and realistic outlook, the less risky an IPO candidate appears and the more generously that firm is likely to be compensated with a higher relative valuation.

While the exact size of the top line, growth rate, or time to cash-flow profitability can vary widely for IPOs, before embarking on the IPO adventure, a potential issuer must have the financial wherewithal to cover the costs of both the process and of being a public company. These costs include, among others, legal and audit fees, compliance fees, advisor fees, the costs of a fully capable finance team, and ongoing investor relations expenses. When the Sarbanes-Oxley rules went into effect, some howled that the incremental expenses were too big a burden for an issuing company. Actually, those costs serve as an important, necessary hurdle. Very simply, if a company cannot afford the cost of having its financial statements audited, it most definitely cannot afford to operate as a public company and should not begin the process.

## WHAT ELSE MATTERS?

Assuming the company is established enough to tell an accurate and compelling story to potential public investors, what else matters? Well, plenty, but two things above all. The easy one is management. The more the team has been together and is fully filled out, the easier the sale to investors. While it is not terribly uncommon to see management changes as a potential IPO approaches—after all, different team members prefer companies at different stages— switching out financial or sales or senior members of management in the months just before a process begins is a suboptimal route. Importantly, the CEO and CFO have to sign personal attestations about the information in the S-1, statements for which they incur personal (that is, no directors and officers coverage) liability. Investors are right to wonder about the finance expert willing to swear all the numbers are accurate after just a month or two on the job. More importantly, an IPO often puts the team under incremental stress. A team that operates cohesively before adding the extra challenges is likely to have an easier go of the process. Furthermore, on this point, mutual fund managers and others repeatedly say that the heart of the "invest-or-don't-invest" decision is the assessment of the team that will run the company. The shorter the team's tenure with the company, the greater the risk to investors and the greater the potential negative impact on valuation.

Secondly, nothing is more important than being able to accurately forecast financial results. Yet this is a swamp of quicksand into which IPO companies fall with stunning and disheartening regularity. Providing a fail-safe forecast for the

year ahead is tremendously challenging for a number of reasons including:

- For most rapidly growing businesses, forecasting out several quarters is very challenging because too many pieces of the P&L are in flux and undoubtedly somewhat uncertain.

- The pricing of the IPO correlates closely to the projected financial results for the next fiscal year, and therefore there is always pressure on the finance department to be optimistic.

- Investors' response to earnings announcements during those first public quarters are highly asymmetrical. A company that outperforms expectations generally receives a hearty round of applause from the market, reflected by the positive reaction of the share price the following day. On the other hand, a company that misses its targets for an early quarter will likely be crushed in the markets by investors who often feel they were somehow misled. To be clear, "crushed" can mean a share price haircut of 20 to 50 percent. The morale impact of that swan-diving share price can have severe and long lasting ramifications for both investors who bought into the deal and the employee base.

Combine genuine uncertainty with strong pressure to be concurrently optimistic (boards) and pessimistic (bankers), and teams have a challenging balance beam for even the most sophisticated finance organizations. The successful navigation of this ledge is a mandatory part of the process and the issuer's future.

Regardless of potential issuer's size and even if management has been together for 10 years, if the company's finance department cannot accurately forecast the P&L several quarters out within a very small margin of error, rethink the timing of the IPO.

## WHAT ABOUT TIMING?

As already explained, much of the timing will be out of the issuer's control, and planning to "hit the window" is a waste of time. The size of that window varies directly with the strength of a company's financial prospects. The stronger the numbers, the closer to profitability, the less important a window is. It is true that during periods of economic meltdown such as the 2008–2009 period, investors may have no interest in new issues. This is because new issues involve greater investment risk than established or "seasoned" public companies. During times of greater overall market volatility, the largest of the public investors tend to minimize risk in their portfolios by moving into more proven, less volatile stocks. Consumer staples and utilities tend to outperform faster growing, unprofitable technology stocks when markets are risky. Furthermore, sometimes the bluest of the blue chips are "on sale" in these periods, and many a portfolio manager prefers shifting money into proven performers at a discounted price rather than into an unproven "trust me it will be great" new issue.

Market volatility is measured by an index, the VIX. The VIX, also called the "fear index" is calculated by the Chicago Board of Trade as an estimate of the market's near-term (30-day) volatility. When the VIX is up, the IPO count goes down. Who wants added risk on top of the market's already heightened level of indigestion-inducing daily swings? When markets are relatively more stable, the IPO count climbs.

The challenge for issuers is that the VIX readjusts daily. It simply isn't possible today to predict how volatile markets will be in six months. The only time companies trying to time the market can have any impact is when they make the "go" or "no go" decision for the roadshow kickoff. Even then, timing the market is almost impossible; swings happen daily. That said, there are times during the year that are suboptimal for an IPO. Companies should assume there will be fewer institutional buyers in the market during the last two weeks of August, traditionally a vacation time for many investors and similarly, the last two weeks of December. Beyond that, all timing conversations are guesses that could be prescient or completely misguided, with the answer clear only in hindsight.

The best strategy for management is to begin preparations when the company's fundamentals are solid, forecasting competent, and the team is in place. Potential issuers can always choose to slow the process down if internal or external factors dictate that to be the prudent choice, but accelerating the process can be done only on the margin because the SEC review process generally takes not less than 90 days from the initial filing and often takes significantly longer. Solid advance preparation of parts of the S-1 and an early start on audits can meaningfully reduce the time spent leading up to the initial document filing. However, even then, the IPO registration and execution process takes the better part of a year.

This chapter covers just the visible portion of the IPO prep iceberg but offers some elements to consider. Summarizing those:

- Exactly what a company aims to accomplish with an IPO should influence the process.

- Companies should:

  - meet with investment bankers judiciously, when and if they want. When the time comes, bankers will be fully attentive and ready.

  - choose IPO timing based on internal pre-paredness, not an externally influenced target or an imaginary "window."

  - not share too many financial details too early. There will be plenty of time for more effective leveraging of those numbers later in the process.

  - befriend a few institutional investors early. There is much to be learned from them that will serve an issuer well when the time comes.

  - should not publicly complain about the cost of Sarbanes-Oxley. If it is too big a hurdle, the company isn't ready.

An IPO is the brass ring (or a college graduation) for entrepreneurial ventures with a bright, independent future. A strategic approach to the process of becoming public can deliver enormous benefits down the road.

# 34

# INTRODUCTION TO IPO READINESS

**Gunderson Dettmer Stough Villeneuve Franklin & Hachigian, LLP**

Richard C. Blake, Corporate Partner

Heidi Mayon, Corporate Partner

As an entrepreneurial company's growth begins to gain scale and accelerate, a natural question is, What's next? Of the typical answers—continue to grow as a private company, be acquired, or conduct an initial public offering (IPO)—the IPO is the one path that eventually requires a company to fundamentally change its stockholder base, governance structure, internal and external reporting, and compliance framework. These changes take time, and at some point in an entrepreneurial company's lifecycle it should begin to consider IPO readiness, even if staying private or selling the company remain viable possibilities.

This introduction to the IPO readiness process outlines what companies should think about and address beginning several years before the IPO organizational meeting—the official "kickoff" for an IPO—to prepare for that transition.

## BEGIN WITH THE END IN MIND, AND BEGIN AS EARLY AS IT MAKES SENSE

The companies that most successfully transition to public companies realize from the beginning that the IPO is not an event unto itself but just one step along a maturing company's lifecycle. Both before and after the IPO, the company has corporate strategies and objectives that transcend the IPO. Companies must simultaneously execute their business and begin to put in place the people, processes and systems that will allow them to successfully conduct an IPO and grow as a public company.

It would be too trite, and not entirely accurate, to say that it is never too early to start preparing for an IPO. Many companies, however, start too late and are forced to "catch up" after making definitive IPO plans. Deciding when to start IPO planning is very company specific, but in most cases, beginning some activities two to three years before an IPO organizational meeting is appropriate.

## THE FUNDAMENTAL PRINCIPLE OF IPO READINESS: BEGIN TO RUN YOUR COMPANY IN KEY WAYS AS IF IT WERE ALREADY A PUBLIC COMPANY

The companies that most successfully transition to life as a public company are the ones that start acting like a public company by the time of the IPO organizational meeting in certain key ways, particularly:

- Setting, achieving, and reporting quarterly and annual financial targets

- Building a finance, accounting, and legal team that is capable of meeting the timelines and substance of public company periodic reporting with the Securities and Exchange Commission (SEC)

- Recruiting a public company quality management team and board of directors

If companies can successfully transition to public company readiness in these areas before an IPO, they can avoid any embarrassment and stock price drop from stumbling early on as a public company. Further, public statements from the SEC clarify that it expects private companies— particularly ones aspiring for an IPO—to improve their transparency with investors, controls on financial reporting, and corporate governance, even as private companies.

## BEGIN TO ASSEMBLE THE TEAM

It will take a small army of internal and external advisors to work on a company's IPO. In the early days of IPO preparation, when the company is still several years away from an IPO, an internal working group of key employees from executive management, finance, and legal typically lead the process, particularly the chief financial officer, controller, general counsel, and others from the legal team. The external group of advisors is also usually smaller at this point, consisting primarily of:

- External legal counsel, who can advise on the IPO process and IPO readiness generally, and on SEC reporting requirements, corporate governance, and stock exchange listing standards, due diligence, and other legal matters specifically

- Independent auditors, who will audit your historical financial statements and ensure that they meet SEC reporting requirements as well as advise on the company's internal control environment and on readiness of the finance team to meet SEC reporting requirements

- Consulting accountants, who can assist the company in finance and accounting tasks that the independent auditors are unable to perform because of SEC auditor independence rules. These include accounting advisory services, assisting to draft historical financial statements, designing and implementing enhanced accounting controls and systems, and supplementing the company's internal finance and accounting team until the company has internally hired all necessary staff to function as a public company

While there is no legal impediment to switching advisors on a company's path to an IPO, the process of doing so is distracting and time consuming and is best avoided by selecting the right advisors at the outset. Each advisor should have experience successfully guiding companies through the IPO process and advising public companies after the IPO.

The companies that most successfully execute IPO preparation have "regular" meetings of the internal and external working group. These meetings are a time for internal education about the IPO process and public company readiness, as well as a time to assign and report on IPO readiness tasks. In the years before an IPO organizational meeting is held, the meetings may be held less frequently; in the year before the organization meeting, the meetings are typically held more frequently—eventually weekly—to ensure that everyone is staying on track with assignments.

The company's underwriter selection is also key for its IPO. A company will want to select underwriters with a strong reputation in the vestment community. In addition to reputation, ompanies should consider:

*Expertise and experience*: Choosing an investment bank with a track record of executing IPOs for similarly situated companies is essential. A company will also want to select an investment bank with expertise in that company's particular industry and sector. Those investment banks will have good relationships with long-term investors interested in that industry, will be able to introduce the company to those investors in pre-IPO "testing the waters" meetings, and will have greater success in placing the company's IPO shares in the hands of those investors.

*Individual bankers*: The individual bankers working on the IPO will be key in drafting the company's story that will form the basis of the investment thesis for new investors. Bankers with expertise and experience in a particular industry will be able to anticipate the questions new investors may have with respect to a company's story, answer those questions preemptively, and drive the new investment community's understanding of the company in the proper direction.

*Research analysts*: A company should also pick an investment bank that has a research analyst who clearly understands the company and the industry in which it operates. While underwriters are not able to promise specific analyst coverage following an IPO, most research analysts at investment banks that served as underwriters begin covering the company. Good research analyst coverage is a requirement to support a stock in the public market.

iscussions with potential underwriters should egin a year or more prior to the organizational heeting. A company will want time to develop relationship with the individual bankers and nderstand the capabilities of a particular bank s well as the research analyst. The final decision n which bank to actually engage for the IPO hay be delayed until approximately a month rior to the actual organizational meeting.

Other advisors who begin assisting in IPO preparation in the year before an IPO include:

- Compensation consultant
- IPO consultant
- Investor relations consultant
- Financial printer and electronic data room provider

During the IPO, additional IPO and post-IPO advisors join the team:

- Roadshow coach
- Transfer agent
- Stock option administrator
- Electronic roadshow provider

## GET YOUR FINANCIAL HOUSE IN ORDER

One tremendous change between being a private company and being a public company is financial reporting, both historical as well as forward looking. Getting your financial house in order can take several years before the IPO organizational meeting, so understanding the financial statement requirements in an IPO and what is expected of public company finance teams after an IPO is a key area of IPO preparation.

In the registration statement that is filed in connection with an IPO, the company will need to include:

- Audited financial statements for the three most recently completed fiscal years or the two most recently completed fiscal years if the company is an emerging growth company under the JOBS Act of 2012 (i.e., one with less than $1 billion in annual revenue), as most entrepreneurial companies are
- Unaudited interim financial statements for the most recently completed three-, six-, or nine-month interim period and the corresponding period of the preceding year
- Management's discussion and analysis (MD&A) of the audited and unaudited interim financial

statements included in the registration statement

- Selected financial information for up to the five most recently completed fiscal years

- Selected quarterly financial data for up to the eight most recently completed fiscal quarters

- Key financial and operational metrics, if any, that the company uses to analyze and manage its business decisions

- Separate audited and interim financial statements and pro forma financial information of certain significant acquisitions

- Other financial information, such as segment reporting and financial statements schedules, depending on the company's circumstances

After an IPO, the company must file a quarterly report with the SEC within 40 to 45 days of the end of the fiscal quarter, including the unaudited interim financial statements and the related MD&A. Within 60 to 90 days of the end of the fiscal year the company will be required to file an annual report with the SEC with audited financial statements.

As a private company, the company may have worked with its independent auditors to complete audits of past annual fiscal periods, but those audits likely were not completed in accordance with SEC requirements for public companies or within the time periods required for annual reports due after an IPO. In addition, private companies typically do not "close the books" each quarter or prepare interim financial statements, nor do they design, document, and test their internal controls at the level required by Section 404 of the Sarbanes-Oxley Act of 2002.

As a result, a major component of a company's IPO preparation involves:

- Identifying and preparing the annual and interim financial statements that would be required in an IPO registration statement

- Building the internal financial reporting staff necessary to prepare these financial statements, as well as closing the company's books each quarter and preparing the

quarterly and annual reports to be filed with the SEC

- Beginning the process of designing, documenting, and testing the company's internal control over financial reporting

The other key area of financial IPO preparation is building a financial planning and analysis (FP&A) team that can prepare forward-looking financial models, identify key performance indicators (KPIs) the company will use to analyze and manage its business, and work with the financial reporting team to report the company's quarterly and annual results. During the course of its IPO, a company will begin to share its projections and model with the research analysts at the investment banks that make up the underwriting syndicate. This model will serve as the preliminary basis in determining the company's IPO price range and gives the research analysts a starting point from which to build their own models that will become the basis for their research reports on the company following the IPO. The company's ability to set and achieve attainable quarterly and annual financial targets is crucial to a newly public company's credibility with these research analysts and public investors.

The companies that most successfully transition to life as a public company are the ones that start the FP&A process early and test the company's ability to forecast, project, and achieve its quarterly and annual KPI targets while the company is still private and not subject to the scrutiny of public analysts and investors. Many companies go so far as to "issue quarterly guidance" to its board or audit committee and then prepare a quarterly earnings press release and hold a mock quarterly earnings call with its board or audit committee and its external advisors to prepare to be in the public spotlight.

## BOARD, MANAGEMENT, AND GOVERNANCE

### BOARD RECRUITMENT AND COMPOSITION

According to "By the Numbers: Venture-backed IPOs in 2016," a Gunderson Dettmer survey of key corporate governance and disclosure topics in IPOs (IPO Survey), at IPO closing boards of emerging growth companies usually range from five to nine persons and average approximately seven persons. Both the New York Stock Exchange and the Nasdaq listing rules require that within 12 months of an IPO closing, a majority of a listed company's board be "independent directors." The IPO Survey, however, found that 94 percent of venture-backed IPO companies in 2016 had a majority of independent directors at the time of IPO closing.

In addition, both stock exchanges require listed companies to have adopted audit, compensation, and nominating committees by the time of the IPO. The audit and compensation committee members must meet heightened independence requirements from the standards applicable to the board in general. In addition, an audit committee must have at least one "audit committee financial expert." There are phase-in periods for meeting the required committee independence tests:

- One committee member must be independent at IPO closing.

- A majority of committee members must be independent within 90 days of IPO closing.

- 100 percent of committee members must be independent within 12 months of IPO closing.

The IPO Survey found, however, that nearly all venture-backed IPO companies in 2016 had entirely independent board committees at the time of IPO closing, as well as at least one audit committee financial expert.

Ideally, the process of on-boarding additional directors takes place over time, one by one, to minimize disruption to the board. Companies should begin early to analyze the knowledge, backgrounds, and skills sets—as well as personalities—that will be needed on the board to effectively execute a company's business strategy as well as operate as a public company.

In the process of assembling its post-IPO board, we recommend that companies prioritize

recruiting an audit committee financial expert who has certain specialized experience and training that enable a deep understanding of financial results and accounting. There is a high demand for such persons, and identifying one who also has the right personality and professional experience to contribute to the board can be time consuming.

Venture-backed companies going public also need to shift from a VC-investor-centric board to one with more operational, accounting, and industry expertise. A few key considerations when evaluating the composition of a future public company board are:

- The number of directors with experience operating or advising a public company

- The specific regulatory and financial expertise of directors

- Industry expertise of directors that enables issue spotting and unique viewpoints

- Directors that are focused on governing for the benefit of all of a company's investors

## MANAGEMENT TEAM

A company should begin evaluating the capabilities of its management team more than a year prior to the time of its IPO, asking whether each has the expertise and ability to scale into a public company executive, and whether additional personnel should be recruited. Often, a company will need to bring on a CFO who has experience reporting financial information of a public company and communicating those results to public investors. A general counsel, COO, and additional finance and sales personnel are also often added in the year leading up to an IPO.

## CORPORATE GOVERNANCE

By the time a company goes public, it will be required to adopt a number of new "public company" policies and procedures to comply with SEC and stock exchange listing standards. Many companies, particularly those with a larger number of employees or broader geographical scale, begin this process in the year or so before the IPO by adopting several key policies, including:

- Code of business conduct, which sets the company's expectations regarding honest and ethical conduct, including handling conflicts of interest; compliance with applicable laws, rules, and regulations; prompt internal reporting of violations to an appropriate person; and accountability for adherence to the code

- Compliance policy and hotline, which gives employees a means by which to make confidential and anonymous reports regarding concerns

- Public communications policy, which addresses who may act as a company spokesperson and what type of information the company may disclose publicly, which may include policies regarding use of social media

## LEGAL PREPARATION

Ideally the company has been working closely with external counsel since it was incorporated to make sure it has complied with legal formalities. No later than the year before a company goes public, however, it should begin working with its external counsel to make sure it is prepared on two main legal fronts for its IPO, due diligence and registration statement drafting. Ideally, the company can walk into the IPO organizational meeting with its due diligence data completely prepared and a draft of the registration statement ready.

Following the IPO organizational meeting, the underwriters and their counsel will want to ensure that the company's historical legal and other documents have been reviewed and that information included in the registration statement has sufficient factual support. In advance of the organizational meeting, the company, working with external counsel, typically prepares a "virtual data room" containing electronic copies of these documents, which can take some time to compile and upload. In advance of creating a data room, the company and external counsel typically review the company's records to ensure whether any corporate housekeeping should be

done in advance of the IPO. Most importantly, this housekeeping review would include the following:

- Reports on past board, committee, and stockholder actions to ensure they are complete and accurate

- Historical issuances of stock and options to ensure that they comply with state and federal corporate and securities requirements and that the company's capitalization records are accurate and complete

- Organizational documents and material agreements to understand which may be required to be filed with the SEC in connection with the IPO, what approvals are necessary for the IPO, whether the IPO triggers any rights or responsibilities for the company, and whether anything else limits the company's business in any way

- Intellectual property protection and status

External counsel can also assist the company to prepare the registration statement that will be required to be filed with the SEC. Some of the sections of the registration statement— including the section describing the company's business and MD&A—are typically drafted in collaboration with the entire IPO working group and take a great deal of time after the IPO organizational meeting. External counsel, however, usually assists in drafting the remainder of the registration statement before the organizational meeting, including the risk factors, description of management and the board, executive compensation, principal stockholders, related party transactions, and description of capital stock.

## FINAL PRACTICAL ADVICE

It is easy to become overwhelmed at the amount of work that an IPO will take. Entrepreneurs who begin IPO planning early, start running their company like a public company in advance of the organizational meeting, and address the key lead-time items discussed above will put their companies in a better position to successfully execute their IPOs and continue to grow as a public company.

# 35

# GETTING YOUR PRE-IPO ACCOUNTING HOUSE IN ORDER

**KPMG**

Aamir Husain, National IPO Readiness Leader

Dean Bell, Partner in Charge and U.S. Head of Accounting
  Advisory Services

Brian Hughes, National Partner in Charge of Private Markets &
  National Venture Capital Co-Leader

Mike Meara, Director, Accounting Advisory Services

A company that is planning to go public is subject to a host of new and complex accounting requirements. These range from issues with financial statements, to providing sufficient key performance indicators (KPIs) in management's discussion and analysis (MD&A), to providing data concerning highly technical accounting issues. Pre-IPO companies will frequently be dealing with many of these items for the first time and can find the SEC requirements to be quite burdensome. However, we have found that companies can tackle the process much more effectively by planning early and by focusing on several accounting issues that have historically raised the most red flags.

A company that has a coherent IPO plan and understands the accounting issues that have historically raised difficulties will substantially limit any surprises during the IPO process. Focusing on these accounting items early on will help to minimize any delays during the SEC comment phase. As recent volatile markets have shown, companies need to have the flexibility to file an IPO when the best market conditions are present. Having key issues resolved early, especially those that involve complex accounting rules, can make it much easier for a company to file at the most opportune moment.

## BEWARE OF THE MORE COMMON ACCOUNTING COMPLEXITIES

Frequently, the accounting issues that are the most problematic are those that are particularly complex or subject to conflicting or subjective interpretations. In our experience, there are several accounting areas that warrant extra attention and that need to be considered early in the planning process. Giving these five accounting areas adequate focus can help minimize problems as the IPO date approaches. These areas include the **registrant's financial statements, SEC S-X Rule 3-05, KPIs, certain technical accounting issues,** and *pro forma* **financial information.**

# 1. THE REGISTRANT'S FINANCIAL STATEMENTS

Prior to an IPO, management needs to consider the appropriate structure for the entity that will be going public. It may choose to restructure to gain tax advantages or for other business reasons. For example, multiple entities may be combined to form the registrant (also known as a roll-up or put-together transaction) or corporate divisions can be carved out or spun off. The legal entity structuring used to form the registrant can add complexity and may trigger the requirement for additional financial statements to be presented in the registration statement if a "predecessor" entity exists.

The definition of "predecessor" in Rule 405 of SEC Regulation C is very broad for purposes of financial statements required in a registration statement. The designation of a "predecessor" is required when "a registrant succeeds to substantially all of the business (or a separately identifiable line of business) of another entity (or group of entities) and the registrant's own operations before the succession appears insignificant relative to the operations assumed or acquired." In order to determine if an entity is a predecessor entity, management should consider the order in which the entities were acquired, the size and value of the entities, and ultimately whether the acquired entity will be the main driver of the entire business's operations.

When a predecessor is identified, the registration statement must include the predecessor's financial information. Pre-IPO companies should be cognizant of this requirement as they are finalizing their corporate structure. This can be a tricky area since significant judgment may be required in identifying a predecessor, and it can be challenging to identify the proper set of financial statements to include for a predecessor in a registration statement.

# 2. S-X RULE 3-05—FINANCIAL STATEMENTS OF OTHER ENTITIES

Under this potentially burdensome rule, a public company must include audited financial statements in its SEC registration statements for any "significant" business it has acquired. (This rule also applies to any planned acquisitions.) These audited statements must be submitted for either one, two, or three years, depending on the significance of the acquisition and must include a balance sheet, a statement of income, a statement of cash flows, and related disclosures.

A pre-IPO company needs to ask the following questions under Rule 3-05 to determine if financial statements are required and for what time period they will be required:

- Is a "business" being acquired?
- How significant is the acquired business?
- Has the acquisition occurred or is it probable?

Once the company has determined that an acquisition has taken place, the significance of that acquisition must be determined. The SEC uses three tests to make that determination:

1. *The investment test:* The total purchase price of the target (adjusted for certain items) is compared to the acquirer's pre-acquisition consolidated total assets.

2. *The asset test:* The asset test compares the target's consolidated total assets to the acquirer's pre-acquisition consolidated total assets.

3. *The income test:* Under this test, the target's consolidated income from continuing operations before taxes, extraordinary items, and cumulative effect of a change in accounting principles and exclusive of any amounts attributable to any noncontrolling interest ("pretax income") is compared to the acquirer's pre-acquisition consolidated pretax income.

All three of the tests must be performed, and the significance level of the target is ultimately calculated based on the highest percentage reached *in any* of the three tests. Therefore, pre-IPO companies should be aware that an acquisition that appears insignificant under one test may be significant under another test and will therefore trigger the reporting requirements under Rule 3-05 (see Figure 1: Number of Years Financial Statements are Required for Targets).

**FIGURE 1** Number of Years Financial Statements are Required for Targets

| > 20% | > 40% | > 50% |
| 1 Year | 2 Years | 3 Years |

Companies with under $1 billion in revenues that qualify for filing under the JOBS Act will be required to submit only up to two years of financial statements for recent, significant acquisitions.)

Why is this rule so problematic? This requirement tends to pose significant challenges for pre-IPO companies because the targets that they purchase are frequently young companies themselves, with a less sophisticated approach towards financial statement requirements. Any company that is considering going public needs to understand these rules and analyze their impact at the time of the acquisition. Financial statements for the target should be reviewed as soon as feasible. If no adequate financial statements exist and are required under the rules, the pre-IPO company should be prepared to create them in conjunction with the target's financial team.

Other circumstances that could require the inclusion of separate financial statements are S-X Rule 3-09, which can require separate financial statements for significant equity method investments of the registrant, and, in the case of the registration of a debt offering, S-X Rule 3-10, which can require separate financial statements of subsidiaries that are guarantors of the registrant's debt being registered.

## 3. DEFINE KEY PERFORMANCE INDICATORS TO SUPPORT MANAGEMENT'S REPORTING REQUIREMENTS

Companies seeking to go public are required to prepare an MD&A for inclusion in the S-1, which discusses the historical performance of the business from which investors can draw guidance on future performance. This is achieved through a narrative explanation of the financial statements and other statistical data to enhance an understanding of the company's business performance. The MD&A should provide insight through discussion of a company's financial statements that enables investors to see the company through the eyes of the management, to enhance overall financial disclosure by providing contextual information with which financial information can be analyzed, and provide information on quality and variability of a company's earnings and cash flows.

It is essential that management selects and prepares KPIs that effectively communicate business performance in a clearly understood manner that can be used to measure historic trends, compared with other peer companies within the same industry, and provide information necessary for an understanding of likely future business developments.

The starting point for choosing appropriate KPIs should be those that management currently uses to manage the business. These should be evaluated through a balanced view of common practice of other public companies in the industry and those needed to adequately measure and communicate achievements of management's stated strategies. Management should be prepared to discuss their choice of KPIs and how these are relevant to the business, especially if they include metrics not commonly used in their industry.

There has been increased usage of non-GAAP (generally accepted accounting principles)

measures by registrants to supplement other metrics that management considers important in running the business. While non-GAAP measures are allowed to be presented in SEC filings, the SEC has issued guidelines and has prohibited practices concerning their use and has increased scrutiny in this area recently. If a registrant considers using non-GAAP measures in a registration statement, it needs to ensure the SEC guidelines are followed.

The SEC has steadily expanded the line-item disclosure requirements for the MD&A, adding specific requirements for off-balance sheet arrangements, long-term contractual obligations, and certain derivatives contracts and related-party transactions, as well as critical accounting policies.

While the requirements of the MD&A are detailed and may seem straightforward, pre-IPO companies frequently struggle to produce a document that meets the SEC's requirements. Companies that are not used to meeting the expectations of stockholders or analysts may have a hard time adequately explaining their business model, which seems intuitive to the management team. In addition, many pre-IPO companies may use unique metrics that are not used by similar companies in their industries. That tends to be a mistake. The SEC is looking for MD&As where the metrics are benchmarked against industry norms and that conform to the industry standard or to those used by the company's closest competitors. This is not an area where creativity is appreciated.

Creating future projections is always a difficult process. Growth and profit projections need to be based on realistic assumptions that are shared by at least a portion of the industry. Starting early is advantageous as well; if a company is making assumptions that are different from its peers, those assumptions can be explained or possibly changed in response to SEC comments.

## 4. TECHNICAL ACCOUNTING ISSUES

In our experience, certain technical accounting issues demand added attention from the pre-IPO

finance team. We have found that these areas have become SEC favorites when it comes to added scrutiny. These accounting issues usually involve new rules and/or those areas that may be subject to multiple or subjective interpretations. Companies who do not spend enough time on these issues risk a complicated comment period and may even find themselves subject to issuing a restatement. A restatement issued in the first few quarters after a company has gone public can result in a huge loss of public confidence, a decline in stock price, and questions from suppliers and/or customers. Recovering from such a public event may take months or even years. Our advice—get it right the first time.

### Revenue Recognition

Revenue recognition rules have always been subject to SEC scrutiny for newly public companies. New revenue recognition rules have been issued by the Financial Accounting Standards Board (FASB) and will soon become effective. Companies need to ensure that they are complying with the new rules and are using established and accepted mechanisms for recognizing revenue, even in cases where new business models are being used. We anticipate that this is one area that will receive even more attention from the SEC moving forward. In addition, adoption dates vary for public and private companies, and newly public companies need to ensure that they are ready to meet the public company timelines.

### Segment Reporting

In addition to all of the consolidated financial information, companies that are engaged in more than one line of business or operate in more than one geographic area may also be required to include separate revenues and operating data for each of their business lines or geographic areas.

Generally, an operating segment is defined as a component of a larger enterprise that engages in business activities from which it may earn revenues and incur expenses; whose operating esults are regularly reviewed by the enterprise's hief operating decision maker; and for which iscrete financial information is available.

he aim of segment reporting is to align public nancial reporting with a company's internal eporting in order to permit financial analysts nd the public to see the overall enterprise the ame way management sees it. The SEC has onsistently focused on segment reporting, and nese accounting issues may be particularly crutinized in the pre-IPO context since it is ommon for organizational changes to take place re-IPO.

he most critical factor in determining whether n issuer has more than one operating segment how management runs its business. Whether n issuer can aggregate operating segments is ghly fact specific, involves certain judgment alls, and depends on factors such as economic milarity, the similarity of the products or ervices sold, the nature of the production rocess, customer type, distribution methods, nd the regulatory environment for the usiness.

## he Issue of "Cheap Stock"

nother technically challenging SEC favorite is o-called "cheap stock." Questions may arise hen a pre-IPO company awards stock to mployees during the 12 months before the IPO t valuations that are substantially lower than ne IPO offering price. ASC 718 requires that ne fair value of the equity given to employees e established on the grant date of the award; nat the fair value must be determined based n available information on the grant date; and nat the grant date value will be recognized as compensation expense during the employee's mployment.

a pre-IPO context, the value of a stock ward can vary greatly in a very short period f time, and assumptions and projections may e subject to large variances. Some companies nd themselves stumbling when they need to xplain how a particular stock award was valued. ompanies are advised to understand the

accounting rules before making any stock-based compensation awards in the period leading up to an IPO and to use justifiable assumptions and/ or an independent entity to evaluate the award. Documenting all assumptions is key.

## Impairment Issues

We have found that pre-IPO companies have been challenged with asset value impairment issues. Impairment issues tend to be industry specific. However, in general, companies have recently been finding it much more difficult to value their businesses and their underlying assets. Global economic uncertainty and rapid shifts in interest rates and commodity prices, among other factors, have made it tougher than ever to accurately predict future revenue and profit numbers and underlying asset assumptions.

As they prepare to go public, companies need to evaluate on a quarterly basis whether there have been any impairment triggers. If there is an impairment triggering event, companies should be prepared to calculate any impairment charge under U.S. GAAP.

## 5. *PRO FORMA* FINANCIAL INFORMATION

Another accounting area where companies are urged to spend added time concerns *pro forma* information. *Pro forma* financial information needs to be provided to reflect the impact of any IPO structuring transaction. In addition to a material acquisition, S-X Article 11 also requires *pro forma* financial information in a number of other situations, such as:

- Disposition of a significant portion of a business;

- Acquisitions of one or more real estate operations;

- Roll up transactions;

- The registrant was previously part of another entity; and

- Any other financial events or transactions that would be material to investors.

*Pro forma* financial information is intended to illustrate the continuing impact of a transaction by showing how the specific transaction might have affected historical financial statements had it occurred at the beginning of the issuer's most recently completed fiscal year or the earliest period presented.

In particular, the rules require:

- A condensed *pro forma* balance sheet as of the end of the most recent period for which a consolidated balance sheet of the issuer is required, unless the transaction is already reflected in that balance sheet; and

- A condensed *pro forma* income statement for the issuer's most recently completed fiscal year and the most recent interim period of the issuer, unless the historical income statement reflects the transaction for the entire period.

*Pro forma* adjustments can involve some degree of judgment calls and are therefore just the kind of accounting issue that the SEC staff may question. The finance team needs to determine whether *pro forma* financial information will be required and make sure that it is using widely accepted metrics when developing the company's *pro forma* financial statements.

## CONCLUSION

Going public has tremendous advantages. However, the process itself is quite time-consuming and complex. Companies that are contemplating an IPO need to plan early and understand all of the requirements and challenges. Management can easily lose control of the process because of problems with complex accounting issues, which can cause delays or even a major loss of shareholder confidence. While all filing requirements are important, paying particular attention to some of the more difficult accounting issues, and doing so as soon as possible, can help a company develop a coherent and effective IPO readiness plan that may avoid some of the most common accounting pitfalls.

In addition to focusing on these potentially perilous accounting issues, pre-IPO companies need to be cognizant of all post-IPO reporting and listing requirements. They should be prepared to establish an effective investor relations function, to issue accurate and timely 10-Ks and 10-Qs, to meet SOX compliance rules, and to meet all other rules and expectations that public companies need to follow.

# 36

# GUIDEBOOK TO A SUCCESSFUL IPO

Morgan Stanley

Colin R. Stewart, Head of Global Capital Markets Technology
   Group, Vice Chairman

## MARKET BACKDROP

*Increasingly selective IPO market over the last 2 years:* Since 2001 (exclusive of crisis years in 2002, 2003, 2008, and 2009), we have averaged around 40 tech IPOs amounting to $8 billion in issuance annually. The tepid tech IPO activity over the last two years meant that there were only 23 and 16 IPOs in 2015 and 2016, respectively. Companies are now staying private for longer as they focus on scaling their business towards a critical mass and closer to profitability. Notwithstanding the vibrant private financing market that has been useful in funding long-term growth aspirations, investors are also exercising more restraint, preferring companies with seasoned management teams that operate under a more stable competitive landscape.

*Multiyear expansion of M&A activity continues to exacerbate scarcity in investment opportunity*: Since 2015, the technology sector in the United States has lost a net of more than $200 billion of publicly traded free float. This number is a net number that takes into account only cash, mergers and acquisitions (M&A) transactions, and all IPOs and follow-on transactions completed. The confluence of the increase in pace, volume, and size of M&A transactions, and the abysmally low new issuance volumes have dramatically reduced the investable universe of tech companies (especially those with growth) in the sweet spot of $1 billion to $10 billion in equity value. The lack of investing choices is particularly acute across the software and Internet sectors. These will lead to favorable demand dynamics for the tech IPO market over

**TABLE 1**  IPO Overview Across Different Time Periods

|  | 1997–1998 | 1999–2000 | 2001–2008 | 2009–2016 |
|---|---|---|---|---|
| IPO Size ($MM) | 130 | 162 | 212 | 347 |
| Market Cap ($MM) | 711 | 1140 | 920 | 2156 |
| LTM Revenue ($MM) | 224 | 107 | 339 | 23 |
| LTM Operating Margin (%) | (84%) | (1942%) | 8% | 8% |
| Growth Rate (%) |  |  | 125% | 45% |

the next two years, as the current class of tech unicorns matures into companies with growth, profitability, and scale.

## IPO SUCCESS FACTORS FOR PROSPECTIVE PUBLIC COMPANIES

*"History does not repeat itself, but it does rhyme."* – Mark Twain/Joseph Anthony Wittreich

We applied our magnifying glass to analyze more than 250 tech companies that have gone public since 2010. There were a number of key takeaways from the subsequent pattern recognition for successful public companies.

*Growth rate trends (primarily revenue before other measures of profitability):* It was not too long ago that the "growth at all cost" mentality was in vogue. Investors now adopt a more holistic approach in sizing companies, often scrutinizing the quarter-on-quarter (QoQ) and year-on-year (YoY) pace of growth (deceleration). Once bitten, twice shy. They now demand the pain associated with revenue decelerations to be offset by accelerations in free cash flow and/or profitability.

Having said that, our sample analysis still suggests a minimum threshold of 40 percent YoY growth in quarterly revenue in order to stand out from the madding crowd. This is imperative, given the global scarcity of high-growth stocks with decent scale (market cap between $1 billion and $10 billion) in the tech sector (mostly Internet and software). For instance, of the 160+ Internet companies with market cap between $1 billion and $10 billion globally, there are only 9 companies that are expected to grow their respective revenues above 30 percent YoY. In the equivalent software universe, there are only 8 out of 195 companies.

*Revenue scale:* Revenue scale is indicative of a company's ability to capture its addressable markets (serviceable and total) and its competitive edge vis-à-vis peers. Gems are often uncovered for companies with trailing 12-month revenues that are greater than $150 million because they usually are able to generate enough top line and

become operationally feasible (breakeven) from the subsequent operating leverage. This threshold has been raised recently, driven as the quest for faster growth.

For instance, the older class of IPOs used to break even at about $200 million to $250 million in revenue. Now we are seeing some companies break even at $400 million to $500 million in revenue. This is also attributable to the increasingly intense competitive landscape, especially in verticals that have large total available markets (TAMs) but niche serviceable available markets (SAMs), which all create execution issues in allowing companies to punch through to $200 million to $250 million, let alone $400 million to $500 million, at a sustainable revenue growth rate of 30 percent.

*Profitability:* The perennial question for both investors and companies in regards to which lens to view the world is, profitability versus growth. Does it have to be one or the other, or is there a way to balance the two? As the paradigm shifts from the "grow, expand" mentality, as it has been doing over the last few years, we have seen broad-based multiple compression, especially for companies which do not have GAAP (generally accepted accounting principles) earnings. In that regard, investors have flocked towards perceived safe havens in the form of larger $100 billion or more market cap companies that continue to accrue a disproportionate amount of value in the public markets via consistent outperformance in delivering both top and bottom lines.

Beyond longer term considerations around the ability of nascent public companies to augment their profitability profiles, we have found that prospective public companies with better than 20 percent operating margin at time of listing often have a better chance of success, in terms of longer-term value creation for shareholders

*Business model:* Growth rates, revenue scale, profitability—in our view, all these ultimately collapse into a point of singularity in the form of your business model. How do you expect to make money? What are your unit economics? Why are you special? Impressive growth rates and revenue scale may arouse investor interest, but a clear articulation of your business model will ultimately command buy-side interest. Technology may change with time, but investors have always preferred predictability, visibility, and maturity of the business model. These translate into convincing investors that their risk is low through consistent execution, a sticky user base through cohort behavior over time, attractive lifetime value to customer acquisition cost, efficient marketing spend, low user churn, and an upside that can be achieved with low friction.

## UNDERSTANDING THE BUY-SIDE PSYCHE: "RISK VS. REWARD"

In recent years, the tech IPO market has been dominated by software and Internet, 89 percent of the issuance in 2014 to 2016, compared to a decade ago when it was 44 percent. The IPO market is likely to have a similar composition in the near future, especially looking at which companies have been funded over the past few years. We examined the dataset of software and Internet IPOs since 2004. The playing field has been pretty even, with 121 Internet IPOs versus 116 software IPOs.

An investor who invested in the entire basket of 237 Internet and software IPOs would have more than doubled the S&P's performance since 2014 (up 194 percent for software/Internet IPOs vs. 85 percent for the S&P). While that is a lot of alpha or outperformance over a couple of market and economic cycles relative to existing public companies, not all Internet and software companies are created equal in regards to public market returns and risk profiles.

*Internet investing:* Internet investing is best characterized by a paraphrased quote from William Faulkner: "You cannot swim for new horizons (returns) until you have courage to lose sight of the shore (value)." Internet investing is not for the faint-hearted, with the return profiles barbelled towards massive value creation for a few companies but value destruction for many.

Having the attention of billions of users while continuing to innovate to maintain engagement

(video, virtual reality, messaging, health, e-commerce, autonomous driving) and at the same time delivering massive cash flow, GAAP earnings to acquire key technologies or companies (YouTube, Android, Whatsapp, Instagram, Qunar, etc.), and hire top talent is akin to tackling the impossible trinity—the ultimate juggling act that ultimately will yield very few winners.

Despite $900 billion of value being created by 121 Internet companies, the concentration of performance has been from a very small number of IPOs, with 74 percent of the value being created by Google (Alphabet), Facebook, and Baidu. Excluding these three companies, we saw only $69 billion of net value creation by 118 Internet companies. Meanwhile, 64 Internet companies (54 percent) lost $54 billion in shareholder value.

*Software investing:* Software investing magnifies the virtues of compounding in the form of lower returns but has lower beta and lower risk. Compared to Internet companies, the switching cost for software is higher (harder to rip out) and relationships are typically contracted over a period of years, providing a stable and visible base to anchor revenue growth. Add that to the "land and expand" component of successful software companies, and we would have a set of companies that are able to consistently compound growth on a yearly basis. The next generation of software companies are also valuable in an M&A context to legacy software companies because they provide them with much needed growth and access to new technologies/ business models, thereby introducing a valuation floor for newly public software companies.

Of the 116 software IPOs that we have seen since 2004, there has been $174 billion of value creation, with Salesforce being the largest value creator at $51 billion (29 percent). Excluding Salesforce, the 115 other companies created $123 billion in value, arguably a more diverse set of positive data. Meanwhile, only 39 software companies are currently trading below IPO price, having experienced $11 billion of value destruction.

## FINAL THOUGHTS AND TAKEAWAYS

"I am awfully greedy; I want everything from life (investing) . . . You see, it is difficult to get all (returns) which I want. And then when I do not succeed I get mad with anger." – Simone de Beauvoir

Regardless of economic market climate, investors will always seek the path of least (seemingly) resistance, i.e., strong returns with limited risk. For Internet companies, this means higher returns but lower beta and overall riskiness. For software companies, this means dial up the returns but keep the low volatility and predictability. In other words, investors all want to buy growth and scale that are inherent in Internet winners but with the predictability and stability of enterprise.

While utopia in the form of perfect investment does not exist in the real world, the following translate into a few key organizing principles as you move toward being a public company:

- Do your best to articulate your company's story, particularly the overall riskiness of the business. In that line, scale matters as much as your company's path towards profitability.

- With a prevailing "show-me" approach, investors would need to be convinced that the risk is low through execution, solid business model, defensible TAM, expanding SAM, as well as a team that understands the tradeoff between profitability and growth and has a handle on growth as you execute towards $1 billion of revenue and beyond.

- Have a team that is able to focus as much on the qualitative aspects (vision, mission, long-term strategy, competition) as much as the quantitative side of things (TAM and SAM sizing, user data, cohort behavior, salesforce efficiency, daily active users/monthly active users [DAU/MAU], engagement, renewal rates). Our recent experience suggest that investors have come to expect user data as they build long-term models that take into account the ramp-up in sales.

- Size matters but is not everything. This is especially true when it comes to TAM sizing. Time and time again, we have seen "too good to be true" TAM sizing being heavily discounted by the Street. What matters is leaving enough margin of safety in terms of the bottom-up sizing in order for you to consistently deliver a beat-and-raise quarter.

# 37

# THE NYSE'S VIEW OF GOING PUBLIC AND SELLING SECURITIES IN THE CAPITAL MARKETS

New York Stock Exchange

As you go through the process of leading a high-growth company through an IPO, one of the most important decisions is selecting the right market for listing the company's securities.

## GLOBAL EXCHANGE OVERVIEW

According to the World Federation of Exchanges, as of December 31, 2016, the Americas had the highest domestic market capitalization, which reached $31 trillion, followed by Asia Pacific at $23 trillion. The New York Stock Exchange (NYSE) is the largest and most liquid exchange compared to all other exchanges globally. As of December 31, 2016, NYSE had cumulative domestic capitalization of $19.6 trillion, with the Nasdaq second at $7.8 trillion. In addition, as of December 31, 2016, the NYSE leads as the most liquid exchange, trading 20 percent of total cash equity, followed by Nasdaq at 13 percent. This can be attributed to NYSE's unique market model that is designed to maximize liquidity, encourage market activity, and help participants trade more efficiently. See Figure 1.

## WHY LIST IN THE UNITED STATES?

U.S. capital markets are viewed as the destination of choice for investors and companies alike as they provide unparalleled liquidity, diversity, cross-border capability, and, as a result of the 2012 JOBS Act, regulatory and financial reporting

**FIGURE 1** Top Five Total Domestic Market Capitalization and Liquid Cash Equity Trading as of December 31, 2016

| Total Domestic Market Cap ($T) | |
|---|---|
| NYSE | $19.6 |
| Nasdaq-US | $7.8 |
| Japan Exchange Groups Inc. | $5.1 |
| Shanghai Stock Exchange | $4.1 |
| LSE Group | $3.5 |

| Liquid Cash Equity Trading ($M) | |
|---|---|
| NYSE | $1,353.6 |
| BATS Global Markets | $1,032.2 |
| Nasdaq-US | $875.2 |
| Shenzhen Shock Exchange | $767.9 |
| Shanghai Stock Exchange | $642.4 |

**FIGURE 2** Top Five Exchanges by IPO Proceeds Raised and Median Proceeds Raised from 2014 to 2016

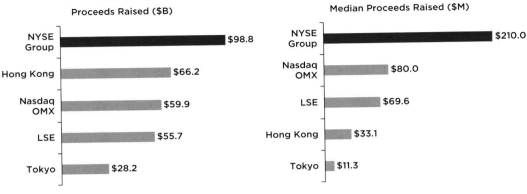

relief. From 2014 to 2016, $522 billion was raised from IPOs. With 619 IPOs, U.S. exchanges represented 28 percent of proceeds raised. There are currently four exchanges in the United States where companies can raise capital. The NYSE led with $98 billion in proceeds raised for the same time period. See Figure 2.

For companies backed by venture capital (VC) or private equity (PE), follow-ons also become an important decision factor. Follow-on activity remains equally strong in the United States. See Figure 3.

## DOES EQUITY MARKET STRUCTURE MATTER?

The U.S. equity market structure rules are developed and enforced by the Securities and Exchange Commission (SEC). An underlying

principle of these rules is to ensure that market participants executing orders on behalf of investors seek out the best execution for that order—this often translates to the best available price, and it is the broker's responsibility to secure it.

SEC rules implemented in 2007 placed a regulatory emphasis on achieving the best price for each order by promoting competition among exchanges. In order to compete, the SEC required exchanges to become fully automated and immediately accessible. This led to a proliferation of electronic exchanges and other more opaque electronic trading platforms known as dark pools. Today there are 13 exchanges and more than 50 dark pools available for executing orders.

The growth of the number of trading venues has increased the level of competition among trading

**FIGURE 3** Top Five Exchanges for Marketed Follow-on Proceeds Raised and Median Proceeds Raised from 2014-2016

**TABLE 1**    Comparison of the NYSE and Nasdaq as of December 31, 2016

|  | NYSE | Nasdaq |
| --- | --- | --- |
| Market Structure | Only hybrid model combining technology with human insight, accountability, and capital support | 100% electronic trading optimized to be fast, automated, and anonymous order execution |
| Listed companies | 2,024 | 2,475 |
| Total market cap | $25.3T | $8.5T |
| Median market cap | $2.8B | $349M |
| Average daily volume (shares) | 1,807,792 | 658,288 |
| Average daily volume (dollars) | $66.9M | $27.1M |
| Market cap distribution | Small cap: 37% | Small cap: 57% |
|  | Mid cap: 36% | Mid cap: 31% |
|  | Large cap: 27% | Large cap: 13% |
| Exchange-traded volume | 37.7% | 27.8% |
| Capital obligations | $75M | $1M |

venues and reduced costs to trade; however, this has also resulted in a more fragmented marketplace. Although this has achieved lower costs of trading, it has increased the fixed costs associated with connecting to multiple venues. Such fragmentation also makes it harder for institutional investors to source liquidity. Table 1 provides a brief comparison of the U.S. listing exchanges.

## OTHER EXCHANGE CONSIDERATIONS

In addition to the market structure and access to capital, there are other key considerations when deciding on the listing venue.

### TRADING MODEL

The NYSE is the only exchange in the world that combines leading technology with human judgment to prioritize price discovery and stability over speed. Nasdaq offers electronic trading optimized to be fast, automated, and anonymous. The cornerstone of the NYSE market model is the Designated Market Maker (DMM). DMMs have obligations to maintain fair and orderly markets for their assigned securities.

They operate both manually and electronically to facilitate price discovery during market opens, closes, and during periods of trading imbalances or instability. This high-touch approach is crucial in order to offer the best prices, dampen volatility, add liquidity, and enhance value.

### GLOBAL REACH AND VISIBILITY

The two main U.S. exchanges, NYSE and Nasdaq, are well known. Being listed on the NYSE or Nasdaq may help companies find new investors more easily, add credibility with customers and vendors, and inspire confidence in their overall market position.

The opening and closing of the trading day garner concentrated media attention and provide a company on its listing day unique opportunities to gain immediate global visibility. For example, the NYSE's Opening Bell is broadcast across 33 channels. Furthermore, many listed companies return to the exchanges after their IPO multiple times a year to use their facilities for analyst, investor, or board meetings as well as corporate announcements, media interviews, and events.

## NETWORK AS A BUSINESS PLATFORM

In addition to the important company debut on the occasion of a company's IPO, another key venue consideration is to list among peers, customers, and partners. That commonality may facilitate better connections to help drive business objectives. Additionally, exchanges also host events that provide networking opportunities and relationship development within its listed company community.

Many of the leading established companies from technology and health care to energy and industrial are traded on the Big Board. For example, 90 percent of the Dow Jones Industrial Average and 77 percent of the S&P 500 are listed on the New York Stock Exchange. Furthermore, between 2014 and 2016, NYSE continued to list the larger companies, where 57 percent and 45 percent of the IPOs that chose to list on NYSE had a market capitalization greater than $700 million and $1 billion, respectively. In contrast for the same time period, 56 percent and 41 percent of the IPOs that listed on Nasdaq had a market capitalization of less than $300 million and $200 million respectively.

From an industry sector perspective, both exchanges are highly diversified. See Figure 4.

However, as noted previously, the size of the companies is significantly different between the two exchanges where the median market capitalization of the listed companies for NYSE and Nasdaq is $2.8 billion and $349 million, respectively.

## INVESTOR RELATIONS SERVICES

Another important factor when considering a listing venue is the quality of customer service and the solutions that will help the management team after its IPO. Being a public company offers increased access to the capital needed to continue innovating and growing, but it also places new requirements on companies. Executives and investor relations officers (IROs) are on the front line, delivering corporate strategy and financial reports to shareholders and facilitating shareholder feedback and insights back to corporate boards. Companies are increasingly relying on chief financial officers (CFOs) in developing corporate strategy, in addition to their being responsible for capital management, financials, audits, and strategic investments. IR teams are also becoming more involved in internal and external communications, competitive intelligence, media relations, and other corporate initiatives in addition to financial reporting. Thus, the exchanges' ability to provide

**FIGURE 4** Market Share Comparison of Listed Companies by Industry for NYSE and Nasdaq as of December 31, 2016 by Market Capitalization

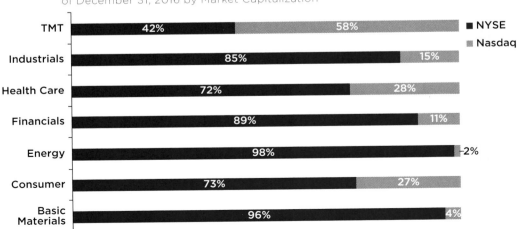

robust analytics and shareholder intelligence, as well as to provide direct access to market traders, as part of the IR toolkit, is paramount to helping a company manage a well-run investor relations program.

## SIDEBAR

Elements in evaluating the quality of the IR toolkit include:

*Best-in-class versus one-stop shop*: The NYSE teams up with the leading providers of webhosting/website design solutions, market analytics, surveillance services, and news distribution. Nasdaq has chosen a different strategy of acquiring various companies over the years to provide these stand-alone services directly.

*Direct access to traders to gain market information and insights:* For NYSE-listed companies, IROs and CFOs can directly contact the designated market maker who has specific obligations related to each issuer's stock and

can provide real time information to evaluate the stock.

*Ongoing issuer services program:* Each exchange provides access to data and analytical tools, but with varying degrees of functionality and cost. The NYSE, however, is the only exchange to provide complimentary issuer services (webhosting, market analytics, surveillance services) for qualified listed companies, based on the shares outstanding.

*Community events:* Access to the IR community through summits, webinars, and roundtables helps foster sharing best practices and networking.

*Venue for investor events:* The NYSE recently completed a significant renovation of its landmark building and increased event capacity by 40 percent. Furthermore, the space is complimentary to the listed community and can be used to hold various business functions including analyst and investor days, board meetings, and customer events.

# 38

# 409A VALUATIONS AND OTHER COMPLEX EQUITY COMPENSATION ISSUES

KPMG

Anthony Doughty, CFA, Managing Director

Michael Notton, CFA, CPA, Senior Manager

## BACKGROUND

Valuation of various equity classes issued by an enterprise, sometimes within a complex capital structure, can be a daunting but necessary exercise for a private company when certain key milestones occur (e.g., exploring another round of financing or granting share-based compensation to employees) or for meeting tax and financial reporting requirements. The sections below will offer a thorough explanation of the valuation process and will describe the key features of various instruments commonly encountered when valuing equity classes within a complex capital structure. This article is not intended to provide specific accounting or tax guidance. Moreover, given the complexities involved, this article will focus on the overall goal and intent of the valuation techniques versus extensive discussion on option theory or nuances underlying the approaches.

## BASICS

Securities within complex capital structures predominantly include preferred stock, common stock, and share-based awards.

*Preferred stock*: The rights of preferred stock can be divided into two broad yet distinct categories—economic rights and control rights. Economic rights offer an advantage to preferred stockholders as compared to common stockholders, since these rights directly correlate with the timing, preference, and amounts of returns these preferred stockholders receive. Control rights ensure that preferred stockholders can influence or control the enterprise in ways that are disproportionate to their ownership percentages.

*Common stock:* Common stock represents the residual claim on enterprise value after debt and preferred equity holders have been repaid. Common stock is typically the foundation for benchmarking the relative ownership percentage of the various classes: ownership interests related to preferred equity and share-based awards are often expressed as a percentage of their fully diluted common share equivalents.

*Share-based compensation:* This may include various derivative instruments; chief among these instruments are options, which allow holders to purchase or sell a certain amount of equity shares in a company at a predetermined price, referred to as the "strike price" or "exercise price." It may also include awards of restricted or nonvested stock (i.e., stock that is not fully transferable until certain conditions, such as years of service or certain performance targets, have been met).

## WHEN AND WHY IS A VALUATION NEEDED

Valuations play a critical role in tax reporting, financial reporting, and in informing strategic decisions. Additionally, stakeholders who have made an investment in a private enterprise or an investment in a subset of a public entity may require a valuation to understand the performance of their investment on an interim basis.

### TAX PURPOSES

A timely valuation of an enterprise's shares may be required for tax compliance if management plans to issue share-based awards in the form of options or restricted stock. Here are two common examples:

*IRC 409A Nonqualified Deferred Compensation Plans:* Section 409A of the Internal Revenue Code (IRC) calls for a holder of an in-the-money option (i.e., the fair market value (FMV) of the underlying share exceeds the exercise price) at the grant date to recognize taxable income equal to the difference between the FMV of the shares and the exercise price as they vest. The applicable combined federal and state tax rate upon vesting may be as high as 85 percent or more in some cases. Option holders who receive awards that cannot be shown to be at- or out-of-the money on the grant date may face immediate tax upon vesting at the rates described previously. Therefore, it is particularly important for companies to establish the FMV of the shares at the option grant date using valuation methodologies presented within this article.

*IRC 83(b):* The recipient of an equity interest subject to vesting may elect to be taxed upon the FMV of the shares at the grant date by providing notice to the IRS within 30 days of the grant date. If no election is made, the recipient would typically pay ordinary income tax based on the FMV of the shares upon vesting.

### FINANCIAL REPORTING PURPOSES

Financial reporting guidelines frequently recommend disclosures to aid investors. Accounting guidance may require companies to disclose the value associated with derivative instruments.

Valuations of grants of share-based awards are often required to establish compensation expense (in the case of grants to employees under Accounting Standards Codification (ASC) Topic 718, *Compensation—Stock Compensation*) or to account for distributions to shareholders under ASC Topic 505, *Accounting for Distributions to Shareholders with Components of Stock and Cash.*

In addition, situations may arise when warrants may be required to be valued separately from the instruments to which they were attached in accordance with ASC Topic 815, *Derivatives and Hedging* and ASC Topic 820, *Fair Value Measurement.*

### STRATEGIC PURPOSES AND GOALS

Valuation can be essential to the process of raising capital. A valuation of the enterprise is a key consideration in the amount, ownership interest, and form of an equity raise. A valuation of the enterprise or certain assets may also be helpful to secure debt financing. Moreover, the techniques described later in the article are helpful to understand the value exchanged or potential dilution associated with issuances of subordinated securities—either to motivate employees or to attract investors with higher return targets.

## TOTAL EQUITY VALUATION APPROACHES

When appraising various security interests within a private entity, specialists typically establish the value of total equity by first valuing the enterprise. Valuation specialists employ a variety of methods to determine value, but each of these methods may be classified as variations on one of three approaches—market, income, and asset-based approaches. Generally, valuation specialists will consider the result from one or more methods in determining value based on the needs of the particular client and situation.

*Income approach:* This approach recognizes that an investment's value is determined by the potential receipt of future economic benefits. The discounted cash flow (DCF) method—which involves estimating the future cash flows of a business and discounting them to their present value—is a form of the income approach that is commonly used to value business interests. The discount rate applied in the DCF Method is established based on the risks inherent in the investment and market rates of return; these risks are determined by a careful consideration of alternative investments that are of a similar type and quality.

*Market approach:* This approach assumes that companies operating in the same industry will share similar characteristics and that the company values will correlate with those characteristics. Therefore, a comparison of the subject company to similar companies whose financial information is publicly available may provide a reasonable basis to estimate the subject company's value. There are two commonly applied forms of the market approach:

- *The guideline public company (GPC) method:* The GPC method provides a value estimate by using multiples derived from the stock prices of publicly traded companies. The GPC method involves developing earnings or book value multiples based on the market value of the guideline companies and applies these multiples to the corresponding metrics of the subject company to estimate value.

- *The guideline merged and acquired company (GMAC) method:* This method is conceptually similar, but the multiples are developed based on observed transaction prices rather than the market capitalization of publicly traded peer companies.

*The asset approach:* This approach considers reproduction or replacement cost as an indicator of value. This approach assumes that a prudent investor wouldn't pay more for any entity than the amount that he or she could use to replace or re-create it. Valuation professionals will use historical costs to estimate the current cost of replacing the entity valued. In the asset approach, the equity value of a business enterprise is calculated as the appraised value of the individual assets and liabilities that comprise the business.

Once enterprise value is determined, as described above, the specialists can subtract the value of debt to arrive at the total equity value.

## EQUITY ALLOCATION APPROACHES

The valuation techniques and examples described in the remainder of this article leverage heavily upon discussion in the revised AICPA practice aid, *Valuation of Privately-Held-Company Equity Securities Issued as Compensation.* This publication is often referred to as the "cheap stock" practice aid.

### SIMPLE CAPITAL STRUCTURE

In the context of a simple capital structure (i.e., comprised of only one class of equity), total equity is divided by the number of shares outstanding to derive the share price.

### COMPLEX CAPITAL STRUCTURE

Complex capital structures, which have multiple equity classes, require more complex allocation methodologies to derive the value of each equity class. This section highlights the techniques utilized to determine the value of distinct equity classes in a complex capital structure.

*Current value method (CVM):* This allocation methodology is based on an estimate of total equity value on a controlling basis assuming an immediate sale or liquidation of the enterprise. Once that estimate is established, specialists allocate value to the various series of stock based on those series' liquidation preferences or conversion values, whichever would be greater.

The fundamental assumption of the CVM is that each class of stockholders will exercise its rights and achieve its return based on the enterprise value as of the valuation date, rather than at some future date. Accordingly, preferred stockholders will participate either as preferred stockholders or, if a conversion feature is available and would be more economically advantageous, as common stockholders. Common shares are assigned a value equal to their *pro rata* share of the residual amount (if any) that remains after the liquidation preference of preferred stock is considered.

However, because the CVM focuses exclusively on the present, it is generally appropriate to use in two very specific circumstances:

1. When a liquidity event in the form of an acquisition or a dissolution of the enterprise is imminent, and expectations about the future of the enterprise as a going concern are virtually irrelevant; or

2. When an enterprise is at such an early stage of its development that (a) no material progress has been made on the enterprise's business plan, (b) no significant common equity value has been created in the business above the liquidation preference on the preferred shares, and (c) no reasonable basis exists for estimating the amount and timing of any such common equity value above the liquidation preference that might be created in the future.

In situations in which the enterprise has progressed beyond the venture stage, valuation specialists will use other allocation methods.

## FACT PATTERN I: ILLUSTRATIVE EXAMPLE USING CVM

To illustrate, consider the purchase of a business on January 1, 2016, with a capital structure and buy-in details as shown below:

| Intial Purchase Price (Equity Value) as of 1/1/2016 | $40,000,000 |
|---|---|
| **Series A Preferred Stock** | |
| Stock Issuance Price | $35,000,000 |
| Shares Issued | 1,000,000 |
| Liquidation Preference | $35.00 |
| **Common Stock** | |
| Shares Outstanding | 5,000,000 |
| Common Stock Value Per Share | $1.00 |

For simplicity, assume the preferred stock is not entitled to dividends, nor does it have any conversion or participation rights. Now, consider a valuation for the enterprise is performed as of January 1, 2017. The common equity value implied under the CVM is as follows:

| Current Value Method (CVM) | |
|---|---|
| Equity Value as of 1/1/2017 | $35,000,000 |
| Preferred Stock Fair Market Value | $35,000,000 |
| Common Stock Fair Market Value | $0 |

Because the preferred shareholders have liquidation preference equal to the value of the enterprise, no residual value is available to the common shares under the CVM. Note this assumes there was an imminent liquidity event at the time the enterprise was valued.

*The option pricing method (OPM):* This allocation methodology treats common stock and preferred stock as call options on the enterprise's equity value, basing exercise prices on the liquidation preferences of the preferred stock. Common stock has value only if the funds available for distribution to shareholders exceed the value of the liquidation preferences at the time of a liquidity event such as a merger or sale—assuming the enterprise has funds available to make a liquidation preference meaningful and collectible by the shareholders. The common stock is modeled as a call option that gives its owner the right, but not the obligation, to buy the underlying equity value at a predetermined or exercise price.

The OPM has commonly used the Black-Scholes option pricing model to price the call option.

This method considers the various terms of stockholder agreements—including the level of seniority among the securities, dividend policy, conversion ratios, and cash allocations—that can impact the distributions to each class of equity upon a liquidity event. The OPM also implicitly considers the effect of the liquidation preference as of the future liquidation date, not as of the valuation date. Many practitioners believe this makes it the most appropriate method to employ when specific future liquidity events are difficult to forecast.

## FACT PATTERN II: ILLUSTRATIVE EXAMPLE USING OPM

For the same business described in the earlier example, management anticipates an exit in five years. The following assumptions are necessary to complete the Black-Scholes option pricing model:

| Black-Scholes Option Pricing Model Assumptions | |
| --- | --- |
| Liquidation Preference | $35,000,000 |
| Expected Holding Period  (Years) | 5.0 |
| Expected Volatility | 35.0% |
| Risk-Free Rate of Interest | 1.0% |

The OPM would allocate the equity value between the preferred stock and common stock as follows:

| Option Pricing Method (OPM) | |
| --- | --- |
| Equity Value as of 1/1/2017 | $35,000,000 |
| Anticipated Exit | 1/1/2022 |
| Preferred Stock Fair Market Value | $23,732,579 |
| Common Stock Fair Market Value | $11,267,421 |

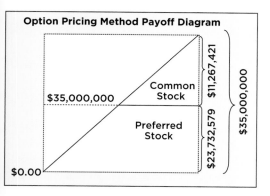

Option Pricing Method Payoff Diagram

As shown in the figure, this model assumes the common stock would have a claim on any

appreciation in the equity value above $35 million. Intuitively, the preferred stock is now worth less than the original purchase price because the equity value declined by 12.5 percent since purchase and due to anticipated future dilution from common. In contrast, the common stock continues to hold an option to participate in the appreciation of the business over the holding period.

*The probability-weighted expected return method (PWERM):* This allocation methodology estimates the value of the various equity securities through an analysis of future values for the enterprise, assuming various future outcomes. Share value is based upon the probability-weighted present value of expected future investment returns, which considers each of the possible future outcomes available to the enterprise as well as the rights of each share class. Although the future outcomes in any given valuation model will vary based upon the enterprise's facts and circumstances, common future outcomes modeled might include an IPO, a merger or sale, a dissolution, or continued operation as a private enterprise. This method involves a forward-looking analysis of the potential future outcomes; it also estimates the ranges of future and present value under each outcome and applies a probability factor to each outcome as of the valuation date.

## FACT PATTERN III: ILLUSTRATIVE EXAMPLE USING PWERM

Continuing the fact pattern from the previous example, management anticipates the following exit opportunities:

| Scenario | Probability | Timing | Exit Value |
| --- | --- | --- | --- |
| IPO Price | 50% | 4 | $75,000,000 |
| Private Sale | 40% | 3 | $50,000,000 |
| Liquidation | 10% | 5 | $1,000,000 |

The application of the PWERM with these exit opportunities is illustrated below:

|  | IPO | Private Sale | Liquidation |
|---|---|---|---|
| Expected Equity Value at Exit | $75,000,000 | $50,000,000 | $1,000,000 |
| Preferred Liquidation Preference | $35,000,000 | $35,000,000 | $35,000,000 |
| Distributions to Preferred | $35,000,000 | $35,000,000 | $1,000,000 |
| Distributions to Common (Residual) | $40,000,000 | $15,000,000 | $0 |
| **Present Value of Distributions to Preferred** | | | |
| Timing (Years) | 4.0 | 3.0 | 5.0 |
| PV Factor at 8% | 0.735 | 0.794 | 0.681 |
| PV of Expected Cash Flows | $25,726,045 | $27,784,128 | $680,583 |
| Probability | 50% | 40% | 10% |
| Probability Weighted PV of Expected Cash Flows to Preferred | | | $24,044,732* |
| **Present Value of Distributions to Common** | | | |
| Timing (Years) | 4.0 | 3.0 | 5.0 |
| PV Factor at 26% | 0.398 | 0.501 | 0.316 |
| PV of Expected Cash Flows | $15,902,470 | $7,510,082 | $0 |
| Probability | 50% | 40% | 10% |
| Probability Weighted PV of Expected Cash Flows to Common | | | $10,955,268* |
| **Total Present Value of Equity** | | | $35,000,000* |

*equals the sum of the indicated subtotals

In the application of the PWERM, it may be necessary to assess the risk profile of the various classes separately. If the sum of the present values for the various classes does not reconcile to the equity value as of the valuation date, that may indicate the assumptions around the amount, timing, probability, or risk associated with the exit events should be reconsidered.

In the application of the OPM and PWERM, an appraiser would also take into account considerations for the relative control position and marketability of the various classes and any applicable discounts. For simplicity, this has not been illustrated in the earlier examples.

In certain situations, an appraiser may utilize a combination of the OPM and PWERM methodologies in tandem. This is referred to as the hybrid method.

To recap, the following image illustrates the results under the CVM, OPM, and PWERM:

| Current Value Method (CVM) | FMV |
|---|---|
| Preferred Stock | $35,000,000 |
| Common Stock | $0 |
| **Option Pricing Method (OPM)** | **FMV** |
| Preferred Stock | $23,732,579 |
| Common Stock | $11,267,421 |
| **Probability Weighted Expected Return Method (PWERM)** | **FMV** |
| Preferred Stock | $24,044,732 |
| Common Stock | $10,955,268 |

As you can see, in the context of a going concern not bound by an imminent liquidity event, the use of a CVM may understate the value of the subordinated securities (which are able to participate in the upside of a business).

# CONCLUSION

The valuation process helps enterprises prepare for major transitions and milestones, such as IPOs, mergers and acquisitions, and regulatory compliance. Valuation professionals provide organizations with a clear, unbiased understanding of the value of their enterprise. Conducting a valuation of any enterprise requires a thorough understanding of the various methods to be employed. This article has provided an overview of the methods commonly employed to value various equity classes within a complex capital structure; however, it is, so to speak, the tip of the iceberg in terms of the myriad procedures that must be considered for a successful valuation.

The stakes for any organization that has reached a valuation stage are high, which is why these organizations should consider the expertise of third-party valuation specialists. The specialists should conduct each component of an intricate, complex process in a way that allows the enterprise owners the freedom to continue on with their business as usual—all while ensuring that the results are defensible and that there is no suggestion of any conflict of interest. Relying on a third-party specialist may ultimately be more cost- and time-efficient than attempting to undertake a valuation internally.

# 39

# THE JOBS ACT

Fenwick & West LLP

Jeffrey R. Vetter, Co-Chair, Securities and Corporate Finance;
and Partner, Corporate

## EMERGING GROWTH COMPANIES AND OVERVIEW OF THE IPO PROCESS FOR THESE COMPANIES

### BACKGROUND

The Jumpstart Our Business Startups Act (the JOBS Act) has had the effect of increasing the number of companies electing to pursue an initial public offering (IPO) and to provide those companies a transition period or "on-ramp" to the public markets, allowing them to focus resources on growth of their businesses before having to expend resources toward complying with many of the regulations often cited as costly and burdensome for newly public companies. The so-called "IPO on-ramp" provisions, which are contained in Title I of the JOBS Act, reduce a number of existing financial disclosure, corporate governance, and other regulatory burdens on a new category of issuer, referred to as an "emerging growth company." The JOBS Act was supplemented by the passage of the Fixing America's Surface Transportation Act (FAST Act) in December 2015, which further streamlined the IPO process for emerging growth companies.

### QUALIFYING AS AN EMERGING GROWTH COMPANY

Subject to certain exceptions, an emerging growth company (EGC) is defined as an issuer of securities that had gross revenues of less than $1 billion during its most recently completed fiscal year. An issuer would qualify as an EGC even if its gross revenues exceeded $1 billion in years prior to its most recent fiscal year. In some instances, companies that began (and had not yet completed) the IPO process as an emerging growth company would lose that status on the first day after achieving $1 billion in revenues. This required companies that were EGCs to add significant amounts of additional disclosure during the IPO process. With the passage of the FAST Act, these companies would not lose the benefit of EGC status during the IPO process as long as the IPO occurred within one year.

Gross revenues are measured with reference to total revenues as presented on the income statement presentation under U.S. Generally Accepted Accounting Principles (GAAP) or International Financial Reporting Standards (IFRS) as issued by the International Accounting Standards Board (IASB), if used as the basis of reporting by a foreign private issuer. If the financial statements of a foreign private issuer are presented in a currency other than U.S. dollars, total annual gross revenues for purposes of this test should be calculated in U.S. dollars using the exchange rate as of the last day of the most recently completed fiscal year. When calculating gross revenues, financial institutions may exclude gains and losses on dispositions of investment portfolio securities.

## LENGTH OF TRANSITION PERIOD

An issuer that is an EGC as of the first day of that fiscal year will continue to maintain that status until the earliest of:

- the last day of the fiscal year in which it achieves $1 billion of gross revenues;

- the last day of the fiscal year that includes the fifth anniversary of its IPO;

- the date on which it has issued more than $1 billion in nonconvertible debt during any previous rolling three-year period (excluding issuances in A/B debt exchange offers); or

- the date on which it is deemed to be a "large accelerated filer" (which requires, among other things, having common equity held by nonaffiliates with a market value of $700 million or more).

## ADVANTAGES OF EMERGING GROWTH COMPANY STATUS
### OVERVIEW

The IPO on-ramp provisions of the JOBS Act offer EGCs a number of advantages during the IPO process, including:

- confidential submission and review of IPO registration statements;

- reduced financial statement audit and disclosure requirements;

- reduced executive compensation disclosure requirements;

- the ability to engage in oral or written "test-the-waters" communications with certain types of potential investors to gauge interest before or after filing; and

- liberalizing the use of research reports and easing restrictions on analyst communications.

The IPO on-ramp provisions of the JOBS Act also reduce the costs and burdens of being a public company for EGCs after completion of their IPOs by providing:

- an exemption from the public accounting firm attestation to issuer internal controls required by Section 404(b) of the Sarbanes-Oxley Act of 2002 (SOX);

- scaled-back financial and compensation disclosure requirements for future registration statements, periodic reports, and other reports to be filed with the Securities and Exchange Commission (SEC);

- exemptions from "say-on-pay" vote (and votes on the frequency of "say on pay" votes), certain other required shareholder actions, and certain proxy statement disclosures;

- exemptions from mandatory audit firm rotation and any auditor's discussion and analysis requirements; and

- relief from the requirement to comply with any update issued by the Financial Accounting Standards Board (FASB) to its Accounting Standards Codification until the date that a company that is a private company is required to comply with such new or revised accounting standard if such standard does not apply to private companies.

In this regard, EGCs that are foreign private issuers and reconcile their home country GAAP financial statements to U.S. GAAP may also take advantage of the extended transition period for complying with updates issued by the FASB to its Accounting Standards Certification in their U.S. GAAP reconciliation.

### CONFIDENTIAL SUBMISSIONS

EGCs have the option to confidentially submit to the SEC a draft registration statement for confidential, nonpublic review by the SEC prior to public filing. This allows an EGC to explore the possibility of an IPO without exposing any confidential information to its competitors or the market generally until 15 days (after the passage of the FAST Act) before the date on which it begins to conduct its roadshow, and without risking the embarrassment associated with pulling the IPO should the EGC do so.

The confidential submission process is only available for EGCs that have not already completed a public offering of common equity securities, including offerings under employee benefit plans or pursuant to a resale registration statement. EGCs that have completed public offerings of debt securities may use the confidential submission process. Foreign private issuers may also be eligible to submit their draft registration statements on a non-public basis under existing policies of the SEC's Division of Corporation Finance; however, the benefits of this policy are not available to foreign private issuers that take advantage of any benefit available to EGCs.

## SCALED DISCLOSURES

EGCs may "scale back" financial and compensation disclosures in their IPO registration statements and subsequent filings under the Securities Exchange Act of 1934. In particular, IPO registration statements for EGCs may contain:

- two years of audited financial statements, including those of acquired businesses, rather than the standard three-year statement;

- with the FAST Act, this two-year period is based on the time of the effectiveness of the IPO. As a result, EGCs would not be required in initial submissions to the SEC to include audited financial statements for years that would not be required if the two-year period were determined from the effective date;

- selected financial information for the years including and after the earliest audited period presented (i.e., as little as two years of selected financial information), rather than the traditional five-year period;

- management's discussion and analysis (MD&A) of the periods covered by the audited financial statements (i.e., as little as two years plus

"stub" periods), rather than the required three-year period; and

- the streamlined and simplified compensation disclosures required of smaller reporting companies, meaning that that the registration statement need not include, among other things, a detailed compensation discussion and analysis section or tabular information for more than three executive officers and certain executive compensation tables.

With respect to the scaled executive compensation disclosure requirements, ECGs must still consider whether there is additional, material compensation disclosure that would be useful to investors to understand how the EGC's executive compensation programs operate.

EGCs may follow all or some of these "scaled" disclosure provisions, except that in their initial filing or submission they must decide whether to take advantage of the extended transition period for complying with any of the FASB's updates to its Accounting Standards Codification. If an EGC decides to take advantage of such extended transition period, it may later choose to reverse its election. Most EGCs have not been electing to take advantage of these extended periods.

Although the JOBS Act refers to domestic company rules and forms, a foreign private issuer that qualifies as an EGC may comply with the scaled disclosure provisions to the extent relevant to the form requirements for foreign private issuers.

While these changes are designed to reduce costs, EGCs may find that providing the traditional level of historical financial disclosure is helpful in the IPO marketing process. Most EGCs have still elected to present financial statements for a full three years and also five years of selected financial data.

## TEST-THE-WATERS COMMUNICATIONS

Issuers must avoid illegal offers and not engage in communications and activities that might be viewed as impermissibly affecting the market for the securities to be offered. The JOBS Act amends Section 5 of the Securities Act of 1933 to add a new Section 5(d), which permits EGCs to engage in oral and written communications with institutional or highly sophisticated prospective investors to gauge their interest in a contemplated securities offering before or during the "quiet period" or during the "waiting period." Issuers should pay careful attention to the timing, content, and delivery mechanism of each communication. In particular, written communications are subject to SEC review and could complicate the IPO process if they are inconsistent with the prospectus or roadshow presentation. As a matter of standard practice, the SEC requests copies of any "testing the waters" communications made in reliance on Section 5(d) as well as any research reports.

## OTHER BENEFITS

The "IPO on-ramp" provisions make becoming a public company more attractive by reducing costs and burdens for EGCs after they go public, often by simplifying and streamlining disclosures. One of the most significant of these benefits is an exemption from the requirement contained in Section 404(b) of SOX to obtain an internal controls attestation and report from a registered independent public accounting firm while the issuer remains an EGC. For many, perhaps most, companies seeking to complete an IPO, this will delay by at least three years the need to comply with this requirement of SOX. It should be noted, however, that EGCs will still be required to establish and maintain "disclosure controls and procedures" and internal controls, and their principal executive officer and principal financial officer will still be required to certify Form 10-Q and 10-K filings.

## PROCESS TIMELINE

The time-intensive process of submitting confidentially and executing an IPO as an EGC can take 12 to 16 weeks from initial filing to effectiveness, which is typical for a non-EGC issuer to complete the IPO process as well. As with IPOs of non-EGC issuers, the exact time

taken to complete an IPO for an EGC can vary widely and depends on market conditions, the complexity of the transaction, the EGC's readiness prior to embarking on the IPO process, and many other factors. The IPO process for EGC can be broken down into the following stages.

## PRIOR TO OFFICIAL IPO PROCESS LAUNCH

*Decision to go public:* While the EGC should still evaluate its internal readiness, including industry position and growth prospects, it also has the flexibility to assess investor interest in a contemplated offering of its securities to determine whether it is ready to go public.

*Testing the waters:* The EGC and its advisors should consider whether to engage in test-the-waters communications with "qualified institutional buyers" or "accredited investors to gauge interest in a contemplated offering of its securities.

*Internal controls:* Once the decision has been made to prepare for an IPO, the EGC should still take the actions other issuers take: select an appropriate board of directors, prepare audited financials (with a qualified independent registered public accounting firm), and begin establishing internal controls.

*Selection of advisors:* The EGC should still carefully select its IPO advisors, including the right investment bank and counsel experienced in the industry and types of initial public offerings of the EGC.

## WEEK 1

*Organizational meeting:* The traditional organizational meeting would still occur in the case of an IPO for an EGC. However, if an EGC is uncertain of its ultimate timing for its IPO, it may decide to work more informally with a few underwriters to prepare for an eventual formal kickoff of the IPO process with the organizational meeting.

## WEEKS 2 TO 4

*Drafting:* The EGC would still prepare the same Form S-1 registration statement and prospectus.

The drafting process is also largely the same as that for traditional IPOs. The contents of the S-1 registration statement are different in the following ways:

- the financial statements may include two (rather than three) years of audited financial statements and select financial statement info for the previous two (rather than five) years;

- the MD&A of the EGC's performance need not cover more than the past two (rather than three) years plus any "stub" periods;

- the compensation disclosure and analysis for executives and board members need not include more information than is required of a smaller reporting company, meaning that the document need not include, among other things, compensation discussion and analysis or tabular information for more than three executive officers, and may omit certain compensation-related tables such as the grant of plan-based awards, and option exercise tables; and

- the EGC must make affirmative disclosure in the registration statement as to whether it will elect to "opt out" of new accounting standards that are not also applicable to private companies.

*Due diligence:* The due diligence process for an IPO of an EGC is the same as that for traditional IPOs. Because this process is time-intensive, an EGC should consider its overall readiness to complete an IPO before embarking on the IPO process.

*Legal and other documentation:* In addition to the prospectus, the EGC and underwriter's counsel will work with the investment bank, the EGC, and the auditors to draft the underwriting agreement, auditor's comfort letter, and other documentation. The primary differences in the documentation of traditional IPOs and those of an EGC include:

underwriting agreement will contain additional representations and warranties relating to a company's status as an EGC and representations and covenants relating to test-the-waters communications; and

- the lock-up agreements for existing shareholders no longer need contain what are known as "booster shot" provisions—where the typical 180-day lock-up period can be extended if the EGC issues an earnings or other material press release or if material news about the EGC is released prior to the expiration of the lock-up period.

*Determine listing venue:* The EGC should still determine earlier in the process whether it is eligible to list on the NYSE or other exchange and reserve a ticker symbol.

## WEEK 5

*Confidential submission:* A draft Form S-1 registration statement should be submitted confidentially to the SEC. In general, draft registration statements submitted through the confidential submission process are the same as registration statements filed outside of it, and until an EGC publicly files its S-1 registration statement, these submissions remain confidential.

## WEEKS 6 TO 7

*Testing the waters:* The EGC and its advisors should consider whether to engage in test-the-waters communications with "qualified institutional buyers" or "accredited investors" to gauge interest in the contemplated offering of its securities. In addition to helping the EGC gauge investor interest, such communications could provide valuable information and experiences and impact the crafting of the marketing story for the impending roadshow. Most EGCs do engage in "testing the waters" meetings at least once before or during the IPO process. It is important to note that the SEC will require that the EGC provide copies of any materials, such as PowerPoint presentations displayed or used in these meetings, and therefore these materials should be reviewed carefully, even if the meetings occur months prior to an IPO.

*Roadshow presentation:* The preparation of the roadshow presentation and the roadshow itself is not notably different for EGCs than it is for companies engaging in traditional IPOs. Before finalizing the key roadshow messages, the EGC should consider taking advantage of the testing-the-waters provisions of the JOBS Act to help further refine the roadshow messaging.

## WEEK 8

*Initial comments on prospectus from SEC:*
The SEC comment process for confidential submissions takes a similar amount of time as traditional IPOs—with the SEC taking approximately 30 days to review and provide comments to the initial submission. Subsequent rounds of comments can take a range of time depending on the complexity of the issues and additional disclosures included by the EGC. Comment letters and related correspondence for completed IPOs of EGCs are made public within a few months of the effective date of the registration statement.

## WEEKS 9 TO 12

- Continue submitting confidential draft Form S-1 amendments, responding to SEC comments confidentially, and receiving incremental confidential comment letters until SEC comments are resolved.

- A Form S-1 registration statement should be filed publicly with the SEC at least 15 days before roadshow launch.

- Lock-up agreements and Financial Industry Regulatory Authority (FINRA) questionnaires should be widely circulated shortly before the public filing. At this stage, the employees and existing investors of the EGC would then know of the proposed IPO.

- Continue to consider engaging in test-the-waters communications.

*Discuss offering structure:* The EGC and the investment bank should determine if there will be more than sufficient investor demand for

the contemplated offering of its securities, so that the EGC can determine whether to make the decision to publicly file the registration statement.

## WEEK 12-13

- Finalize offering size and structure and convey valuation information to the SEC in order to resolve any issues regarding valuation of the EGC's common stock in prior equity transactions, such as grants of employee stock options.

- Publicly file S-1 Registration Statement if not yet previously filed.

## WEEKS 14 TO 16

- File a Form S-1 amendment with the red herring prospectus that includes price range and offering size.

- Launch roadshow.

- Price the IPO.

- The next day, the EGC begins publicly trading on the NYSE, rings the opening bell, and hosts other key marketing events associated with being a public company.

- Closing of the IPO.

## CONCLUSION

The JOBS Act and FAST Act have helped relieve some of the burdensome requirements smaller companies face in accessing the U.S. capital markets and made going public more attractive by reducing the associated costs and burdens for a period of transition while these companies grow. Many EGCs are benefiting from being able to explore an IPO without incurring as many of the costs, without disclosing confidential information, and avoiding any embarrassment associated with publicly withdrawing the IPO should the EGC do so.

# 40

# M&A—WHY IT MATTERS

Morgan Stanley

Anthony Armstrong, Managing Head of Global Technology
    Mergers & Acquisitions

The Myth: "Great companies are bought, not sold."

The Reality: Great companies are sold—after a carefully orchestrated process.

Mergers and acquisitions (M&A) is term used to describe buying and selling of companies. And in the case of most startups and private companies, it usually refers to the act of selling your company. But most entrepreneurs, executives, and investors are rightfully focused on building a great company, not selling it. This, combined with the belief in the above myth that your company is not for sale because it is/will be great, leads to the common question: why do I need to think about M&A now?

While there are lots of reasons to think about M&A now, the simplest reason is that a sale is the most likely exit for your company. In the United States, private technology companies valued at $100+ million are more than three times more likely to sell than issue an IPO. And for companies under $100 million in value, a sale is about the only successful exit opportunity. So while blazing a stand-alone path in pursuit of an IPO is oftentimes the best value-maximizing strategy, the odds say an M&A outcome is more probable. Once you understand the odds, you'll realize being prepared for a sale is less like preparing for the thousand-year flood and more like being prepared for a rainstorm.

As a lifelong M&A professional who now leads Morgan Stanley's Global Technology M&A practice, I have been in hundreds of board meetings discussing the decision to buy and sell companies. From that experience, I can tell you that the decision to sell your company is the most important and challenging professional decision you're likely to ever make. And just like any important decision, you want to be prepared and thinking about it well before the moment comes when you have to make it. You also want to have a general understanding of how a sale transaction may play out, so you can manage and optimize the outcome.

## BE PREPARED—SKATE TO WHERE THE PUCK IS GOING TO BE

Being prepared is the best way to minimize the risk of M&A. Companies have enough risk as it is: execution, financing, competition, vendor/customer, regulatory, etc. So the best thing companies can do is "de-risk" wherever they can. The good news is, there are several easy things you can do to be prepared for and de-risk M&A.

*Have a plan:* M&A deals usually have a long lead time and require thought and tactics, so having a plan early is important. For example, most processes start with an approach by a buyer, so having a plan in place to quickly respond and decide what to do (e.g., engage with other potential buyers) is critical. If you're not prepared by the time you're approached, then you're probably suboptimizing the outcome. As the famous ice hockey player Wayne Gretzky said, "skate to where the puck is going to be, not where it has been."

*Have advisors:* Recognize that M&A is likely not your core area of expertise. So surrounding yourself with advisors you trust on M&A is just as important as surrounding yourself with a good board or good legal counsel. Early on these advisors are likely to be your board members or investors who have been through several sale processes before. As the company grows, M&A situations can get more complex, so having an outside advisor who you know and trust is also important.

## THE M&A PROCESS AND TRANSACTION

No two M&A situations are exactly the same. Each has its own strategic and financial context, constituents (e.g., shareholders, decision makers, influencers, employees, customers, partners, and vendors), potential buyers, history, and timing. So while you can't prepare for every scenario, there are some general things you can do to understand how the M&A process usually works and how you can successfully navigate it.

### ENGAGE EARLY WITH POTENTIAL BUYERS

Buyers tend to fall in love slowly with companies; it's not love at first sight. It can take months, years, or even decades for a buyer to decide to acquire a company. This means you should have a plan for cultivating dialogues and relationships with potential buyers well in advance of a potential sale. Having your first-ever call into a potential buyer be "I'm selling my company,

would you like to buy it?" is not a recipe for success.

Here are some key guidelines for engaging early with potential buyers:

Prioritize meetings where there is legitimate commercial/partnering opportunity. This way you have multiple reasons to meet and can adjust the conversation in real time as appropriate.

Limit meetings to your executives only. Don't outsource it to your junior corporate development team. Your company is like your product. You need to sell it, and you want to be in control of making the most important sales pitch in the history of the company.

Similarly, make sure you're meeting with a decision maker, key person, or influencer on the other side. Taking the right meeting is more important than taking just any meeting.

Don't assume a potential buyer really understands your business. It can be difficult for a third party to truly understand what your business does, the value proposition you provide customers, the secret sauce that differentiates you, and the huge market opportunity being addressed. Unless there are competitive reasons not to, take the time to educate strategic parties. This way you are known by the ecosystem of buyers. If you're not known, you may get passed up on the M&A chessboard.

And remember, the best time to take these meetings is when you're not for sale. Allow buyers to get to know you without the pressure of a transaction and without you seeming eager to sell.

### KNOW THE BUYER UNIVERSE

The good news is, the universe of potential buyers for technology companies is bigger today than it has ever been. So if you think your company may appeal only to a few potential buyers, you may be pleasantly surprised to learn there are likely more. And more buyers can mean more competitive tension and a higher valuation. The bad news is, with more buyers it takes more time and effort to get on everyone's radar screen.

Technology buyers can generally be placed into four categories:

*U.S technology:* For the past 20 years, the main buyers of technology companies were U.S. technology companies. Amazon, Cisco, Facebook, Google, IBM, Intel, Microsoft, Oracle, and Salesforce are examples of these serial acquirers. In 2005 U.S. technology companies represented approximately 60% of technology acquisitions, but now they represent only 25%. The reduction of volume isn't because this group is slowing down on M&A but instead because new groups are ramping up their technology M&A efforts.

*Cross-industry:* Many large established companies in other industries such as industrials, retail, and telecom are being disrupted by technology. As this happens, these incumbents need to enhance their own capabilities or risk being dislocated. M&A is becoming a common solution, with examples including General Electric buying ServiceMax, Walmart buying Jet.com, and Verizon buying Fleetmatics. The technology M&A volume of this group has increased almost 300 percent since 2012 and now represents approximately 20 percent of technology acquisitions.

*Foreign buyers:* A new wave of international buyers has also emerged for technology companies. Notably, Chinese buyers have been extremely active increasing their annual technology M&A volume from $300 million per year in 2012 to over $40 billion in 2016. Examples of this include HNA buying Ingram Micro, Tencent buying Supercell, and Canyon Bridge acquiring Lattice Semiconductor. While there can be increased regulatory risks with cross-border deals, there continues to be strong international demand and this group now represents approximately 25 percent of technology acquisitions.

*Private equity:* The traditional private equity model is to pay low or reasonable prices for a company, add a bunch of debt, focus on cost controls instead of growth, and drive profitability. This model has not historically fit with buying technology companies who seek higher valuations, are not well suited for significant debt, are growing rapidly, and are less focused on optimizing near-term profitability. However, as private equity has to put more money to work, and the value creation opportunity in technology companies continues to outpace other industries, a new private equity model is emerging. This new model believes revenue growth is key, paying higher valuations is okay, no debt is fine, and the goal is to position the business for an even bigger sale or IPO. Examples of this include Vista Equity acquiring Cvent, Vista Equity acquiring Marketo, and EQT acquiring SiteCore. Private equity now represents approximately 30 percent of technology acquisitions.

## DESIGN A PROCESS

If you've successfully cultivated these relationships, then it's likely one of these parties will eventually approach you with M&A interest. This is usually how a process starts. Designing the right process for your circumstances and goals is important. That process should address questions such as: How many other parties are you calling? What is the script for those parties? What do you tell the existing interested party? What information do you provide interested parties? What is the timeline?

A good process will create options, reveal information, and allow you and your board to make an informed decision. For the potential buyers, a good process will create competitive tension and get them to pay as much as possible. But even if you have a good process, you still need to have a good negotiation.

## NEGOTIATE

Like any deal, good negotiations are important in arriving at a good outcome. While there are many different ways to successfully negotiate an M&A deal, having done hundreds of deals, my main piece of advice is to have your company speak with one voice to the potential buyer(s).

That one voice could be you, another executive, an investor, a board member, or most commonly, a financial advisor, but choose who you want negotiating and stick with them. This strategy helps keep a consistent message. It's okay and healthy to have different points of view on selling or not, valuation, or other key considerations in the boardroom, but telling a buyer all of those points of view can expose you to a weakened negotiating position. For example, if you tell the buyer you'll only sell for $1 billion and take a hard stance on that, but one of your investors goes behind your back and tells the buyer $100 million because they just want to sell at any price, that is value-destroying for you.

## ADVOCATE YOUR VALUATION

There are hundreds of books on corporate valuations. You could spend years reading about academic views on DCFs, WACCs, trading multiples, and precedent transactions. But here's the secret: M&A valuation is just as much about tactics as it is science. Balancing the two is important, and here's a simple way to frame a company's value proposition to a potential buyer that combines tactics and science:

*Stand-alone value (science):* This is the value of the company on its current trajectory. This is what you could reasonably expect to get in a financing round. It reflects the company's financials, market opportunity, competitive position, team, and technology.

*Synergy value (tactics supported by science):* If a strategic party acquires your firm, then there are most likely synergies, or joint opportunities, that don't exist in your stand-alone value.

Be able to articulate and quantify the value-creating synergy opportunities. These include accelerating your sales, enhancing the acquirer's sales, and/or or reducing duplicative costs. A strong synergy case is usually a key reason a party is interested in acquiring you. Since every potential buyer has a different synergy opportunity, think about custom synergy opportunities for each one.

*Scarcity value (tactics):* There is only one of your company, and the more buyers believe you are unique or a "category of one," the more they'll pay. For example, LinkedIn was a category of one, which helped it achieve a $26 billion sale to Microsoft.

## CONCLUSION

As you build and grow your successful company it can be easy to forget about what history tells us is the most likely outcome: a sale. While a sale doesn't need to happen and shouldn't be a main focus of yours yet, you'd also be adding risk if you totally ignored it today. One solution is to find the right advisor. The right advisor should help you today to formulate a long-term M&A plan that can unfold over the course of several years. The advisor should be able to provide you access to all four categories of potential technology buyers, be able to articulate your strategic fit and synergies with potential buyers, be able to provide you valuation and negotiation advice, and help you navigate a potentially complex M&A situation. This carefully orchestrated process may lead to the successful sale of your great company one day.

# 41

# EXITING THE BUSINESS: WHAT ARE THE TAX IMPLICATIONS?

**KPMG**

Brian Hughes, National Partner in Charge of Private Markets Group & National Venture Capital Coleader

Andrew Cherry, Tax KPMG Managing Director

You've worked long and hard to build your business. Now it's time to retire—or perhaps move onto another endeavor.

You're ready to sell the business; that much is certain. But how to do it is another matter, and it involves a host of decisions and considerations. Some are personal, some are financial. For example:

Are you able to negotiate a lump sum cash payout?

Does the buyer want to make payments that continue over time?

Are you willing to take back a promissory note from the buyer?

Do you want to stay involved in business operations (and does the buyer want you to)?

A key consideration impacting your decision that should not be overlooked is: What are the tax consequences of your exit strategy? While tax implications should not *control* what you eventually do, they should be a significant factor in how you try to structure the exit transaction. It can make a big dollars-and-cents difference in the amount of money you actually end up with.

In this section, we will be exploring the tax implications of various exit strategies.

## IT'S A NEGOTIATION

What may be a favorable tax outcome for you, as a seller, may work to the tax disadvantage of the eventual purchaser (and vice versa). As a practical matter, typically there is a lot of give-and-take and intense negotiations between you and the buyer. Tradeoffs may be made on tax benefits in return for concessions on the purchase price or other deal terms.

This is one of the reasons that entrepreneurs need a tax adviser who can guide and advise them on federal, state, estate and in some cases, international, tax consequences of a sale. And, again, taxes are just one aspect of the overall transaction. There are a host of nontax considerations that must be factored in as well. In any case, selling a business is not a do-it-yourself job.

## BUSINESS ENTITY DICTATES TRANSACTION STRUCTURE

The type of entity under which you operate your business will likely dictate the form of the exit transaction you would prefer.

Generally, entrepreneurs operate their businesses as a C Corporation (C Corp), a limited liability corporation (LLC) treated as a partnership, or an S Corporation (S Corp).

*C Corp:* If the business operates as a C Corp owned by an individual, tax considerations often dictate that the exit transaction be structured as a stock sale (as opposed to a sale of the assets of the business). When this occurs, the buyer is purchasing the owner's shares of the corporation.

*LLC and S Corp:* Tax considerations for an entity owned by an individual may be more flexible if the business is operated as an LLC or an S Corp. The sale transaction can be structured either as a sale of units (LLC) or stock (S Corp) *or* as a sale of the assets of the business to the purchaser with a favorable tax result. Assets can include real estate, buildings, equipment, fixtures, trade secrets, good will, inventory, receivables, and so on.

## DOUBLE TAXATION FACTOR

The C Corp is subject to what's referred to as "double taxation" on earnings and, specifically, gain when it sells its assets to a buyer. That is, the C Corp initially is subject to income tax on gain upon the asset sale. Then, a noncorporate shareholder is subject to income tax when the after-tax cash is distributed by the C Corp. (However, if the C Corp has net operating losses (NOL) carry-forwards, it may offset the gain and, thereby, reduce income tax at the corporate level. Note that there may be limitations, such as those of Internal Revenue Code (IRC) Section 382 on how much gain NOLs can offset.)

However, if the transaction is structured as a straight stock sale, there is no taxation at the corporate level; only the shareholder is subject to income tax on the gain on sale of his or her

shares. Thus, there is no double taxation. What's more, the proceeds are taxed at tax-favored capital gain rates (currently as low as 15 or 20 percent, depending on your tax bracket).

And if the C Corp meets certain requirements, a portion of the gain—or in some cases all of the gain—can be excluded from federal income tax under the "qualified small business stock" rules. (For example, Section 1202 of the Tax Code allows for qualified business stock treatment for C Corps that meet certain thresholds, such as not having more than $50 million in assets before and immediately after the setup date, the stock was held for at least five years, and the C Corp was an active business.)

Generally, there are no double tax consequences when dealing with pass-through entities such as an S Corp or LLC. Only the owner of the entity is subject to tax on gains. (An exception here is if the S Corp formerly was a C Corp and the sale takes place within the so-called five-year built-in gains (BIG) tax recognition period. In this case, an asset sale by the S Corp could trigger corporate-level BIG taxes (IRS Sec. 1374).)

## BUYER'S PERSPECTIVE ON STOCK VERSUS ASSET SALE

Buyers generally prefer transactions to be structured as an asset sale. There are several tax as well as nontax reasons for this.

*Amortization:* The buyer of assets can *depreciate* or *amortize* (i.e., write off) the purchase price of the assets over a number of years. The length of time for the write-off depends on the nature of the assets purchased. However, a buyer of stock is not entitled to depreciate the cost of its stock.

For example, the purchase price is allocated to tangible assets purchased based on their fair market values. The purchase price paid in excess of the value of tangible assets (i.e., the "premium") is allocated to intangible assets, which are amortized straight-line over 15 years. The purchase price allocated tangible assets, such as machinery and equipment, is depreciated over five or seven years.

*step-up in basis:* This principle allows the basis of an asset to be adjusted to its cost upon a taxable purchase. For example, say that in 2000, the seller bought a building for $1 million in which his business operates; a buyer pays $10 million for it today. The buyer will "step up" the basis of the building to its $10 million cost.

Result: If the buyer decides to sell the building, he would be subject to tax on the difference between the selling price and $10 million, not the original $1 million purchase price.

What's more, the buyer is able to claim depreciation write-offs based on the building's stepped-up $10 million basis. With a stock sale, while the buyer will take a cost basis in the acquired stock, stock is not a depreciable asset. Moreover, while the target corporation in a stock sale will be able to continue to depreciate its assets, it will not step up the basis of its assets as a result of the buyer's purchase of the target stock. If the target had already depreciated some of the assets down to zero, they can't be depreciated any further.

This inability to recover the purchase price of a business for tax purposes through depreciation deductions could create a cash-flow issue, particularly for a buyer just launching the business.

*Assumption of liability:* When the transaction is structured as a stock sale, the buyer is acquiring the owner's shares of a legal entity (C Corp or S Corp). This also means that the legal entity's existing and contingent liabilities (e.g., contractual, unrecorded, and otherwise) remain within the entity and are transferred to the buyer within the target, unless the parties negotiate and agree to some other arrangement. This same liability concern generally does not apply to an asset sale unless the sale is engineered as a merger. (Note that there are federal and state "successor liability" laws that may hold buyers responsible for certain liabilities, regardless of the terms negotiated between the buyer and seller.)

*Tax attributes:* If a buyer acquires assets in a taxable transaction, the buyer will not inherit the tax attributes (e.g., net operating losses, credits, earnings, and profits) of the selling corporation. If the buyer acquires stock, the attributes will remain in the target. However, the target's ability to use certain favorable attributes may be limited after the acquisition.

Bottom line: If you operate your business as an S Corp or LLC, then an asset sale may be most efficient from both your and the buyer's perspectives. You qualify for capital-gain treatment on the gain and there are no double-tax consequences; and the buyer receives a step-up basis on depreciable acquired assets.

Note that if the seller uses the cash-basis method of accounting for tax purposes, accounts receivable that are sold will result in ordinary income. In addition, there may be depreciation recapture on fixed assets based on how the purchase price is allocated. However, depending on the facts and circumstances, the majority of the gain should qualify for capital-gains treatment.

Also, if you sell the stock of a C Corp, the buyer won't be able to amortize its purchase price. In that case, the buyer may argue that the purchase price should be reduced based on some or all of the amount it *could* have written off had it been able to buy assets.

## ACQUISITION CONSIDERATION: CASH VERSUS EQUITY

The buyer's payment, or "consideration," for your company may consist of cash, buyer debt and/or equity, or a combination of some or all of these. In any case, if a nonrecognition provision doesn't apply, the proceeds you receive are subject to tax. But how it's taxed—ordinary income, capital gains, or tax-free—and when it's taxed, depends on several factors.

*Cash:* Regardless of the type of business entity you're operating, if you sell stock or assets for cash, the gain is subject to income tax.

*Equity:* If you sell stock and you take back an equity component—in other words, an ownership interest in the buyer's business—the equity component may be tax free or tax deferred if the transaction is structured properly.

There are a number of ways to structure a transaction so the seller won't recognize gain or loss on the receipt of equity in an acquiring corporation. For example, if you exchange the stock in your company for stock in the buyer's company and the transaction qualifies as a "corporate reorganization," it may be treated as a tax-free exchange. (This same principle may apply when an LLC is the buyer; the LLC can give back the seller "interests" in the LLC, which may be tax-free.)

This means that the seller doesn't have to pay tax on the value of the shares received on the date of sale. Rather, the tax is paid when you sell the buyer's stock at some point in the future.

However, if you receive a cash payment from the buyer in addition to the stock in a transaction otherwise qualifying as a reorganization, you are subject to tax on that portion of the proceeds.

From a tax perspective, purchasers may have less incentive to undertake a reorganization transaction compared to a taxable transaction because they generally will not adjust the basis of their assets to cost. On the other hand, the acquiring entity in a reorganization may be able to preserve certain tax attributes of the target (albeit potentially subject to limitation) that otherwise would not be acquired in a taxable transaction.

The rules that address nonrecognition transactions are complex and should be undertaken with care, as failure to satisfy their requirements potentially could subject a seller to both a corporate and a selling shareholder tax.

*Taking a risk:* When you take back the buyer's stock, you run the risk of the stock declining in value or the business going under. So, while your potential gain is tax deferred, if the value of the business and its stock goes down (or becomes worthless), you may wind up with little or nothing of value.

In some cases, the buyer may want or require a seller to stay on as an employee and offer him an equity interest in the company. Giving the seller "skin in the game" provides an incentive for him to continue performing well and maintaining or enhancing the value of the company.

The nature of the consideration—cash versus equity—is another one of the negotiating points between a buyer and seller and may be reflected in the ultimate sales price and terms.

## ALLOCATING PURCHASE PRICE TO ASSETS PURCHASED

This is often a major point of negotiation when the exit is structured as an asset sale. The seller and the buyer have to agree on the allocation of the sales price among the various assets. This allocation can determine whether gain recognized by the seller is ordinary income or capital gain income. And with current capital gains tax rates of 15 to 20 percent, compared to the top ordinary income tax rate of 39 percent, this can make a significant bottom line difference.

It also impacts the amount and timing of the depreciation and amortization the buyer may be entitled to take. For example, a buyer typically prefers to have the purchase price allocated to fixed tangible assets (such as property, plant, and equipment) because it allows for a faster write-off period (between five and seven years). Conversely, a buyer generally would want less of the purchase price allocated to intangible property, such as goodwill, going concern value, or trademarks, which has a longer write-off period (i.e., 15 years). Depreciation of certain assets may result in ordinary income tax treatment on the portion of the proceeds allocated to those assets. The IRS and the courts generally will respect a buyer and seller's allocation agreement if it's reasonable and negotiated at arm's length.

*Cash basis business:* There is less room for negotiation on the allocation of unrecognized accounts receivable for a seller of a cash-basis business. These receivables must be valued at their fair market value (FMV) and are subject to ordinary income tax.

# DEFERRED PURCHASE PRICE

There are several ways to arrange for deferred payment of the purchase price, and each one carries different tax consequences for both the buyer and the seller. In general, if structured properly, deferred payments allow you to recognize taxable gain only as payments from the buyer are received. Depending on your overall tax situation, this might make sense. And from the buyer's perspective, it may allow for a better cash flow, particularly in the early stages of the new business.

There also are nontax reasons for certain payment deferral arrangements, particularly from the buyer's point of view. First, a portion of the purchase price may be put into escrow (e.g., held by an attorney or third-party custodian) or otherwise held back for an agreed-upon period of time. This may be done to protect the buyer from a seller's breach of representation or warranties or if certain financial metrics are not met. (Note that with a contingent purchase price or escrow arrangement, the IRS may impute an interest rate (if one is not stated in the agreement) and require the seller to pay ordinary income on the interest portion of the deferred purchase price; see IRC Code Sec. 7872.)

Second, the parties may negotiate a contingent purchase price that will be paid only if the seller's business meets certain financial milestones after the acquisition. This arrangement often is used if the parties are unable to agree on a value of the business at the time of sale (e.g., if the business is subject to significant subsequent contingencies, such as government approval of a key product). This is also considered a form of installment sale.

*Installment sales:* Many sellers help finance the sale of their business by taking back a promissory note from the buyer as part of the purchase price. For example, your buyer pays you $5 million in cash on the date of the sale and gives you a note promising payment of $5 million a year for the next five years. This installment sale arrangement allows you to pay tax on your gain over a five-year period, which could be advantageous if tax rates (and your income) go

down. However, if the deferred amount *exceeds $5 million*, you may have to pay the IRS interest on the deferred tax liability on the amount above that $5 million. (See IRC Code Sec. 453.)

From a nontax perspective, as with any arrangement where you don't receive full payment at closing, there's the risk of partial payment or nonpayment if the buyer and/or the buyer's business run into financial difficulties.

*Contingent payments:* There are times when a seller and buyer structure the exit transaction to include contingent payments with no maximum stated purchase price. An example of this type of arrangement is when the buyer agrees to pay you a stated percentage of revenue annually from the acquired business or based on some other period of time. Note that if there's no end date for payments, you may be jeopardizing your ability to accelerate the recovery of your basis. So, for these types of contingent payment arrangements, you should consider including a maximum term for the payments so you can start recovering your basis from day one.

# STOCK OPTIONS AND RESTRICTED STOCK

Your company may have granted stock options or given restricted stock to employees as a reward or as a performance incentive. What happens to these instruments when you sell your company, and what are the tax implications?

As a rule, the terms of the stock option or restricted stock agreement dictate what can or must happen. In some cases, your obligations can be assumed by the buyer and replaced by the buyer with buyer's stock options or restricted stock, typically with similar terms. In most cases, however, employees prefer to cash out. After all, one of the reasons they were granted the stock or stock options was to allow them to share in the company's success in the event the business was sold or if there were a change in control.

With the cash-out option and unvested restricted stock, you generally get a tax deduction for these payments. And the value of the restricted stock or stock options gets reported as wages on the employees' Form W-2s. These amounts are also subject to income and employment withholding (e.g., Social Security, unemployment, FICA) taxes.

## FINAL THOUGHTS

At the end of the day, the manner in which you have set up your company goes a long way in dictating the structure of the sale transaction when you exit the business. For example, a C Corp generally has a strong incentive to push for selling its stock rather than its assets. There is more flexibility when the target is an S Corp, LLC, or other pass-through entity.

The parties may achieve a more favorable tax result if the seller is an S Corp, LLC, or other pass-through entity, and the buyer wants to purchase the assets of the business. Then, as with most business matters, everything

else is a negotiation and almost everything is negotiable.

While the owners of a C Corp benefit from a stock sale, the buyer might not. In that case, the buyer might negotiate for a lower purchase price based on the present value of tax benefits it would have gained if the transaction were structured as an asset sale.

A seller may agree to take equity as a form of consideration from a buyer but may negotiate for a higher purchase price than if it were a straight cash deal and must be cognizant of the tax-free transaction rules. The same give-and-take can apply with respect to allocation of the purchase price among assets or deferred purchase price arrangements.

These are all factors that you and your adviser should consider when planning for and negotiating the sale of your business.

# 42

# COMPENSATION STRATEGIES FOR EMERGING PUBLIC COMPANIES

**Korn Ferry Hay Group**

Bob Wesselkamper, Senior Client Partner and Global Head,
Rewards and Benefits Solutions

How does an emerging public company establish a compensation and rewards strategy that satisfies its organizational needs and its obligations to shareholders while also serving to support one of its most valuable assets—its people? How does a newly public company establish a fair and equitable strategy that optimizes the execution and people-spend associated with a new public company opportunity? The answer is by positioning the company for growth and predictability, which are attributes most valued by capital markets.

For any growing company, especially one on the verge of going public, there is a fine balance between the structure of overhead and expenses (selling, general, and administrative, SG&A), which can limit the scale, speed, or agility of operations, and the demands of a frequent driver of value—the employees. Almost every public company comes out of its initial public offering wanting to be perfect in its delivery of predictable people costs. But in fact it's not easy, nor does anyone ever do it perfectly.

It is in this striving for perfection that we gain insights into cost drivers and learn and improve on pay delivery, as well as challenge operating business models to deliver the next disruptor in an industry. For most new companies, the buildup of staff in the first three to five years, along with balancing growth to align with and anticipate the market demand and operational performance of the company, is a critical deliverable for any executive team. This chapter will outline how newly public companies can best approach aligning and optimizing the people costs within a new public entity with respect to the pressures and demands associated with delivering value to shareholders.

## WHAT

The first step for an emerging public company in creating an effective rewards program that serves the needs of all stakeholders—shareholders, customers, and employees— is to create a total rewards strategy. This approach encompasses nonmonetary and monetary rewards and incentives, including base-pay considerations. An effective total rewards approach seeks to align reward programs with the business across all of its regions, business units, and functions as well as all categories of employees, from C-suite executives and line managers to rank-and-file employees and contract and contingent workers.

Intangible rewards can include training and development programs that allow workers to grow and advance in their careers so that their sense of engagement, skills, and base compensation can routinely grow during their careers. A meaningful rewards program will encompass not merely calculating a bonus program but also integrating an employee-rewards perspective throughout the company, from hiring policies and pay levels to policies on transfers and promotions. Other intangible bonuses include social rewards, such as company picnics and holiday celebrations, employee discounts, or company-sponsored social clubs and activities—many of the things that reflect the "culture" of the company.

While ensuring that rewards are broadly designed to work across all functions and business units for all employees, employers must also ensure that the measurement system put in place for earning specific rewards be designed to balance several different types of performance measures; these include financial results, customer satisfaction, operation efficiency, and human capital. Such measurements can range from budget efficiency and revenue production to customer wait-time in a call center, to waste and rework ratio on the plant floor, to employee turnover in an individual business unit.

In this light, an effective rewards strategy can offset its costs by first utilizing already existing business functions, such as training and advancement practices. These strategies can also create savings by increasing efficiency in recruiting and retention of highly talented and motivated employees. Certain types of intangible rewards can also boost the company brand if some rewards, such as creative annual celebrations and employee giveaways, are highlighted in local media. Finally, research by Korn Ferry Hay Group found that implementing rewards strategies that are clearly aligned with organizational goals, strategy, and culture enabled a cross section of FORTUNE World's Most Admired Companies to pay five percent less in base salaries for management and professional jobs versus a comparison group.

## HOW

A critical element for the success of any effective total rewards program is executive support under the new public entity structure for an emerging public company. If executives and managers fail to understand the rewards programs clearly, they will likely not buy into the strategy and thus may not deliver the long-term results shareholders demand. For that reason, it's vital to ensure that rewards programs are communicated and characterized as a shared investment, not a cost.

When the total reward structure is considered a cost, the goal will be to minimize it. But when seen as an investment, leaders seek to optimize it and leverage rewards, maximizing participation and recognition to achieve company goals that directly benefit shareholders and customers.

Those organizations where senior leaders, managers, and HR operations embrace a total rewards outlook will function quite differently from those that look only at keeping rewards costs as low as possible. When managers view rewards in this light, the incentives may be considered expensive employee entitlements and become separated from the performance goals that good rewards programs support.

One factor that strongly encourages executives to buy into the total rewards approach is that in companies with effectively aligned rewards programs, Korn Ferry Hay Group research found the FORTUNE World's Most Admired Companies top executives receive above-average pay—about 10 percent more at the function-head level and above. When bonuses are taken into account, senior managers in the world's top companies can earn 20 percent more than their peers. These people are being rewarded for their ability to deliver and ensure their company stays at the top of its sector—given then are the ones who are driving the strategy and leading their people to perform. This allows the business to attract and maintain the best key executives to deliver shareholder and customer results.

Beyond support, managers at all levels need to be actively involved in implementing and reinforcing rewards strategies, especially being sure to engage line managers in the rollout of reward programs. The role of line managers in promoting and integrating the rewards strategy into daily operations is crucial, and it is a mistake to define rewards strategy as simply an HR function. The design of a rewards strategy isn't the biggest element in making the program succeed; in fact, there is no magic answer or universal set of best rewards practices for achieving results.

What does make the difference in effective programs is a relentless focus on excellence in execution. This means building reward platforms and fine-tuning them in practice over time rather than undertaking wholesale changes or switching to a completely new rewards strategy, which can erode employee enthusiasm for any rewards program.

## WHO

To be effective in a post-IPO operation, any total rewards strategy will need to be flexible, and it is likely to need to change over time from the rewards strategy of a nonpublic company, especially a startup. In addition, an effective total rewards strategy has to be able to respond to the company's operating cycles, the larger business cycle, and the ways in which the company and its market grow and evolve over time.

In the initial surge of activity, a startup may be focused on grabbing a large portion of market share, increasing name and brand recognition, and scaling up rapidly. However, the post-IPO company culture will need to shift to that of a firm that can manage costs in a predictable fashion to give shareholders the certainty they need in a forward-looking business. This includes controlling and maximizing the people spend in a way that supports certainty and shareholder demand for profitability. It's important to remember that in establishing the newly public firm's priorities as first clients, shareholders, and then employees, it is the employees doing the actual day-to-day work who drive value to shareholders.

An effective total rewards program means a company can align those costs, needs, and incentives that produce results by nurturing and developing talent; by frequently promoting from within, companies can actually pay less for talent than other organizations do. Korn Ferry Hay Group found on average, promoting from within costs about five percent less in base pay for management and professional positions.

That's because stronger talent development programs incorporated into a total rewards framework encourage the development of internal candidates, resulting in less need to hire more expensive talent from outside the company. This integration of talent management and rewards makes it easier for the company to attract and recruit the right people, reduces turnover, and, by aligning incentives and rewards with business strategy and goals, creates a more efficient culture that creates increased return on investment.

Newly public companies will find that rewards and incentives will shift at all levels in the company to align with shareholder priorities on forward-looking certainty in the business. For example, top-level executives were once wooed with large grants of stock options in the startup culture, but public companies instead focus on regular grants more strictly tied to performance. As the company grows and looks to manage costs with contingent workers, those employees also should be tied in to the rewards structure, giving the company an opportunity to develop and recruit from that workforce as well.

## WHY

The value of creating an effective total rewards strategy is that it can effectively align the tangible and intangible goals of the workforce at all levels of the company with the corporate goals of satisfying customers and shareholders. An effective strategy also helps reduce personnel costs as compared with those of competitors and can help provide the stability and certainty the new public entity will need to provide to its shareholders.

Keep in mind all the global elements of rewards—from tangible elements, such as cash compensation, to intangible rewards, such as a healthy work-life balance. In fact, noncash rewards have been found to be more compelling incentives over salaries and other factors such as benefits, which many workers view as an entitlement. In fact, the constraints on financial elements of reward programs mean a broader definition of "reward" has become more commonplace in the market over the past decade; rewards include perks such as a company gym to the inspirational value of a company's work for employees who want to feel they are making a difference in the world. Intangible rewards are not merely soft "nice to haves," such as the ping-pong tables at tech startups. Instead, they have become a core component of employer branding and the backbone of the employer's "value proposition" to employees.

The value of an effectively managed total rewards program to emerging public companies is that when properly structured, these incentives aren't simply costs to be minimized by investments that position the company for the growth and predictability shareholders demand. In a growing company, the potential for personnel overhead expenses to limit the ability of the firm to grow and respond to the volatile, ever-changing marketplace can be critical. By turning what has often been viewed as necessary overhead into a core piece of corporate strategy, rewards ranging from base salaries to on-the-job training can become an essential element that controls cost, supports strategy, produces satisfied customers and shareholders, and positions a post-IPO company for growth and success.

# 43

# EXAMINING THE ROLE OF THE BOARD OF DIRECTORS

New York Stock Exchange

The board of directors is a governing body elected to represent the interests of a company's shareholders. Board members serve in a twofold capacity: to advise management on strategy and to oversee risk. These roles are carried out with a fiduciary responsibility to shareholders. The board of directors delegates day-to-day management duties of the corporation to various executives, whom the board selects and who are then accountable to the board. In addition, directors have legal obligations under federal securities laws as well as state corporate laws.

In its broadest definition, the role of the board of directors comprises the following:

- Act in best interests of shareholders.
- Oversee strategy and risk management.
- Provide CEO oversight and succession planning.

## DUTIES AND RESPONSIBILITIES
### FIDUCIARY DUTIES

Board members have a legal obligation to act in the interest of the corporation. Their primary fiduciary duties, which are principally derived from Common Law of Delaware, include the following:

*Duty of loyalty:* The basic definition of the duty of loyalty is the obligation to take only those actions that are within the best interests of the corporation and not in the fiduciary's own interest. The duty of loyalty also precludes acting for unlawful purposes and affirmatively requires directors to make a good faith effort to monitor the corporation's affairs and compliance with law. Therefore, a company's directors must ensure the following:

- that the company has policies that comply with laws and regulations and that management adheres to them;
- that all actions taken by management have the interests of shareholders above all others;
- that directors remain independent and do not take advantage of their positions to act in their own interests, i.e., partake in self-dealing.

It is generally accepted under Delaware law that a director's duty of confidentiality falls under the duty of loyalty. All companies should have comprehensive corporate confidentiality policies that apply to employees as well as directors. Three broad categories of confidential information exist:

- proprietary information that is of competitive, commercial value;
- inside information about finances and strategy; and
- sensitive information regarding board proceedings and deliberation.

*Duty of care:* The duty of care requires that directors act in good faith and with the care an ordinarily prudent person in a like position would exercise under similar circumstances and in a manner the director reasonably believes to be in the best interests of the corporation. To satisfy the duty of care, it is critical to

- have reasonable knowledge of the company's business;
- act on an informed, good-faith basis;
- obtain credible information on each issue;
- adequately deliberate the relevant issues; and
- understand the consequences that will flow from each decision before making a decision, which may require the advice of legal or financial experts.

Some corporations have in their charter a provision immunizing directors from personal monetary liability for violating their duty of care. However, a company cannot shield directors from liability if duty of loyalty is breached.

## Confidentiality

Information in any category that is material and nonpublic may be disclosed by company insiders only in specific ways prescribed by federal securities laws, including Regulation FD. For these reasons, all companies should have comprehensive corporate confidentiality policies that apply to employees as well as directors. The authorized processes and channels for disclosure of confidential corporate information should be well defined and understood within the company, because improper disclosures can lead to criminal and civil liability in certain circumstances.

There are legal ramifications for some breaches of confidentiality. A damaging leak of confidential material could, in certain circumstances, amount to a breach of the duty of loyalty, which could result in personal liability for damages and limit the director's legal and contractual protections against such liability.

## Director Independence

Both NYSE and Nasdaq require that the majority of directors be independent; however, the definition of independence differs for each exchange. Factors for independence include the director's or a member of the director's family relationship to the company or to auditors, clients, and other third parties of the company. Additionally, the IRS and several regulations (including Sarbanes-Oxley and Dodd-Frank) define independence requirements. Companies are required to report director independence in proxy statements. The nominating/governance committee often reviews independence to ensure the board is in compliance with all requirements and regulations.

## DIRECTOR LIABILITY

*The business judgment rule*: In a practical sense, courts have rarely ruled against a company for a breach of duty of care. Even if a board's decision turned out in hindsight to be wrong or resulted in a situation that was not in the best interest of shareholders, if a board can show that it followed the standards of the duty of care, courts will not find against the company under the so-called "business judgment rule." The Delaware Chancery Court has noted that the business judgment rule focuses on the board's decision-making process rather than on a substantive evaluation of the merits of the decision. Thus, according to the ruling, the business judgment rule "prevents judicial second-guessing of the decision if the directors employed a rational process and considered all material information reasonably available—a standard measured by concepts of gross negligence."

Various legal indemnifications are afforded to boards of directors that can help shield them from liability, including corporate indemnification as set out by Delaware law, statutory indemnification, and private directors and officers (D&O) liability insurance.

## OVERSIGHT OF STRATEGY AND RISK

Contributing to corporate strategy—and ensuring the proper oversight of management's execution of that strategy—is a core responsibility of the board of directors. There are several foundational aspects to the board's role in this regard. It must first define the corporate strategy and then work with executive management to develop a business model that translates the strategy into shareholder value. Once that model is in place, the board has a responsibility to monitor management's execution of the strategy through evaluative means that provide measurable indicators of performance.

Implicit in the board's role to develop and monitor strategy is a coinciding role to measure and oversee risk. Every corporate strategy involves risk, and each company's unique appetite for risk may be found on a spectrum from risk averse to risk tolerant. The board must agree on the proper appetite for risk and make sure that the corporate strategy remains in balance with that tolerance. Finally, overarching all these considerations is an imperative to ensure the corporate strategy is designed to create long-term value for shareholders.

To fulfill their role to oversee strategy and risk, directors are often confronted with making decisions that are, by nature, affected by underlying economic, geopolitical, market, financial, and technological trends. Therefore, it is critical for board members to understand these macro trends as well as challenges and opportunities related to capital allocation, market position, and operations.

## CEO OVERSIGHT

One of the most critical jobs of the board of directors is to ensure the company has the right leadership at the helm to carry out the agreed-upon strategic objectives as well as to oversee a sound CEO succession plan. Doing so ensures continuity of leadership if a CEO unexpectedly departs or is subject to a forced turnover; provides confidence to shareholders and the market; and creates a sense of stability to employees and other stakeholders during times of transition.

Along these lines, the board also participates in an objective evaluation of the CEO on a regular basis to ensure performance and leadership expectations are being met. While financial measures are used quite often to benchmark and measure CEO performance, CEOs are, at their essence, decision makers that must be able to lead, inspire, and garner respect. Thus, the board must be confident that the CEO is making decisions using an informed, objective process and setting the appropriate tone at the top for the entire organization.

Much like its role with regard to CEO oversight and evaluation, it is the board's role to set and oversee the executive compensation plan for the CEO and other named officers, in accordance with appropriate performance targets and in strategic alignment with the overall goals for the company. The environment for executive compensation is constantly evolving to respond to shareholders, the public, and legislative and regulatory oversight of compensation matters. The ways in which executive compensation plans are structured can have far-reaching implications because they set the tone for performance expectations and cultural alignment.

## BOARD STRUCTURE

The organizational structure of a board of directors is dictated by state law, federal regulations, its corporate charter, and by exchange listing rules, but certain aspects are also determined by the needs of each individual company.

## BOARD SIZE

There is no regulatory or legal mandate with regard to board size. Rather, each company must take into consideration independence requirements and desired compositional mix when determining board size. Therefore, boards must continually evaluate their composition to ensure they have a good balance of perspectives based upon skills, experience, diversity, age, and tenure, as well as to respond to the changing business environment. Robust evaluations of board effectiveness are key to ensuring boards have the proper mix of skills and objectivity to oversee strategy, monitor risk, and fulfill their fiduciary responsibilities.

## DIRECTOR ELECTIONS

Traditionally, board members are elected for one-year terms; some boards have adopted two- or three-year terms with elections of members staggered so that an entire board cannot be replaced in any single year. Increasingly, however, staggered boards (also known as "classified boards") have fallen out of favor with investors, and today the vast majority of companies hold election of the full board at each annual meeting.

In general, directors are elected by the shareholders either by majority voting, which requires a simple majority of all outstanding votes, or plurality voting, where a director may be elected by virtue of receiving the most votes. The outcomes of these two methods can be vastly different: In a majority vote, even an uncontested director must affirmatively be voted in by a majority of shareholders; with a plurality vote, only one vote is needed to elect an uncontested director. In recent years, there has been a widespread push by shareholders for boards to adopt the majority voting standard.

## BOARD EVALUATIONS

To evaluate the effectiveness of the board's oversight, the majority of boards conduct annual assessments of the board's performance. Types of evaluations include those of the full board, committees, and individual directors. In 2015, 52 percent of the S&P 500 evaluated the full

board and committees and 33 percent evaluated the full board, committees, and individual directors annually. Some boards perform the evaluations in house either through surveys or interviews, while others bring in independent third parties to perform the assessment.

## DIRECTOR COMPENSATION

In recent years, the acceleration of regulatory changes and required disclosures have increased the time commitment and workload directors must undertake to effectively perform their fiduciary duties. Consequently, director compensation packages have changed in both design and execution. Typical director compensation arrangements include a mix of cash and equity retainers plus board and committee meeting fees. Most companies provide for additional retainers for nonexecutive chairmen/lead directors and committee chairmen. Stock ownership guidelines and holding requirements are consistent with requirements for senior executives.

## BOARD LEADERSHIP ROLES

The roles of the board chairman, lead director, and corporate secretary are all germane to an understanding of the board's operations and governance structure.

The chairman of the board presides over board meetings and is responsible for scheduling meetings, planning and prioritizing agendas, and distributing materials in advance. The person in this role also must communicate internally and externally as to board priorities, policies, and concerns. In addition, the chairman is expected to preside over discussions involving strategic planning, enterprise risk management, director compensation, succession planning, director recruitment, and mergers and acquisitions.

In some cases a company will have a nonexecutive board chairman; in others, the board has opted to allow the role to be combined with that of the CEO. Despite strong arguments that splitting these two roles results in a higher functioning board, more independence, and more CEO accountability, most studies to date have been unable to correlate corporate performance with having a separate CEO and board chairman. In cases where the roles are combined, there is a lead director who is designated to carry out the same responsibilities as the board chairman.

## BOARD MEETINGS

Most companies require formal, in-person board meetings between four and six times per year, not including committee meetings and additional telephone meetings needed to address pressing concerns. In addition, the Sarbanes-Oxley Act dictated that boards meet in so-called "executive session"—that is, only with nonmanagement members of the board present—at least once a year.

Board actions are debated at board meetings and resolutions are passed when they receive a majority vote, either in person or by written consent. Boards rely on management to provide adequate material, in a timely fashion, to allow them the appropriate amount of debate on the issues at hand. Boards are expected to act independently, without being swayed by management's views or having been compromised by any conflict of interest.

Boards do not make decisions on the day-to-day operation and management of the company but rather focus on issues that are related to strategy and risk. A typical board agenda, often drafted by the CEO and/or the chairman, would include items such as review of financial performance and targets, budgets, executive compensation, capital management, succession planning, competitive strategy, compliance oversight, litigation, R&D, large-scale capital expenditures, mergers and acquisitions (M&A), and governance matters such as resolutions and bylaws, among others.

## BOARD COMMITTEES

Many agenda items are deliberated by the full board, but to allocate the oversight of the vast array of board matters most efficiently, certain areas and responsibilities are delegated to three standing committees: audit, compensation, and

nominating/governance. These committees perform discrete, specific duties, then make recommendations and report back to the full board.

## AUDIT COMMITTEE

The rise of the audit committee in scope and responsibility occurred immediately after the passage of Sarbanes-Oxley, when all eyes were focused on the ways in which boards provided checks and balances on financial reporting and independent risk oversight. Today, audit committees play a vital role in the capital markets' investor protection framework through their oversight of the audit engagement and their company's financial reporting process. As corporate risks continue to evolve, so does the scope of the audit committee's purview, and it has often become the committee charged with oversight of various risks, such as cyber, operational, compliance, and many others that could impact shareholder value.

The primary role of the audit committee is to provide oversight and ensure integrity of the company's financial reporting, audit process, the system of internal controls, disclosures, and compliance with laws and regulations. Both NYSE and Nasdaq listing requirements require audit committees be composed of entirely independent members; the SEC adopted final rules in 2003 also requiring each audit committee to have a designated "financial expert."

## COMPENSATION COMMITTEE

Much like the transformation of the audit committee, the scope and workload of the compensation committee has also increased dramatically in the last few years as a result of a slew of new requirements and disclosures related to compensation, spawned by the 2010 Dodd-Frank Act. Today, compensation committees meet year-round to review and assess pay and performance targets, to analyze and review disclosures, and to ensure effective shareholder communication with regard to equity plans, incentives, goal-setting, and much more.

The compensation committee's primary responsibility is to set objectives and goals by which the CEO's performance will be measured, review CEO performance, recommend executive compensation packages to the board, set board compensation, and hire compensation consultants as appropriate.

The compensation committee, composed of or including independent directors, recommends to the full board the executive compensation plan, which should be designed to attract, retain, and motivate qualified executives. (NYSE requires compensation committees to be composed entirely of independent directors; Nasdaq rules require at least two independent directors.) Shareholders then are given a chance to approve these plans on a regular basis (every one to three years) during the annual shareholders meeting in a "say on pay" vote under final rules adopted by the SEC in 2011.

## NOMINATING/GOVERNANCE COMMITTEE

Shareholder expectations regarding the selection, retention, and succession of the right executive leadership, along with heightened scrutiny about the skills and effectiveness of corporate boards, have brought new levels of awareness about the importance of the work of the nominating/governance committee. Today, this committee often finds itself squarely in the

spotlight of many hotly debated governance issues and policies such as the separation of the chairman and CEO, board diversity, the efficacy of director evaluations, CEO succession planning and others.

The nominating/governance committee is responsible for oversight of composition, governance structure, operations, and evaluation of the board and its committees; assisting the board with CEO succession planning; and identifying, evaluating, and recommending director candidates to the board.

*Other committees:* Although not required by regulation or exchange listings rules, boards may organize other committees to assist with specific oversight duties such as executive, finance, risk, technology, corporate social responsibility, and other matters.

**BOX 1** Board Demographics

| | |
|---|---|
| • Average number of board seats held per director | 1.26 |
| • Average tenure | 6.2 years |
| • Average number of directors on a board | 8.49 |
| • Average Age | 60 |
| • Male/female % | 86.5%/13.5% |

# 44

# RECRUITING A BOARD OF DIRECTORS

New York Stock Exchange

When a company decides to go public, one of the most important initial decisions to be made involves the structure and composition of its board of directors. The board of directors represents the interests of a company's shareholders and has a legal fiduciary duty to act in their interests in all matters. In doing so, directors are tasked with advising management on the company's strategic direction and overseeing organizational risk. Shareholders therefore have a vested interest in how the board is structured and how effectively it discharges its duties, which makes the selection and recruitment of board members one of the most critical obligations of a nascent public company.

## FORMATION REQUIREMENTS

A public company board is subject to many more strictures than that of a private company board, among them, requirements imposed by applicable stock exchange listing requirements, the Securities and Exchange Commission (SEC), and in some cases additional federal regulatory bodies.

The New York Stock Exchange requires all listed companies to have a board of directors, the majority of whom are independent members, within one year of listing. In addition, the board's audit committee and its compensation committee must comprise a majority of independent members. Other rules that relate to "interlocking directorships," that is, applying to directors who serve on multiple companies, also apply under SEC and U.S. tax rules. (For a complete list of NYSE requirements related to corporate governance and board structure, companies should refer to the New York Stock Exchange Listed Company Manual, which can be accessed at http://nysemanual.nyse.com.)

Beyond these requirements, there is a great deal of flexibility and discretion on how a public company board is structured, both quantitatively and qualitatively. As an overarching principle, good governance dictates that a public company board be composed of individuals whose combined skill sets, viewpoints, knowledge areas, and professional and social capital allow for both autonomous and synergistic oversight of current corporate leadership and operations as well as the future needs of the company.

## REGULATORY DISCLOSURES

In 2009, the SEC adopted amendments to Regulation S-K of the Securities Act of 1933 that require U.S. public companies to enhance their disclosures in proxy statements regarding the qualifications of director nominees. According to the SEC, these amendments "provide investors with more meaningful disclosure that will help them in their voting decisions by better enabling them to determine whether and why a director candidate is an appropriate choice for a particular company."

The amendments were part of a package of new SEC disclosure rules aimed at improving the overall quality of information in proxy statements. Specifically, companies must provide investors with detailed biographical information on each nominee, including the following:

- particular qualifications, attributes, skills, or experience that led the board to conclude that the person should serve as a director;

- any directorships of public companies and registered investment companies that each director nominee held at any time in the previous five years; and

- legal proceedings against the nominee going back 10 years.

The rules also require boards to discuss whether and how they consider diversity in the nomination process.

## RECRUITING BOARD MEMBERS

In the last two decades, public company boards have come to be viewed through a much more critical lens, and consequentially the composition and ongoing refreshment of the board has never held more importance. Companies must ensure boards have adequate bench strength and depth of knowledge to be able to discuss new and emerging risks that can impact their organization and to ask critical questions of management regarding those risks. Only then can directors provide a prudent review of strategic risk and corporate objectives that ensures they are meeting their fiduciary duties to shareholders.

When a company is newly formed, the board must follow the guidelines set out in the corporate bylaws. Those tenets will generally cover the board's size, terms, chairperson, meetings, vacancies, powers, and compensation. In addition, many companies draft a board of directors agreement. The agreement outlines the specific responsibilities of a board member to both the board and the corporation as well as specific responsibilities of the corporation to each board member. It should detail the minimums expected of the directors and the consequences of directors' failure to adhere to those minimums.

Often, newly formed boards consist of investment principals and/or founders, but broadening the mix of perspectives and experiences should be a goal early on. As a general rule, the nominating/governance committee has responsibility to exercise general oversight with respect to the governance of the board of directors; review the qualifications of and recommend proposed nominees to the board of directors; evaluate and recommend to the board corporate governance practices applicable to the corporation; and to appraise the framework for assessment of board performance and board self-evaluation. This committee also defines onboarding and succession-planning criteria that factor in shareholder concerns and interests, as well as known gaps of experience and skill sets related to the current and future needs of the company.

To assist in this endeavor, outside consultants and executive search firms often play a key role in working with the nominating/governance committee or the full board to identify qualified individuals for open board seats. Such firms have outreach capabilities that can tap into diversified markets and geographies and also have the benefit of having their fingers on the pulse of individuals who are actively pursuing board service.

To achieve the desired compositional mix of directors, boards often create a matrix that provides a framework for the particular skills and expertise the board has deemed to be both necessary and optimal. While sitting CEOs are the type of individual most sought after to fill board seats, such individuals are in short supply. Often then, the search for a new member must widen to consider other C-suite-level executives who can bring considerable breadth of experience to the board. In addition, the topic of diversity is often prominent when creating or reviewing a board's composition. While diversity of gender or race is often the touchstone, it is equally if not even more important to ensure the board is composed of members who bring diversity of thought, perspective, and experience to bear on the board as a whole.

Beyond these tenets, it is worth noting that the last decade has brought heightened risks that heretofore had not existed within the board's purview—such as cybersecurity, liability related to the Internet of Things (IoT), and increased market globalization and disintermediation. These dynamics have created additional complexities for corporate governance well beyond what were once traditional board matters. As a result, boards are under immense pressure to stay up to date on a wide range of topics and have begun to seek individuals who are well versed in these emerging dynamics.

Therefore, it is more important than ever before for boards to regularly undergo examination to identify potential gaps and proactively take steps to evolve and adapt to this changing reality. Boards whose composition isn't reflective of the new paradigm run the risk of jeopardizing future growth opportunities that can create shareholder value.

## BOARD TERMS AND ASSESSMENTS

As part of a board's ongoing operations, an annual assessment to identify—and rectify—potential gaps in board composition is necessary, especially as changes in strategy, technology, or the industry itself occur. NYSE listing requirements state that every board should conduct a self-evaluation at least annually to determine whether it and its committees are functioning effectively. Such assessments help

measure and substantiate directors' acclimation to a rapidly evolving corporate reality and ensure that the board is performing effectively to serve the needs of the company and its shareholders.

Yet in the face of an evolving corporate landscape, turnover on U.S. boards remains low. In a given year, roughly 7 to 8 percent of S&P 500 board seats turn over. At most companies, mandatory retirement drives director succession, and for 30 percent of the S&P 500, the retirement age is 75 or older. With so little turnover and amid so much rapid change, it is no wonder investors question whether boards have the relevant experience to advise management about the company's market, geographic, and product directions.

Indeed, retirement age is still the most popular trigger for board turnover—with good reason. Term limits create an expected, nonconfrontational, even collegial manner of dealing with rotating members off a board. Yet for those same reasons, such policies continue to be debated. The experience that comes with tenure can be an invaluable asset to a board, and many directors insist age should not be the sole determinant that forces the retirement of an otherwise highly qualified, well-functioning member of the board. Some observers have posited that requiring companies to replace directors after some (implicit) period of time will result in the loss of talent and drag down results. Another argument says it creates a lazy way of effecting change because if there is a nonperforming director, the path of least resistance would be to "wait it out" until the director in question reaches retirement age. Some companies are addressing the issue head on. State Street Corp., a financial services company, for example, states in its current governance guidelines that while term limits can help ensure a refreshment of ideas and viewpoints, they simultaneously create the disadvantage of losing the contribution of directors who have developed valuable insight into the company.

## SHAREHOLDER CONCERNS

Investors have become a potent voice in recent years on matters related to board composition. Increasingly, activists and long-term shareholders are demanding more information about the specific skills and experience individual directors bring to the board—and how these skills relate to the needs of the business. Correspondingly, they have become more strident about issues such as director tenure and turnover.

While a board's process for determining the most relevant and optimal mix is something best left to individual companies to establish, it is critical that companies develop clear and understandable communications that allow shareholders to understand the rationale related to board composition. The use of a summary chart or table in the proxy disclosure is often the best tool a company can use to give shareholders a big-picture view of the criteria the company considers in selecting candidates and to clearly explain how the criteria support the company's business and strategy.

Another shareholder concern relates to directors who are "overboarded," that is, those who hold multiple board seats, which brings their effectiveness into question. The proxy advisory firm Institutional Shareholder Services (ISS), which makes recommendations to large institutional shareholders on corporate governance, has said that, starting in 2017, it will issue a negative recommendation if a director serves on more than five corporate boards. Some companies have addressed this issue by adopting directorship limits in their governance guidelines.

The attention on overboarding exemplifies a widespread recognition that board service has become increasingly time intensive and complex, with many directors anecdotally noting that prep time and meeting length have greatly increased. Interestingly, NYSE's data shows that just 5 percent of directors sit on more than two public boards, suggesting that the support for overboarding policies, while logical, does

not speak to the root cause of a lack of board efficiency or effectiveness.

Finally, it's worth noting that when it comes to the effective functioning of a board, the whole is indeed worth more than the sum of its parts. Recent studies suggest that not only do synergistic boards have a greater impact on profitability, but, according to research by the International Finance Corporation (IFC), a member of the World Bank Group, well-governed companies with high levels of transparency and disclosure can also more easily command a premium and typically outperform their peers by about 19 percent over a two-year period. Therefore, if superior corporate governance practices ultimately result in increased market valuation, a rigorous and well-managed evaluation process can go a long way toward achieving the ultimate goal of higher corporate performance.

### FIVE BEST PRACTICES

With momentum quickly shifting in favor of greater board refreshment and rigor around composition, NYSE has identified five best practices related to board composition.

### 1. View director recruitment in terms of ongoing board succession planning, not one-off replacements.

Investors expect boards to evaluate board composition holistically, in the context of the company's long-term strategy and the current business environment. Led by the nominating/governance committee, boards should periodically review the skills and expertise on the board to identify gaps based on changes in strategy or the business context, as well as skills that may be lost to director departures. Boards also may want to consider valuable soft skills: Do we have someone who asks the tough questions of management? A creative thinker who views issues with a fresh perspective? Who helps to bring closure on discussions? Who has experience with business transformation?

## 2. Proactively communicate the skill sets and expertise in the boardroom—and the roadmap for future board succession.

Investors want to understand the board's approach to board renewal and be confident that it regularly evaluates the contributions and tenure of current board members as well as the relevance of their experience. Publishing a skill matrix and sharing the board's thinking about the types of expertise needed on the board—and how individual directors provide that expertise—are increasingly considered best practices.

## 3. Set expectations for appropriate tenure, both at the aggregate and individual levels.

One way boards can combat the perceived stigma attached to a director leaving a board before the mandatory retirement age kicks in is to set term expectations when new directors join. Furthermore, the best boards create an environment where directors are willing to think critically about their own contributions and acknowledge when different expertise would be valuable.

## 4. Establish a robust process for evaluating the contributions of individual directors.

Consensus is growing in support of conducting individual director assessments as part of the board effectiveness assessment—not to grade directors but to provide constructive feedback that can improve performance. High-performing boards expect directors to stay engaged and contribute fully and are willing to address underperformance.

## 5. Think like an activist and identify vulnerabilities in board renewal and performance.

Activists often conduct side-by-side comparisons of directors' skill sets and experiences against the company's strategic agenda, looking for weaknesses in expertise or performance. The annual board evaluation is an important platform for thinking critically about board performance and composition and identifying potential vulnerabilities.

# 45

# WEALTH MANAGEMENT AND ESTATE PLANNING: FINDING AN ADVISORY FIRM THAT CATERS TO YOUR TYPE OF CAREER AND LIFESTYLE

**Intellectus Partners**

David J. La Placa, Founder and CEO

Wealth management means something very different for an entrepreneur, or at least it should. The lifecycle, behavioral profile, and tolerance for risk of entrepreneurs are unlike that of non-entrepreneurs. These considerations need to be accounted for before embarking on a program to create a proper financial advisory structure.

*The entrepreneurial lifecycle:* Investment management and wealth management are not the same thing. Often, clients come to a wealth management firm at or near an exit and expect the firm to just step in and work "magic." A firm can certainly help and add value at that point, but wealth management for entrepreneurs needs to begin much earlier. Ideally it should line up temporally with their business lifecycle. Those who come to us near their exit are often limiting their outcomes. They are also reducing the value creation that comes from wealth management to returns on invested capital or just investment management. That is but one component of wealth management, not the whole thing, and often not the most impactful.

When properly prepared clients engage a wealth management or multifamily office firm, they do it at the moment that they are considering leaving their existing job to launch Newco. That is where the process begins. At that time, long-term planning needs to be executed along with their new business plan. In fact, how you structure your Newco, including the corporate structure, method of issuing shares, how shares are held, tax structures, holding entities, and the like can all have an incredibly meaningful impact on your future financial outcome. A wealth management firm that works exclusively or mostly with serial entrepreneurs can provide the greatest insight and value to entrepreneurs.

It is imperative that successful executives and entrepreneurs consider the sheer magnitude of the responsibility of managing their own large pool of wealth. Managing your wealth is very similar to running a business itself. Organization, process, and resources should not be overlooked. In fact, these are the base components of a well-thought-out plan. Clients should take the time to consult with an appropriate wealth management firm as early as possible if they think some form of change may be coming. Aligning yourself with a firm that has a broad and diverse group of partnerships delivering value-added resources such as custodians, strategies, investment products and vehicles, research, trust services, and back-office solutions and can integrate all of this into a comprehensive solution can be invaluable.

We live in an age of increased specialization and segmentation. "Generalist" wealth managers are usually not appropriate for an entrepreneur because they do not have the experience and expertise to handle the intricacies of the responsibilities. Just as there are wealth advisors for certain wealth levels, there are definitely advisors with specialized expertise to help entrepreneurs. On a personal note, I will readily admit, that now that I have lived the life of a startup CEO, I am better suited to advise other CEOs. The sheer experience, terror, joys, and challenges of the startup life and being a CEO have dramatically improved my ability to advise other CEOs and entrepreneurs on the intricacies of their wealth, careers, and businesses.

As the entrepreneurial lifecycle grows and evolves, there will be numerous opportunities along the way to affect outcomes. They could be related to personal or familial changes in the person's life events. They could be changes at the company such as hockey stick growth or challenges leading to pivots. Each of these requires detailed analysis and evaluation of possible strategies in the wealth plan. As the executive achieves greater success and wealth is created, even if illiquid, new possibilities emerge. Having an ongoing, honest dialogue with your advisory team is critical. Your advisory team should be able to identify unique opportunities and how to apply innovative resources for you to capitalize on and achieve your personal financial goals.

The points in time where a professional advisory firm can have the greatest impact are:

1. Business

    a. At business creation

    b. As the company attempts to raise institutional money

    c. As the company begins to scale

    d. Pre-exit/IPO

    e. Post-exit/IPO

2. Personal and family life events

    a. New career/company

    b. Birth/death/disability

    c. Marriage/divorce

    d. Pre- and post-retirement

    e. Generational planning

3. Economic

    a. When forecasting is required

    b. Managing complexities of the economic cycle

    c. Periods of volatility

## YOU CANNOT SEPARATE ENTREPRENEURS FROM THEIR BUSINESS AND THUS THEIR BUSINESS FROM THEIR WEALTH

An entrepreneur has a personal balance sheet comprised of two halves. One half is what is traditionally thought of in Wealth Management, the public traded securities, funds etc. The other is the nonliquid assets. In the "old model" of wealth management, the client might find an advisor who has some expertise regarding Securities Investing and asset allocation. That economic model is based upon charging fees on the assets that reside in an investment account with that broker-dealer. Thus the interests of the advisor/broker are solely related to that pool of assets, and that is where he or she focuses all their attention. To the extent that they do have any expertise to begin with, it revolves around stocks, bonds, maybe third-party investment managers, etc. But, if you were to ask any entrepreneur where his or her wealth is likely to come from in the next five to ten years, they will generally tell you that it will come from the half of their balance sheet that is the company that they are building and the other related business endeavors and deals associated with that, which is generally illiquid and not sitting in an investment account. But a typical advisor just does not have ny real-world expertise to help with that side. It is just not "what they do." This is an important distinction. Providing advice around the entire balance sheet, including the "assets" that are not sitting in an investment account can often be where real long-term success comes from.

Alignment of interests is another critical component of success. This relates of course to economic models, fees, products, conflicts of interest, and incentives. The days of hiring an advisor who pitches you only the firm's vertically integrated products and their firm's ideas are numbered. Working with an advisory firm that has access to many different views of the world, investment managers, products, and resources is incredibly valuable.

In the "old model" a client found an advisor and moved his or her assets to that advisor's firm. That firm was generally a big bank that is leveraged sometimes 10:1 or more. The client then would receive ideas and strategies from just one firm's perspective. As we all know, no one firm will always see every opportunity or risk, so a broader access to safer custodians, research, and perspectives can be really powerful. An advisory firm that has partnerships with a multitude of un-levered and more stable custodians, as well as the top research firms and their views, is key.

So, the clients become "captive" to that advisor, that bank, and all of the risks associated with that. Frequently, the smart clients would have accounts at a few different firms for "diversification" purposes. That is no longer necessary.

The world is changing. The advent of Registered Investment Advisory (RIA) firms as a dominant force in the wealth advice world has leveled the playing field in favor of the client. It has shifted the leverage away from the big bank to the client. It is our view that in the future it will move ever further to where the clients will be the ones with all the leverage because they are the ones with the capital in the first place. It will be the advisory firms that will come to them. The advisors will compete online and off to attract clients so that advisors can go to the client, not vice versa. Those clients will have an

open architecture, including a disparate team of advisors and of products and services from which they can choose and integrate into one platform that they control.

*The behavioral biases:* Most clients do not have an appreciation for the recent advances in finance theory, especially behavioral finance. Based upon our research, it is clear that the most impactful component of a personal financial model are behavioral biases (both the clients' behavioral biases as well as those of the advisors). We all have biases and tendencies, and they are driven by our own personality types and personality dimensions. These lead to our own decisions and outcomes.

You might be a procrastinator, impetuous, or risk-averse—these are behavioral types. First, knowing where you fit in on this spectrum is critical. It is very similar to knowing your strengths and weaknesses in your golf game before you go to play or your advantages and disadvantages in a negotiation before you enter into one. If you have proper awareness of your situation and yourself, you will likely fare far better. Finances and managing wealth are no different. Methodologies are emerging today that accomplished wealth advisors and technology companies are utilizing to significantly improve client understanding, self-awareness, and ultimately outcomes through behavioral technology.

As the former MIT and Harvard Professor in Behavioral Economics and Chief Scientist from HintBox.ai*, a leading technology company that offers a Behavioral Artificial Intelligence Personal Finance platform, describes, "Like all human behavior, making an investment decision involves a multilevel, complex interplay of processes: the cognitive (how you think; for example, how you process facts and information about the markets), the affective (what emotions you experience; for example, the regret you feel about not having bought the stock that made your neighbor a fortune), and the perceptual (how you perceive the outside world; for example, to what specific events and possible consequences of the recent presidential elections you pay attention). Moreover, as investors, we don't live in an isolated dark room that keeps us immune to the influence of others. Rather, we read the news, we talk to our friends, and we observe, in conscious and less-than-conscious ways, what others do in the markets and how they understand what is happening. To this list, add social factors like conformity and groupthink, then you discover what may lead people astray in their financial decision making!

"Next, consider that only very late in the course of evolution did humans come up with the concept of money and start acting as investors and financial decision makers. Compare this financial decision making to how people deal with stress in modern life, and you realize that from an evolutionary perspective, we are not equipped to deal optimally with either challenge. For example, when we feel threatened by a sudden, unexpected stressor in the environment, our evolutionary response is to either flee from the stressor or to engage in an immediate fight. While this fight-or-flight reflex had survival value in the world of the hunter-gatherers (think of the sudden sight of an approaching tiger), in today's world simply running away and hiding or attacking to destroy the source of stressors is usually not adequate (think of your financial advisor breaking the bad news of an unexpected investment loss). Similarly, our hard-wired, innate tendencies in financial and investment decision situations may also be limited."

## THE POINT IS THAT WE ALL NEED TO UNDERSTAND OUR OWN CAPABILITIES, LIMITATIONS, AND NEEDS, ESPECIALLY IN MANAGING OUR OWN WEALTH!

*Technology, tools, and new models:* Indexing, passive investing, and robo-advisors have captured the zeitgeist of the personal finance world for the past two years. The media have certainly boosted their status, and for good reason. These tools have expanded the available options to investors and allowed many smaller investors to participate in the markets with

greater ease and essentially index more easily. While we are fans of anything that makes it easier for investors to achieve their goals, these are but one small step in the direction of where the world of finance is going. But they have their own limitations. The long-run returns on stocks as an example annualize at rates near 10 percent, but average investors generally do not come close to that. Thus the argument for passive/index investing is a strong one. But these numbers benefit from the fact that stocks have been in a bull market for years. By definition, index investing, robo-advisor models, and the like are long-term strategies that carry uneven risks in more challenging periods. Thus an all-of-the-above strategy can be a wise one.

In fact, if you look at the numbers of the robo industry, it is doing a good job of helping the smaller investor, but the numbers are still relatively very small. The technology curve is steepening and the exponential nature of it scaling before our eyes. We are on the cusp of far greater advances in technology that will enable greater financial outcomes. These advances will create services that employ artificial intelligence and data science to better analyze (satellite and UAV/Drone imagery, Sentiment analysis and Quant models), and improve decision making; provide greater transparency, reporting, aggregation, and safety; and all around better returns and outcomes. We allude to the positive impact that the emergence of behavioral AI is having on the industry, and this is a result of the confluence of regulatory change, technological shifts in big data, data science, mobility, and artificial intelligence. The future of an actual AI-based advisor is just about upon us.

*Structural planning:* Structural planning is one of the game changers in outcomes. It is the very first and most important component of risk management. We view taxes, creditors, and predators as primary risks to a successful personal financial plan. It is also, unfortunately, the one that is almost universally overlooked. This is a category that relates to every single turn in the lifecycle. Some refer to this as estate planning, but for us it is far more integral and involved in almost every facet of your plan.

As we referred to throughout, events will arise in your life that have planning consequences. Whether is it the new business, having a child, marriage, divorce, or retirement, to name a few, there are impacts to your structural planning. Frequent areas of iteration and discussion include financial planning, stock-based compensation, and liquidity considerations. More traditional areas are tax (income, estate, capital gains), philanthropic, and legacy planning.

The inherent complexity and the intensely personal nature of these items generally lead people to avoid these topics. However, the costs of procrastination are often very high. As you build your team of advisors, it is critical to make sure that there is a specialist, preferably an attorney, as part of the team with deep expertise in structural planning. We believe that the best method to achieve an integrated and

unified outcome is to allow your trusted advisor to arrange for the key participants and service providers to provide advice and services. Our view is to integrate this with and do not outsource this from your wealth management advisor.

In conclusion, the best approach to the creation and development of a successful wealth management plan is to use your business skills and approach it in a similar manner. Rely upon your business experience and instincts to research the firm, understand its value proposition, and make sure that its specializations align with your needs and goals. Once you build your team, be certain to properly communicate as much as possible on an ongoing basis to maximize the resources and talent at your disposal. If you take this approach, your odds of success in creating a successful and sustainable Wealth Management model for you and your family are far greater.

# SUCCESSFUL SUCCESSION PLANNING

**Korn Ferry Hay Group**

James Peters, Senior Client Partner, Global Head of
    Succession Management

As companies grow and mature, one of the most important considerations for the future is succession management. Succession today means far more than finding that one person to step in and take over a position. Rather than simply looking for replacements, succession planning requires a broad and deep talent pipeline—that is, developing and supplying talent at the top and at other key levels of the organization.

Too often, when organizations address succession planning, they engage in a common practice known simply as "replacement planning." The primary purpose of replacement planning is to identify immediate successors to take over a specific position in the organization should an emergency occur in which the existing executive (the "incumbent") can no longer continue to serve. Sometimes, the replacement is referred to as a "truck candidate"; if the incumbent is "hit by a truck," someone has been identified to take over and assume the responsibilities and requirements of the position. Replacement planning is most frequently focused on C-suite roles: CEO, chief operating officer (COO), chief financial officer (CFO), and so forth.

As a practice, replacement planning is a worthy pursuit. However, the primary fault with it is a lack of choice: the replacement is one person, and frequently this person may be the replacement for multiple positions. The replacement is often taken at face value, regardless of the changing issues, problems, and challenges confronting the organization—let alone the changes in competitive dynamics or the requirement for shifting strategies requiring skills, behaviors, and capabilities. The replacement plan is devoid of developmental considerations because it typically is not created or implemented to prepare the replacement for future needs.

Succession planning goes deeper. Its focus is not simply on preparing for an emergency replacement, but also considers multiple candidates for a given role in the organization. (The common practice is three successors identified for each role.) Successors are given comprehensive and rigorous assessments to identify their current strengths and weaknesses, the results of which are compared to anticipated requirements and capabilities of the role, and the strategic requirements of the organization. Any gaps are closed through the creation and implementation of a development plan.

**FIGURE 1** Moving Toward Succession Management

| Talent Strategy | Toward Succession Management | | |
|---|---|---|---|
| | Replacement Planning | Succession Planning | Succession Management |
| Identification of Successors | Yes | Yes | Yes |
| Development of Successors | Little or none | Yes (Top Talent Pools) | Yes (All Talent Pools) |
| Managerial Levels | Top two or three | Top two or three | All levels |
| Decisions and Analytics | Individual-level analytics to decide:<br><br>• Who is ready right now?<br>• Is the best talent internal or external? | Group and Individual analytics to decide:<br><br>• Which leaders should be successors?<br>• Are they ready? How do we develop them? | Enterprise, Group, and Individual analytics to decide:<br><br>• Where do gaps exist in talent pools?<br>• How long will talent gaps take to fill? |

In this chapter, we will look at why and how companies can move toward *succession management* as a best practice to prepare for their leadership talent needs in the future.

## UNDERSTANDING SUCCESSION MANAGEMENT

Succession management looks at talent at all levels of the organization. The practice views talent as "pools" located along a pipeline, and the pools are aggressively managed to enhance performance, build skills and capabilities, and improve leadership candidates' overall agility to respond to rapidly changing competitive dynamics.

In contrast, succession planning is usually an annual activity. Succession plans rarely change but rather are "dusted off" from the previous year, discussed again, and then put back on the shelf. Successors are identified through nomination, which typically is a "one up" process: the incumbent identifies a potential list of successors, which is not challenged, calibrated, or validated. The list is taken on face

value. Development plans may or may not be implemented.

Another way to think of succession management is that it assists the organization in evaluating its "supply" of talent against the "demand" for talent. This approach is very different from replacement planning and succession planning.

With succession management, the succession agenda is omnipresent, on an ongoing basis. Development is monitored, measured, and managed, just as the organization would do with any other resource crucial to achieving its strategic objectives. At the same time, organizations today are confronted by rapid changes: technological innovations, shifting customer expectations, new competitors, new business models, and globalization, as well as public policy issues such as environmental sustainability. Because of this evolving landscape, what makes a CEO successful today may be different in a few years. That's why succession planning cannot involve only identifying a "replacement" CEO but also anticipating the appropriate candidate pool for the future.

**FIGURE 2** Toward Succession Management

| | From | To | Towards |
|---|---|---|---|
| | Replacement Planning | Succession Planning | Succession Management |
| Identification of Successors | Yes | Yes | Yes |
| Development of Successors | Little or none | Yes (Top Talent Pool) | Yes (All Talent Pools) |
| Managerial Levels | Top two or three | Top two or three | All levels |

Most important, succession management allows the organization is to begin identifying what I call its "seven CEOs." This concept is just as important within maturing and advance stage companies as in a large multinational.

With *seven CEOs* identified—the current senior leader, plus six others at various stages in career development—organizations can meet the demands of robust succession management.

Every organization needs to consider to key questions: *Who are your seven CEOs? What should you do to prepare them?*

## THE SEVEN CEOs

A useful analogy for understanding the concept of the seven CEOs is what air traffic controllers refer to as "a string of pearls" visible in the night sky around any major metropolitan airport. The landing flight path reveals a string of airplanes preparing to land, staged miles apart, but visible due to their landing lights. This string of pearls is a visual representation of the plan to control the flow of planes into the airport, which may be altered in response to contingencies.

Similarly, enterprises today need a "string" of seven CEOs to respond to current and future leadership talent needs. Succession management is designed to identify, assess, develop, and retain the seven CEOs within every organization. These candidates, often found deep in the leadership pipeline, are assessed to determine their strengths and weaknesses. Development plans are crafted to close any gaps, and experiences are provided to ensure that each is able to address the strategies, issues, problems, and challenges of the organization 3, 5, 7, 12, or 20 years from today. Succession management oversees this flow of talent through the pipeline to ensure the organization has the requisite talent ready and able—thus reducing the leadership risk within the organization.

One of the primary reasons for the heightened interest in succession planning and management is "Bulletin 14E" issued by the Securities and Exchange Commission in 2009. This bulletin essentially put the boards of directors of publicly traded companies on notice. Instead of the historical view that succession management was a prerogative of the C-suite, Bulletin 14E notified directors of publicly traded companies that they had a fiduciary responsibility for a company's effort at succession management.

271

Subsequently, the National Association of Corporate Directors (NACD) assembled a blue-ribbon panel to focus on the board's responsibility for the development, retention, onboarding, and succession of the enterprise's talent. In its report, *Talent Development: A Boardroom Imperative*, the panel described the world in which organizations are operating today as volatile, uncertain, complex, and ambiguous—and confounded by a rapidly emerging shrinkage of experienced senior management and executives as a result of demographic shifts. The report notes:

> Having the right leadership in place to drive strategy, manage risk, and create long-term value is essential to an enterprise...the talent management challenge goes well beyond CEO succession. Do the company's talent development efforts support its strategy and fit its risk profile? Is there a clear view of management's bench strength—and any gaps in the pipeline—in critical areas of the business? Does the company understand what its talent needs will be in three years—or five years—in a landscape that may look very different from today's?

## SEVEN CRITICAL ROLES

The idea of identifying *seven* CEOs may be daunting for companies that not so long ago were lean organizations in which everyone was wearing multiple hats. Like all good practices, it begins with a process, implemented over time. Generally speaking there are seven critical roles that can be found within organizations. They are:

- Enterprise leadership, more commonly referred to as the C-suite

- Managers of businesses, who have a portfolio of businesses

- Manager of a business, a classic general managerial role

- Functional leader

- A manager of managers

- A manager

- Individual contributor

As you go down the talent pipeline, pools of potential CEO candidates expand from 3, to 10, 50, 100, 500, and/or 1,000 or more. Their readiness (their "landing," to recall the airport "string of pearls" metaphor) may be years apart; nonetheless, they are identified, and their development can be shifted as organizational strategies and challenges alter.[1]

Those who are "high potentials" could become part of succession management plans all the way to the enterprise level. Those who are "high performer/profession" (High Pro) are still part of the talent pipeline, but upward mobility may be more limited. Thinking in these terms allows organizations to view the leadership pipeline within an organization as repositories, or pools, of talent. Further downstream in the pipeline, the "pool" becomes broader with more potential candidates.

## THE VALUE OF THE LEADERSHIP PIPELINE

A compelling example of the value of the leadership pipeline construct to assist in identifying the seven CEOs was the 2001 succession at General Electric, when Jeffrey Immelt succeeded Jack Welch. The process was well documented and reported in the popular financial press. What is less well known is that Immelt had first been identified in 1982 as having the potential to be a GE leader at the enterprise level—though not necessarily CEO.

Immelt's career experiences were then carefully evaluated and guided through the leadership pipeline in preparation—as were the careers of hundreds of other executives within GE. After 19 years of preparation, Immelt was one of the three primary internal candidates. He was chosen by the GE board as the best equipped to address the strategic challenges of the company (Figure 3).

As the GE example shows, succession management is an enterprise-wide practice to optimize the flow of management talent through the talent pipeline for the benefit of the organization and its individual employees. The

**FIGURE 3** Who is your organization's next
"Jerey Immelt"?

Early identification of high potential talent is critical.
Consider the example of Immelt's career at GE:

- 1982 – Identified as a high potential
- Guided through a series of "DIVA" (diversity, intensity,
  variety, and adversity) experiences
- 1997 – On list of 8 CEO candidates
- 2000 – On list of 3 CEO candidates
- 2001 – Named CEO

primary focus of this practice is to ensure that
executive, managerial and, most importantly,
pivotal roles in the organization are filled at
all times with competent internal candidates.
To accomplish this, succession management
includes processes to identify, develop, and
deploy talent. The process also assists in the
mitigation of risk for the organization and
individuals. The organization wants to confirm
it has the requisite talent to accomplish its
strategic objectives while not placing internal
candidates in harm's way by moving them into
positions that exceed their capabilities. The goal
is to ensure the organization has the right people,
with the right behaviors and skills, in the right
place at the right time.

The process of succession management has at its
core some well-developed practices, including:

Alignment to the overall leadership and talent
strategy of the organization.

Rigorous and consistent onboarding process,
assuring a seamless transition into increasingly
more challenging roles for the benefit of the
individual and the organization.

Robust talent reviews that are honest,
facilitated, calibrated, transparent, and based
on strong performance expectations.

Identification of the capabilities of all talent
within the organization, not just a select few.

Map of talent in which both high potential and
high professional talent are identified.

Creation and implementation of research-
based development plans that can be
accelerated through experiential, relational,

and educational approaches, often referred to
as 70/20/10 development (see below).

- Transparent process and the brokering of
  talent for developmental purposes that occurs
  across the organization.

## INTERNAL CANDIDATES AND APPROPRIATE DEVELOPMENT PLANS

The formula for developing successful executives
is quite clear: 70 percent of development comes
from experience, 20 percent from feedback and
people, and 10 percent from courses or training
events.

Corporate directors must understand this
paradigm. Experience should be the core of
leadership and executive development, and
those experiences should provide sufficient
"development heat." Interesting and thought-
provoking courses at leading educational
institutions have their use, but development
plans need to be loaded with assignments—such
as leading a startup or working internationally—
designed to create well-tested executives.
High-potential executives also should get
comprehensive, multi-rater feedback each year.

Another critical component is providing coaching
for *emerging executives*. During the next decade,
the global population of 35- to 50-year-olds—the
prime age of emerging executive talent—will
decrease in number by 15 percent. As a result of
this drop-off, companies will be forced to move
talent through the leadership pipeline faster.
The danger here is if unseasoned managers are
put into positions of authority too quickly. If that
happens, these managers may very well lack
some of the competencies and skills needed in
assuming the roles of senior managers and CEOs.
To avoid this deficit, emerging business leaders
would benefit significantly from assistance
provided by a skilled executive coach with a blend
of leadership expertise, human development
knowledge, and strong business acumen.

Talent management plans should be monitored
and measured. Here, the adage "what gets

measured gets done" should ring in the ears of corporate directors. Executives devote their attention to how they are measured for merit raises, bonuses, stock awards, and recognition. Therefore, if the C-suite executives are evaluated on talent-development metrics, they are more certain to ensure talent development throughout the firm keeps flowing.

Organizations should also have in place formal assessment processes to evaluate internal candidates—with "formal" being the operative word. For those organizations that actually have one, a succession planning process typically is driven by a one-up talent review, e.g., the general manager for Brazil provides the head of Latin America with a short list of succession candidates. Typically, this list is passed upward and onward. This notoriously subjective approach is rife with documented problems, such as the "halo effect" (one can do no wrong) and personal biases toward a given person. Rather, objectivity and transparency should drive succession plans within a framework of possible strategic scenarios. These criteria can be met through a formal assessment approach.

Many companies use a performance/potential matrix, which plots where an executive sees his or her direct reports. The vertical axis is sustained performance, which takes into account a three- to five-year period, and not just the last year's results. High performance means superior—the best performance people have seen. Middle performance indicates someone is meeting the expectations of the role. Lower performance indicates that there are conditions interfering with a person's ability to meet the requirements.

On the horizontal axis is *learning agility*, which Korn Ferry views as the foremost indicator of leadership success. Learning agility is the ability and willingness to apply past experiences and lessons learned to unfamiliar or changing situations. At the intersection of the two axes— superior sustained performance and high learning agility—is high-potential talent.

A talent review using the performance/potential matrix is an invaluable exercise. Organizations also should include a 360-degree feedback process. In this approach, an immediate boss, peers, and direct reports proffer their perspectives on the current skills of the executive in question. This not only provides executives with valuable feedback, it also can measure in great detail the degree of "fit" with future requirements of the organization.

## SUCCESSION PLANNING FOR THE FUTURE

As this discussion shows, succession today means far more than finding one person to step in and take over a particular position, especially at the top of the organization. What's needed is a succession management approach that deepens the talent pipeline.

At a time when boards of directors have a clear fiduciary responsibility for succession, a robust process is needed to identify, evaluate, and develop a broad slate of candidates. Often found deep within the organization, these candidates are assessed to determine their strengths and weaknesses, and provided with development plans for the short and long term. By identifying their "seven CEOs," organizations ensure they have the requisite talent ready and able to step into top roles, which reduces leadership risk. At every stage of the process, assessment and development are key components. Strengths and weaknesses of individual candidates are identified. Based on these insights, and with an understanding of the company's evolving leadership needs, development plans are crafted to close gaps and provide experiences to prepare for future positions. With a "seven CEOs" approach, both growth- and late-stage companies can ensure they have the talent pipeline in place to support their future success.

## REFERENCE

1. Charan, Ram, Drotter, Steve, and Noel, Jim, *The Leadership Pipeline: How to Build the Leadership Powered Company* (2nd Edition), 2011, San Francisco: Jossey-Bass.

# PART V

## A FRONTLINE PERSPECTIVE

# A COMPANY BASED ON IMPACTFUL PRODUCTS AND A UNIQUE CULTURE

## Penumbra, Inc.

### Adam Elsesser, Chairman, Chief Executive Officer, and President

Dr. Arani Bose and I started Penumbra, Inc. (NYSE:PEN) in 2004 with a very simple mission. We wanted to make medical devices that could dramatically improve the lives of people throughout the world suffering from devastating diseases. Having already sold our first company to a large medical device company, we understood the power of singular focus at a startup. The real challenge for us was to determine how we could permanently capture that startup energy and focus so we could unleash it on multiple products at the same time and then build an enterprise that continues to innovate as it grows.

One of the first focus areas for PEN was ischemic stroke, which results from a blood clot blocking an artery in the brain and is a leading cause of adult disability and death in the United States. When Penumbra was founded, it was only the second company working on a minimally invasive approach to remove clots quickly. In 2008, Penumbra introduced a product that enabled physicians to remove clots using aspiration, sometimes described as a minimally invasive "vacuum" inside the artery.

At the time, many clinicians were skeptical about the device's value. We knew we needed to continually improve and iterate the device and prove the clinical benefit of removing blood clots using aspiration.

We also knew that in order to capture the energy and focus necessary to drive real clinical change, we had to promote and encourage team success, without any fear of retribution for failing. And we needed time.

One of the most important early decisions was to forego traditional venture capital funding in order to pursue a longer-term vision, including both time to develop the device market for stroke patients and time to build a multiproduct company that addresses multiple unmet clinical needs. We raised substantial capital from friends who believed in our vision and had the patience to wait for their investment to pay off.

After deciding not to take traditional venture capital, our first task was to look at the typical corporate structures, policies, hierarchies, and decisions and determine if they worked for or against our goals. The second task was to relentlessly model behavior that supported our goals.

## STRUCTURES DESIGNED WITH INNOVATION IN MIND

Often in the medical device field, innovation suffers as companies grow and bureaucracy increases. So we established some basic corporate structures that promoted the culture we believed would allow innovation to thrive as the company grew.

First, we did not adopt a typical "bonus" system for the professional staff. These systems generally hold back a certain amount of compensation and distribute it at the end of the year to the employees based on a ranking system comparing the "value" or "contribution" of employees. We determined that such a system creates unnecessary competition among the same employees we ask to cooperate and work as a team. At Penumbra, we simply pay people fairly and take into account extraordinary effort as appropriate. Our system has removed all the effort and emotion expended on year-end reviews. This structure has resulted in a high retention rate for our employees. It also helps promote cooperation and teamwork.

Another corporate structure that PEN approached differently was departmental budgets. It is obviously critical to manage a company with fiscal discipline, and Penumbra has been known for running its business profitably for most of the years it has been commercial. Typically, companies determine each department's budget in advance and then authorize and empower the departmental manager to run the department within that budget. This structure provides certainty. What it does not always provide is the best spending decisions and cross-functional teamwork.

Penumbra keeps the budgeting process centralized and empowers functional heads to spend money on mission-critical items but not on other things. There are several benefits of this structural change. First, it limits turf wars, silos, and hierarchies that can be created when departmental heads are fighting over budget increases, allowing for a more cooperative, respectful environment in which the entire team

is working together to get the right answer and develop the best products. Second, it frees up many senior people with significant technical skills to be directly involved in the day-to-day work of their departments rather than in administration.

Finally, the third example involves internal meetings. Other than meetings required by the regulations that govern our work, Penumbra does not rely on standing or prescheduled meetings. Meetings are called only when necessary. A great deal of work and communication is done informally, making a regular or standing meeting less relevant. This approach has had the effect of streamlining communication and promoting less posturing and grandstanding at meetings. The result is a much more efficient product development process.

## MODEL BEHAVIOR WITH INNOVATION IN MIND

Another big initiative at Penumbra was to have everyone model the type of cooperative behavior we all wanted. This effort would then give permission to all the new employees joining over the years to follow suit. There are countless things we do to develop our culture, but the four most critical are summarized here:

*Risk:* When building a company with the mission of making innovative products, it is critical to know this fundamental truth—if you're going to do something that's never been done before, you're going to fail along the way. As companies grow, they traditionally become more risk-averse. That change in risk profile pushes companies away from innovation. At Penumbra, we empower our teams to take risks and fail. If things do not work right away or a product does not develop as hoped, it is not considered a negative. This permission to take risks and fail also needs to be clearly and constantly communicated.

*Jargon:* Sometimes people in business settings speak in jargon. Unfortunately, no one responds emotionally to jargon. I don't respond to it, so how would I expect anyone else to respond to those types of terms? At Penumbra, we encourage everyone to talk in the most fundamental terms. Say what you want to say as if you were a real human being—because you are! When everyone follows this approach, everyone understands the goals and vision because they are clearly stated.

A good example of this happened when we went public a year ago. An expert advising us was trying to get me to talk about Penumbra's opportunity in terms of the huge market "size" or "opportunity" for our products. I was a little taken aback at first because I've never talked about what we do in terms of a market opportunity—that felt like a buzzword. We always think about our efforts in terms of people and the positive impact we have on their lives. I told this expert that if we stick to what is most important to us, investors can get the same information, and it does not frame our work in purely financial terms but rather in the human terms that matter to all of us.

*No tiptoeing:* It is common for people, particularly those at a senior level, to communicate about company issues in a scripted manner. This is a big mistake—employees can immediately tell and then lose faith in the mission. Tiptoeing around issues does not build a strong, trusting culture. This is evident in performance reviews. If you are kind but painfully fair and direct during reviews, people ultimately see the value in those honest conversations and feel good that their challenges or issues have been identified and that there is a pathway to improving and succeeding in their work.

*Great ideas:* Another pillar of Penumbra's culture is that great ideas can come from anywhere in the company. We have created a culture of openness that allows for great ideas to come to light. Everyone at the company has adopted an open-door policy in order to encourage people to share their amazing ideas. Instead of getting in the way for great ideas to surface, the hierarchy or chain of command encourages these ideas. Several years ago, a 23-year-old engineer who didn't know that it "couldn't be done" rewrote the rules around product engineering to develop a breakthrough version of our stroke product. With no barriers, she accomplished what was thought to be impossible. Great ideas are critical to our success and can thrive only when everyone on the Penumbra team can be heard—and gets credit for his or her great idea.

Over the 12 years since it was founded, Penumbra has scaled to become a successful publicly traded company. We now have about 1,600 employees, occupy a six-building campus in Alameda, California, and manufacture all of our products in the United States. The most important measure of our success, however, is the fact that our products have played an important role in positively impacting hundreds of thousands of patients and their families over the years.

# CONTRIBUTOR PROFILES

# New York Stock Exchange

1 Wall Street
New York, New York 10005
**Tel:** +1 212 748 4000
**Web:** www.nyse.com

## THOMAS FARLEY

President, NYSE Group

Tom Farley is President of the NYSE Group, which includes the New York Stock Exchange and a diverse range of equity and equity options exchanges, all wholly owned subsidiaries of Intercontinental Exchange, Inc. (NYSE: ICE). Farley joined the NYSE in November 2013 when ICE acquired NYSE Euronext. He served as the Chief Operating Officer before becoming President in May 2014. Prior to that, he served as SVP of Financial Markets at ICE, where he oversaw the development of several businesses and initiatives across ICE's markets. Farley joined ICE in 2007, where he served as the President and COO of ICE Futures U.S., formerly the New York Board of Trade. He currently represents ICE on the Options Clearing Corporation Board of Directors.

Previous to joining ICE, Farley was President of SunGard Kiodex, a risk management technology provider to the derivatives markets. Before becoming President of SunGard Kiodex, Farley served as the business unit's Chief Financial Officer and Chief Operating Officer. Farley has also held various positions in investment banking at Montgomery Securities and in private equity at Gryphon Investors.

Farley holds a Bachelor of Arts degree in Political Science from Georgetown University and is a Chartered Financial Analyst.

# Revolution LLC

1717 Rhode Island Avenue NW
Suite 1000
Washington, DC 20036
**Tel:** +1 202 776 1400
**Web:** www.revolution.com

## STEVE CASE

Chairman and CEO
**Email:** TheThirdWave@revolution.com

Steve Case is one of America's best-known and most accomplished entrepreneurs and philanthropists and a pioneer in making the Internet part of everyday life. Case cofounded AOL in 1985 and under his leadership and vision, AOL became the largest and most valuable Internet company, driving the worldwide adoption of a medium that has transformed business and society. He is chairman and CEO of Revolution, a Washington, D.C.-based investment firm he cofounded in 2005, as well as Chairman of the Case Foundation, which he established with his wife Jean in 1997. Case was the founding chair of the Startup America Partnership, an effort launched at the White House to accelerate high-growth entrepreneurship throughout the nation. He is also a Presidential Ambassador for Global Entrepreneurship and was a member of President Obama's Council on Jobs and Competitiveness, where he chaired the subcommittee on entrepreneurship. Case is also the author of the *New York Times* bestselling book, *The Third Wave: An Entrepreneur's Vision of the Future.*

# 104°West

## 104 West Partners

1925 Blake Street
Suite 200
Denver, Colorado 80202
**Tel:** +1 720 407 6060
**Web:** www.104west.com

### PATRICK WARD

CEO
**Email:** patrick.ward@104west.com

Patrick Ward has been advising clients and companies and executives on communications issues and practices for over 30 years. He has worked with major brands, including Twitter, HP, AOL/MapQuest, NTT, and Canon, as well as innovators such as Webroot, Magisto, Rapt Media, and Digital Chocolate, among many others. He has worked with some of the most accomplished founders and CEOs in the technology industry, including Jack Dorsey, Trip Hawkins, Nolan Bushnell, John Sculley, Jeremy Jaech, Lew Platt, and Eckhardt Pfeiffer, as well as numerous other entrepreneurs and executives. He has been called one of the Top 50 Tech PR people by *Business Insider* and one of the Top 100 Tech PR Professionals in the World by *Hot Topics*. His firm, 104 West, was named one of the best firms for startups by HubSpot.

## Bessemer Venture Partners

535 Middlefield Road #245
Menlo Park, California 94025
**Tel:** +1 650 853 7000
**Web:** www.bvp.com

### BYRON DEETER

Managing Partner
**Email:** Byron@bvp.com

Byron Deeter is an experienced CEO and founder, having first worked with Bessemer when he raised venture capital for the Series A of Trigo Technologies in 2000. Working closely with BVP, Trigo went on to become one of the first global SaaS companies, reached profitability, and successfully sold to IBM in one of the largest outcomes of its vintage. Having seen the potential of cloud computing early, Byron returned to venture capital in 2005 to lead BVP's global cloud practice and has been actively involved in a portfolio that now includes over 100 cloud investments worldwide. Byron directly led investments in numerous IPOs including Box, CornerstoneOnDemand, Criteo, Eloqua, Instructure, and Twilio, as well as many existing private industry leaders such as GainSight, Intercom, Procore, SendGrid, Tile, and Vidyard.

## CARNEY BADLEY SPELLMAN

## Carney Badley Spellman, P.S.

701 Fifth Avenue
Suite 3600
Seattle, Washington 98104-7010
**Tel:** +1 206 622 8020
**Web:** www.carneylaw.com

### SUSAN SCHALLA

Attorney
**Email:** schalla@carneylaw.com

Susan Schalla works with startup and emerging growth companies through their entire lifecycle and represents venture capital, private equity, and other investors. Susan serves as outside general counsel for businesses with regard to entity formation and structuring, shareholder or partnership agreements, equity compensation, and angel and venture capital financing. Susan represents both buyers and sellers in merger and acquisition transactions and has worked with private equity firms in their purchase and sale of portfolio companies. She has a graduate degree in tax law and uses her knowledge of both corporate and tax issues to achieve the most efficient tax results for businesses at startup, as they grow, and at the exit stage. Susan holds an LLM degree in Taxation from New York University School of Law, a JD from the University of California at Los Angeles School of Law, and a BA from the University of Chicago.

## JOSEPH M. WALLIN
Attorney
**Email:** wallin@carneylaw.com

Joseph Wallin focuses his practice on startups and emerging high growth companies. Joe frequently represents companies in angel and venture financings, mergers and acquisitions, and other significant business transactions. Joe also represents investors in businesses and provides general counsel services for companies from startup to post-public. He initially drafted what became Washington State's new crowdfunding bill and helps startups navigate federal and state securities laws and exemptions. Joe frequently publishes articles in the press and on his blog and hosts a weekly podcast called "The Law of Startups." He holds an LLM degree in Taxation from New York University School of Law, a JD from Seattle University School of Law, and a BA from the University of Washington.

# CBRE

## CBRE Group, Inc.
400 S. Hope Street, 25th Floor
Los Angeles, California 90071
**Tel:** +1 213 613 3333
**Web:** www.cbre.com

## LENNY BEAUDOIN
Senior Managing Director
**Email:** Lenny.Beaudoin@cbre.com

Lenny Beaudoin oversees CBRE's Global Workplace practice and jointly manages the business in the Americas. A recognized leader in the industry, Lenny has worked on engagements across a wide range of markets and industries, giving him an informed perspective on leading global trends. Known for challenging the status quo in pursuit of bold outcomes, Lenny's creative approach to finding and solving problems blends his love of data with his talent for facilitating unique client experiences.

## NINA CHARNOTSKAIA
Director
**Email:** Nina.Charnotskaia@cbre.com

Nina Charnotskaia is a Director in CBRE's Workplace and leads the team's Research Discipline. She connects her experience in design, workplace strategy, and change management to help organizations create unique, engaging workplace environments. She approaches workplace strategy through both a quantitative demand analysis and an understanding of qualitative culture and experience, ensuring successful implementation of workplace programs. For her, a successful workplace experience creates the kind of connections and community that make coming to work the easy and most appealing choice for employees.

## GEORGIA COLLINS
Senior Managing Director
**Email:** Georgia.Collins@cbre.com

Georgia Collins jointly manages CBRE's Workplace practice in the Americas, with specific responsibility for nurturing the team's research and development efforts. An expert at helping people understand and link business objectives with real estate strategy, Georgia thinks the office should play an integral role in building and maintaining organizational culture, and so is focused not just on the physical place but also on the total experience of what it means to go to work.

## Class V Group, LLC

3130 Alpine Road #288-414
Portola Valley, California 94028
**Web:** www.classvgroup.com

### LISE BUYER
Partner
**Email:** lb@classvgroup.com

Lise Buyer is the founder and a Partner of Class V Group, providing strategic and logistical guidance to companies preparing for an IPO. She founded Class V to leverage her unique perspective on the equity markets gained from firsthand experience as an institutional investor, investment banker, venture capitalist, board member, and internal IPO strategist. Lise was an early member of Google's finance department, where she was one of the chief architects of the company's innovative IPO and a recipient of a Google Founders' Award. Previously she was a buy-side investor for T. Rowe Price, a sell-side equity analyst, and venture capitalist. As a public company board member, she served as a financial expert. She holds a BA from Wellesley College and an MBA from Vanderbilt University as an Owen Merit Scholar. She is a member of the TED Braintrust and a former Fellow of the Davos World Economic Forum.

### LESLIE PFRANG
Partner
**Email:** Leslie@classvgroup.com

Leslie Pfrang is a Partner at Class V Group, where she leads the Eastern U.S. practice advising companies as they prepare for and execute successful IPOs, navigate the markets once companies go public, and manage through future liquidity and public company events. Prior to joining Class V Group Leslie spent 20 years on Wall Street, most recently building relationships with top institutional investors and leading the sale and trading of equity transactions including hundreds of IPOs and follow-on offerings. She sat on the equity commitment committees at leading investment banks and brings unbiased

market perspective and an insider's knowledge of the underwriting and syndicate process to the companies Class V Group advises. Leslie's career includes time in investment banking, where she led debt, equity, M&A, and restructuring transactions. She is a securities attorney and CPA and began her career as an auditor for Ernst & Young.

## Fenwick & West LLP

801 California Street
Mountain View, California 94041
**Tel:** +1 650 428 4800
**Web:** www.fenwick.com

### JEFFREY R. VETTER
Co-Chair, Securities & Corporate Finance
   Partner, Corporate
**Email:** JVetter@fenwick.com

Jeffrey Vetter concentrates his practice on public and private offerings of securities, mergers and acquisitions, counseling public and late-stage private companies, and other securities law matters.

Jeff has worked on more than 75 IPOs. His recent issuer-side IPOs include LendingClub, King Digital Entertainment, Workday, Facebook, Nimble Storage, Proofpoint, Marin Software, and Responsys. Jeff also represents underwriters of numerous IPOs, including Tableau Software, Mobile Iron, Rocket Fuel, Veeva Systems, Jive Software, Fusion-io, Salesforce.com, New Relic, Barracuda, and Omniture. He has experience with other public and private offerings of debt and equity securities and stock exchange listings, NYSE Euronext and Frankfurt Stock Exchange, corporate governance matters, and joint ventures.

Jeff's M&A experience includes transactions with total announced deal value well in excess of $40 billion, for transactions such as Responsys' $1.6 billion acquisition by Oracle, SuccessFactors' $3.4 billion acquisition by SAP, and SuccessFactors' $290 million acquisition of Plateau Systems.

## First Round Capital

1040 Locust Street
Philadelphia, Pennsylvania 19104
**Tel:** +1 917 843 2023
**Web:** www.firstround.com

### CHRIS FRALIC

Partner
**Email:** chris@firstround.com

Chris Fralic has been a Partner at First Round since 2006. He has focused on a number of the firm's investments in areas such as advertising and marketing technology, social/mobile, Commerce/travel, connected devices, and gaming.

Some of his investments that have been acquired include Flurry (Yahoo!), Invite Media (Google), and Demdex (Adobe), and two are now public companies, ScanScout/Tremor (NYSE:TRMR) and MyYearbook (NYSE: MEET). Another two, Arbor.io and Circulate, were acquired by the same company (Acxiom) on the same day. Some of the current investments he works directly with include Warby Parker, Hotel Tonight, and Refinery29. Chris has 30 years of technology industry experience, with significant Internet business development roles since 1996. He was VP of Business Development at social bookmarking and tagging company del.icio.us through the Yahoo! acquisition. He was also one of the early employees and VP of Business Development at Half.com starting in 1999, and after the eBay acquisition spent six years with eBay in a variety of business development, media, and entertainment roles. Chris has attended the TED Conference for over 20 years and worked with it in 2006 to help launch TEDTalks, which have now been viewed over 4 billion times.

# FIRSTMARK

## FirstMark Capital

100 Fifth Avenue
New York, New York 10011
**Tel:** +1 212 792 2200
**Web:** www.firstmarkcap.com

### RICK HEITZMANN

Founder and Managing Director
**Email:** Rick@firstmarkcap.com

Rick Heitzmann is a founder and Managing Director of FirstMark Capital, an early-stage venture capital fund based in New York City. Rick invests in consumer and enterprise technology companies in the media, gaming, commerce, software as a service, advertising, and data services sectors. Rick has led successful investments in market leaders in commerce (StubHub, acquired by eBay), gaming (Riot Games, acquired by Tencent), data services (First Advantage, NASDAQ: FADV; acquired by First American), advertising technology (Tapad), media (Pinterest), and more. Prior to founding FirstMark, Rick was an entrepreneur including being a founding member of the senior management team at First Advantage, which he helped grow, take public (NASDAQ: FADV), and sell to First American (NYSE: FAF). He serves on the Board of Directors of the New York Venture Capital Association. Rick has been featured as a business leader and prominent venture capitalist on radio and television and in the *Wall Street Journal*, *New York Times*, and Bloomberg, among others. Rick holds a BS from Georgetown University and an MBA from Harvard Business School.

## CAITLIN STRANDBERG
Vice President
**Email:** Caitlin@firstmarkcap.com

Caitlin Strandberg is a Vice President at FirstMark Capital, an early-stage venture capital fund based in New York City. As a member of the investment team, she focuses on the sourcing and due diligence of new investments as well as supporting the FirstMark platform. Prior to joining FirstMark, Caitlin was a member of the investment team at Flybridge Capital Partners and worked as an early employee at LearnVest (acquired by Northwestern Mutual) and Behance (acquired by Adobe). Caitlin holds a BA from Cornell University and an MBA from Harvard Business School.

## Flybridge Capital Partners
31 St. James Avenue, 6th Floor
Boston, Massachusetts 02216
**Tel:** +1 617 307 9295
**Web:** www.flybridge.com

## JEFFREY J. BUSSGANG
Cofounder and General Partner
**Email:** jeff@flybridge.com

Jeff Bussgang is cofounder and general partner at Flybridge Capital, an early-stage venture capital firm based in Boston and New York City. He also serves as a Senior Lecturer at Harvard Business School and has coauthored 15 HBS cases and notes regarding startup management and entrepreneurship. In 2010, Jeff authored a book on venture capital and entrepreneurship, *Mastering the VC Game*, to provide entrepreneurs an insider's guide to financing and company-building. Prior to Flybridge, Jeff cofounded Upromise, a loyalty marketing and financial services firm that was acquired by Sallie Mae. He also served as an executive team member at Open Market, an Internet commerce software leader that went public in 1996. Prior to Open Market, Jeff was with the strategy consulting firm, The Boston Consulting Group. Jeff holds a BA in Computer Science from Harvard University and an MBA from Harvard Business School.

## Founder Central, University of Southern California
514 Fertitta Hall
Los Angeles, California 90089
**Web:** www.noamwasserman.com

## DR. NOAM WASSERMAN
Founding Director, Founder Central and
   Professor of Clinical Entrepreneurship
**Email:** nwasserman@mba1999.hbs.edu

Noam Wasserman is founding director of the Founder Central initiative at the University of Southern California. Before returning home to Los Angeles, he was a professor at Harvard Business School for 13 years. His book, *The Founder's Dilemmas: Anticipating and Avoiding the Pitfalls That Can Sink a Startup,* was an Amazon #1 bestseller in Management and won the Academy of Management's Impact on Practice award. It has now spent more than half a decade on Amazon's Strategy bestseller list. The book's quantitative backbone is a dataset of 10,000 founders collected annually since 2000. Noam created HBS's most popular entrepreneurship elective, "Founder's Dilemmas," for which he won the Faculty Teaching Award and the Academy of Management's Innovation in Entrepreneurship Pedagogy award. He also taught the course at Stanford Engineering and Columbia Business School, where he received perfect teaching ratings. Noam's research has been published in top academic journals and national periodicals.

## Foundry Group

1050 Walnut Street
Suite 210
Boulder, Colorado 80302
**Tel:** +1 303 642 4080
**Web:** www.foundrygroup.com

### BRAD FELD
Managing Director
**Email:** brad@foundrygroup.com

Brad Feld has been an early-stage investor and entrepreneur since 1987. Prior to cofounding Foundry Group, he cofounded Mobius Venture Capital and, prior to that, founded Intensity Ventures. Brad is also a cofounder of Techstars. In addition to his investing efforts, Brad has been active with several nonprofit organizations and currently is chair of the National Center for Women & Information Technology, cochair of Startup Colorado, and on the board of Path Forward. Brad is a nationally recognized speaker on the topics of venture capital investing and entrepreneurship and writes the widely read blogs Feld Thoughts, Startup Revolution, and Ask the VC. Brad holds BS and MS degrees in Management Science from the Massachusetts Institute of Technology. Brad, an avid art collector, lives in Boulder, Colorado, and Homer, Alaska, with his wife and is on a quest to run a marathon in every state in the U.S. He has completed 23 marathons as part of his goal.

### JASON MENDELSON
Managing Director
**Email:** Jason@foundrygroup.com

Jason Mendelson is a cofounder and managing director at Foundry Group, a Boulder, Colorado-based venture capital firm focused on making early-stage technology investments, participating in select growth rounds, and identifying and supporting the next generation of venture fund managers. Prior to cofounding Foundry Group, Jason was a cofounder of SRS Acquiom and a Managing Director and General Counsel for Mobius Venture Capital. Prior to

this, Jason was an attorney with Cooley. Early in his career, Jason was a software engineer at Accenture. Jason holds a BA in Economics and a JD from the University of Michigan. He is an adjunct professor at the University of Colorado Law School. He is also an active musician with his band Legitimate Front. He also coauthored the best-selling book, *Venture Deals–Be Smarter Than Your Lawyer and Your Venture Capitalist.* He is on Twitter @jasonmendelson.

# Frankfurt Kurnit

## Frankfurt Kurnit Klein & Selz PC

488 Madison Avenue
New York, New York, 10022
**Tel:** +1 212 826 5578
**Web:** www.fkks.com

### JAY S. RAND
Partner and Cochair of the Corporate & Finance Group
**Email:** JRand@fkks.com

Jay S. Rand is a partner and cochair of the Corporate & Finance Group and a member of the Technology Group at Frankfurt Kurnit. He is widely recognized as a leading advisor to emerging tech and tech-enabled companies and their investors. He has extensive experience advising on entity formation, corporate governance, venture capital, and other types of financing. He also advises clients on M&A transactions, strategic partnerships, and licensing arrangements. Jay's practice focuses in particular on clients in high-growth industries, such as digital media, FinTech, software, health and life sciences, and consumer goods and technologies. He also represents venture capital funds, private equity funds, angel investors, and accelerators in investment and other transactional matters. He is a member of the adjunct faculty at Columbia Law School, where he teaches a course in High-Growth Entrepreneurship. He is also a frequent speaker and author of articles on issues critical to emerging companies, entrepreneurs, and investors. He has been admitted to the New York Bar.

## Gunderson Dettmer Stough Villeneuve Franklin & Hachigian, LLP

1200 Seaport Boulevard
Redwood City, California 94063
**Tel:** +1 650 321 2400
**Web:** www.gunder.com

### RICHARD C. BLAKE

Corporate Partner
**Email:** rblake@gunder.com

Richard C. Blake leads the Public Offerings, Public Company Representation, and Corporate Governance practice group at Gunderson Dettmer, LLP. Richard has vast experience preparing companies for public offerings, as well as counseling companies and boards of directors on complex public company matters. Richard has led public offerings for companies across a broad range of industries, including enterprise software, Internet, media, ad-tech, retail, life sciences, telecommunications, semiconductors, entertainment, energy and clean technology, and automobiles. He assisted as counsel to the NYSE's Commission on Corporate Governance and is a frequent speaker at conferences for the Society of Corporate Governance, NIRI, PLI, and NYSE Euronext. Richard is coauthor of "By the Numbers: Venture-backed IPOs in 2015."

He has clerked for judges on the United States Court of Appeals for the Ninth Circuit, and the Utah Supreme Court. He holds a BA with honors and a JD with honors from Brigham Young University.

### ANDREW BRADLEY

Corporate Partner
**Email:** abradley@gunder.com

Andy Bradley is a corporate and securities partner in Gunderson Dettmer's Silicon Valley office. He specializes in the representation of emerging growth companies throughout their lifecycles. He represents a wide variety of technology companies from consumer Internet, software, telecommunications, and entertainment technology industries, as well as a number of leading venture capital firms. Prior to attending law school, Andy cofounded The Hive Group, an information visualization software company. In his five-year tenure as head of marketing and product development, Andy coinvented the company's patented Honeycomb technology, worked closely with the sales team to close and manage industry and government customers, and participated directly in the management and fundraising efforts of the company. He received his JD from Columbia Law School and MA and BA degrees from Stanford University.

### JEFFREY ENGERMAN

Corporate Partner
**Email:** jengerman@gunder.com

Jeff Engerman is a corporate and securities partner in Gunderson Dettmer's Boston office. His practice focuses on the representation of private and publicly held emerging growth companies in a variety of industries. He also devotes a substantial amount of time to the representation of venture capital and private equity funds. Jeff specializes in all areas of corporate, securities, and partnership law. His work with companies spans the entire corporate lifecycle, including company formation and entity selection, general corporate representation and counseling, venture capital financings of equity and debt securities, initial public offerings, and mergers and acquisitions. In addition, Jeff represents venture capital and private equity firms of all stages. He is also an active participant in the venture law community and has assisted with the development of the form agreements used by the National Venture Capital Association. Jeff has previously cochaired the Venture Capital and Emerging Companies Committee of the Boston Bar Association. He received his JD from Harvard Law School and his BA from The Evergreen State College.

## HEIDI MAYON

Corporate Partner
**Email:** hmayon@gunder.com

Heidi Mayon is a partner in the Public Offerings, Public Company Representation, and Corporate Governance practices at Gunderson Dettmer. Heidi has represented corporations, investment banks, and investors in more than 100 initial public offerings, follow-on offerings, confidentially marketed offerings, and PIPE transactions. She regularly advises late-stage private companies on a wide variety of topics relevant to the IPO process. Heidi serves on the Capital Markets Advisory Committee of Law360, is a member of the California Corporations Commission, and is a frequent speaker on topics relating to capital markets transactions. She is coauthor of several chapters discussing the IPO process in the widely used treatise *Venture Capital and Public Offering Negotiation* and is a coauthor of "By the Numbers: Venture-backed IPOs in 2015." Heidi holds a BA from the University of San Diego and a JD from the University of San Francisco and is licensed to practice in California.

## Harvard Business School

### WILLIAM R. KERR

Professor of Business Administration
Rock Center 212
Boston, Massachusetts 02163
**Tel:** +1 617 496 7021
**Web:** www.hbs.edu/wkerr
**Email:** wkerr@hbs.edu

William Kerr is a Professor at Harvard Business School. He is the faculty chair of the Launching New Ventures program for executive education, and he has received Harvard's Distinction in Teaching award. Bill focuses on how companies and economies explore new opportunities and generate growth. He considers the leadership and resources necessary to identify, launch, and sustain dynamic and enduring organizations, and his recent work on launching global ventures especially emphasized global opportunities. He is a recipient of the Ewing Marion Kauffman Prize Medal for Distinguished Research in Entrepreneurship and works with companies worldwide on the development of new ventures and transformations for profitable growth. He also advises governments about investments in the innovative capacities of their nations.

## Intellectus Partners

1050 Battery Street
Suite 150
San Francisco, California 94111
**Tel:** +1 415 795 7831
**Web:** www.intellect.us

### DAVID J. LA PLACA

Founder and CEO
**Email:** david@intellectuspartners.com

David La Placa has led Intellectus Partners since its founding in 2015, keeping client-centric solutions, relationship banking, and innovation at the forefront of his leadership. He leads the Global Executive Investment & Operating committees and oversees all investment strategies. David's energy, vision, and hands-on experience in multiple ventures solidify his connection to entrepreneurs. He speaks not from a distance to their needs but from a vital understanding of the satisfactions and challenges of entrepreneurship today. David has extensive experience at the intersection of entrepreneurial advisory, wealth creation, and investment management. He has been recognized as a "Top Advisor" by *Fortune* and *Research Magazine*. *Barron's* has named him one of the "Top Advisors in America" for several years.

Prior to founding Intellectus Partners, David was a member of the Client Advisor Executive Committee and a Managing Director with Deutsche Bank Alex. Brown. He joined Deutsche Bank in 2004 and quickly became one of the top financial advisors in Silicon

Valley. Within Deutsche Bank, David served as a portfolio manager, led the firm's Private Wealth Management West Coast effort within Venture Services, and was the lead advisor for its Internet & Digital Media outreach. Previously, David was Senior Vice President, Private Wealth Management, and cohead of the Venture Services Group at Lehman Brothers in Menlo Park, California. He was responsible for coverage of ultra-high-net-worth entrepreneurs, as well as trading and distribution of venture capital and private equity fund portfolio securities. He is extremely active in the venture community within Silicon Valley and sits on boards, advises, and invests in startup and growth companies. Current associations include Orbital Insight, Scientific Revenue, CareCloud, Navdy, TheHintBox!, Moon Express, Jukely, Fan Compass, Union Sports, Intellectus Ventures, and Doc.ai, among others. David graduated from Temple University's Fox School of Business, with a concentration in Real Estate, Finance, and International Marketing.

## Ipreo

1359 Broadway
New York, New York 10018
**Tel:** +1 212 849 5000
**Web:** www.ipreo.com

### CHARLIE YOUNG
Executive Vice President and Managing Director
**Email:** charlie.young@ipreo.com

As a global leader in the financial technology space, Ipreo's software, data, and analytics power the mission-critical connections between every participant in today's capital markets. As a EVP and Managing Director, Charlie Young leads Ipreo's Private Company Solutions ("PCS") business. PCS empowers private companies to manage the increasingly complex challenges of data management, investor reporting, equity administration, and capital raising. Prior to driving the PCS business, Charlie ran M&A and Corporate Strategy at Ipreo. In that role, Charlie acquired

and integrated a series of assets that combined to establish Ipreo's Private Capital Markets business, which now serves over 450 of the world's leading private market investors. He joined Ipreo from the private equity firm KKR, where he partnered with portfolio company management teams to drive value creation opportunities. Prior to KKR, Charlie was a consultant with McKinsey & Company. Charlie holds a BA from Harvard University.

## KASOWITZ
KASOWITZ BENSON TORRES LLP

### Kasowitz Benson Torres LLP
333 Twin Dolphin Drive
Suite 200
Redwood Shores, California 94065
**Tel:** +1 650 453 5414
**Web:** www.kasowitz.com

### STEVEN C. CARLSON
Managing Partner, Silicon Valley Office
**Email:** scarlson@kasowitz.com

Steve Carlson is an intellectual property litigator. He focuses on patent, trade secret, and trademark disputes, representing individuals, startup companies, and multinational corporations. He litigates cases through trial in the courts and at the Patent Trial and Appeal Board and offers strategic advice for strengthening IP portfolios and diligence services for fundraising and acquisitions. His cases span the spectrum of technologies, include chemistry, biotechnology, software, machine learning, databases, and mechanical inventions. He clerked for the Honorable Roderick McKelvie of the U.S. District Court for the District of Delaware and for the Honorable Paul Michel of the U.S. Court of Appeals for the Federal Circuit. He obtained a chemistry degree from Reed College and his JD from Yale Law School. He is a coauthor of the *Patent Case Management Judicial Guide* (provided to all federal judges) and the book *Patents in Germany and Europe: Procurement, Enforcement, and Defense.*

# KeyBanc Capital Markets

## KeyBanc Capital Markets

1301 5th Avenue
Seattle, Washington 98101
**Tel:** +1 206 684 6226
**Web:** www.pacific-crest.com/debt-capital-markets/

### GABRIELLA BLUNK

Analyst
**Email:** gabriella.blunk@key.com

Gabriella Blunk is an analyst on KeyBanc's Debt Capital Markets team. She joined KeyBank working in credit administration in 2013 and eventually moved to the technology sector, supporting the sector specialists on the Pacific Crest Securities Technology team. She received her BA in International Relations-Global Business and her MA in International Relations from the University of Southern California.

### JOHN BROCK

Managing Director
**Email:** jbrock@key.com

John Brock is a Managing Director and Head of Technology Debt Capital Markets for KeyBanc Capital Markets, the corporate and investment banking subsidiary of KeyCorp. He joined KeyCorp over 30 years ago. For the last 20 years he has founded and built both a direct lending platform for emerging growth technology companies and a debt capital markets business that annually acts as lead bookrunner for billions of dollars of debt transaction for larger technology firms. Working closely with the sector specialists on the Pacific Crest Securities Technology team, he has executed transactions for public, private, and financial sponsor clients across a broad range of technology verticals including software, Internet, communications, FinTech, and technology services. John has an MBA from Case Western Reserve and BS in Finance and Accounting from Miami University (Ohio).

### SARAH HILL

Director
**Email:** sarah.hill@key.com

Sarah Hill is a Director for KeyBanc's Debt Capital Markets team, working closely with the sector specialists on the Pacific Crest Securities Technology team. She began her career with KeyBank and has over 15 years of debt capital markets transaction experience across a broad set of technology verticals. She received a BA in Business Administration from Washington State University and an MBA from Pacific Lutheran University.

## Korn Ferry

1900 Avenue of the Stars
Suite 2600
Los Angeles, California 90067
**Tel:** +1 310 552 1834
**Web:** www.kornferry.com

### DEBRA A. NUNES

Senior Client Partner, Korn Ferry Hay Group
**Email:** deb.nunes@kornferry.com

Debra Nunes is a Senior Client Partner for Korn Ferry Hay Group, based in the firm's Boston office. Ms. Nunes has consulted to global companies for more than 30 years. She has partnered with CEOs to build the capability of their teams to effectively develop and execute strategy. This includes entering new markets, integrating major acquisitions, and reshaping the company's portfolio. She assists companies in developing the leadership capability necessary to align the organization and implement strategies. She has partnered with CHROs to enhance the skills of HR professionals to support the development of their senior leaders and teams. Debra is the coauthor of *Senior Leadership Teams: What It Takes to Make Them Great*, published by Harvard Business School Press. Using this framework, she works with executive leadership teams to improve the performance of the companies they lead. She holds an MBA from Boston University, a master's degree in counseling and personnel from Western Michigan University, and a bachelor's degree in psychology from Westfield State University in Massachusetts.

## JAMES PETERS

Senior Client Partner, Global Head of Succession
    Management, Korn Ferry Hay Group
**Email:** james.peters@kornferry.com

Jim Peters is a Senior Partner and Global Lead for Succession Management for Korn Ferry Hay Group, based in the firm's Minneapolis office. Previously, he was the Global Managing Director of Lominger Consulting, Inc. (LCI), responsible for the overall practice leadership for LCI's global consulting engagements. His clientele has included Fortune 500 companies and many other diverse organizations. He has consulted with companies in over 25 countries. Jim is considered an expert in strategic human resource management, with a specific emphasis on strategic staffing, development, and succession planning. He is the cocreator of Lominger's proprietary Succession Architect tool set and its Talking Talent process for enhancing executive talent reviews. Jim is an adjunct staff member for the Center for Creative Leadership and is certified in Benchmarks and Tools for Developing Successful People. He is a master certifier in the Leadership Architect Suite of Tools and was the editor/owner of HR Strategies and Tactics newsletter. He holds a master's degree in organization science from the University of Wisconsin.

## MARK ROYAL

Senior Principal, Korn Ferry Institute
**Email:** mark.royal@kornferry.com

Mark Royal is a Senior Principal within the Korn Ferry Institute. His particular areas of focus include relating employee engagement metrics to individual and organizational performance measures and structuring work environments to translate high levels of employee motivation into improved results. Mark also plays a leading role in directing Korn Ferry Hay Group's annual research with *Fortune* magazine to identify the World's Most Admired Companies and uncover the business practices that make these companies highly regarded and highly successful. Mark has coauthored the book *The Enemy of Engagement*, which gives managers new insights and research-based tools for ensuring their teams are both willing and able to make maximum contributions. Mark holds a doctorate of philosophy and a master's degree in sociology from Stanford University and a bachelor's degree in sociology from Yale University.

## BOB WESSELKAMPER

Senior Client Partner and Global Head, Rewards
    and Benefits Solutions
**Email:** Bob.Wesselkamper@kornferry.com

Bob Wesselkamper leads efforts to continue to expand the focus of Korn Ferry's full reward and benefit offerings, including broad-based reward strategy, executive rewards, job evaluation and leveling, reward benchmarking, and pay data. He has more than 25 years of experience as a senior global human resource consultant, working with senior management and boards on all aspects of their rewards, benefits, and HR service delivery needs. His industry focus includes media, automotive, manufacturing, professional, and financial services. Bob has worked across Europe, Asia, Latin America, the Middle East, and Africa. During his career he has focused on the business needs of mature and emerging multinational companies with a deep emphasis on operational improvement, mergers and acquisitions support, new venture startup, and change management leadership. He received his undergraduate degree in economics from DePauw University.

## KPMG

345 Park Avenue
New York, New York 10154
**Tel:** +1 212 758 9700
**Web:** www.kpmg.com

### MARK BARNES

Partner in Charge of International Corridors
**Email:** mbarnes1@kpmg.com

Mark Barnes leads KPMG's initiative focused on
International Corridors and High Growth Markets
(HGM). He has many years of experience working
across a diverse range of sectors with companies
investing to and from growth markets such as
China, India, Korea, Brazil, Russia, and ASEAN.
The HGM practice is made up of dedicated
teams helping FORTUNE 1000 enterprises better
understand opportunities in rapidly developing
markets and work across Global Corridors in
areas that include market entry or expansion
strategy, buying and selling businesses, risk
frameworks, protecting intellectual property, Tax,
and regulatory to name just a few.

During Mark's tenure, the High Growth Markets
practice has grown significantly to provide
a broad range of practical services helping
businesses achieve their growth ambitions across
the investment lifecycle, from initial strategy and
market entry to expansion or consolidation.

Mark is a frequent public speaker, contributor to
news publications, and regularly hosts webcasts
on topics such as cross border investments;
updates on business and regulatory climate in
growth markets, risk, and regulatory framework
models; and managing culture.

### DEAN BELL

Partner in Charge and U.S. Head of Accounting
 Advisory Services
**Email:** dbell@kpmg.com

Dean Bell is the Partner in Charge and U.S.
Head of Accounting Advisory Services in
KPMG's Deal Advisory practice. He has been
with the firm for 19 years and also serves as
the accounting advisory services leader for the
Americas. In addition to his leadership role, Dean
has executed the complete spectrum of AAS
product offerings with a particular emphasis on
accounting change and accounting assistance in
consolidations, fair value, business combinations,
impairments, financial instruments, and SEC
reporting.

### ANDREW CHERRY

Managing Director
**Email:** acherry@kpmg.com

Andy Cherry is a Managing Director in the Tax
practice of KPMG's Philadelphia office. He is a
member of the American Institute of Certified
Public Accountants and Pennsylvania Institute
of Certified Public Accountants and sits on the
Board of Directors of the Philadelphia Alliance
for Capital and Technology and the Board of
Directors of The Enterprise Center. Andy's
client experience includes early-, middle-, and
late-stage growth companies that are backed
with private equity and venture capital and
middle-market public and private companies.
His experience includes advising clients on
transactional tax planning for matters involving
a broad range of corporate and partnership/
limited liability company issues. Andy also assists
his clients with their day-to-day federal income
tax matters, which include tax compliance,
general corporate tax planning, tax accounting
methods, and the tax aspects of merger and
acquisition transactions, and he represents
clients before the Internal Revenue Service at the
examination and appeals level.

## ANTHONY DOUGHTY, CFA
Managing Director
**Email:** adoughty@kpmg.com

Anthony Doughty is a Managing Director in KPMG's Economic and Valuation Services practice. He has more than 20 years of experience in performing valuations for firms in the consumer and industrial products, pharmaceutical/medical device, technology, and financial services industries. He has led complex valuation engagements on domestic and international transactions, including public offerings, for financial reporting purposes and for tax purposes. Anthony has participated in a wide range of valuation assignments including pretransaction analyses and financial modeling to drive management decision making, and valuation consulting services for coinvestment purposes, corporate restructurings, and SEC reporting purposes. He is a national resource within KPMG's Complex Securities Valuation Practice and a Chartered Financial Analyst.

## BRIAN HUGHES
National Partner in Charge of Private Markets &
    National Venture Capital Co-Leader
**Email:** bfhughes@kpmg.com

Brian Hughes is the National Partner in Charge of Private Markets Group & National Venture Capital Co-Leader. He is a member of the American Institute of Certified Public Accountants and Pennsylvania Institute of Certified Public Accountants and sits on the Board of Directors of the Philadelphia Alliance for Capital and Technology and the Board of Directors of the New Jersey Technology Council. Brian has over 30 years of diversified experience in public accounting, and his career has been focused primarily on public and nonpublic technology, software, business services, venture capital, private equity funds, and portfolio companies. Brian has significant experience with initial public offerings, as well as acquisitions and divestitures. In addition, he has considerable experience with the international operations of U.S.-based companies, as well as the U.S. operations of foreign-based multinational corporations. Brian's client experience includes working with high-growth companies in the development stage, through subsequent rounds of financings and other capital formation transactions, or to an initial public offering or acquisition by a larger market participant.

## AAMIR HUSAIN
National IPO Readiness Leader
**Email:** ahusain@kpmg.com

Aamir Husain is KPMG's National IPO Readiness Leader. He is a recognized and respected subject matter expert on IPO Readiness and brings over 23 years' experience in advising companies on all aspects of going public including financial reporting, the JOBS ACT, filing for an S-1, and SOX compliance. He has been a continuing partner and contributing author with the NYSE, including coleading its joint IPO Bootcamp series and coauthoring both the 2010 and 2013 IPO Guides. He has been featured in numerous high-profile publications including *The Deal*.

## PHIL ISOM
Global Head of M&A
**Email:** pisom@kpmg.com

Phil Isom leads KPMG's Global M&A practice as well as Corporate Finance and Restructuring for KPMG in the U.S. and is a member of the Global Corporate Finance executive committee. Phil leads over 2,600 professionals operating in 156 member-firm countries, providing wide-ranging M&A advisory services, including mergers, acquisitions, divestments, strategic and financial advice, distressed M&A process or restructuring, leveraged buyouts, and structured financing. Phil has over 24 years of experience in investment banking, investing, and restructuring. During his tenure, Phil has led the transformation and growth of the firm's Corporate Finance practice by building industry-focused teams and expanding inorganically via three acquisitions. The practice has since added capital advisory, real estate, an international desk, a private wealth desk, and fairness opinions to its product suite. KPMG Corporate Finance was recognized as investment bank of the year in 2015 by the *M&A Advisor* and is consistently ranked the #1 global middle market bank by Thomson Reuters.

## MIKE MEARA
Director, Accounting Advisory Services
**Email:** mmeara@kpmg.com

Mike Meara is a member of KPMG's Accounting Advisory Services group and a director in the firm's New York office. He has worked on a variety of equity offerings, including IPOs and other SEC-registered offerings and cross-border transactions to assist companies to list on exchanges in the U.S., Hong Kong, and London. He regularly advises public companies on financial reporting and regulatory issues including SEC filings, IFRS conversions, and post-merger integration. Prior to joining Accounting Advisory Services, he held financial management positions in Fortune 1000 companies, where he was responsible for SEC reporting and corporate financial reporting areas. He received his MBA and BBA degrees from Thunderbird and the University of Texas at Austin, respectively.

## MICHAEL NOTTON, CFA, CPA
Senior Manager
**Email:** mnotton@kpmg.com

Michael Notton is a Senior Manager in KPMG's Economic and Valuation Service (EVS) Practice. He is based in the Chicago office, providing a range of valuation services for financial reporting, tax, and strategic planning purposes. These include valuations of business interests, derivatives, and intangible assets in support of business combinations, restructurings, and capital raises as well as for interim reporting purposes. In addition, he regularly values awards with nonlinear payouts as part of KPMG's Complex Securities Valuation Practice. He is a Chartered Financial Analyst and Certified Public Accountant.

## Lighter Capital
1501 4th Avenue #1180
Seattle, Washington 98101
**Tel:** +1 206 455 9633
**Web:** www.lightercapital.com
**Email:** info@lightercapital.com

Lighter Capital is a fintech company revolutionizing the business of startup finance. They provide tech entrepreneurs up to $2M in capital to grow their startups while retaining equity and control. Their application and underwriting processes are powered by proprietary technology that lets entrepreneurs spend less time fundraising and more time building their businesses. Based in Seattle, Lighter Capital invests in companies across the U.S.

## Morgan Stanley
2725 Sand Hill Road, Suite 200
Menlo Park, California 94025
**Tel:** +1 650 234 5500
**Web:** www.morganstanley.com

## ANTHONY ARMSTRONG
Managing Head of Global Technology Mergers & Acquisitions
**Email:** Anthony.Armstrong@morganstanley.com

Anthony Armstrong is Co-Head of Global Technology M&A, and he has 20 years of M&A experience. Over his career, Mr. Armstrong has served in the following senior roles:

From 2011 to 2015, he served as Head of Americas M&A for Credit Suisse, based in New York and San Francisco.

From 2009 to 2010, he served as Head of Direct Investing / M&A for the Qatar Invest Authority— one of the world's largest sovereign wealth funds (and Credit Suisse's largest shareholder) based in London.

From 2005 to 2008, he served as Head of West Coast M&A for Credit Suisse.

Anthony began his investment banking career at a sellside M&A boutique before joining DLJ in its M&A Exclusive Sales Group, which at the time was the preeminent sellside franchise on Wall Street. He joined Credit Suisse's M&A group as part of CS's acquisition of DLJ.

Anthony has been involved in approximately 100 sellside transactions over the course of his career, during which time he has represented multinational corporations, sovereign wealth funds, private equity firms, and entrepreneurs.

Anthony received his MBA from Northwestern University with highest distinction, where he graduated first in his class. He received his undergraduate degree in business from Colorado State University.

## COLIN R. STEWART

Head of Global Capital Markets Technology
   Group, Vice Chairman
**Email:** Colin.R.Stewart@morganstanley.com

Colin Stewart is a Managing Director of Morgan Stanley, a Vice Chairman of Global Capital Markets, and runs the equity financing business for the Global Technology Group. He has been involved in and led over 150 IPOs on 5 continents including Google, Facebook, China Mobile, Alibaba, Salesforce.com, Workday, Seagate, LinkedIn, Servicenow, Zalando, and Snap.

Colin holds a BA degree in History (major) and Asian Studies (minor). He has worked at Morgan Stanley for over 28 years in various roles in Asset Management, Institutional Equity Division, Firm Management, and Investment Banking. Colin spent 10 years in Asia working in Morgan Stanley's Hong Kong, Tokyo, and Beijing offices. In 1997 and 1998 he was deputy CEO of China International Capital Corporation, a Morgan Stanley joint venture and the first international style investment bank in China.

## TED TOBIASON

Managing Director and Head of Private Capital
   Markets
**Email:** Ted.Tobiason@morganstanley.com

Ted Tobiason is currently Co-Head of Private Capital Markets and the Head of Technology Private Capital Markets at Morgan Stanley. In these capacities, Ted has led the Morgan Stanley team in private placements for Uber, Airbnb, Domo, Apttus, ForeScout, Financial Force, Simplivity, Xero, Oportun, Adyen, and Klarna. His public equity transaction experience includes working with Rally Software, SunEdison Semiconductor, Trulia, Twitter, Veeva, and VIP Shop. Ted has 21 years of Investment Banking Experience. Prior to Morgan Stanley, Ted spent eight years as Head of Technology ECM at Deutsche Bank and served as a senior research analyst concentrating on the technology sector for Cypress Funds. He holds an MBA from Columbia Business School and an AB from Princeton University.

## Moving Brands

100 Crosby Street
Suite 509
New York, New York 10012
**Tel:** +1 646 650 2300
**Web:** www.movingbrands.com
**Email:** info@movingbrands.com

Moving Brands is a global, creative company with offices in San Francisco, New York, London, and Zurich. It works with some of the world's most interesting businesses (including Netflix, Apple, Google, and Sony) as well as the most innovative startups (such as Flipboard, Asana, and Housing). Moving Brands' services span brand strategy and identity design, UI&UX for digital products and services, business design and transformation, communications campaigns, film, and animation. Its multidisciplinary teams partner with startups to enable them to scale up and with global businesses to help them innovate.

# Penumbra

## Penumbra, Inc.

One Penumbra Place
Alameda, California 94502
**Tel:** +1 510 748 3200
**Web:** www.penumbrainc.com

### ADAM ELSESSER

Chairman, Chief Executive Officer, and President
**Email:** aelssesser@penumbrainc.com

Adam Elsesser cofounded Penumbra and has
served as Chief Executive Officer and a member
of the board of directors since its inception in
2004 and as President and Chairman of the
board of directors since January 2015. Prior to
Penumbra, Adam led SMART Therapeutics, Inc., a
medical device company focused on devices for
neurointervention, as its Chief Executive Officer
from 2000 to 2002 and, after its acquisition
by Boston Scientific Corporation, President of
SMART Therapeutics within Boston Scientific
Corporation from 2002 to 2005. Before his work
in the medical device industry, Adam was a
partner in the law firm of Shartsis Friese LLP. He
received a BA from Stanford University and a JD
from Hastings College of the Law.

## Pioneer Square Labs

240 2nd Avenue S
Suite 300
Seattle, Washington 98104
**Tel:** +1 206 462 1827
**Web:** www.pioneersquarelabs.com

### GEOFF ENTRESS

Cofounder and Managing Director
**Email:** geoff@pioneersquarelabs.com

Geoff Entress is a cofounder and Managing
Director of Pioneer Square Labs, a Seattle-based
studio that creates and launches technology
startups. Geoff is also an active angel investor
in the Pacific Northwest, focusing broadly on
investments in information technologies. A
current venture partner with Voyager Capital and
a former venture partner with Madrona Venture
Group, he is a current investor in over 100 private
companies in the region and is a board member
of several of those companies. Geoff is a member
of the executive committee of the Alliance of
Angels and is an advisory board member of the
entrepreneurship programs at the University of
Washington, the University of Notre Dame, and
the Tepper School of Business at Carnegie Mellon
University. Geoff is a graduate of the University
of Michigan Law School, the Tepper School of
Business at Carnegie Mellon University, and the
University of Notre Dame.

# SAPPHIRE VENTURES

## Sapphire Ventures

3408 Hillview Avenue
Building 5
Palo Alto, California 94304
**Tel:** +1 650 849 3950
**Web:** www.sapphireventures.com

### JAI DAS

Managing Director
**Email:** jai@sapphireventures.com

Jai Das is a Managing Director at Sapphire
Ventures who invests in startups he believes
are developing ground-breaking products and
services in the areas of pervasive analytics,
next-gen AI, software defined infrastructure,
cloud and mobile computing, IoT, and AR/VR.
He has more than 15 years of experience helping
companies innovate their product and marketing
strategies in order to scale and become market
leaders.

Jai has led the firm's investments in and is a
member of the board at CloudHealth, Cyphort,
JFrog, Mirantis, Mulesoft, Narrative Science,
PayTM, Portworx, PubNub, and Socrata. He is
also closely involved with Catchpoint, Iron.io,
Mirantis, Newgen Software, OpenX, and

Splashtop. His exits and IPO's include Alteryx, Apigee (acquired by Google), Box (BOX), Control4 (CTRL), ExactTarget (acquired by Salesforce), Five9 (FIVN), GroundWork (acquired by Parallax), Jaspersoft (acquired by TIBCO Software), JustDial (JUSTDIAL), MuleSoft (MULE), MySQL (acquired by Oracle), Nutanix (NTNX), Tealeaf (acquired by IBM), and Square (SQ).

Prior to joining Sapphire Ventures in 2006, Jai worked at Intel Capital, Agilent Ventures (formerly Hewlett Packard), and MVC Capital (a Draper Fisher Jurvetson affiliate). He began his career as a software engineer at Oracle and then moved into product management. Jai has a BS in electrical engineering from Brown University and an MBA from University of Chicago's Booth School of Business, where he received the George Hay Brown Prize for academic excellence.

## Schox Patent Group

500 3rd Street
Suite 215
San Francisco, California 94107
**Tel:** +1 888 775 9990
**Web:** www.schox.com

### JEFFREY SCHOX
Founding Member and Patent Attorney
**Email:** Jeffrey@Schox.com

Jeffrey Schox is the founding member of Schox Patent Group, which he founded in 2004 after spending 10,000 hours in large patent law firms. Jeffrey and his team, recruited directly from his course at Stanford, have developed the patent strategy and crafted the patent applications for Twilio (NYSE:TWLO), Cruise ($1B acquisition), and 250 startups that have collectively raised over $2B in venture capital. In addition to being a patent attorney and an entrepreneur, Jeffrey is also an Adjunct Professor at Stanford, the Chairman of the Advisory Board at the University

of Michigan Center for Entrepreneurship, and an active mentor in several of the top incubators, including Y Combinator. Jeffrey lives and works in San Francisco.

## SoftTech VC

4 Palo Alto Square 2nd Floor
Palo Alto, California 94306
**Tel:** +1 650 688 1801
**Web:** www.softtechvc.com

### JEFF CLAVIER
Managing Partner
**Email:** jeff.clavier@softtechvc.com

Jean-Francois "Jeff" Clavier is the Founder and Managing Partner of SoftTech VC, one of the original seed VC firms in Silicon Valley, having closed 185+ investments since 2004. An early angel investor in Web 2.0, Jeff and his team have backed successful startups such as Mint (Intuit), Brightroll (Yahoo), LiveRamp (Acxiom), Milo (eBay), Wildfire (Google), Bleacher Report (Turner), Gnip (Twitter), Fitbit (NYSE:FIT), Curse (Amazon), Eventbrite, Sendgrid, Poshmark, Hired, Postmates, Vungle, Shippo, Front, and Molekule. The firm has $300M+ under management and is currently investing out of its $100M Fund V, making on average 15 seed commitments of $1M per year in mobile/cloud SaaS, consumer services, connected devices, marketplaces, and healthcare IT. One of the early VC bloggers in 2004, Jeff is now a popular conference speaker and social media/TV commentator (as @jeff). When he is not spending time with SoftTech's portfolio companies, Jeff enjoys traveling, skiing, collecting wine, and hanging out with friends.

## Sphero
4772 Walnut Street
Suite 206
Boulder, Colorado 80301
**Tel:** +1 720 930 7650
**Web:** www.sphero.com

### PAUL BERBERIAN
CEO
**Email:** paul@sphero.com

Paul Berberian is an experienced chief executive
and entrepreneur who has founded and run
seven high-tech companies over the last
18 years. In 2010 he became the CEO of
Boulder-based Sphero. In 2005, he cofounded
Market Force Information, a consolidation
of leading customer experience, mystery
shopping, and market research firms. Paul is
the former CEO and cofounder of Raindance
Communications (NASDAQ: RNDC), a web and
phone conferencing services company acquired
by West Corporation in 2006. Before founding
Raindance, he was cofounder and CEO of LINK-
VTC, a video teleconferencing company, which
was sold in 1995 to Frontier Communications.
Paul is a distinguished graduate of the U.S. Air
Force Academy.

## STANFORD
### GRADUATE SCHOOL OF BUSINESS

## Stanford Graduate School of Business
655 Knight Management Way
Stanford, California 94305
**Tel:** +1 650 725 9663
**Web:** www.gsb.stanford.edu/faculty-research/
faculty/stefanos-zenios

### STEFANOS ZENIOS
Investment Group of Santa Barbara Professor of
 Entrepreneurship and Professor of Operations,
 Information, and Technology
Co-Director, Center for Entrepreneurial
 Studies, Graduate School of Business,
 Stanford University
**Email:** stefzen@stanford.edu

Stefanos Zenios is the Investment Group of
Santa Barbara Professor of Entrepreneurship
and Professor of Operations, Information,
and Technology at the Stanford University
Graduate School of Business. He is also the
faculty codirector of Stanford GSB's Center for
Entrepreneurial Studies. An innovative teacher
and researcher, Stefanos is the main architect
of Startup Garage, a popular GSB course that
each year helps hundreds of Stanford GSB
students and executives learn and apply the
innovation processes that are at the center of
the Silicon Valley ecosystem. He also oversees
the Stanford GSB Venture Studio, a vibrant
learning facility for Stanford graduate students
across all disciplines who want to learn about
designing and creating sustainable, high-impact
ventures by testing what they are learning in the
classroom. He previously designed and cotaught
Biodesign Innovation, a project-based course on
designing and launching new medical devices,
and is one of the senior authors of a textbook
with the same name.

## Techstars

1050 Walnut Street #202
Boulder, Colorado 80302
**Web:** www.techstars.com

### DAVID COHEN
Co-CEO
**Email:** david@techstars.com

David Cohen is the Founder and Co-CEO of Techstars and has been an entrepreneur and investor for his entire life. He has had only one job interview in his career, successfully got that job, but then quit shortly thereafter to start his first company. Since then, he has founded several companies and has invested in hundreds of startups such as Uber, Twilio, SendGrid, FullContact, and Sphero. In total, these investments have gone on to create more than $80B in value.

Prior to Techstars, David was a cofounder of Pinpoint Technologies, which was acquired by ZOLL Medical Corporation (NASDAQ: ZOLL) in 1999. This experience is recounted in his memoir *No Vision, All Drive*. Later, David was the founder and CEO of earFeeder, a music service that was sold to SonicSwap. He also had what he likes to think of as a "graceful failure" in between. David is the coauthor (with Brad Feld) of *Do More Faster: Techstars Lessons to Accelerate Your Startup*. David also enjoys reading nonfiction books and playing tennis. He is married to the coolest girl he's ever met and has three amazing kids who always seem to be teaching him something new. He tweets at @davidcohen and blogs at DavidGCohen.com.

## VLP Law Group LLP

555 Bryant Street
Suite 820
Palo Alto, California 94301
**Tel:** +1 650 293 9131
**Web:** www.vlplawgroup.com

### MARK D. BRADFORD
Partner
**Email:** MBradford@VLPLawGroup.com

Mark Bradford is a partner at VLP, specializing in executive compensation, equity compensation, and employee benefits for clients ranging from startups to emerging growth public companies. He also represents individual executives in negotiating employment agreements, terminations and severance, and entire management teams in significant M&A transactions. Mark has over 16 years of experience as an executive compensation and employee benefits attorney. He has represented buyers and sellers in over 200 cross-border and domestic M&A deals, with transactions ranging in size from a $1 million acquihire to a $7 billion sale of a major client. In connection with these transactions, Mark has negotiated and drafted deal-related agreements, including employment, incentive, retention, severance, and noncompetition, and worked on post-closing integration matters. He has also worked with more than 35 companies on compensation matters arising out of their initial public offerings. Mark has drafted hundreds of executive employment, equity and cash incentive, change in control, retention, and severance plans and arrangements for emerging growth companies. He brings a wealth of experience and perspective regarding the culture and business needs of Silicon Valley companies when providing counsel to in-house legal, human resource, finance, tax, and stock administration professionals.

**WOODRUFF
SAWYER &
COMPANY**

## Woodruff-Sawyer & Co.

50 California Street, 12th Floor
San Francisco, California 94111
**Tel:** +1 415 391 2141
**Web:** www.wsandco.com

### PRIYA CHERIAN HUSKINS

Partner and Senior Vice President
**Email:** Phuskins@wsandco.com

Priya Cherian Huskins is a partner at Woodruff-Sawyer & Co., a full-service insurance brokerage. She is a recognized expert in D&O liability risk and its mitigation. In addition to consulting on D&O insurance matters, she counsels clients on ways to reduce their exposure to shareholder lawsuits and regulatory investigations. Priya is a frequent speaker on corporate governance and risk mitigation issues. She is regular lecturer at director education events such as Stanford's Annual Directors' College. She's also the author of the popular D&O Notebook blog.

Priya serves on the board of directors of an S&P 500 public company, a large private company, a FinTech startup, and a nonprofit. She also serves on the advisory board of the Stanford Rock Center for Corporate Governance. Priya began her career as a corporate and securities attorney at Wilson Sonsini Goodrich & Rosati (WSGR), one of Silicon Valley's leading law firms.

### WADE PEDERSON

Partner and Senior Vice President
**Email:** Wpederson@wsandco.com

Wade Pederson is a partner at Woodruff-Sawyer & Co., a full-service insurance brokerage. A member of Woodruff-Sawyer's P&C Technology and Corporate & Executive Protection practices, Wade specializes in property and casualty and management liability exposures. Wade plays a key role in managing client relationships while working directly with insurance markets to negotiate and place insurance programs. The breadth of Wade's practice allows him to provide clients with a holistic approach to insurance coverage. Over Wade's career he has worked with companies of all sizes, ranging from startups to multinational firms, giving him expertise with companies in all stages of growth and risk complexities. Wade also works with a variety of industries, with a particular focus on the technology, biotechnology, and clean technology sectors. Clients on the cutting edge of technological innovation benefit from Wade's deep expertise when it comes to assessing and effectively mitigating business risk through insurance.